全国外贸技能竞赛实战演练

——单证缮制

（2012 年版）

主　编　刘长声

总顾问　刘宝荣　王乃彦

主　审　姚大伟

中国商务出版社

图书在版编目（CIP）数据

全国外贸技能竞赛实战演练：单证缮制：2012 年版
/ 刘长声主编. —2 版. —北京：中国商务出版社，
2012.4

　　ISBN 978-7-5103-0674-7

　　Ⅰ.①全… Ⅱ.①刘… Ⅲ.①国际贸易–票据–资格
考试–习题集 Ⅳ.①F740.44－44

　　中国版本图书馆 CIP 数据核字（2012）第 058722 号

全国外贸技能竞赛实战演练——单证缮制（2012 年版）
QUANGUO WAIMAO JINENG JINGSAI SHIZHAN YANLIAN—DANZHENG SHANZHI（2012NIANBAN）
主编　刘长声　总顾问　刘宝荣　王乃彦　主审　姚大伟

出　版：中国商务出版社
发　行：北京中商图出版物发行有限责任公司
社　址：北京市东城区安定门外大街东后巷 28 号
邮　编：100710
电　话：010—64269744（编辑室）
　　　　010—64266119（发行部）
　　　　010—64263201（零售、邮购）
网　址：www.cctpress.com
邮　箱：cctp@cctpress.com
照　排：北京开和文化传播中心
印　刷：北京密兴印刷有限公司
开　本：787 毫米×980 毫米　1/16
印　张：25.5　字　数：461 千字
版　次：2012 年 4 月第 2 版　　2012 年 4 月第 2 次印刷

书　号：ISBN 978-7-5103-0674-7
定　价：60.00 元

前　言

　　全国职业院校外贸技能竞赛是中国国际贸易学会和全国外经贸职业教育教学指导委员会主办的一项全国性赛事。竞赛的宗旨是：学习贯彻《国家中长期教育发展规划纲要》，促进职业院校外经贸类专业内涵发展，展示近年来外经贸职业教育风采和技能人才培养的特点，激发外经贸类专业学生学习职业技能、提高实践能力的热情，进一步促进职业院校外经贸人才培养水平的全面提升，为国际商务事业发展提供坚强的人才保障。

　　自 2008 年以来，此项竞赛已连续举办了四届，取得了很好的社会效应，也受到了越来越多的职业院校的重视，参赛院校逐年增加。为了满足参赛院校培养学生实际动手能力和基本技能的需要，为参赛选手提供更多的赛前辅导，我们严格按照外贸技能竞赛大纲的要求，编写了《全国外贸技能竞赛实战演练——单证缮制》一书，并于 2012 年重新修订出版。

　　本书是针对参加全国职业院校外贸技能竞赛选手进行赛前辅导使用的演练习题集，包括外贸单证基础理论知识与单证缮制两部分的内容。全书共分为三个篇章：信用证篇、单据篇和综合篇，所选习题基本涵盖了竞赛大纲所要求掌握的知识和技能要点，侧重于对基础知识的训练，同时加入了重点及难点习题，并附有详细的习题答案。

　　本书不仅适用于参加全国职业院校外贸技能竞赛的选手，也适用于参加国际商务单证员考试的考生，同时还是国际商务单证实务课程的重要参考书。

　　在本书的编写和出版过程中，得到了各级领导、专家、学者的支持和帮助，得到了各参赛院校指导教师的大力协助，他们提供了很多素材和修改建议，在此谨表敬意和感谢。

　　本书由全国外经贸职业教育教学指导委员会秘书长刘长声担任主编，天津商务职业学院赵明、许彦斌、辛文琦、杨金玲老师参加了本书的编写。

　　由于编者水平有限，错误在所难免，恳请专家和同行赐教。

编者

2012 年 2 月

目　　录

信 用 证 篇

综 合 篇

参 考 答 案

信 用 证 篇

一、认知信用证

(一) 信用证中英文条款互译

1. FULL SET OF CLEAN "ON BOARD" BILLS OF LADING MADE OUT TO ORDER AND ENDORSED IN BLANK NOTIFY APPLICANT CALLING FOR SHIPMENT FROM CHINA TO HAMBURG MARKED "FREIGHT PREPAID".

2. BENEFICIARY'S ORIGINAL SIGNED COMMERCIAL INVOICES AT LEAST IN 3 COPIES ISSUED IN THE NAME OF THE BUYER INDICATING THE MERCHANDISE, COUNTRY OF ORIGIN AND ANY OTHER RELEVANT INFORMATION.

3. WE HEREBY ENGAGE WITH THE DRAWERS, ENDORSERS AND BONA-FIDE HOLDERS OF DRAFT(S) DRAWN UNDER AND IN COMPLIANCE WITH THE TERMS OF THE CREDIT THAT SUCH DRAFT(S) SHALL BE DULY HONOURED ON DUE PRESENTATION AND DELIVERY OF DOCUMENTS AS SPECIFIED (IF DRAWN AND NEGOTIATED WITH IN THE VALIDITY DATE OF THIS CREDIT).

4. THE BENEFICIARY IS TO CABLE MR. SMITH STATING L/C NO., QUANTITY SHIPPED NAME & ETA OF VESSEL WITHIN 5 DAYS AFTER SHIPMENT, A COPY OF THIS CABLE MUST ACCOMPANY THE DOCUMENTS FOR NEGOTIATION.

5. 买方应通过为卖方可接受的银行开立于装船月份前 40 天寄至卖方的不可撤销的即期信用证，有效期至装运后 21 天在中国议付，但须在信用证有效期之内。

6. 2009 年 1 月 31 日前从上海港运至香港，不允许分批装运和转运。

7. 由卖方以发票金额的 110％投保一切险和战争险，根据中国人民保险公司 1981 年 1 月 1 日的海洋运输货物保险条款。

8. 每 30 件装于一个盒子，20 个盒子装于一个纸箱，共 200 个纸箱。

（二）问答题

请阅读信用证：

From：VOLKSBANK SCHORNDORF, HAMBURG, GERMANY

To：BANK OF CHINA，HEBEI BRANCH

Form of Doc. Credit	*40A：	IRREVOCABLE
Doc. Credit Number	*20：	08-4-1520
Date of Issue	31C：	080201
Applicable rules	40E：	UCP LATEST VERSION
Expiry	*31D：	DATE：080415 IN THE COUNTRY OF BEN-EFICIARY
Applicant	*50：	LUCKY VICTORY INTERNATIONAL STUTTGART STIR. 5, D-84618，SCHORNDORF，GERMANY
Beneficiary	*59：	HEBEI MACHINERY IMP. AND EXP. CORP（GROUP） 720 DONGFENG ROAD, SHIJIAZHUANG, CHINA
Amount	*32B：	Currency USD Amount 57 600.00
Pos. /Neg. Tol.（％）	39A：	5/5

Available with/by   * 41A：ANY BANK BY NEGOTIATION
Draft at…   42C：DRAFTS AT 30 DAYS SIGHT
FOR FULL INVOICE VALUE
Drawee   42A：VOLKSBANK SCHORNDORF
                         HAMBURG，GERMANY
Partial Shipments   43P：ALLOWED
Transshipment   43T：ALLOWED
Loading in Charge   44A：TIANJIN
For Transport to   44B：HAMBURG
Latest Date of Ship.   44C：080331
Descript. of Goods   45A：
STAINLESS STEEL SPADE HEAD，
ART. NO. S569，4 800 PCS，USD 5. 60 PER PC.，
ART. NO. F671，3 200 PCS，USD 9. 60 PER PC.，
AS PER S/C NO. 08HM256 DATED JAN. 01，2008.
CIF HAMBURG
Documents required 46A：
   ＋ SIGNED COMMERCIAL INVOICE IN TRIPLICATE.
   ＋ FULL SET OF CLEAN ON BOARD OCEAN BILLS OF LADING
MADE OUT TO ORDER OF SHIPPER，MARKED "FREIGHT PREPAID"
AND NOTIFY APPLICANT.
   ＋ GSP CERTIFICATE OF ORIGIN FORM A
   ＋ PACKING LIST IN TRIPLICATE.
   ＋ INSURANCE POLICY COVERING RISKS AS PER INSTITUTE
CARGO CLAUSE（A）INCLUDING WAREHOUSE TO WAREHOUSE
CLAUSE UP TO FINAL DESTINATION AT SCHORNDORF，FOR 110
PCT OF THE CIF VALUE，MARKED PREMIUM PAID，SHOWING
CLAIM PAYABLE IN GERMANY.
   Additional Cond. 47A：
   1. A HANDING FEE OF USD 80. 00 WILL BE DEDUCTED IF DIS-
      CREPANCY DOCUMENTS PRESENTED.
   2. ALL DOCUMENTS MUST BE IN ENGLISH.
   3. ALL DOCUMENTS INDICATING THIS L/C NUMBER.
Presentation Period 48：

DOCUMENTS TO BE PRESENTED WITHIN 15 DAYS AFTER THE DATE OF SHIPMENT, BUT WITHIN THE VALIDITY OF THE CREDIT.

Details of Charges 71B：

ALL BANKING CHARGES AND EXPENSES OUTSIDE THE ISSUING BANK ARE FOR BENEFICIARY'S ACCOUNT.

回答 1～4 题：

1. 本信用证的附加条款中提出了哪几点要求？

2. 在此信用证业务结汇时，受益人应向银行提交哪些单据？

3. 此信用证对于分批装运、转船及装运期的要求是什么？

4. 此信用证对提单缮制的要求有哪些规定？

（三）单选题

1. 在托收业务中，进口商可凭信托收据向银行借单提货的托收方式是（　　）。

    A. D/P at sight　　　　　　　　　B. D/P after sight

    C. D/A　　　　　　　　　　　　　D. D/A after sigh

2. 接受汇出行的委托将款项解付给收款人的银行是（　　）。

    A. 托收银行　　　B. 汇入行　　　C. 代收行　　　　D. 转递行

3. 信用证规定议付时扣除佣金 100 美元，发票和报关单上的收回金额显示为 USD 100 000.00，实际收汇 USD 98 000.00（国外扣除费用 100 美元），出口收汇核销单上的金额一览应该填写为（　　）。

    A. USD 98 000.00　　　　　　　　B. USD 99 000.00

    C. USD 100 000.00　　　　　　　　D. USD 100 100.00

4. 如果信用证规定"shipment on or about 15 Oct. 2000"，那么装运期应为（　　）。

    A. 9 天　　　　　B. 10 天　　　　C. 11 天　　　　　D. 12 天

5. 根据《URC522》，D/A 180 天远期，代收行应在什么时候交单（　　）。

    A. 收到单据后 7 个工作日内　　　B. 承兑后交单

　　　C. 船到港后交单　　　　　　　　D. 承兑后付款时交单

6. 在国际贸易支付方式中,信用证是银行信用,使用的通常是(　　)。

　　A. 商业汇票　　　B. 银行汇票　　　C. 银行本票　　　D. 支票

7. 在托收项下,单据的缮制通常以(　　)的依据。如有特殊要求,应参照相应的文件或资料。

　　A. 信用证　　　B. 发票　　　C. 合同　　　D. 提单

8. 根据《UCP 600》,信用证的第一付款人是(　　)。

　　A. 进口人　　　B. 开证行　　　C. 议付行　　　D. 通知行

9. 根据《跟单信用证统一惯例》(国际商会第 600 号出版物)的规定,如买卖合同规定立即装运,开来信用证的装运期规定为"尽速"装运,该装运期应理解为(　　)。

　　A. 开证行开出信用证之日起 30 天内装运

　　B. 通知行通知信用证之日起 30 天内装运

　　C. 受益人收到信用证之日起 30 天内装运

　　D. 银行将不予至理

10. 在补偿贸易中条件下,一般最适宜采用(　　)。

　　A. 对开信用证　　　　　　　　B. 保兑信用证

　　C. 循环信用证　　　　　　　　D. 议付信用证

11. 如果信用证对出单人未做明确规定,我出口企业可以自行缮制的单证有(　　)。

　　A. 保险单　　　　　　　　　　B. 提单

　　C. 一般原产地证　　　　　　　D. 普惠制原产地证

12. 我通过某公司与美国的 M 公司达成一笔进口交易,合同规定通过中国银行开立不可撤销转让信用证,中国银行在证内对转让费未做规定,按惯例此项费用应由(　　)。

　　A. 我进口公司负担　　　　　　B. 第一受益人负担

　　C. 我进口用户负担　　　　　　D. 第二受益人负担

13. 以下国际港口:Amsterdam, Manila, HongKong 所在国家代码分别依次为(　　)。

　　A. PH,HL,CN　　　　　　　　B. HL,PH,CN

　　C. PH,CN,HL　　　　　　　　D. HL,CN,PH

14. 海运出口货物的发货人或其代理人根据海关规定,应当在货物运抵海关监管区后(　　),向海关申报出口货物。

　　A. 船离境 36 小时前　　　　　B. 船离境 48 小时前

    C. 船离境 12 小时前   D. 船离境 24 小时前

15. 在出口业务中,如采用托收支付方式,我方应争取使用以下贸易术语中的
    (　　);而在(　　)贸易术语下,从谨慎角度出发,需要投保卖方利益险?
    A. FOB,CFR   B. CFR, FOB
    C. FCA, CIF   D. CIF, FOB

16. "the credit does not bear our confirmation and does not invoice any under-taking on our part" 信用证上的这一条款通常是(　　)所加的?
    A. 开证行   B. 通知行
    C. 保兑行   D. 开证申请人

17. 下列品质规定方法,正确的是(　　)。
    A. 彻底消灭皱纹的某某牌皮鞋
    B. 荞麦水分 10%、杂质 3%
    C. 木薯片 1998 年产,大路货,水分最高 10%
    D. 柳酸甲醇,按英国药典规定

18. 信用证要求提供"land-sea combined transport B/L"但又规定不可转运,货从内地装火车到香港装海轮,此操作与规定(　　)。
    A. 有矛盾
    B. 无矛盾
    C. 有无矛盾主要看收货人与银行的意思

19. 下列被称为装货单,即下货纸的是(　　)。
    A. S/O   B. S/C   C. D/P   D. P/I

20. In Octuplicate 在信用证英语中的意思是表示单据的(　　)。
    A. 种类   B. 名称   C. 份数   D. 时间

21. 一份 SWIFT 信用证有下列内容:31D:080415 CHINA,44C:080331,46A:B/L telex released,Consigned to applicant,notify consignee,Copy of B/L required. 信用证没有 48 栏位,受益人于 2008 年 3 月 15 日装船完毕,请问下列哪个日期是受益人可以交单的最晚日期? (　　)
    A. 3 月 30 日   B. 4 月 5 日   C. 3 月 31 日   D. 4 月 15 日

22. 信用证规定 shipping documents must show p/o No. 5237. 出口商制作单据时,下列哪种单据可不显示此 p/o 编号? (　　)
    A. 保险单   B. 发票   C. 汇票   D. 提单

23. 沃尔玛总部与中国某大型日用品生产工厂签订采购合同,所购商品用于供应其中国门店,那么采用下列哪个贸易术语较为合适? (　　)
    A. EXW   B. DAT   C. DAP   D. DDP

24. 某批货物的保险金额为 USD 110 000.00,货物在运输途中一共损失了 USD 5 000.00,且属于保险公司的承保范围。如果是分别按下列三种情况投保: irrespective of percentage、in excess of 2.5%、with 2.5% franchise,那么这次出险保险公司各应该赔付多少金额?（　　）
    A. USD 5 000，USD 2 250，USD 5 000
    B. USD 2 250，USD 5 000，USD 5 000
    C. USD 5 000，USD 5 000，USD 2 250
    D. USD 5 000，USD 5 000，USD 2 750

25. L/C 规定:DOCS MUST BE PRESENTED WITHIN 21 DAYS AFTER B/L DATE,禁止分批装运。提交的正本 B/L 不止一套,装运港为一个或一个以上港口(L/C 特别允许或在 L/C 规定的特定地理范围内),B/L 显示同船,同航程同目的地,而装运期不同,则下列哪项日期被用来计算交单期?（　　）
    A. B/L 上显示最早的那个装运日
    B. 最早的 B/L 出具日
    C. B/L 上显示最晚的那个装运日
    D. 最晚的 B/L 出具日

26. 根据《UCP 600》,信用证中下列哪一项措词不是表明需要提交至少一份正本?（　　）
    A. in duplicate　　　　　　　　B. in two fold
    C. in two copies　　　　　　　　D. in two photocopies

27. 根据《UCP 600》,银行可接受有下列哪项批注的提单?（　　）
    A. TWO BAGS BROKEN
    B. ONE BOX CRASHED, CONTENTS EXPOSED
    C. SAID TO CONTAIN
    D. CONTENT LEAKING

28. 信用证中下列哪项表述不属于《UCP 600》所述及的 honour?（　　）
    A. by sight payment　　　　　　B. by deferred payment
    C. by acceptance　　　　　　　　D. by negotiation

29. 信用证规定要提供注有实际发运日期的空运提单,以下形式哪种是注明了发运日期的?（　　）
    A. 空运提单有效的出具日期
    B. 注有航班号以及在预先打好的填有"For carrier use only"的格式注有日期
    C. 发运日期必须特别注明

30. 可转让信用证的某一部分是否可被分开转让？（　　）

    A. 可以，只要分批装运是允许的并且信用证的总金额没被超过

    B. 任何情况下也不可以

    C. 只有信用证金额可以

31. 一份开出的不可转让的信用证的受益人是否可以要求将此信用证已产生的收益或将产生的收益分给第三者？（　　）

    A. 可以

    B. 他不允许向任何人转让任何收益

    C. 可以，但只有在信用证规定分批装运是允许的情况下

32. 备用 L/C 是（　　）。

    A. 跟单 L/C 的一种

    B. 一种特殊形式的光票 L/C

    C. 既可是跟单 L/C，又可是光票 L/C

33. 某公司以 CIF 条件出口一批货物，在广州港装上船只"DONGFENG"号运往香港，在香港装上第二程船"NATA"号后运往旧金山，该公司在保单的载运输工具栏"PER CONVEYANCE S. S."应填写为（　　）。

    A. DONGFENG

    B. NATA

    C. DONGFENG/NATA

    D. DONGFENG/NATA W/T HONGKONG

34. 某公司出口乒乓球，信用证规定："乒乓球 10 000 打，单价每打 2.38 美元，总金额 23 800.00 美元，禁止分批装运"。根据《UCP 600》规定，卖方交货的（　　）。

    A. 数量和总金额均可在 5% 的范围内增减

    B. 数量和总金额均可在 10% 的范围内增减

    C. 数量可以有 5% 的范围内增减，但总金额不得超过 23 800.00 美元

    D. 数量和金额均不得增减

35. 进出口许可证制度是一种管理进出口贸易的手段，就其职能和实施范围来说（　　）。

    A. 它只能限制进出口商品的数量

    B. 它只能限制进出口商品的质量

    C. 它既能限制进出口商品的数量，又能限制进出口商品的质量

    D. 它既能限制进出口商品的数量，又能限制价格，市场等方面

36. 使用假远期信用证，实际上是套用（　　）。

    A. 卖方资金　　　B. 付款银行资金　　　C. 买方资金　　　D. 收款银行资金

37. 信用证规定：SHIPMENT FROM NANJING FOR TRANSPORTATION
TO USA BEFORE AUG. 8，2004 PARTLAL SHIPMENT：PROHIBT-
TEDDOCUMENTS REQUIRED：COURIER RECEIPT ISSUED BY
DHL CONSIGNED TO THE APPLICANT EVIDENCING POSTAGE
PAID

两份 DHL 快邮收据提交给银行。

第一份 DHL 快邮收据显示：

FROM NANJING TO NEW YORK

PLACE AND DATE OF PICK—UP：AUG. 7，2004 9：10AM，NANJING

第二份 DHL 快邮收据显示：

FROM NANJING TO BOSTON

PLACE AND DATE OF PICK—UP：AUG. 8，2004 9：10AM，NANJING

根据《UCP 600》，以下关于快邮件陈述正确的是（　　　）。

　A. 分批装运，因为提交了两份 DHL 快邮收据

　B. 分批装运，因为两份 DHL 快邮件收据的日期不同

　C. 未产生分批装运，因为两份 DHL 快邮收据的启运地与信用证的规定相符

　D. 未产生分批装运，因为两份 DHL 快邮收据的目的地相同

38. 进出口货物是收、发货人或其代理人向海关申报，交验规定的单据和证件，
请求办理海关放行手续的行为被称为（　　　）。

　A. 报关　　　　B. 放行　　　　C. 通关　　　　D. 结关

39. 一张每期用完一定金额后，需等开证行通知到达，才能恢复到原金额继续使
用的信用证是（　　　）。

　A. 非自动循环信用证　　　　　B. 半自动循环信用证

　C. 自动循环信用证　　　　　　D. 有时自动，有时非自动

40. 香港某公司出售一批商品给美国 ABC Co.，美国银行开来一份不可撤销可
转让信用证，香港某银行按香港公司委托，将信用证转让给我某进出口公
司，如信用证未对转让费用做明确规定，按惯例应由（　　　）。

　A. 我某进出口公司负担　　　　B. 香港某公司负担

　C. 美国 ABC C0. 负担　　　　　D. 香港某银行负担

41. 以下不是 EDI 必须包括的内容是（　　　）。

　A. 纸单据和电子单据同时传递　　B. 按统一的标准编制资料

　C. 电子方式的传递信息　　　　　D. 计算机应用程序之间的连接

42. 在下列业务中，不属于托收行责任的是（　　　）。

　A. 对邮寄单据遗失负责

B. 按委托人指示办事

C. 按业务常规选择代收行

D. 以应有的勤勉和谨慎处理业务

43. 在跟单信用证中,议付行的索汇路线有向开证行或向(   )索汇。

  A. 通知行 B. 托收行 C. 偿付行 D. 代收行

44. 以下关于信用证修改业务的描述正确的是(   )。

  A. 由申请人向原开证行提出修改要求

  B. 修改通知书的传递途径和方式可以与原证不同

  C. 受益人对修改通知必须明确表示是否接受

  D. 受益人可以部分接受修改书内容

45. 以下词语中用于确定装运期限时,(   )不包括所述日期。

  A. until B. from C. between D. before

46. 承兑交单的起算日应为(   )。

  A. 出票日   B. 付款人见票承兑日

  C. 付款日   D. 托收日

47. 首都国际机场的代码为(   )。

  A. PEK B. PVG C. NRT D. ORD

48. 开立信用证必须以对外签订的正本合同为依据。为保证"证同一致",正确的做法是(   )。

  A. 在信用证中注明"参阅＊＊＊＊＊号合同"

  B. 在信用证中列明合同要求明确的所有条款

  C. 在信用证中注明"系＊＊＊＊＊号合同项下货物"

  D. 将合同副本作为附件附在信用证后

49. 某份可转让信用证开证金额为 USD 22 000.00,同时规定保险单据的投保金额是发票金额的 110％,禁止分批装运。第一受益人拟将 USD 12 100.00 通过银行转让给第二受益人。为了满足原信用证规定的保额,则应规定保险单据的投保比例为(   )。

  A. 100％ B. 110％ C. 200％ D. 210％

50. 出口商安排海运托运的正确排序是(   )。

  A. 办理托运,领取装运凭证/装货、装船/换取提单/向买方发出装船通知

  B. 向买方发出装船通知/办理托运/领取装运凭证/装货、装船/换取提单

  C. 办理托运/装货、装船/领取装运凭证/换取提单/向买方发出装船通知

  D. 向买方发出装船通知/办理托运/装货、装船/领取装运凭证/换取提单

51. 我出口孟加拉国一批货物,以 CFR 价格条件成交,该货于 8 月 15 日开始装

船,8月18日装毕,8月20日起航,9月6日抵达目的港,9月8日客户提货,我交货日期是( )。

A. 8月15日   B. 8月18日

C. 8月20日   D. 9月6日

E. 9月8日

52. 程租船下,租船合约规定为FIO,则( )。

A. 船方不负担装卸费,港口费用,船员工资、伙食,但负担燃料费

B. 船方不负担装卸费,负担港口费用、船员工资、伙食、燃料费

C. 船方负担装货费,不负担卸货费,港口费用、船员工资、伙食、燃料费

D. 船方负担卸货费,不负担装货费,负担港口费用、船员工资、伙食、燃料费

53. OCP条款适用的范围为( )。

A. 远东出口到北美OCP地区   B. 远东出口到美国

C. 远东出口到美国OCP地区   D. 美国OCP地区出口到远东

54. 以下关于LINER TERMs的陈述正确的是( )。

A. FOB LINER TERMs是指装船费用按照班轮的做法处理,即买方负责承担装船的有关费用;CFR LINER TERMs指卸货费用按照班轮的做法处理,即买方不负担卸货费

B. FOB LINER TERMs是指装船费用按照班轮的做法处理,即卖方负责承担装船的有关费用;CFR LINER TERMs指卸货费用按照班轮的做法处理,即买方负担卸货费

C. FOB LINER TERMs是指采用班轮运输,即买方负责承担装船的有关费用;CFR LINER TERMs指卸货费用按照班轮的做法处理,即买方不负担卸货费

D. FOB LINER TERMs是指装船费用按照班轮的做法处理,即卖方负责承担装船的有关费用;CFR LINER TERMs指卸货费用按照班轮的做法处理,即买方负担卸货费

55. 我国甲公司要与比利时某公司签订销售合同出口服装到比,要采用海陆联运方式,甲公司将货物运至目的地的运费并支付保险,根据《INCOTERMS 2000》,应采用的贸易术语是( )。

A. FOB   B. CIF   C. EXW   D. CIP

56. 我方出口一批钢铁到也门,按CIF HODEIDAH成交,合同规定我方不承担卸货费,该术语应变形为( )。

A. CIF Liner Terms Hodeidah   B. CIF Landed Hodeidah

C. CIF Ex Ship's Hold Hodeidah   D. CIF Ex Tackle Hodeidah

57. 卖方必须在合同规定的期间,在指定装货港,将货物交至买方指定的船上,并负担货物越过船舷为止的一切费用和货物灭失或损坏的风险。这种情况的术语应是(   )
   A. DES   B. FAS   C. FOB   D. CIF

58. 采用FOB变形,主要是解决在(   )条件下货物的装船费用问题。
   A. 班轮   B. 程租船   C. 期租船   D. 光船租船

59. 某出口商品每件净重30千克,毛重34千克,体积每件为45cm×35cm×22cm,如班轮运价运费计算标准为W/M10级,船公司计算运费时(   )。
   A. 按净重计收运费   B. 将由托运人自由选定
   C. 按体积计收运费   D. 将由承运人自由选定

60. 班轮从价运费的计算是按货物的(   )。
   A. CIF价   B. FOB价   C. CFR价   D. 进货成本

(四) 多选题

1. 出口信用证的融资方式有(   )。
   A. 汇票贴现   B. 红条款信用证
   C. 出口押汇   D. 打包放款

2. 下列信用证条款中属于软条款的是(   )。
   A. 三份正本已装船海运提单,做成"凭指定"抬头,通知买方
   B. 一份开证申请人手签的质量检验证书,字迹须和开证行预留签字样本相符
   C. 待进口商取得进口许可证后,开证行以信用证修改形式通知信用证生效
   D. 所装船名和船期由进口商通知开证行,开证行以信用证修改形式通知受益人
   E. 货物运抵目的港后,待进口地商检机构检验合同并出具书面证书后开证行才付款

3. 根据《UCP 600》规定,不能使信用证成为可以转让的措词有(   )。
   A. ASSIGNABLE   B. TRANSMISSIBLE
   C. TRANSFERABLE   D. DIVISIBLE

4. 托收结算方式的主要当事人(   )。
   A. REMITTING BANK   B. PRINCIPAL
   C. NEGOTIATING BANK   D. COLLECTING BANK
   E. PAYER

5. 关于信用证中英语"Date and place of expiry",说法正确的是(   )。
   A. 表明该证的到期日期和到期地点

B. 信用证的到期地点可以在开证行所在地也可以是受益人的所在地

C. 可以推算出信用证的开证日期

D. 如果是开证行所在地,那么审单员一定要把握好交单时间和邮程,防止信用证失效

6. 如果信用证没对货物数量订有增减条款,只要同时符合下列哪些条件,该货物的出运数量允许有 5% 的增减幅度(   )。

A. 信用证未规定数量不得增减

B. 支取金额不超过信用证金额

C. 货物的数量不是按包装单位或个数计数的,如长度(米、码),体积(立方米),容量(升,加仑),重量(吨,磅)

D. 信用证不准分批

E. 支取金额可超过信用证金额的 5%

7. 在国际贸易中,常用于中间商转售货物交易的信用证是(   )。

A. 对背信用证   B. 对开信用证

C. 可撤销信用证   D. 可转让信用证

E. 循环信用证

8. 国际贸易中采用保付代理方式收取货款,对出口人的好处是(   )。

A. 保理商负责进口人资信调查   B. 出口商承担信贷风险

C. 保理商承担信贷风险   D. 保理商向出口人提供奖金融通

E. 保理商向进口人提供奖金融通

9. 下列关于信用证与合同关系的表述正确的是(   )。

A. 信用证的开立以买卖合同为依据

B. 信用证业务受买卖合同的约束

C. 合同是审核信用证的依据

D. 银行按信用证规定处理信用证业务

10. 备用信用证与跟单信用证的相同点是(   )。

A. 受益人只要提交与信用证要求相符的单据,即可向开证银行要求付款

B. 开证行所承担的付款义务都是第一性的

C. 均凭符合信用证规定的凭证或单据付款

D. 以符合信用证规定的货运单据为付款依据

E. 都是在买卖合同或其他合同的基础上开立的,但是,一旦开立就与这些合同无关,成为开证行对受益人之间的一项独立的义务

11. 在我国出口业务中,信用证项下制单结汇的方式有(   )。

A. 收妥结汇   B. 押汇   C. 定期结汇   D. 电提   E. 保理

12. 由上海运往底特律、芝加哥的一批货物,若采用 OCP 条款,应满足下列条件（　　）。

    A. 必须在美国西海岸港口转船

    B. 必须在提单上注明"OCP"字样

    C. 必须在提单的目的港一栏填写西海岸港口城市名,以及底特律、芝加哥最终目的地名称

    D. 必须是美国急需的货物

13. 已装船提单的签发期为 7 月 15 日,信用证规定的有效期为 8 月 15 日,交单期限为装运日后的 15 天,如果信用证要求卖方提交保险单,则保险单的出单日期可以为（　　）。

    A. 7 月 30 日　　B. 7 月 15 日　　C. 7 月 25 日　　D. 7 月 10 日

    E. 8 月 15 日

14. 申请出口退税须提供两单两票是（　　）。

    A. 盖有海关"验讫"章的出口报关单

    B. 银行收汇核销单

    C. 出口销售发票

    D. 出口产品购进发票（＝增值税发票）

    E. 出口结汇水单（银行证明外汇到账的证明）

15. 假远期信用证的主要特点是（　　）。

    A. 由开证行开出延期付款信用证

    B. 由受益人开出远期汇票

    C. 由指定的付款行负责贴现汇票

    D. 由进口人负担贴现息和费用

16. 国际多式联运必须（　　）。

    A. 依据多式联运合同

    B. 至少有两种不同的运输方式

    C. 将货物从一国境内运至另一国境内

    D. 海/海、陆/陆、空/空联运

17. CIF 和 CIP 这两个贸易术语的相同点是（　　）。

    A. 买卖双方的报关责任相同　　　　B. 主运费的责任方相同

    C. 保险费的责任方相同　　　　　　D. 货物风险转移界点相同

    E. 使用的运输工具可以相同

18. 假远期信用证与远期信用证的区别是（　　）。

    A. 开证基础不同　　　　　　　　　B. 信用证条款不同

C. 利息的负担者不同 　　　　D. 收汇的时间不同

19. 以下对贸易术语变形的正确说法是（　　）。
    A. 不改变费用的负担 　　　　B. 不改变交货地点
    C. 不改变风险划分的界限 　　D. 不改变支付条件
    E. 以上均正确

20. 定期租船下，租船人应负担（　　）。
    A. 船员工资 　　B. 港口费 　　　C. 装卸费 　　　　D. 船员伙食
    E. 燃料费

21. 买方采用 FOB 条件进口散装小麦，货物用程租船运输，当买方不愿承担装货费用时，可选用以下价格变形（　　）。
    A. FOB Liner Terms 　　　　B. FOB Under Tackle
    C. FOB Trimmed 　　　　　　D. FOB Stowed
    E. FOB Stowed and Trimmed

22. 构成共同海损的条件有（　　）。
    A. 必须是确实遭遇危难
    B. 必须是自然灾害造成的损失
    C. 必须是有意的、合理的措施造成的损失
    D. 必须是为船、货共同安全而采取的措施
    E. 必须是属于非常性质的损失

23. 构成实际全损的情况有（　　）。
    A. 保险标的物全部灭失
    B. 保险标的物完全变质
    C. 保险标的物不可能归还保险人
    D. 施救费用和救助费用超过保险价值

（五）判断题

（　　）1. 买卖合同规定："交货数量 5 000 吨，1999 年 9/10 月份装运"，那么出口在 9 月 1 日至 10 月 31 日这段时间内任何一天将货物装运，但不得分批装运。

（　　）2. 联合国设计推荐使用的国际标准化地名代码中上海为 CNSHG。

（　　）3. 根据《UCP 600》规定，如遇法定节假日，信用证到期日、交单日或提单的装运日可以顺延至下一个银行工作日。

（　　）4. 转让信用证项下，只要受益人提交合格单据，转让银行就应承担与开证行相同的付款责任。

（　　）5. 来证规定装运期限位"after 12th May, 2009"，则应理解为 2009 年 5 月 12 日或以后装运。

（　　）6. 备用信用证条件下，如果开证申请人按期履行了合同的义务，则该信用证必须被使用。

（　　）7. 信用证是一种银行开立的无条件承诺付款的书面文件。

（　　）8. 背对背信用证与未经保兑的可转让信用证一样对供货方有利。

（　　）9. 一份报关单可以填报多个许可证号。

（　　）10. 《UCP 600》规定，标明"正本"（original）字样的单据为正本单据，须经出单人签署方为有效。标明"副本"（copy）或不标明"正本"字样的单据为副本单据，无须签署。

（　　）11. 根据《UCP 600》规定，保兑行保兑信用证后，对随后接到的修改书可自行决定是否将保兑责任扩展至修改书。

（　　）12. 一项发盘如表明是不可撤销的，则意味着发盘人无权撤销该发盘。

（　　）13. 按《UCP 600》规定，银行接受 7 种运输单据，除非另有约定，一般银行不接受卖方提交的快递收据。

（　　）14. 如果信用证只规定最迟装运期，未列有效期，受益人应按双到期来操作。

（　　）15. 若信用证要求"packing list to be made out in neutral form" 即是指装箱单做成中性的形式。也就是说，装箱单上不显示买方的名称或任何可以显示出买方身份的标记、符号等。

（　　）16. 开证行收到倒签提单，并有根据，开证行可以以伪造单据为由提出拒付。

（　　）17. 从西欧某商进口在当地通常可买到的某化工产品。约定交货前该商所属生产上述产品的工厂之一因爆炸被毁，该商要求援引不可抗力免责条款解除交货责任。我方应予同意。

（　　）18. 根据《联合国国际货物销售公约》，一方发盘，另一方表示接受但同时要求提供原产地证明时，发盘人只要立即向对方表示确认，合同关系就能确立。

（　　）19. 信用证中 43P 域为 prohibited，44E 域为 Chinese port，那么如果货物在中国 A 港没装够，同一艘船同一航次到中国 B 港装足信用证所要求数量的货物后同一航线到达同一目的地，在 A 港与 B 港取得的两套提单同时交给银行，银行认为这样的交单行为虽然符合《UCP 600》第 31 条 b 款规定，但却不符合信用证本身 44E 域的单一港口要求，故不能接受这样的单据。

（　　）20. 如果信用证中的 44F 域是一个地理区域，信用证要求的提单的卸货港栏可照抄此区域无须填列具名港口。

（　　）21. 受益人收到修改通知后，原信用证的条款失效。

（　　）22. FOB LINER TERMs 价格会比 FOB 更高。

（　　）23. CFR LINER TERMs 价格会比 CFR 更高。

（　　）24. 信用证项下单证不符，开证行可以拒付货款；托收项下单据不符，买方可以拒付货款。

（　　）25. 电汇或者信汇需通知收款人取款，收款人经过背书可以转让汇票。

（　　）26. 见索即付保函的担保人承担的是第二性、附属的付款责任。

（　　）27. 备用信用证是跟单信用证。当开证申请人未能如期按合同条款履约时，凭受益人出具的完全符合信用证条款规定的汇票及/或证明申请人违约的书面文件，开证行即应履行担保责任。

（　　）28. 出口单证工作的基本程序可以归纳为信用证登录、审核、制（出）单、交单、结汇和档案管理。

（　　）29. 为保证单据的整洁要求，应当尽量减少在单据中进行涂改。一旦出现制单错误，如发票上的货品编号、汇票上的付款到期时间等，应当加盖出口企业的校正章。

（　　）30. 采用信用证方式结算货款，只对卖方有利。

（　　）31. 托收业务中，提单的收货人应为代收行。

（　　）32. 来证规定的数量已装完，而发票金额还有一些多余，在议付行表示接受的情况下，可采取"扣除"、"放弃"的办法处理，即在总额下面减除差额零头，减除后的发票总额不超过信用证所允许的金额。

（　　）33. FOB 条件下，如合同中未规定"装船通知"条款，卖方则在货物装船后允许不发装船通知。

（　　）34. 美国陆桥运输主要包括 OCP、MLB 和 IPI 三种运输方式，因为这三种运输方式都是国际多式联运方式，所以可以要求货运代理签发国际多样式联运提单。

（　　）35. 程租船运输方式，F. I. 条款指船方不管装。

（　　）36. 只有在 CFR 条件下才需要在装船以后及时发出装船通知，其他价格术语条件下并不要求一定要发发运通知。

（　　）37. 在 CFR 条件下，卖方在货物装船后必须发出装船通知，以便买方办理投保手续。否则卖方不能以风险在船舷已转移为由免除责任。

（　　）38. 按 CIF 术语成交，尽管价格中包括至指定目的港的运费和保险费，但卖方不承担货物必然到达目的港的责任。

（　　）39. 根据《INCOTERMS 2000》，在 FAS 贸易术语下，如买方所派的船不能靠岸，则卖方只要将货物装上驳船即可。制单是单证工作的基础，是按照信用证、合同和其他的要求，根据货物实际情况缮制有关单据。

（　　）40. Documents must be presented for negotiation within10 days, from B/L date，或 after B/L date，若 B/L 为某月 1 日，则最晚交单期分别为该月 10 日。

（　　）41. 国外 A 银行开来一张保兑信用证，请国内 B 银行加保兑，B 银行将该证通知受益人 C 公司，未加任何批注，这是默示，它对信用证的保兑已经认可。

（　　）42. 香港某客户开来一张信用证，号码为 123，购买衬衫 1 千打，"不准分批"，因货未备妥，经修改为"允许分批"，该 L/C 项下 1 000 打衬衫后来分两次出运，随后，该客户又开来第二张信用证，除数量、金额、装效期与第一张信用证有所不同，其余条款套用第一张信用证"Similar to L/C NO. 123"，这张信用证项下货物可分批出运。

（　　）43.《海牙规则》规定，向船公司提出索赔的期限是货物到达目的港交货的后一年。

（　　）44. 根据联合国贸发会 1996 年通过的《电子商务示范法》的解释，通过以数据电文交换而订立的合同，符合法律上所要求的书面合同的性质。

（　　）45. 我国对外经济活动中达成和履行合同必须符合法律的规范，其中包括有关的双边或多边国际条约，与我国进出口货物出口贸易关系最大的一项国际条约是《国际货约》。

（　　）46. 根据《UCP 600》的规定，信用证经修改后，开证行即不可撤销地受该修改的约束。

（　　）47. 根据《UCP 600》，在交易磋商中，当一方发盘，另一方作出有效的接受后，合同即告示成立。

（　　）48. 在 CIF 条件下，卖方办理保险，在 CFR 条件下，买方办理保险，因此在货运过程中货物发生损失，前者由卖方负责，后者由买方负责。

（　　）49. 按 CIF Landed 条件成交，卖方应负担货物卸到岸上的一切费用和风险。

（　　）50. 佣金是卖方按原价给予买方的一定百分比的减让，也就是在价格上给予一定的优惠。

（　　）51. F 组贸易术语的交货点/风险点与费用点是分离的，C 组贸易术语的交货点/风险点与费用点是重合的。

二、开立信用证

（一）依据合同，按照业务规范自行填制信用证开证申请书

销 售 合 同
SALES CONTRACT

卖方 **SELLER**：	DESUN TRADING CO., LTD. HUARONG MANSION RM2901 NO. 85 GUANJIAQIAO, NANJING 210005, CHINA TEL：0086-25-4715004 FAX：0086-25-4711363	编号 **NO.**：	NEO2009026
		日期 **DATE**：	Feb. 28, 2009
买方 **BUYER**：	NEO GENERAL TRADING CO. P. O. BOX 99552, RIYADH 22766, KSA TEL：00966-1-4659220 FAX：00966-1-4659213	地点 **SIGNED IN**：	NANJING, CHINA

买卖双方同意以下条款达成交易：

This contract Is made by and agreed between the BUYER and SELLER, in accordance with the terms and conditions stipulated below.

1. 品名及规格 **Commodity & Specification**	2. 数量 **Quantity**	3. 单价及价格条款 **Unit Price & Trade Terms**	4. 金额 **Amount**
		CFR DAMMAM PORT, SAUDI ARABIA	
SHANGHAI COUNTRY BICYCLE. ART SH28 INCH	300 PCS	USD 100	USD 30 000. 00
Total：	**300 PCS**		**USD 30 000. 00**

5. 总值 **Total Value**	USD THIRTY THOUSAND ONLY.
6. 包装 **Packing**	PACKED IN ONE CARTON OF 10 PCS EACH
7. 唛头 **Shipping Marks**	N/M
8. 装运期及运输方式 **Time of Shipment & means of Transportation**	Not Later Than Apr. 30, 2009 BY VESSEL
9. 装运港及目的地 **Port of Loading & Destination**	From：SHANGHAI PORT, CHINA To：DAMMAM PORT, SAUDI ARABIA

续表

10. 保险 　　Insurance	TO BE COVERED BY THE BUYER.
11. 付款方式 　　**Terms of Payment**	The Buyers shall open through a bank acceptable to the Seller an Irrevocable Letter of Credit payable at sight of reach the seller 30 days before the month of shipment，valid for negotiation in China until the 15th day after the date of shipment.
12. 备注 　　**Remarks**	

<table>
<tr><td align="center">The Buyer
NEO GENERAL TRADING CO.
(signature)</td><td align="center">The Seller
DESUN TRADING CO.，LTD.
(signature)</td></tr>
</table>

IRREVOCABLE DOCUMENTARY CREDIT APPLICATION

TO：×× BANK　　　　　　　　　　　　DATE：

Beneficiary(full name, address)	L/C No. Ex Card No. Contract No.：
	Date and place of expiry：
Partial shipments （ ） allowed （ ）not allowed	Transhipment （ ）allowed （ ） not allowed	（　）Issue by airmail （　）With brief advice by teletransmission （　）Issue by express delivery （　）Issue by teletransmission （which shall be the operative instrument
Loading on board/dispatch/taking in charge at/from Not later than For transportation to		Amount：（both in figures and words）：
Description of goods：		Credit available with （　）by sight payment （　） by acceptance （　） 　　by negotiation （　） by deferred payment at 　　against the documents detailed herein （　） and beneficiary's draft for 100% of invoice value
		（　）FOB （　） CFR （　） CIF （　） or other terms

续表

Documents required：(marked with ×)

1. ( ) Signed commercial invoice in 3 copies indicating L/C No. and Contract No. _____

2. ( ) Full set of clean on board Bills of Lading made out to   and blank endorsed，marked "freight [ ] prepaid/[ ] to collect[ ] showing freight amount" notifying the applicant

3. ( ) Air Waybills showing "freight [ ]prepaid/[ ] to collect indicating freight amount" and consigned to

4. ( ) Insurance Policy/Certificate in 3 copies for 110％ of the invoice value showing claims payable in China in currency of the draft，blank endorsed，covering[ ] Ocean Marine Transportation/[ ] Air Transportation/[ ] Over Land Transportation) All Risks，War Risks.

5. ( ) Packing list/Weight Memo in 3 copies indicating Contract No. NEO2001026

6. ( ) Certificate of Quantity/Weight in 3 copies issued by [ ] manufacturer/[ ] Seller/[ ] independent surveyor at the loading port，indicating the actual surveyed quantity/weight of shipped goods as well as the packing condition.

7. ( ) Certificate of Quality in 3 copies issued by[ ]manufacturer/[ ] public recognized surveyor

8. ( ) Beneficiary's Certified copy of fax dispatched to the applicant within 2 days after shipment advising the contract number，name of commodity，quantity，invoice value，bill of loading，bill of loading date，the ETA date and shipping Co.

9. ( ) Beneficiary's Certificate certifying that extra copies of the documents have been dispatched to the [ ] applicant/[ ]

10. ( ) Certificate of Origin in 3 copies certifying.

11. ( ) Other documents，if any：

Additional instruction：(marked with ×)

1. ( ) All banking charges outside the opening bank are for beneficiary's account.

2. ( ) Documents must be presented within 21 days after the date of issuance of the transport documents but within the validity of this credit.

3. ( ) Third party as shipper is not acceptable，Short Form/Blank B/l is not acceptable.

4. ( ) Both quantity and amount _____ ％ more or less are allowed.

5. ( ) All documents to be forwarded in one lot by express unless otherwise stated above.

6. ( ) Other terms，if any：

Account No.：   with

Transacted by：

TEL：

（二）依据销售合同填写信用证开证申请书

合同　ABC TEXTILES IMPORT AND EXPORT CORPORATION
127 ZHONGSHAN RD. E. 1 SHANGHAI R. P. OF CHINA
SALES CONFIRMATION
TO：MESSRS TOMSON TEXTILES INC.

3384 VINCENT ST.　　　　　　NO. 23CA1006

DOWNSVIEW, ONTARIO　　　DATE：20080306

M3J, 2J4, CANADA

ARTICLE NO. COMMODITY & SPECIFICATION QUANTITY UNIT PRICE AMOUNT

ART. NO.　　　　TRUERAN DYED JEAN

77111　　　　　　POLYESTES 65%, COTTON 35%

　　　　　　　　20×20, 94×60, 112/114cm,

　　　　　　　　40M AND UP ALLOWING 15% 27.432M

　　　　　　　　AND UP IN IRREGULAR CUTS

　　　　　　　　DWMAKES UP：FULL WIDTH ROLLER ON TUBES

　　　　　　　　　　　　OF 1.5 INCHES IN DIAMETER

　　　　　　　　PACKING：IN SEAWORTHY CARTONS

　　　　　　　　　　　　　　　　　　　　CIF TORONTO

COL.	M.	USD/M	USD
RED	4 000	1.56	6 240.00
SILVER	3 000	1.32	3 960.00
FIESTA	4 000	1.56	6 240.00
DKNAVY	3 000	1.62	4 860.00
WINE	2 200	1.62	3 564.00
ELEPHANT	3 000	1.44	4 320.00
BLACK	4 800	1.62	7 776.00
TOTAL：	24 000		36 960.00

SHIPMENT：BEF. APR. 20TH 2008

　　　　WITH PARTIAL SHIPMENT & TRANSHIPMENT TO BE ALLOWED.

DESTINATION：TORONTO

PAYMENT：BY 100% IRREVOCABLE L/C AVAILAVLE BY DRAFT AT 30 DAYS SIGHT, TO BE OPENED IN SELLERS FAVOUR 15 DAYS BEFORE THE MONTH OF SHIPMENT, L/C TO REMAIN VALID IN CHINA FOR A PERIOD OF 15 DAYS AFTER THE LAST SHIPMENT DATE.

　　　　　　　　　　　　ABC 纺织品进出口公司

IRREVOCABLE DOCUMENTARY CREDIT APPLICATION

TO：   DATE：

Applicant	Beneficiary（full name，address and tel. etc.）
Partial shipments （　）allowed （　）not allowed	**Transshipment** （　）allowed （　）not allowed	issued by（　）teletransmission 　　　　（　）express delivery

Loading on board/dispatch/taking in charge at/from ANY PORT Not later than For transportation to	Contract No.： Credit Amount（both in figures and words）： US DOLLARS　　　　　　　　　　ONLY. Trade Term：（　）FOB（　）CFR（　）CIF（　） others：
Description of goods： SEE ATTACHMENT	Date and place of expiry： Credit available with（　）by sight payment（　）by acceptance（　）by negotiation（　）by deferred payment at against the documents detailed herein（　）by 30 days after sight

Documents required：（marked with ×）

1. （　）Signed commercial invoice in copies indicating L/C No. and Contract No. .
2. （　）Full set of clean on board Bills of Lading made out ［　］to order/［　］to the order of shipper and blank endorsed，marked "freight ［　］prepaid/［　］to collect showing freight amount" notifying ［　］the applicant/［　］
3. （　）Air Waybills showing "freight ［　］prepaid/［　］to collect indicating freight amount" and consigned to
4. （　）Insurance Policy/Certificate in 3 copies for 110% of the invoice value showing claims payable in Canada in currency of the draft，blank endorsed，covering（［　］Ocean Marine Transportation/［　］Air Transportation/［　］Over Land Transportation）All Risks，War Risks. /［　］
5. （　）Packing list/Weight Memo in 3 copies indicating
6. （　）Certificate of Quantity/Weight in 3 copies issued by ［　］manufacturer/［　］Seller/［　］independent surveyor at the loading port，indicating the actual surveyed quantity/weight of shipped goods as well as the packing condition.
7. （　）Certificate of Quality in 3 copies issued by ［　］manufacturer/［　］public recognized surveyor/［　］
8. （　）Beneficiary's Certified copy of fax dispatched to the applicant within 2 days after shipment advising the contract number，name of commodity，quantity，invoice value，bill of loading，bill of loading date，the ETA date and shipping Co.
9. （　）Export license.
10. （　）Certificate of Origin in copies certifying.
11. （　）Other documents，if any：

Additional instruction：（marked with ×）

1. （　）All banking charges outside the opening bank are for beneficiary's account.

2. （　） Documents must be presented within 15 days after the date of issuance of the transport documents but within the validity of this credit.

3. （　） Third party as shipper is not acceptable，Short Form/Blank B/l is not acceptable.

4. （　） Both quantity and amount _____ % more or less are allowed.

5. （　） All documents to be forwarded in one lot by express unless otherwise stated above.

6. （　） Other terms, if any：

For banks use only	我公司承担本申请书背面所列责任及承诺,并保证按照办理。
Seal and/or Signature checked by （　）	
L/C Margin％ checked by （　）	（申请人名称及印鉴章）
Credit Facility checked by （　）	
Ent （　） Ver （　） App （　）	RMB A/C No.
Date：	USD or （　） A/C No.
	联系人：　　　　　　电话：

This L/C is subject to the Uniform Customs and Practice for Documentary Credit（2007 Revision）ICC Publication No. 600

（三）根据下面给出的条件填写开证申请书

合同资料：

THE BUYER：ABC COMPANY

ADDRESS：NO. 529，QUIANG ROAD, TIANJIN, CHINA

THE SELLER：XYZ COMPANY

ADDRESS：NO. 203 LIDIA HOTEL OFFICE 1546-49，DONG-GU, BUSAN, KOREA.

NAME OF COMMODITY：GOLD ROLLED STEEL SHEET IN COIL.

SPECIFICATIONS：JIS G3141 SPCC-SD

SIZE：0. 70MM×1 200 MM×C

QUANTITY：60 MT

PRICE TERM：FOB BUSAN

USD210/MT

TOTAL AMOUNT：USD 12 600. 00

COUNTRY OF ORIGIN AND MANUFACTURERS：REPUBLICE OF KOREA, VICTORY FACTORY

PARTIAL SHIPMENT AND TRANSSHOPMENT ARE PROHIBITTED

PACKING: EXPORT STANDARD PACKING, EACH COIL WEIGHT
5. 0MT MAX

SHIPPING MARK: ST

NO. 1…UP

TIME OF SHIPMENT: BEFORE JULY 15, 2008

PLACE AND DATE OF EXPIRY: CHINA, JULY 30, 2004

PORT OF SHIPMENT: BUSAN

PORT OF DESTINATION: XINGANG PORT, TIANJIN, CHINA

INSURANCE: TO BE COVERED BY BUYER.

PAYMENT: BY IRREVOCABLE FREELY NEGOTIABLE L/C AGAINST
SIGHT DRAFTS FOR 100 PCT OF INVOICE VALUE AND
THE DOCUMENTS DETAILED HEREUNDER.

DOCUMENTS:

1. INVOICES IN TRIPLICATE

2. PACKING LIST IN TRIPLICATE

3. FULL SET OF CLEAN ON BOARD BILL OF LADINGS MADE OUT
TO ORDER AND BLANK ENDORSED NOTIFYING THE APPLICANT
WITH FULL NAME AND ADDRESS MARKED FREIGHT COLLECT.

4. CERTIFICATE OF ORIGIN IN DUPLICATE

5. BENEFICIARY'S CERTIFIED COPY OF FAX TO THE APPLICANT
WITHIN 1 DAY AFTER SHIPMENT ADVISING GOODS NAME,
NAME OF VESSEL, INVOICE VALUE, DATE OF SHIPMENT,
QUANTITY AND WEIGHT.

OTHER TERMS AND CONDITIONS:

1. L/C TO BE ISSUED BY TELETRANSMISSION.

2. THE BUYER SHALL BEAR ALL BANKING CHARGES INCURRED
INSIDE THE ISSUING BANK.

3. ALL DOCUMENTS MUST BE MAILED IN ONE LOT TO THE ISSU-
ING BANK BY COURIER SERVICE.

4. PRESENTATION PERIOD: WITHIN 10 DAYS AFTER THE DATE OF
SHIPMENT.

开证申请书样式：

IRREVOCABLE DOCUMENTARY CREDIT APPLICATION

TO：   DATE：

Beneficiary (full name and address)：		Applicant (full name and address)：
Partial shipment （ ）allowed （ ）not allowed	Transshipment： （ ） allowed （ ） not allowed	Latest date of shipment： Place and date of expiry：
Loading on board/dispatch/taking in charge From： To： Price term：		Amount (Both in figures and words)：

Credit available with （ ）_____

（ ） by negotiation/（ ） by acceptance   with beneficiary's draft for _____ % of the invoice value

at _____ sight on issuing bank.

（ ） by sight payment/（ ） by deferred payment at _____ days

Against the documents detailed herein

Commodity：	Shipping mark：

Documents required：

1. （ ） Signed commercial invoice in _____ folds indicating L/C No. and contract No.

2. （ ） Full set (3/3) of clean on board ocean bills of lading made out to order and blank endorsed marked "（ ） freight prepaid/（ ） to collect" notify the applicant.

3. （ ） Air waybill consigned to the applicant notify the applicant marked "freight（ ）to collect/（ ）prepaid".

4. （ ） Insurance policy/certificate in _____ folds for 110% of the invoice value, showing claims pay in china in the currency of the draft, blank endorsed covering （ ） ocean marine transportation/（ ） air transportation/（ ） overland transportation all risks, war risks as per _____ clause.

5. （ ） Packing list in _____ folds indicating quantity/gross and net weights.

6. （ ） Certificate of origin in _____ folds.

7. （ ） Certificate of quantity in _____ folds.

8. （ ） Certificate of quality in _____ folds issued by （ ） manufacturer/（ ） beneficiary.

9. （ ） Beneficiary's certified copy of telex/fax dispatched to the applicant within _____ day after shipment advising goods name, （ ） name of vessel/（ ） flight. No. date, quantity. Weight and value of shipment.

10. （ ） Beneficiary's certificate certifying that （ ） one set of non-negotiable documents/（ ） one set of non-negotiable documents (including 1/3 original b/l) has been dispatched to the applicant directly by courier/speed post.

11. Other documents，if any

Additional instructions：

1. （ ） All banking charges outside the issuing bank are for beneficiary's account.

2. （ ） Documents must be presented within _____ days after the date of shipment but within the validity of the credit

3. （ ） Both quantity and amount _____ % more or less are allowed

4. （ ） All documents must be sent to issuing bank by courier/speed post in one lot.

5. （ ） Other terms，if any

联系人：   电话号码：   传真号：

（四）根据提供的合同填写开证申请书

汕头服装进出口公司   正 本

SHANTOU GARMENTS IMPORT & EXPORT COMPANY (ORIGINAL)

汕头中山路 106 号

ZHONGSHAN ROAD 106, SHANTOU China

电话(Tel)：0086-754-88587476   传真(Fax)：0086-754-88747698

销 货 合 同   编号 NO. YD-MDSC9811

SALES CONTRACT   日期 DATE：2007/11/8

Buyers：MAURICIO DEPORTS INTERNATIONAL S. A.

Address： RM 1008-1011 CONVENTION PLAZA, 101 HARBOR ROAD, COLON, R. P.

Tel：507-25192334   Fax：507-25192333

The undersigned Sellers and Buyers have agreed to close the following transaction according to the terms and conditions stipulated below：

货物名称及规格 NAME OF COMMODITY AND SPECIFICATTION	数量 QUANTITY	单价 UNIT PRICE	金额 AMOUNT
LADIES SHIRTS	2 000 PCS	CIF USD 10. 000	COLON USD 200 000. 00
	总值 TOTAL AMOUNT：USD 200 000. 00 Say Us Dollars Two Hundred Thousand Only		

PACKING：Each piece in a polybag, then 20 pcs to an export carton.

SHIPMENT：TO be effected during December 2007 from Shanghai allowing partial shipments and transshipment，

INSURANCHE：TO be covered for 110% of invoice value against All Risks as per and subject to Ocean Marine Cargo Clauses of P. I. C. C. dated 1/1/1981.

PAYMENT：The buyers shall open through a first-class bank acceptable to the seller an irrevocable L,/C at 30 days after B/L date to reach the seller November 25, 2007 and valid for negotiation in China until the 15th day after the date of shipment.

卖方 SELLERS
SHANGHAI YUANDA IMP. &
EXP. COMPANY

买方 BUYERS
MAURICIO DEPORTS INTERNA-
TIONAL S. A.

IRREVOCABLE DOCUMENTARY CREDIT APPLICATION

TO:BANK OF CHINA SHANTOU BRANCH	Date:
☐Issue by airmail　☐With brief advice by tele-transmission ☐Issue by express delivery ☐(which shall be the operative instrument)	Credit No. Date and place of expiry
Applicant	Beneficiary (Full name and address)
Advising Bank	Amount

Partial shipments ☐allowed ☐not allowed	Transshipment ☐allowed ☐not allowed	Credit available with By ☐payment　　☐acceptance ☐negotiation against the documents detailed herein
Loading on board/dispatch/taking in charge at/from not later than For transportation to:		☒and beneficiary's draft(s) for　　% of invoice value
☐FOB　　　☐CFR　　　☐CIF ☐or other terms		At　　　　sight drawn on

Documents required:(marked with ×)

1. (　) Signed commercial invoice in _____ copies

2. (　) Full set of clean on board Bills of Lading made out to order and blank endorsed, marked "freight [　] to collect/[　]prepaid [　] showing freight amount" notifying.

　(　) Airway bills/cargo receipt/copy of railway bills issued by showing "freight [　] to collect/ [　] prepaid [　] indicating freight amount" and consigned to _____ .

3. (　) Insurance Policy/Certificate in _____ copies for _____ % of the invoice value showing claims payable in _____ in currency of the draft, blank endorsed, covering All Risks, War Risks and _____ .

4. (　) Packing List/Weight Memo in _____ copies

5. (　) Certificate of Quantity/Weight in _____ copies issued by _____ .

6. (　) Certificate of Quality in _____ copies issued by [　] manufacturer/[　] public recognized surveyor _____ .

7. (　) Certificate of Origin in _____ copies.

8. （　） Beneficiary's certified copy of fax/telex dispatched to the applicant within _____ days after shipment advising L/C No., name of vessel, date of shipment, name, quantity, weight and value of goods.

Other documents, if any

Description of goods:

QUANTITY

PRICE TERM:

Additional instructions:

1. （　） All banking charges outside the opening bank are for beneficiary's account.
2. （　） Documents must be presented within _____ days after date of issuance of the transport documents but within the validity _____ of this credit.
3. （　） Third party as shipper is not acceptable, Short Form/Blank back B/L is not acceptable.
4. （　） Both quantity and credit amount _____ % more or less are allowed.
5. （　） All documents must be sent to issuing bank by courier/speed post in one lot.
6. （　） Other terms, if any

（五）单选题

信用证开立后,应由一家通知行进行通知,确定通知行的做法是(　　)。

A. 由进口商和出口商商定　　　　　B. 由受益人选择

C. 由开证行指定　　　　　　　　　D. 由开证申请人指定

（六）多选题

1. 在信用证业务的有关当事人之间,存在契约关系的有(　　)。

A. 开证申请人与开证行　　　　　　B. 开证申请人与受益人

C. 开证行与受益人　　　　　　　　D. 开证申请人与通知行

2.《UCP 600》适用于以下哪几种信用证(　　)。

A. 保兑信用证　　　　　　　　　　B. 不保兑信用证

C. 光票信用证　　　　　　　　　　D. 备用信用证

E. 自由议付信用证

（七）判断题

(　　)1. 信用证规定起运港为 CHINA PORT,若信用证禁止分批,则信用证中装运港 CHINA PORTS 的实际意义与 CHINA PORT 相同。

(　) 2. 如果信用证修改通知中将装运期和提单的内容进行了修改，那么出口方可以接受装运期部分的修改，而拒绝接受提单内容的修改。

(　) 3. 在信用证业务中，受益人收到信用证修改通知书后，如不同意修改，应立即将信用证修改书退回通知行，否则视为同意接受。

(　) 4. 在进口贸易中，我方对外开证时，一般不主动开出"可转让信用证"，以免被动。

(　) 5. 根据《UCP 600》，对开信用证的第一张信用证和第二张信用证的金额，既可相等，也可以不相等。

(　) 6. 开立银行保函的银行承担第一性的付款责任。

(　) 7. 由于传递造成的逾期接受仍具有效力，发盘人无权拒绝。

三、审核信用证

（一）根据合同审核信用证

1.

售 货 合 同

SALES CONTRACT

NO：2008KG02350

DATE：DEC 28，2008

THE SELLERS： THE BUYERS：

SUCCESS DEVELOPMENT TRADING LTD JYSK AB

39/FL，FLATF，TIANHE FLAZA FOERETA 6 S-23237 ARLOEV

SHANGHAI, CHINA

THIS SALES CONTRACT IS MADE BY AND BETWEEN THE SELLER AND THE BUYER, WHEREBY THE SELLER AGREE TO SELL AND THE BUYER AGREE TO BUY THE UNDER-MENTIONED GOODS ACCORDING TO THE TERMS AND CONDITIONS STIPULATED BELOW：

(1)货号、品名及规格 NAME OF COMMODITY AND SPECIFICATIONS	(2)数量 QUANTITY	(3)单价 UNIT PRICE	(4)金额 AMOUNT
LEATHER GLOVE ART 3900300 ART 3901400	8 400 PCS 15 520 PCS	CIF GOTHENBURG USD 1.25/PC USD 1.02/PC	USD 10 500.00 USD 15 830.40
AS PER S/C NO. 2008KG02350 AND JYSK ORDER 4500341081	TOTAL AMOUNT：		USD 26 330.40

装运港： LOADING IN CHARGE：CHINESE PORT

目的港： FOR TRANSPORT TO：GOTHENBURG，SWEDEN

转运： TRANSHIPMENT：ALLOWED

分批装运：PARTIAL SHIPMENT：ALLOWED

装运期限：THE LATEST DATE OF SHIPMENT：FEB. 28，2009

保险： INSURANCE：BE EFFECTED BY THE SELLERS FOR 110% INVOICE VALUE，COVERING F. P. A RISKS AS PER PICC CLAUSE.

付款方式：PAYMENT：BY IRREVOCABLE L/C，IN FAVOR OF THE

SELLER, TO BE AVAILABLE BY SIGHT DRAFT; REACHING THE SELLERS 30DAYS BEFORE THE SHIPMENT. REMAIN VALID FOR NEGOTIATION IN CHINA UNTIL THE 15TH DAYS AFTER THE FORE-SAID TIME OF SHIPMENT, ALL COMMIOSSION AND OUTSIDE SWEDEN ARE FOR ACCOUNT OF THE SELLERS.

仲裁：　　ARBITRATION：ALL DISPUTE ARISING FROM THE EXECUTION OR IN CONNECTION WITH THIS CONTRACT SHALL BE AMICABLY SETTLED THROUGH NEGOTIATION IN CASE OF NO SETTLEMENT CAN BE REACHED THROUGH NEGOTIATION THE CASE SHALL THEN BE SUBMITED TO THE CHINA INTERNATIONAL ECONOMIC & TRADE ARBITRATION COMMISION. IN SHANGHAI(OR IN BEIJING) FOR ARBITRATION. THE ARBITRAL AWAED IS FINAL AND BINDING UPON BOTH PARTIES FOR SETTLING THE DISPUTES. THE FEE, FOR ARBITRATION SHALL BE BORNE BY THE LOSING PARTY UNLESS OTHERWISE AWARDED.

信用证

THE SELLER   HE BUYER
SUCCUSS DEVELOPMENT TRADING LTD   JYSK AB
　　　　　ISSUE OF A DOCUMENTARY CREDIT
TO   HANGSENG BANK LTD. SHANGHAI BRANCH NORDEA BANK, SWEDEN
FROM
MT700

SEQUENCE OF TOTAL	27：	1/1
FROM OF DA	40A：	REVOCABLE
DC NO	20：	667-01-3042855
DATE OF ISSUE	31C：	090114
APPLICABLE RULES	40E：	UCP LATEST VERSION
EXPIRYDATE AND PLACE	31D：	DATE：MAR 15, 2009 PLACE： SWEDEN
APPLICANT	50：	JYSK AB FOERETA 6 S-23237 ARLOEV SWEDEN
BEBEFICIARY	59：	SUCCESS DEVELOPMENT TRADING LTD.

	39/FL, FLAT F TIANHEPLAZA
	SHANGHAI, CHINA
AMOUNT	32B： USD 26 330. 40
AVAILABLE WITH/BY	41A： ANY BANK BY NEGOTIATION
DRAFT AT…	42C： AT 30 DAYS SIGHT
DRAWEE	42A： ISSUING BANK
PARTIAL SHIPMENT	43P： ALLOWED
TRANSHIPMENT	43T： NOT ALLOWED
LOADING IN CHARGE	44A： CHINESE PORTS
FOR TRANSPORT TO	44B： GOTHENBURG, SWEDEN
LATEST DATE OF SHIPMENT	44C： FEB 08, 2009
DESCRIPTION OF GOODS	45A： LEATHER GLOVE

AS PER S/C NO 2008KG02350 AND

JYSK ORDER 4500341081

8 400 PCS ART 3900300 USD 1. 25/PC

15 520 PCS ART 3901400 USD 1. 20/PC

CIF SHANGHAI (INCOTERMS 2000)

DOCUMENTS REQUIRED 46A： 1 SIGNED ORIGINAL COMMERCIAL INVOICE AND 5 COPIES

PACKING LIST IN 2 COPIES

FULL SET OF CLEAN ON BOARD MARINE BILLS OF LADING, MADE OUT TO ORDER OF ISSING BANK, MARKED "FREIGHT PREPAID" AND NOTIFY APPLICANT (AS INDICATED ABOVE); MENTIONING L/C NO.

GSP CERTIFICATE OF ORIGIN FORM A, CERTIFYING GOODS OF ORIGIN IN CHINA, ISSUED BY COMPETENT AUTHORITIES

INSURANCE POLICY/CERTIFICATE COVERING ALL RISKS OF PICC,

INCLUDING WAREHOUSE TO WARE-HOUSE CLAUSE UP TO FINAL DESTINATION AT GOTHENBURG, FOPR AT LEAST 120 PCT OF CIF VALUE, SHOWING CLAIMS PAYABLE IF ANY IN SWEDEN.

ADDITIONAL CONDITIONS. 47A: ALL DOCUMENTS MUST BE ISSUED IN ENGLISH

MULTIMODAL TRANSPORT DOCUMENTS ACCEPTABLE EVIDENCING SHIPMENT CLEAN ON BOARD ON A NAMED VESSEL

BILL OF LADING MUST SHOW CONTAINER NUMBER

P/L（PACKING LIST）MUST BE SPECIFIED PER ART NO AND CONTAINER NO.

DETAILS OF CHARGES 71 B: ALL COMMISSION AND CHARGES OUTSIDE SWEDEN ARE FOR ACCOUNT OF BENEFICIARY OUR CHARGES WILL BE DEDUCTED/CLAIMED AT THE TIME OF PAYMENT, NEGOTIATION OR EXPIRY.

PRESENTATION PERIOD 48: DOCUMENTS TO BE PRESENTED WITHIN 5 DAYS AFTER THE DATE OF SHIPMENT, BUT WITHIN THE VALIDITY OF THE CREDIT.

CONFIRMATION 79: ON RECEIPT OF MALL ADVICE OF
INSTRUCTIONS NEGOTIATION, WE SHALL COVER AS PER INSTRUCTIONS RECEIVED.

THIS CREDIT IS SUBJECT TO UCP(2007 REVISON), ICC PUUBL NO. 600

审核结果如下：

2. **SALES CONFIRMATION**

BUYERS：BELLAFLORA GARTEN CENTER GE-SELLSCHAFT　NO. 205001
ADDRESS：M. B. H FRANZOSENH-AUSWEG 50 A-4020 LINZ, AUSTRIA　DATE：2006-05-09
SELLERS：DALIAN ARTS&CRAFTS IMPORT&EXPORT CORP.
ADDRESS：NO. 23 FUGUI STR., DALIAN, CHINA

The undersigned buyers and sellers have agreed to close the following transactions according to the terms and conditions stipulated below：

NAME OF COMMODITY & SPECEIFICATION	UNIT PRICE	QUANTITY	AMOUNT & PRICE TERMS
CHRISTMAS GIFTS	CIF HAMBURG	(SET)	CIF HAMBURG
AF-634	USD 0. 66	768	USD 506. 8
AF-655	USD 0. 46	1 600	USD 736. 00
AF-555	USD 1. 01	600	USD 606. 00
AF-629	USD 0. 78	768	USD 599. 04
AF-651	USD 0. 50	1 600	USD 800. 00
AF-673	USD 0. 50	600	USD 300. 00
AF-676	USD 0. 52	672	USD 349. 44
AF-609A	USD 0. 76	420	USD 319. 20
AF-609	USD 0. 90	382	USD 343. 80
AF-609B	USD 0. 95	240	USD 204. 00
AF-705	USD 0. 52	900	USD 468. 00
AF-704	USD 0. 68	648	USD 440. 64
AF-701	USD 0. 58	840	USD 487. 20
AF-702	USD 0. 52	960	USD 499. 20
DL-(EACH 400 DOZ)			
1768B,1756B,1718B,1737B,1691B		(DOZ)	
1679B,1703B,1770B,1771B,1768B,	2. 15	4 000	8 600. 00
DL 1834B	4. 10	400	1 640. 00
(EACH 400 DOZ) DL 1846B,1789	3. 96	800	3 168. 00
TM 4648	0. 54	750 PCS	405. 00
TM-2	1. 54	750 PCS	1 155. 00
A-33	1. 43	600 PCS	858. 00

TOTAL：USD 22 485. 40

PACKING: IN CARTONS

INSURANCE: BY SELLER, FOR THE INVOICE VALUE PLUS 10 PCS, AGAINST ALL RISKS AND WAR&·S. R. RISKS AS PER O. M. C. C OF P. I. C. C CLAUSES

DD. 1981,01,01 FROM WAREHOUSE TO WAREHOUSE.

TIME OF SHIPMENT: JUNE − 1, 2006. PARCIALSHIPMENT AND TRANSHIPMENT ARE ALLOWED.

PORT OF LOADING & DESTINATION: ANY PORT OF CHINA TO HAMBURG.

PAYMENT: L/C AT SIGHT, ARRIVED THE SELLER BEFORE MAY 15TH,2006.

THE SIGNATURE OF BUYERS: THE SIGNATURE OF SELLERS:

ISSUE OF A DOCUMENTARY CREDIT

SEQUENCE OF TOTAL	*27:	1/1
FORM OF DOC. CREDIT	*40A:	IRREVOCABLE
DOC. CREDIT NUMBER	*20:	273. 627
DATE OF ISSUE	31C:	060514
APPLICABLE RULES	40E:	UCP LATEST VERSION
EXPIRY	*31D:	DATE 2006-07-05 PLACE LINZ
APPLICATNT	*50:	BELLAFLORA GARDEN CENTER GESELLSCHAFT M. B. H FRANZ-OSENHAUSWEG 50 A-4020 LINZ, AUSTRIA
BENEFICIARY	*58:	DALIAN ARTS &CRAFTS IMP. & EXP. CORP. NO. 23 FUGUI STRE-ET, ZHONG SHAN DISTRICT, DALIAN, CHINA
AMOUNT	*32B:	CURRENCY USD AMOUNT 21 330. 44
POS. /NEG. TOL. (%)	39A:	10/10
AVAILABLE WITH/BY	*41A:	OBKLAT2L * BANK FUER OBEROEATERREICH

UND

* SALZBURG(OBERBANK)

* LINZ

BY PAYMENT

PARTIAL SHIPMENTS	43P:	NOT ALLOWED
TRANSSHIPMENT	43T:	ALLOWED
LOADING IN CHARGE	44A:	CHINA PORT
FOR TRANSPORT TO	45B:	HUMBURG
LATEST DATE OF SHIPMENT	44C:	060620
DESCRIPT. OF GOODS	45A:	CHRISTMAS GIFTS AS PER SALES CONFIRMATION NO. 96DRA207 OF MAY. 9TH 2006, CIF HAMBURG
DOCUMENTS REQUIRED	46A:	

1. COMMERCIAL INVOICE, 5 FOLD, ALL DULY SIGNED, CERTIFYING THAT THE GOODS HAVE PACKED AND CHINESE ORIGIN.

2. FULL SET OF CLEAN ON BOARD ORIGINAL MARINE BILL OF LADING, MADE OUT TO ORDER, BLANK ENDORSED, NOTIFYING BELLAFLORA

3. CERTIFICATE OF P. R. CHINA ORIGIN TWO ORIGINALS AND ONE COPY AS PER GSP FORM A ISSUED AND MANUALLY SIGNED BY AN AUTHORITY ALSO SHOWING IMPORTING COUNTRY

4. PACKING LIST IN QUINTUPLICATE, IT SHOULD BE COUNTERSIGNED BY BUYER'S AUTHORIZED PERSON AND CERTIFYED BY ISSUING BANK.

经审核,该信用证存在下列错误:

3.

销　售　合　同
SALES CONTRACT

卖方 **SELLER**:	DESUN TRADING CO., LTD. 29TH FLOOR KINGSTAR MANSION, 623JINLIN RD., SHANGHAI CHINA

编号 **NO.**:　SHDS03027

日期 **DATE**:　APR. 03, 2008

地点 **SIGNED IN**:　SHANGHAI

买方 **BUYER**:	NEO GENERAL TRADING CO. ＃362 JALAN STREET, TORONTO, CANADA

买卖双方同意以下条款达成交易:

This contract Is made by and agreed between the BUYER and SELLER, in accordance with the terms and conditions stipulated below.

1. 品名及规格 Commodity & Specification	2. 数量 Quantity	3. 单价及价格条款 Unit Price & Trade Terms	4. 金额 Amount
			CIFC5 TORONTO
CHINESE CERAMIC DINNERWARE			
DS1511 30-Piece Dinnerware and Tea Set	542 SETS	USD 23.50	12 737.00
DS2201 20-Piece Dinnerware Set	800 SETS	USD 20.40	16 320.00
DS4504 45-Piece Dinnerware Set	443 SETS	USD 23.20	10 277.60
DS5120 95-Piece Dinnerware Set	254 SETS	USD 30.10	7 645.40
Total:	**2 039 SETS**		**46 980.00**

允许 With	10%	溢短装,由卖方决定 More or less of shipment allowed at the sellers' option
5. 总值 **Total Value**		SAY US DOLLARS FORTY SIX THOUSAND NINE HUNDRED AND EIGHTY ONLY.
6. 包装 **Packing**		DS2201 IN CARTONS OF 2 SETS EACH AND DS1151, DS4505 AND DS5120 TO BE PACKED IN CARTONS OF 1 SET EACH ONLY. TOTAL: 1639 CARTONS.

续表

7. 唛头 **Shipping Marks**	AT BUYER'S OPTION.	
8. 装运期及运输方式 **Time of Shipment & means of** **Transportation**	TO BE EFFECTED BEFORE THE END OF APRIL 2008 WITH PARTIAL SHIPMENT AND ALLOWED AND TRAN- SHIPMENT ALLOWED.	
9. 装运港及目的地 **Port of Loading & Destination**	FROM: SHANGHAI TO: TORONTO	
10. 保险 **Insurance**	THE SELLER SHALL COVER INSURANCE AGAINST WPA AND CLASH & BREAKAGE & WAR RISKS FOR 110% OF THE TOTAL IN- VOICE VALUE AS PER THE RELEVANT OCEAN MARINE CARGO OF P. I. C. C. DATED 1/1/1981.	
11. 付款方式 **Terms of Payment**	THE BUYER SHALL OPEN THOUGH A BANK ACCEPTABLE TO THE BEFORE APRIL 10, 2008 VALID FOR NEGOTIATION IN CHINA UNTIL THE 15TH DAY AFTER THE DATE OF SHIPMEDNT.	
12. 备注 **Remarks**		

The Buyer	The Seller
NEO GENERAL TRADING CO.	DESUN TRADING CO.,LTD.
（signature）	（signature）

THE ROYAL BANK OF CANADA
BRITISH COLUMBIA INTERNATION CENTRE
1055 WEST GEORGIA STREET, VANCOUVER, B. C. V6E 3P3
CANADA

□CONFIRMATION OF TELEX/CABLE PER-ADVISED　　　　　DATE: APR. 8, 2008
　TELEX NO. 4720688 CA　　　　　　　　　　　　　　PLACE: VANCOUVER

IRREVOCABLE DOCUMENTARY CREDIT	CREDIT NUMBER: 08/0501-FCT	ADVISING BANK'S REF. NO.
ADVISING BANK: SHANGHAI A J FINANCE CORPORATION 59 HONGKONG ROAD SHANGHAI 200002, CHINA	**APPLICANT:** NEO GENERAL TRADING CO. #362 JALAN STREET, TORONTO, CANADA	
BENEFICIARY: DESUN TRADING CO.,LTD. 29TH FLOOR KINGSTAR MAN- SION, 623JINLIN RD., SHANGHAI CHINA	**AMOUNT:** USD 46 980. 00 (US DOLLARS FORTY SIX THOUSAND NINE HUNDRED AND EIGHTEEN ONLY)	

续表

EXPIRY DATE：MAY 15，2008 FOR NEGOTIATION IN APPLICANTS COUNTRY

GENTLEMEN：

WE HEREBY OPEN OUR IRREVOCABLE LETTER OF CREDIT IN YOUR FAVOR WHICH IS AVAILABLE BY YOUR DRAFTS AT SIGHT FOR FULL INVOICE VALUE ON US ACCOMPANIED BY THE FOLLOWING DOCUMENTS：

+ SIGNED COMMERCIAL INVOICE AND 3 COPIED.
+ PACKING·LIST AND 3 COPIES, SHOWING THE INDIVIDUAL WEIGHT AND MEASUREMENT OF EACH ITEM.
+ ORIGINAL CERTIFICATE OF ORIGIN AND 3 COPIES ISSUED BY THE CHAMBER OF COMMERCE.
+ FULL SET CLEAN ON BOARD OCEAN BILLS OF LADING SHOWING FREIGHT PREPAID CONSIGNED TO ORDER OF THE ROYAL BANK OF CANADA INDICATING THE ACTUAL DATE OF THE GOODS ON BOARD AND NOTIFY THE APPLICANT WITH FULL ADDRESS AND PHONE NO. 77009910.
+ INSURANCE POLICY OR CERTIFICATE FOR 130 PERCENT OF INVOICE VALUE COVERING：INSURANCE CARGO CLAUSES(A) AS PER I. C. C. DATED 1/1/1982.
+ BENEFICIARY'S CERTIFICATE CERTIFYING THAT EACH COPY OF SHIPPING DOCUMENTS HAS BEEN FAXED TO THE APPLICANT WITHIN 48 HOURS AFTER SHIPMENT.

COVERING SHIPMENT PF：

4 ITEMS TERMS OF CHINESE CERAMIC DINNERWARE INCLUDING：

    DS1511   30-PIECE DINNERWARE AND TEA SET, 544SETS

    DS2201   20-PIECE DINNERWARE SET, 800SETS,

    DS4504   45-PIECE DINNERWARE SET, 443SETS

    DS5120   95-PIECE DINNERWARE SET, 245SETS

DETAILS IN ACCORDANCE WITH SALES CONTRACT HSDS03027 DATED APR 3，2003.

[ ]FOB/ [ ]CFR/[×] CIF/[ ]FAX TORONTO CANADA.

SHIPMENT FROM	TO	LATEST	PARTIAL SHIPMENTS	TRANSSHIPMENT
SHANGHAI	VANCOUVER	APRIL 30,2008	PROHIBITED	PROHIBITED

DRAFTS TO BE PRESENTED FOR NEGOTIATION WITHIN 15 DAYS AFTER SHIPMENT, BUT WITHIN THE VALIDITY OF CREDIT. ALL DOCUMENTS TO BE FORWARDED IN ONE COVER, BY AIRMAIL, UNLESS OTHERWISE STATED UNDER SPECIAL INSTRUCTION.

SPECIAL INSTRUCTION：ALL BANKING CHARGES OUTSIDE CANADA ARE FOR ACCOUNT OF BENEFICIARY.

+ ALL GOODS MUST BE SHIPPED IN ONE 20'CY TO CY CONTAINER AND B/L SHOWING THE SAME.
+ THE VALUE OF FREIGHT PREP AID HAS TO BE SHOWN ON BILLS OF LADING.
+ DOCUMENTS WHICH FAIL TO COMPLY WITH THE TERMS AND CONDITIONS IN THE LETTER OF CREDIT SUBJECT TO A SPECIAL DISCREPANCY HANDLING FEE OF USMYM35. 00 TO BE DEDUCTED FROM ANY PROCEEDS.

DRAFT MUST BE MARKED AS BEING DRAWN UNDER THIS CREDIT AND BEAR ITS NUM-
BER; THE AMOUNTS ARE TO BE ENDORSED ON THE REVERSE HERE OF BY NEG.
BANK. WE HEREBY AGREE WITH THE DRAWERS, ENDORSERS AND FIDE HOLDER
THAT ALL DRAFTS DRAWN UNDER AND IN COMPLIANCE WITH THE TERMS OF THIS
CREDIT SHALL BE DULY HONORED UPON PRESENTATION.
THIS CREDIT IS SUBJECT TO THE UNIFORM CUSTOMS AND PRACTICE FOR DOCUMEN-
TARY CREDITS（2007 REVISION）BY THE INTERNATIONAL CHAMBER OF COMMERCE
PUBLICATION NO. 600.

Yours Very Truly,

David Jone   **Joanne Hsan**

AUTHORIZED SIGNATURE   AUTHORIZED SIGNATURE

信用证号	
合 同 号	
审证结果	

4.

售货确认书

SALES CONFIRMATION

NO. LT07060

DATE：AUG. 10，2005

THE SELLERS：AAA IMPORT AND EXPORT CO.，THE BUYERS：BBB TRADING CO.，222 JIANGUO ROAD

P. O. BOX 203

DALIAN，CHINA   GDANSK，POLAND

THE UNDERSIGNED SELLERS AND BUYERS HAVE AGREED TO

CLOSE THE FOLLOWING TRANSACTIONS ACCORDING TO THE TERMS AND CONDITIONS STIPULATED BELOW：

品名与规格 COMMODITY AND SPECIFICATION	数量 QUANTITY	单价 UNIT PRICE	金额 AMOUNT
65% POLYESTER 35% COTTON LADIES SKIRTS STYLE NO. A101 STYLE NO. A102 ORDER NO. HMW0501	 200 DOZ 400 DOZ	CIF GDANSK USD 60/DOZ USD 84/DOZ	 USD 12 000.00 USD 33 600.00
TOTAL：	600DOZ		**USD 45 600.00**

总值： 　TOTAL VALUE：US DOLLARS FORTY FIVE THOUSAND AND SIX HUNDRED ONLY.

装运口岸：PORT OF LOADING：DALIAN

目的地： 　DESTINATION：GDANSK

转运： 　TRANSHIPPMENT：ALLOWED

分批装运：PARTIAL SHIPMENT：ALLOWED

装运期限：SHIPMENT：DECEMBER, 2005

保险： 　INSURANCE：BE EFFECTED BY THE SELLERS FOR 110% INVOICE VALUE COVERING F. P. A. RISK OF PICC CLAUSE

付款方式：PAYMENT：BY TRANSFERABLE L/C PAYABLE 60 DAYS AFTER B/L DATE, REACHING THE SELLERS 45 DAYS BEFORE THE SHIPMENT

DAVID KING 　　　　　　　　　　　　　　　苏进
买方 　　　　　　　　　　　　　　　　　　　卖方

LETTER OF CREDIT

FORM OF DOC. CREDIT	*40A：	IRREVOCABLE
DOC. CREDIT NUMBER	*20：	70/1/5822
DATE OF ISSUE	*31：	051007
APPLICABLE RULES	40E：	UCP LATEST VERSION
EXPIRY	*31D：	DATE 060115 POLAND
ISSUING BANK	*51A：	SUN BANK
		P. O. BOX 201 GDANSK,POLAND

```
APPLICANT              *50：    BBB TRADING CO.
                               P. O. BOX 203
                        *      GDANSK，POLAND
BENEFICIARY            *59：    AAA IMPORT AND EXPORT CO.
                               222 JIANCUO ROAD
                               DALIAN，CHINA
AMOUNT                 *32B：   CURRENCY USD AMOUNT
                               45 600. 00
AVAILABLE WITH/BY      *41A：   BANK OF CHINA
                               DALIAN BRANCH
                               BY DEF PAYMENT
DEFFRRED PAYM. DET.    *42P：   60 DAYS AFTER B/L DATE
PARTIAL SHIPMENTS      *43P：   NOT ALLOWED
TRANSHIPMETN           *43T：   ALLOWED
LOADING IN CHARGE       44A：   SHANGHAI
FOR TRANSPORT TO...     44B：   GDANSK
LATEST DATE OF SHIP.    44C：   051231
DESCRIPT. OF GOODS      45A：   65% POLYESTER 35% COTTON
                               LADIES SHIRTS
                               STYLE NO. 101  200DOZ@USD 60/
                               PCE
                               SYTLE NO. 102  400DOZ@USD 84/
                               PCE
                               ALL OTHER DETEILS OF GOODS
                               ARE AS PER CONTRACT NO.
                               LT07060 DATED
                               AUG 10，2005.
                               DELIVERY TERMS：CIF GDANSK
                               (INCOTERMS 2000)
DOCUMENTS REQUIRED      46A：
```

1. COMMERCIAL INVOICE MANUALLY SIGNED IN 2 ORIGINALS PLUS 1 COPY MADE OUT TO DDD TRADING CO.，P. O. BOX 211，GDANSK，POLAND.
2. FULL SET (3/3) OF ORIGINAL CLEAN ON BOARD BILL OF LADING

PLUS ONE 3/3 NEGOTIABLE COPIES, MADE OUT TO ORDER OF IS-SUING BANK AND BLANK ENDORSED, NOTIFY THE APPLICANT, MARKED FREIGHT PREPAID, MENTIONING GROSS WEIGHT AND NET WEIGHT.

3. ASSORTMENT LIST IN 2 ORIGIANLS PLUS 1 COPY.

4. CERTIFICATE OF ORIGIN IN 1 ORIGINAL PLUS 2 COPIES SIGNED BY CCPIT.

5. MARINE ISURANCE POLICY IN THE CURRENCY O THE CREDIT ENDORSED IN BLANK FOR CIF VALUE PLUS 30 PCT MARINE COVERING ALL RISKS OF PICC CLAUSES INDICATING CLAIM PAYABLE IN POLAND.

ADDITIONAL COND.　　　　47A：

+ B/L MUST SHOWING SHIPPING MARKS：BBB, S/C LT07060, GDAND, C/NO.

+ ALL DOCS MUST SHOW THIS L/C NO. 70/1/5822.

DETAILS OF CHARGES 71B：		ALL BANKING COMM/CHRGS OUTSIDE POLAND ARE FOR BENEFICIARY'S ACCOUNT.
PRESENTATION PERIOD	48：	15 DAYS AFTER B/L DATE. BUT WITHIN L/C VALIDITY.
CONFIRMATION	*49：	WITHOUT
SEND TO REC. INFO	72：	CREDIT SUBJECT TO ICC PUBL 600/2007 REV

经审核，信用证存在的问题如下：

5.　　　　　　　　　**SALES CONFIRMATION**

NO：20406

DATE：AUG. 5, 2008

SELLER：SHANGHAI SEWING MACHINE IMP. & EXP. CORPORATION.

BUYER：ABC COMPANY, P. O. BOX NO. 123. KUWAIT.

COMMODITY AND SPECIFICATIONS：

BUTTERFLY BRAND SEWING MACHINE JA-13-DRAWER' FOLDING

COVER

QUANTITY: 5 000 SETS, 5% MORE OR LESS AT SELLER'S OPTION

PACKING: IN CARTONS OF ONE SET EACH

UNIT PRICE: US MYM 58. 00 PER SET CFRC3% KUWAIT

TOTAL VALUE: US MYM 290 000. 00 (U. S. DOLLARS TWO HUNDRED NINTY THOUSAND ONLY)

TIME OF SHIPMENT: DURING OCT. /NOV. 2008 IN TWO EQUAL MONTH-LY LOTS, FROM SHANGHAI TO KUWAIT, AL-LOWING TRANSSHIPMENT.

INSURANCE: TO BE COVERED BY THE BUYER

TERMS OF PAYMENT: BY IRREVOCABLE SIGHT LETTER OF CRED-IT TO REACH THE SELLER 15 DAYS BEFORE THE MONTH OF SHIPMENT AND REMAIN VALID FOR NEGOTIATION IN CHINA UNTIL THE 15TH DAYS AFTER DATE OF SHIP-MENT.

REMARKS: THIS CONTRACT IS CONCLUDED THROUGH AGENT-ABDULLA COMPANY, KUWAIT.

IRREVOCABLE DOCUMENTARY CREDIT

No. 101465

SEPT. 2nd 2008

TO: BANK OF CHINA

SHANGHAI, CHINA

FROM: THE COMMERCIAL BANK OF KUWAIT, KUWAIT

WE OPEN IRREVOCABLE DOCUMENTARY CREDIT

NO. 101465

BENEFICIARY: SHANGHAI SEWING MACHINE IMPORT AND EX-PORT CORPORATION

APPLICANT: ABC COMPANY. P. O. BOX NO. 123 KUWAIT

AMOUNT: US MYM 290 000. 00 (US DOLLARS TWO HUNDRED AND NINTY THOUSAND ONLY)

THIS CREDIT IS AVAILABLE BY BENEFICIARY'S DRAFT AT 30 DAYS AFTER SIGHT FOR 100% OF INVOICE VALUE DRAWN ON THE COM-MERCIAL BANK OF KUWAIT, NEW YORK BRANCH, NEWYORK. U. S. A.

ACCOMPANIED BY THE FOLLOWING DOCUMENTS：

1. SIGNED COMMERCIAL INVOICE IN 3 COPIES.

2. FULL SET OF CLEAN ON BOARD BILL OF LADING MADE OUT TO ORDER AND NOTIFY APPLICANT.

3. INSURANCE POLICY IN DUPLICATE COPIES FOR 120% OF IN-VOICE VALUE COVERING ALL RISKS AND WAR RISK SUBJECT TO CIC DATED JAN 1ST, 1981.

4. CERTIFICATE OF ORIGIN IN DUPLICATE ISSUED BY CHINA IN-TERNATIONAL CHAMBER OF COMMERCE OR OTHER GOVERN-MENT AUTHORITIES.

5. INSPECTION CERTIFICATE OF QUALITY ISSUED BY APPLICANT. 5000 SETS BUTTERFLY BRAND SEWING MACHINE JA-103 DRAW-ERS FOLDING COVER AT US $ 58.00 PER SET CFR KUWAIT AS PER S/C NO. 95406 DATED AU0.5TH, 1995.

LATEST SHIPMENT：OCT. 31ST, 2008 FROM SHANGHAI TO KUWAIT.

PARTIAL SHIPMENTS：ALLOWED

TRANSSHIPMENT：PROHIBITED

THE GOODS SHALL BE CONTAINERIZED

DOCUMENTS MUST BE PRESENTED WITHIN 15 DAYS AFTER THE DATE OF ISSUANCE OF THE B/L, BUT WITHIN THE VALIDITY OF THE CREDIT.

THE COMMERCIAL BANK OF KUWAIT

审证结果如下：

（二）对照合同，指出六处信用证与合同不符的地方

信用证

COMMECIAL BANK OF VANCOUVER

TO：China National Cereals, Oils   Date：Oct. 5，2006
&Foodstuffs Corporation
Beijing，China

Advised Through Bank of China, Beijing

NO. BOC06/10/05

IRREVOCABLE DOCUMENTARY LETTER OF CREDIT

Dear sirs:

We open this by order of Hong Kong Company, Vancouver for a sum not exceeding CAN MYM 120 000 (SAY CAMADIAN DOLLOARS ONE HUNDRED AND TWENTY THOUSAND ONLY) available by drafts drawn on us at sight accompanied by the following documents:

——Full set of clean on board bill of lading made out to order and blank endorsed, marked"freight collect" dated not later than November 30, 2006 and notify accountee.

——Signed commercial invoice in quintuplicate.

——Canadian customs invoice in quintuplicate.

——Insurance policies (or certificates) in duplicate covering marine and war risks.

Evidencing shipment from China port to Montreal, Canada of the following goods:

50 000 tins of 430 grams of Great Wall Strawberry Jam, at CanMYM2.50 per tin CFR C 3% Vancouver, details as per your S/C No. 06/8712

Partial shipment are allowed,

Transshipment is allowed.

This Credit expires on November 30, 2006 for negotiation in China.

销售合同条款

卖方： 中国粮油食品公司(China National Cereals, Oils & Foodstuffs Corporation)

买方： 温哥华香港食品公司(Hong Kong Food Company, Vancouver)

食品名称：长城牌草莓酱(Great Wall Brand Strawberry Jam)

规格： 340 克听装

数量： 50 000 听

单价： CFR 温哥华每听 2.50 加元，并含佣金 3%

总值： 125 000 加元

装运期： 2006 年 11 月自中国港口运往温哥华，允许转船和分批装运

付款条件：凭不可撤销的即期信用证付款，信用证议付有效期应为最后装运期后第 15 天在中国到期。

合同号码：06/8712

审证结果如下：

（三）单选题

1. 根据《UCP 600》规定，若发现单证不符拒受单据时，开证行/保兑行通知寄单行的时间应为收到单据次日起的（　　）内。

   A. 7 个银行工作日　　　　　　　　　　B. 5 个银行工作日

   C. 7 天　　　　　　　　　　　　　　　D. 10 天

2. 某证的装运期是 3 月 30 日，有效期为 4 月 15 日，对交单期未做规定。货物于 3 月上旬出运，取得船公司 3 月 10 日签发的提单。该套单据的最迟交单期为（　　）。

   A. 3 月 21 日　　　　　　　　　　　　B. 3 月 25 日

   C. 3 月 31 日　　　　　　　　　　　　D. 4 月 15 日

3. 如果在制作单据时，将发票人抬头的邮政编码写错，则（　　）。

   A. 必然遭到开证行拒付

   B. 开证行仍应当付款

   C. 是否付款取决于开证行的意愿

   D. 是否付款取决于开证申请人的意愿

（四）多选题

1. 因下列情况开证行有权拒付票款（　　）。

   A. 单据内容与信用证条款不符　　　　　B. 实际货物未装运

   C. 单据与货物有出入　　　　　　　　　D. 单据与单据互相之间不符

   E. 单据内容与合同条款不符

2. 在审核信用证金额与货币时，需要审核的内容包括（　　）。

   A. 信用证总金额的大小写必须一致

   B. 来证采用的货币与合同规定的货币必须一致

   C. 发票或汇票金额不能超过信用证规定的总金额

   D. 若合同中订有溢短装条款，信用证金额应有相应规定

   E. 信用证金额中必须注明折扣率

3. 审核信用证和审核单据的依据是（　　）。

    A. 开证申请书   B. 合同及《UCP 600》的规定

    C. 一整套单据   D. 信用证

4. 通知行对于信用证的审核重点包括（　　）。

    A. 从政策上审核   B. 对信用证本身说明的审核

5. 进出口公司对信用证的审核要点包括（　　）。

    A. 对信用证本身说明的审核   B. 对信用证有关货物记载的审核

    C. 对开证行资信的审核   D. 对单据要求的审核

    E. 对信用证有关时间说明的审核

（五）判断题

（　　）1. 除非信用证另有规定，银行将接受出单日期早于信用证开立日期的单据。

（　　）2. 在信用证付款方式下，只要在信用证的有效期内向银行提交符合合同要求的单据，银行不得拒收单据和拒收货款。

（　　）3. 若受益人逾期交单，则只要其征得开证申请人的同意，仍可要求银行付款。

（　　）4. 根据《UCP 600》，信用证项下单据应在信用证效期和交单期内向银行提交。如果信用证对交单期未做规定，则交单期不得迟于运输单据日期后的 15 天，并且不得迟于信用证的有效期。

（　　）5. 信用证受益人收到来证后，经审核，如发现来证内容与成交合同有不符，可经过通知行转告开证行，要求开证行修改不符处。

（　　）6. "单单一致"对于大小写不予以限制。

四、信用证改证函的书写

(一) Please check the L/C with the contract below and then write a letter to ask for the amendment to the L/C

所给信用证:

Copenhagen Bank

Date: January 4, 2008

To: Bank of China, Beijing

We hereby open our irrevocable letter of credit No. 112235 in favor of China Trading Corporation for account of Copenhagen Import Company up to an amount of GBP 1 455.00 (SAY POUND STERLING ONE THOUSAND FOUR HUNDRED AND FIFTY FIVE ONLY) for 100% of the invoice value relative to the shipment of:

150 metric tons of Writing Paper Type 501 at GBP 97 per M/T CIF Copenhagen as per your S/C No. PO-5476 from Copenhagen to China port.

Drafts to be drawn at sight on our bank and accompanied by the following documents marked "×":

(×) Commercial Invoice in triplicate

(×) Bill of Lading in triplicate made out to order quoting L/C No. 112235, marked FREIGHT COLLECT:

(×) One original Marine insurance Policy or Certificate for All Risks and War Risk, covering 110% of the invoice value, with claims payable in Copenhagen in the currency of draft(s).

Partial shipments and transshipment are prohibited.

Shipment must be effected not later than 31 March, 2008

This L/C is valid at our counter until 15 April, 2008.

所给合同主要条款:

卖方: 中国贸易公司

买方: 哥本哈根进口公司

商品名称:写字纸

规格: 501 型

数量: 150 公吨

单价：　　CIF 哥本哈根每公吨 97 英镑

总价值：　14 550 英镑

装运期：　2008 年 3 月 31 日前自中国港口至哥本哈根

保险：　　由卖方按发票金额的 110％ 投保一切险和战争险

支付：　　不可撤销的即期信用证，于装船前 1 个月开到卖方，并于上述装运期
　　　　　后 15 天内在中国议付有效

（二）根据下列合同审核信用证，指出不符点并草拟改证函

Sales Contract

No.：ss03

Date：May 20，2006

Seller：Shanghai stationery and sporting goods Imp. and Exp. Corp.

Address：5-15 mansion 1230-1240 Zhongshan road，shanghai

Buyer：Smith Co. Ltd.，

Address：The Jane street，Kong zone，London，England

　　　This contract is made by and between the buyers and the sellers，whereby the buyers agree to buy and the sellers agree to sell the undermentioned commodity according to the terms and conditions stipulated below：

Name of commodity：men's gloves

Specification：Model No. 5

Quantity：2000dozens

Unit Price：CFR Amsterdam USD 45. 00 Per dozen

Amount：USD 90 000. 00(Say U. S. Dollars Ninety Thousand Only)

Shipment：From Shanghai, China To Amsterdam, Holland Not Later Than
　　　　　July 30，2006 with transshipment and partial shipment not allowed

Packing：By Seaworthy cartons(CTNS)

Insurance：To be covered by buyers

Terms of Payment：By irrevocable letter of Credit at Sight

Shipping Marks：At sellers' option

信用证

CREDIT NUMBER：　　　A2B9600463

DATE OF ISSUE：　　　　060618

ADVISING BANK：　　　　BANK OF CHINA ZHONGSHAN DONG YI
　　　　　　　　　　　　LU 23 SHANGHAI CHINA

FORM OF DOCUMENTARY CREDIT：IRREVOCABLE

DATE AND PLACE EXPIRY：060830/ON ISSUING BANK'S COUNTERS

APPLICANT：SMITH CO. LTD.，
THE JANE STREET，KONG ZONE，LONDON，ENGLAND

BENEFICIARY：SHANGHAI STATIONERY AND SPORTING GOODS IMP. AND EXP. CORP.

5-15 MANSION 1230-1240 ZHONGSHAN ROAD，SHANGHAI

CURRENCY CODE，AMOUNT：USD 90 000. 00

AVAILABLE WITH…BY…：ANY BANK IN ADVISING BANK'S COUNTRY BY NEGOTIATION

DRAFT：AT 30 DAYS SIGHT DRAFT(S)

DRAWN ON：ABN AMRO BANK NV，LONDON

PARTIAL SHIPMENTS：PERMITTED

TRANSSHIPMENT：PROHIBITED

LOADING ON BOARD/DISPATCH/TAKING IN CHARGE AT/FROM：SHANGHAI PORT

FOR TRANSPORTATION TO：AMSTERDAM PORT

SHIPMENT PERIOD：NOT LATER THAN 060630

DESCRIPTION OF GOODS：2 000 DOZENS MEN'S GLOVES CFR AMSTERDAM AT USD 45. 00 EACH

（三）审证并草拟改证函

1. 合同条款如下：

SALES　CONFIRMATION
销售确认书

THE SELLER：FUZHOU TEXTILES IMP. & EXP. CORP　　　S/C NO：GD25013

20 ZHONGSHAN ROAD E，5. FUJIAN，CHINA　　DATE：APR. 15，2006

TEL：0591-85362168　　FAX：0591-85362168　　　PLACE：FUZHOU

THE BUYER: JOAN& AIM CO., LTD

#304-7 JALAN STREET,

NEW YORK

THE BUYER AND SELLER HAVE AGREEN TO CONCLUDE THE FOLLOWING TRANSACTIONS ACCORDING TO THE TERMS AND CONDITIONS STIPULATED BELOW:

NAME OF COMMODITY AND SPECIFICATION	QUANTITY(PCS)	UNIT PRICE	AMOUNT
80% COTTON 20% POLYESTER LADIES JACKET ART. NO. 49394 (014428) ART. NO. 49393 (014428) ART. NO. 55306 (014429)	600 600 600	US $ 14. 00 US $ 15. 00 US $ 16. 00	CIF NEW YORK US $ 8 400. 00 US $ 9 000. 00 US $ 9 600. 00 US $ 27 000. 00

TOTAL VALUE: SAY US DOLLARS TWENTY-SEVEN THOUSAND ONLY.

TIME OF SHIPMENT: TO BE AFFECTED IN JUNE/JULY, 2006, WITH PARTIAL SHIPMENT NOT ALLOWED AND TRANSHIPMENT ALLOWED.

PORT OF LOADING & DESTINATION: FROM FUZHOU TO NEW YORK

TERMS OF PAYMENT: BY CONFIRMED IRREVOCABLE L/C FOR FULL INVOICE VALUE, AVAILABLE BY DRAFT AT SIGHT, NEGOTIABLE IN FUZHOU VALID IN CHINA UNTILL THE 15 DAYS AFTER DATE OF SHIPMENT, THE L/C TO REACH THE SELLERS ONE MONTH BEFORE THE PRESCRIBED TIME OF SHIPMENT

PACKING: ONE PIECE TO A POLYBAG, EACH 50 POLYBAGS TO ONE CARTON, TOTAL IN ONE 20′ CONTAINER

MARKS & NOS: AT SELLER'S OPTION

INSURANCE：TO BE COVERED BY THE SELLER FOR 110 PERCENT OF INVOICE VALUE COVERING ALL RISKS AND WAR RISKS AS PER AND SUBJECTED TO OCEAN MARINE CARGO CLAUSES OF THE PEOPLE'S INSURANCE COMPANY OF CHINA DATED 1/1/1981

Buyer：	Seller：
JOAN& AIM CO., LTD	FUZHOU TEXTILES IMP. & EXP. CORP
(SIGNATURE)	(SIGNATURE)

收到信用证如下：

APPLICATION HEADER 0700 1547 970225 SAIB FJ. JTC×××3846 992024 001015 1447

◆NATIONAL WESTMINSTER BANK
◆NEW YORK

FORM OF DOC. CREDIT	◆40A：IRREVOCABLE TRANSFERABLE
DOC, CREDIT NUMBER	◆20： 06/0510-FC
DATE OF ISSUE	◆31C：060425
APPLICABLE RELES	◆40E：UCP LATEST VERSION
EXIPRY	◆31D：JUNE 30, 2006 IN NEW YORK
APPLICANT	◆50： JOAN& AIM CO., LTD NEW YORK
BENEFICIARY	◆59： FUZHOU TEXTILES EXP. &. IMP CORP 26 ZHONGSHAN ROAD E, 5. FUJIAN, CHINA
FUJIAN, CHINA AMOUNT	◆32B：CURRENCY USD AMOUNT 27 000. 00
AVAILABLE WITH/BY	◆41A：CITIC BANK, LTD. BY NEGOTIATION
DRAFTS AT…	◆42C：DRAFTS AT 30 DAYS' SIGHT DRAWN ON US FOR FULL INVOICE VALUE
DRAWEE	◆42A：CITIC BANK, LTD.
PARTIAL SHIPMENT：	◆43P：PERMITTED
TRANSHIPMENTS	◆43T：PERMITTED
LOADING IN CHARGE	◆44A：FUZHOU, CHINA
FOR TRANSPORT TO	◆44B：NEW YORK

NOT LATER THAN   ◆44C：JUNE 30，2006

DESCRIPT. OF GOODS   ◆45A：80％COTTON 20％POLYESTER LA-
DIES KNIT JACKET AS PER S/C
NO. GL25013

ART. NO.	QUANTITY	UNIT PRICE
49394(014428)	600 PIECES	USD 14. 00
49393(014429)	600 PIECES	USD 15. 00
55306(014429)	600 PIECES	USD 16. 00

PRICE TERM：CIF NEW YORK

DOCUMENTS REQUIRED   ◆46A：

+ SIGNED COMMERCIAL INVOICE IN 3 COPIES.

+ PACKING LIST IN 3 COPIES SHOWING THE INDIVIDUAL WEIGHT AND MEASUREMENT OF EACH PACKAGE.

+ FULL SET ORIGINAL CERTIFICATE OF ORIGIN ISSUED BY CCPIT.

+ FULL SET CLEAN ON BOARD OCEAN BILL OF LADING SHOWING FREIGHT PREPAID CONSIGNED TO ORDER AND NOTIFY APPLI-CANT.

+ INSURANCE POLICY OR CERTIFICATE FOR 110 PERCENT OF IN-VOICE VALUE COVERING ALL RISKS AND WAR RISKS AS PER AND SUBJECTED TO OCEAN MARINE CARGO CLAUSES OF THE PEOPLE'S INSURANCE COMPANY OF CHINA DATED 1/1/1981.

+ BENEFICIARY'S CERTIFICATE CERTIFYING THAT EACH COPY OF SHIPPING DOCUMENTS HAS BEEN FAXED TO THE APPLI-CANT WITHIN 48 HOURS AFTER SHIPMENT.

PRESENTATION PERIOD   ◆48：DOCUMENTS TO BE PRESENTED WITHIN 5 DAYS AFTER THE DATE OF SHIPMENT, BUT WITH-IN THE VALIDITY OF THE CREDIT.

CONFIRMATION   ◆49：WITHOUT
ADD YOUR CONFIRMATION

2.

售货确认书
SALES CONFIRMATION

NO. LT07060

DATE：AUG. 10，2005

THE SELLERS：AAA IMPORT AND EXPORT CO.，THE BUYERS：BBB TRADING CO.，

222 JIANGUO ROAD　　　　　　　　　　P. O. BOX 203

DALIAN，CHINA　　　　　　　　　　　　GDANSK，POLAND

THE UNDERSIGNED SELLERS AND BUYERS HAVE AGREED TO CLOSE THE FOLLOWING TRANSACTIONS ACCORDING TO THE TERMS AND CONDITIONS STIPULATED BELOW：

品名与规格 COMMODITY AND SPECIFICATION	数量 QUANTITY	单价 UNIT PRICE	金额 AMOUNT
65% POLYESTER 35% COTTON LADIES SKIRTS		CIF GDANSK	
STYLE NO. A101	200 DOZ	USD 60/DOZ	USD 12 000. 00
STYLE NO. A102	400 DOZ	USD 84/DOZ	USD 33 600. 00
ORDER NO. HMW0501			
TOTAL：	600 DOZ		**USD 45 600. 00**

总值：　　　TOTAL VALUE：US DOLLARS FORTY FIVE THOUSAND AND SIX HUNDRED ONLY.

装运口岸：PORT OF LOADING：DALIAN

目的地：　DESTINATION：GDANSK

转运：　　TRANSHIPPMENT：ALLOWED

分批装运：PARTIAL SHIPMENT：ALLOWED

装运期限：SHIPMENT：DECEMBER，2005

保险：　　INSURANCE：BE EFFECTED BY THE SELLERS FOR 110% IN-VOICE VALUE COVERING F. P. A. RISK OF PICC CLAUSE

付款方式：PAYMENT：BY TRANSFERABLE L/C PAYABLE 60 DAYS AFTER B/L DATE，REACHING THE SELLERS 45 DAYS BEFORE THE SHIPMENT

DAVID KING　　　　　　　　　　　　　　　　　　　苏进

买方　　　　　　　　　　　　　　　　　　　　　　卖方

LETTER OF CREDIT

FORM OF DOC. CREDIT	*40A：	IRREVOCABLE
DOC. CREDIT NUMBER	*20：	70/1/5822
DATE OF ISSUE	*31C：	051007
APPLICABLE RULES	40E：	UCP LATEST VERSION
EXPIRY	*31D：	DATE 060115 POLAND
ISSUING BANK	*51A：	SUN BANK
		P. O. BOX201 GDANSK,POLAND
APPLICANT	*50：	BBB TRADING CO.
		P. O. BOX 203
		GDANSK, POLAND
BENEFICIARY	*59：	AAA IMPORT AND EXPORT CO.
		222 JIANCUO ROAD
		DALIAN,CHINA
AMOUNT	*32B：	CURRENCY USD AMOUNT
		45 600.00
AVAILABLE WITH/BY	*41A：	BANK OF CHINA
		DALIAN BRANCH
		BY DEF PAYMENT
DEFFRRED PAYM. DET.	*42P：	60 DAYS AFTER B/L DATE
PARTIAL SHIPMENTS	*43P：	NOT ALLOWED
TRANSHIPMETN	*43T：	ALLOWED
LOADING IN CHARGE	44A：	SHANGHAI
FOR TRANSPORT TO...	44B：	GDANSK
LATEST DATE OF SHIP.	44C：	051231
DESCRIPT. OF GOODS	45A：	65% POLYESTER 35% COTTON
		LADIES SHIRTS

STYLE NO. 101 200 DOZ@USD 60/PCE

SYTLE NO. 102 400 DOZ@USD 84/PCE

ALL OTHER DETEILS OF GOODS ARE

AS PER CONTRACT NO. LT07060 DATED

AUG. 10，2005.

DELIVERY TERMS：CIF GDANSK

(INCOTERMS 2000)

DOCUMENTS REQUIRED 46A:

1. COMMERCIAL INVOICE MANUALLY SIGNED IN 2 ORIGINALS PLUS 1 COPY MADE OUT TO DDD TRADING CO., P. O. BOX 211, GDANSK, POLAND.

2. FULL SET (3/3) OF ORIGINAL CLEAN ON BOARD BILL OF LADING PLUS ONE 3/3 NEGOTIABLE COPIES, MADE OUT TO ORDER OF IS-SUING BANK AND BLANK ENDORSED, NOTIFY THE APPLICANT, MARKED FREIGHT PREPAID, MENTIONING GROSS WEIGHT AND NET WEIGHT.

3. ASSORTMENT LIST IN 2 ORIGIANLS PLUS 1 COPY.

4. CERTIFICATE OF ORIGIN IN 1 ORIGINAL PLUS 2 COPIES SIGNED BY CCPIT.

5. MARINE ISURANCE POLICY IN THE CURRENCY O THE CREDIT ENDORSED IN BLANK FOR CIF VALUE PLUS 30 PCT MARINE COVERING ALL RISKS OF PICC CLAUSES INDICATING CLAIM PAYABLE IN POLAND.

ADDITIONAL COND. 47A:

+ B/L MUST SHOWING SHIPPING MARKS: BBB, S/C LT07060, GDAND, C/NO.

+ ALL DOCS MUST SHOW THIS L/C NO. 70/1/5822.

DETAILS OF CHARGES 71B: ALL BANKING COMM/CHRGS OUT-SIDE POLAND ARE FOR BENE-FICIARY'S ACCOUNT.

PRESENTATION PERIOD 48: 15 DAYS AFTER B/L DATE. BUT WITHIN L/C VALIDITY.

CONFIRMATION *49: WITHOUT

SEND TO REC. INFO 72: CREDIT SUBJECT TO ICC PUBL 600/2007 REV

3. 合同如下所示：

中国国际纺织品进出口公司江苏分公司

CHINA INTERNATIONAL TEXTILES I/E CORP. JIANGSU BRANCH

20 RANJIANG ROAD，NANJING，JIANGSU，CHINA

销售确认书　　　　NO.：CNT0219

SALES CONFIRMATION　　DATE：MAY 10，2008

OUR REFERENCE：IT123JS

BUYERS：TAI HING LOONG SDN，BHD，KUALA LUMPUR.

ADDRESS：7/F，SAILING BUILDING，NO. 50 AIDY STREET，KUALA LUMPUR，MALAYSIA

TEL：060-3-74236211　　　　FAX：060-3-74236212

THE UNDERSIGNED SELLERS AND BUYERS HAVE AGREED TO CLOSE THE FOLLOWING TRANSACTION ACCORDING TO THE TERMS AND CONDITIONS STIPULATED BELOW：

DESCRIPTION OF GOODS	QUANTITY	UNIT PRICE	AMOUNT
100% COTON GREE LAWN	300 000 YARDS	CIF SINGAPORE @HKD 3. 00/YARD	HKD 900 000. 00

SHIPMENT：DURING JUNE/JULY，2008 IN TRANSIT TO MALAYSIA

PAYMENT：IRREVOCABLE SIGHT L/C

INSURANCE：TO BE EFFECTED BY SELLERS COVERING WPA AND WAR RISKS FOR 10% OVER THE INVOICE VALUE.

买方(签章)THE BUYER　　　　　　　卖方(签章)THE SELLER

TAI HING LOONG SDN，BHD，　　中国国际纺织品进出口公司江苏分公司

KUALA LUMPUR.　　　　　　　CHINA INTERNATIONAL TEXTILES

I/E CORP. JIANGSU BRANCH，

买方开来的信用证如下所示：

FROM BANGKOK BANK LTD.，KUALA LUMPUR

DOCUMENTARY CREDIT NO.：08/12345，DATE：JUNE 12，2008

ADVISING BANK：BANK OF CHINA，JIANGSU BRANCH

APPLICANT：TAI HING LOONG SDN，BHD.，KUALA LUMPUR

BENEFICIARY：CHINA NAT'L TEXTILES I/E CORP.，BEIJING BRANCH

AMOUNT：HKD 900 000. 00 （HONGKONG DOLLARS TWO HUNDRED THREE THOUSAND ONLY）

EXPIRY DATE: JUN 15, 2008IN CHINA FOR NEGOTIATION

DEAR SIRS:

WE HEREBY ISSUE THIS DOCUMENTARY CREDIT IN YOUR FAVOR, WHICH IS AVAILABLE BY NEGOTIATION OF YOUR DRAFT(S) IN DUPLICATE AT SIGHT DRAWN ON BENEFICIARY BEARING THE CLAUSE: "DRAWN UNDER L/C NO. 08/12345 OF BANGKOK BANK LTD., KUALA LUMPUR DATED JUNE 12, 2008" ACCOMPAINED BY THE FOLLOWING DOCUMENTS:

+ SIGNED INVOICE IN QUADRUPLICATE COUNTER-SIGNED BY APPLICANT.

+ FULL SET OF CLEAN ON BOARD OCEAN BILLS OF LADING MADE OUT TO ORDER, ENDORSED IN BLANK, MARKED "FREIGHT COLLECT" AND NOTIFY BENEFICIARY.

+ MARINE INSURANCE POLICY OR CERTIFICATE FOR FULL INVOICE VALUE PLUS 50% WITH CLAIMS PAYABLE IN NANJING IN THE SAME CURRENCY AS THE DRAFT COVERING ALL RISKS AND WAR RISKS FROM WAREHOUSE TO WAREHOUSE UP TO KUALA LUMPUR INCLUDING S. R. C. C. CLAUSE AS PER PICC 1/1/1981.

+ PACKING LIST IN QUADRUPLICATE.

+ CERTIFICATE OF ORIGIN ISSUED BY BANK OF CHINA, NANJING.

+ SHIP'S CLASSIFICATION ISSUED BY LIOYDS' IN LONDON.

COVERING:

ABOUT 300 000 YARDS OF 65% POLYESTER, 35% COTTON GREY LAWN AS PER BUYER'S ORDER NO. TH-108 DATED MAY 4, 2004 TO BE DELIVERED ON TWO EQUAL SHIPMENTS DURING MAY/JUNE.

ALL BANKING CHARGES OUTSIDE MALAYSIA ARE FOR THE ACCOUNT OF BENEFICIARY. SHIPMENT FROM CHINA TO PORT KELANG LATEST JULY 31, 2008. PARTIAL SHIPMENTS ARE ALLOWED. TRANSSHIPMENT PROHIBITED.

WE HEREBY ENGAGE WITH DRAWERS, ENDORSERS AND BONA FIDE HOLDERS THAT DRAFTS DRAWN AND NEGOTIATED IN CONFORMITY WITH THE TERMS OF THIS CREDIT WILL BE DULY HONORED ON PRESENTATION. SUBJECT TO *UCP 600*.

　　　　　　　　BANGKOK BANK LTD., KUALALUMPUR (SIGNED)

4. 2006 年 10 月 31 日上海纺织品公司收到创鸿（香港）有限公司通过香港南洋银行开来的编号为 l8959344 的信用证，根据双方签订的合同（CONTRACT NO.：GL0082）对信用证进行审核，指出信用证存在的问题并草拟改证函。

合 同
CONTRACT

ORIGINAL

THE SELLER：SHANGHAI TEXTILES IMP. & EXP. CORP. SHANGHAI

27 ZHONGSHAN ROAD E,1. SHANGHAI, CHINA

TELEPHONE：86-21-63218467   FAX：86-21-63291267

CONTRACT NO.：GL0082

DATE：Oct. 5，2006

PLACE：SHANGHAI

THE BUYER：SUPERB AIM(HONG KONG)LTD.，

RM. 504 FUNGLEE COMM BLDG. 6-8A PRATT AVE., TSIMSHAT-SUI, KOWLOO,HONGKONG

THE BUYER AND SELLER HAVE AGREED TO CONCLUDE THE FOLLOWING TRANSACTIONS ACCORDING TO THE TERMS AND CONDITIONS STIPULATED BELOW：

1. COMMODITY&SPECIFICATION PACKING&SHIPPING MARK	2. QUANTITY (PCS.)	3. UNIT PRICE	4. AMOUNT
80% COTTON 20% POLYESTER LADIES KNIT JACKET		CIF H. K.	
ART. NO. 49394(014428)	600	US $ 14. 25	USD 8 550. 00
ART. NO. 49393(014428)	600	US $ 14. 25	USD 8 550. 00
ART. NO. 55306(014429)	600	US $ 14. 25	USD 8 550. 00

1. COMMODITY&SPECIFICATION PACKING&SHIPPING MARK	2. QUANTITY (PCS.)	3. UNIT PRICE	4. AMOUNT
REMARKS: 1) EACH IN PLASTIC BAGS, 24 BAGS TO A CARTON TOTAL 75 CARTONS 2) SHIPPING MARK: 　 SUPERB 　 H. K. 　 NO. 1-75 　 MADE IN CHINA			TOTAL USD 25 650. 00

TOTAL VALUE: SAY US DOLLARS TWENTY-FIVE THOUSAND SIX HUNDRED AND FIFTY ONLY.

TIME OF SHIPMENT: within 45 days of receipt of letter of credit and not later than the month of Dec. 2006 with partial shipments and transshipment allowed

PORT OF LOADING& DESTINATION: FROM SHANGHAI TO HONGKONG

TERMS OF PAYMENT: BY 100% Confirmed Irrevocable Sight Letter of Credit opened by the buyer to reach the Seller not later than Oct. 31th. 2006 and to be available for negotiation in China until the 15th day after the date of shipment. In case of late arrival of the L/C, the Seller shall not be liable for any delay in shipment and shall have the right to rescind the contract and or claim for damages.

INSURANCE: To be effected by the seller for 110% of the CIF invoice value covering ALL RISKS AND WAR RISK as per China Insurance Clauses.

TERMS OF SHIPMENT: To be governed by "INCOTERMS 2000". For transactions concluded on CIF term, all surcharges including port congestion surcharges, etc. levied by the shipping company, in addition to freight，shall be for the buyer's account

The Buyer： The Seller

SUPERB AIM (HONG KONG) LTD.， SHANGHAI TEXTILES
IMP．& EXP．CORP

国外来证：

06 OCT 20 14：57：32

MT：S700 ISSUE OF DOCUMENTARY CREDIT　　PAGE 0001

FUNC SWPR3

UMR 00182387

APPLICATIONG HEADER 0700 1547 9700225 SAIB H. K. JTC×××3846
992024 001015 1447

- NANYANG COMMERCIAL BANK LTD.
- HONGKONG

USER HEADER	SERVICE CODE 103：
	BANK PRIORITY 113：
	MSG USER REF 108：
	INFO. FROMC1　115：
SEQUENCE OF TOTAL	• 27：　1/2
FORM OF DOC. CREDIT	• 40：　REVOCABLE
DOC. CREDIT NUMBER	• 20：　L8959344
DATE OF ISSUE	• 31C：061020
APPLICABLE RULES	• 40E：UCP LATEST VERSION
EXIPRY	• 31D：DATE 061231 AT NEGOTIATING BANK'S COUNTER
APPLICANT	• 50：　SUPERB AIM(HONG KONG)LTD. HONG KONG
BENEFICIARY	• 59：　SHANGHAI TEXTILES IMP & EXP CORPORATION 27 ZHONGSHAN ROAD E，1 SHANGHAI，CHINA
AMOUNT	• 32B：CURRENCY USD AMOUNT 256 500.00
AVAILABLE WITH/BY	• 41A：NANYANG COMMERCIAL BANK，

LTD. H. K.

BY NEGOTIATION

DRAFTS AT… • 42C：DRAFTS AT 20 DAYS' SIGHT FOR FULL INVOICE VALUE

DRAWEE • 42A：NANYANG COMMERCIAL BANK, LTD.

PARTIAL SHIPMENTS • 43P：ALLOWED

TRANSSHIPMENT • 43T：PROHIBITED

LOADING IN CHARGE • 44A：SHIPMENT FROM CHINESE PORT(S)

FOR TRANSPORT TO • 44B：SINGAPORE/Hong Kong

LATEST DATE OF SHIP • 44C：061215

DESCRIPT. OF GOODS • 45A：80% COTTON 20% POLYESTER LADIES KNIT JACKET AS PER S/C NO. GL0082

ART. NO.	QUANTITY	UNIT PRICE
49394(014428)	600 PIECES	USD 14. 25
49393(014428)	600 PIECES	USD 14. 25
55306(014429)	600 PIECES	USD 14. 25

PRICE TERM：CIF H. K.

DOCUMENTS REQUIRED • 46A：

+ 3/3 SET OF ORIGINAL CLEAN ON BOARD OCEAN BILLS OF LADING MADE OUT TO ORDER OF SHIPPER AND BLANK ENDORSED AND MARKED"FERIGHT COLLECT" NOTIFY APPLICANT(WITH FULL NAME AND ADDRESS)

+ ORIGINAL SIGNED COMMERCIAL INVOICE IN 5 FOLD INDICATING S/C NO.

+ INSURANAL POLICY OR CERTIFICATE IN TWO FOLD ENDORSED IN BLANK, FOR 120 PCT OF THE INVOICE VALUE INCLUDING：THE INSTITUTE CARGO CLAUSE （A）, THE INSTITUTE WAR CLAUSE, INSURANCE CLAIMS TO BE PAYABLE AT DETINATION IN THE CURRENCY OF THE DRAFTS.

+ CERTIFICATE OF ORIGIN GSP FORM A IN ONE ORIGNAL ONE COPY.

+ PACKING LIST IN 3 FOLD
+ BENEFICIARY'S CERTFICATE STATING THAT ALL DOCUMENTS HAS BEEN SENT WITHIN 10 DAYS AFTER SHIPMENT.

ADDITIONAL COND. • 47：

　　1. T. T. REIMBURSEMENT IS PROHIBITED.

　　2. THE GOODS TO BE PACKED IN EXPORT STRONG COLORED CARTONS.

　　3. INSPECTION IS TO BE EFFECTED BEFORE SHIPMENT AND RELEVANT CERTIFICATE/REPORTS ARE REQUIRED FROM THE INSPECITING AGENCY OR INSPECTOR DESIGNATED BY THE BUYER.

DETAILS OF CHARGES • 71B：

ALL BANKING CHARGES OUTSIDE HONG KONG INCLUDING REIMURSEMENT COMMISSION ARE FOR ACCOUNT OF BENEFICIARY.

PRESENTATION PERIOD • 48：

　　DOCUMENTS TO BE PRESENTED WITHIN 15 DAYS AFTER THE DATE OF SHIPMENT, BUT WITHIN THE VALIDITY OF THE CREDIT

CONFIRMATION • 49：WITHOUT

INSTRUCTION • 78：

　　THE NEGOTIATION BANK MUST FORWARD THE DRAFTS AND ALL DOCUMENTS BY REGISTERED AIRMNIL DIRECT TO US (NANYANG COMMERCIAL BANK, LTD. WESTERN DISTRICT BILLS CENTER 128BONHAM STRAND E. HONG KONG)IN ONE LOT, UPON RECEIPT OF THE DREFTS AND DOCUMENTS IN ORDER, WE WILL REMIT THE PROCEEDS AS INSTRUCTED BY THE NEGOTIATING BANK

（四）根据合同审核信用证

售 货 合 同
SALES CONTRACT

NO.：2008KG02350

DATE：DEC. 28, 2008

THE SELLERS：　　　　　　　　　　THE BUYERS：

SUCCESS DEVELOPMENT TRADING LTD　　JYSK AB

39/FL, FLAT F, TIANHE FLAZA　　FOERETA 6 S-23237 ARLOEV

　　　　　　　　　　　　　　SWEDEN

SHANGHAI，CHINA

THIS SALES CONTRACT IS MADE BY AND BETWEEN THE SELLER
AND THE BUYER，WHEREBY THE SELLER AGREE TO SELL AND
THE BUYER AGREE TO BUY THE UNDER-MENTIONED GOODS AC-
CORDING TO THE TERMS AND CONDITIONS STIPULATED BELOW：

(5)货号、品名及规格 NAME OF COMMODITY AND SPECIFICATIONS	(6)数量 QUANTITY	(7)单价 UNIT PRICE	(8)金额 AMOUNT
LEATHER GLOVE ART　3900300 ART　3901400	 8 400 PCS 15 520 PCS	CIF GOTHENBURG USD 1. 25/PC USD 1. 02/PC	 USD 10 500. 00 USD 15 830. 40
AS PER S/C NO 2002KG02350 AND JYSK ORDER 4500341081	TOTAL AMOUNT：		USD 26 330. 40

装运港：　LOADING IN CHARGE：CHINESE PORT
目的港：　FOR TRANSPORT TO：GOTHENBURG，SWEDEN
转运：　　TRANSHIPMENT：ALLOWED
分批装运：PARTIAL SHIPMENT：ALLOWED
装运期限：THE LATEST DATE OF SHIPMENT：FEB. 28，2009
保险：　　INSURANCE：BE EFFECTED BY THE SELLERS FOR 110%
　　　　　　　　INVOICE VALUE，COVERING F. P. A RISKS AS
　　　　　　　　PER PICC CLAUSE.
付款方式：PAYMENT：BY IRREVOCABLE L/C，IN FAVOR OF THE
SELLER，TO BE AVAILABLE BY SIGHT DRAFT；REACHING THE
SELLERS 30DAYS BEFORE THE SHIPMENT. REMAIN VALID FOR
NEGOTIATION IN CHINA UNTIL THE 15TH DAYS AFTER THE FORE-
SAID TIME OF SHIPMENT，ALL COMMIOSSION AND OUTSIDE SWE-
DEN ARE FOR ACCOUNT OF THE SELLERS.
仲裁：　　ARBITRATION：ALL DISPUTE ARISING FROM THE EXE-
CUTION OR IN CONNECTION WITH THIS CONTRACT SHALL BE
AMICABLY SETTLED THROUGH NEGOTIATION IN CASE OF NO
SETTLEMENT CAN BE REACHED THROUGH NEGOTIATION THE
CASE SHALL THEN BE SUBMITED TO THE CHINA INTERNATION-
AL ECONOMIC & TRADE ARBITRATION COMMISION. IN SHANG-

HAI (OR IN BEIJING) FOR ARBITRATION. THE ARBITRAL AWAED IS FINAL AND BINDING UPON BOTH PARTIES FOR SETTLING THE DISPUTES. THE FEE, FOR ARBITRATION SHALL BE BORNE BY THE LOSING PARTY UNLESS OTHERWISE AWARDED.

THE SELLER   THE BUYER
SUCCUSS DEVELOPMENT TRADING LTD   JYSK AB
ISSUE OF A DOCUMENTARY CREDIT

TO   HANGSENG BANK LTD. SHANGHAI BRANCH
FROM   NORDEA BANK, SWEDEN
MT700

SEQUENCE OF TOTAL	27:	1/1
FROM OF DA	40A:	REVOCABLE
DC NO.	20:	667-01-3042855
DATE OF ISSUE	31C:	090114
APPLICABLE RULES	40E:	UCP LATEST VERSION
EXPIRYDATE AND PLACE	31D:	DATE: MAR. 15, 2009 PLACE: SWEDEN
APPLICANT	50:	JYSK AB
		FOERETA 6 S-23237 ARLOEV SWEDEN
BEBEFICIARY	59:	SUCCESS DEVELOPMENT TRADING LTD.
		39 /FL, FLAT F TIANHE PLAZA SHANGHAI,
AMOUNT	32B:	USD 26 330. 40
AVAILABLE WITH/BY	41A:	ANY BANK BY NEGOTIATION
DRAFT AT…	42C:	AT 30 DAYS SIGHT
DRAWEE	42A:	ISSUING BANK
PARTIAL SHIPMENT	43P:	ALLOWED
TRANSHIPMENT	43T:	NOT ALLOWED
LOADING IN CHARGE	44A:	CHINESE PORTS
FOR TRANSPORT TO	44B:	GOTHENBURG, SWEDEN
LATEST DATE OF SHIPMENT	44C:	FEB. 08, 2009
DESCRIPTION OF GOODS	45A:	LEATHER GLOVE

AS PER S/C NO. 2008KG02350 AND JYSK ORDER 4500341081

8 400 PCS ART 3900300 USD 1. 25/PC

15 520 PCS ART 3901400 USD 1. 20/PC

CIF SHANGHAI (INCOTERMS 2000)

DOCUMENTS REQUIRED　　46A：1 SIGNED ORIGINAL COMMERCIAL

INVOICE AND 5 COPIES

PACKING LIST IN 2 COPIES

FULL SET OF CLEAN ON BOARD MARINE BILLS OF LADING, MADE OUT TO ORDER OF ISSING BANK, MARKED "FREIGHT PREPAID" AND NOTIFY APPLICANT (AS INDICATED ABOVE); MENTIONING L/C NO.

GSP CERTIFICATE OF ORIGIN FORM A, CERTIFYING GOODS OF ORIGIN IN CHINA, ISSUED BY COMPETENT AUTHORITIES

INSURANCE POLICY/CERTIFICATE COVERING ALL RISKS OF PICC, INCLUDING WAREHOUSE TO WAREHOUSE CLAUSE UP TO FINAL DESTINATION AT GOTHENBURG, FOR AT LEAST 120 PCT OF CIF VALUE, SHOWING CLAIMS PAYABLE IF ANY IN SWEDEN.

ADDITIONAL CONDITIONS.　　47A：ALL DOCUMENTS MUST BE ISSUED IN ENGLISH

MULTIMODAL TRANSPORT DOCUMENTS ACCEPTABLE EVIDENCING SHIPMENT CLEAN ON BOARD

ON A NAMED VESSEL

BILL OF LADING MUST SHOW

CONTAINER NUMBER

P/L（PACKING LIST）MUST BE

SPECIFIED PER ART NO AND

CONTAINER NO.

DETAILS OF CHARGES   71B： ALL COMMISSION AND CHARG-

ES OUTSIDE SWEDEN ARE FOR

ACCOUNT OF BENEFICIARY

OUR CHARGES WILL BE DE-

DUCTED/CLAIMED AT THE

TIME OF PAYMENT, NEGOTIA-

TION OR EXPIRY.

PRESENTATION PERIOD   48： DOCUMENTS TO BE PRESENTED

WITHIN 5 DAYS AFTER THE

DATE OF SHIPMENT,BUT WITHIN

THE VALIDITY OF THE CRED-

IT.

CONFIRMATION INSTRUCTIONS 79： ON RECEIPT OF MALL ADVICE

OF NEGOTIATION, WE SHALL

COVER AS PER INSTRUCTIONS

RECEIVED.

THIS CREDIT IS SUBJECT TO UCP（2007REVISON），ICC PUUBL NO. 600

（五）审证并改证

请你以单证员王力的身份,根据售货确认书对信用证进行审核,将不符点列出, 并发英文函电致客户提出改证要求。

售货确认书

SALES CONFIRMATION

Sellers：SICHUAN CHANGHONG ELECTRIC CO.，LTD

35 EAST MIANXING ROAD，HIGH-TECH PARK，MIANYANG，SICHUAN，CHINA

S/C No. JXIN04006

Date：FEB. 15，2005

Signed at：MIANYANG，CHINA

Fax No. 86-760-3138616

Buyers：ABC CORPORATION LIMITED

CTRADE XABIA，KM5 53620 GATA DE GORGOS

ALICANTE，SPAIN

兹 经 买 卖 双 方 同 意，按 下 列 条 款 成 交。

The undersigned Sellers and Buyers have agreed to close the following transaction according to the terms and conditions stipulated below.

货号 Article No.	品名及规格 Description of Goods	数量 Quantity	单价 Unit price	金额 Amount
80230019	AIR CONDITIONER KFR-35GW/NL，MODEL，R407C，220V	10 000 SETS	CIF VALENCIA USD 160. 00/SET	USD 1 600 000. 00

数 量 及 总 值 允 许 5% 的 增 减，由 卖 方 决 定 。

With 5% more or less both in amount and quantity allowed at the Sellers' option.

Total Value：US DOLLARS ONE MILLION SIX HUNDRED THOUSAND ONLY.

Packing：ONE SET IN TWO CARTONS，TOTAL 20 000 CARTONS

Time of shipment：3 000 SET BY 31ST，MARCH 2005 AND 7 000 SET BY 15TH，APRIL，2005

PARTIAL SHIPMENT AND TRANSSHIPMENT ARE ALLOWED.

Loading port & Destination：FROM SHANGHAI TO VALENCIA SPAIN

Insurance：TO BE COVERED BY THE SELLERS COVERING FPA AND WAR RISK FOR 110% OF INVOICE VALUE AS PER CIC.

Terms of payment：BY IRREVOCABLE LETTER OF CREDIT TO BE AVAILABLE BY 30 DAYS AFTER SIGHT DRAFT TO REACH THE SELLERS BEFORE MAR. 13，2005 AND TO REMAIN VALID FOR NEGOTIATION IN

CHINA UNTIL THE 15TH DAY AFTER THE AFORESAID TIME OF SHIPMENT.

Shipping Mark：N/M

卖方	买方
SELLERS	BUYERS

2005FEB20   Logical Terminal CDPF

MT S5700   **Issue of a Documentary Credit**   Page 00001

Func JSRVP

User Header	Service Code	103：
	Bank Priority	113：
	Msg User Ref.	108：
	Info. From CL	115：
Sequence of Total	*27：	1/1
Form of Doc. Credit	*40A：	IRREVOCABLE
Doc. Credit Number	*20：	C20050226
Date of Issue	31C：	050220
APPLICABLE RULES	40E：	UCP LATEST VERSION
Expiry	*31D：	050415
Applicant	*50：	ABC CORPORATION LTD.,SPAIN
Beneficiary	*59：	SICHUAN GHANGHONG ELECTRIC CO.,LTD
		35 EST MIANXING ROAD, HIGH-TECH PARK MIANYANG,SICHUAN, CHINA
Amount	*32B：	Currency Amount 1 600 000. 00
Pos. /Neg. tol. (%)	39A：	05/05
Available with/by	*41D：	ANY BANK BY NEGOTIATION
Draft at…	42C：	45 DAYS AFTER SIGHT
Drawee	42D：	OURSELVES
Partial Shipments	43P：	ALLOWED
Transshipment	43T：	ALLOWED
Loading in Charge	44A：	ANY CHINESE PORTS
For Transport to…	44B：	VALENCIA PORT
Shipment Period	44C：	LATEST MAR. 30，2005

Descript. of goods	45A：

AIR CONDITIONER

KFR-35GW/NL，MODEL，R407C，220V，10 000 SETS，
@USD 160.00，

CIF VALENCIA 3 000 SETS SHIPMENT BY 31ST，
MARCH 2005，7 000 SETS SHIPMENT BY 15TH，
APRIL 2005.

OTHER DETAILES AS PER S/C NO. 800678

Document required	46A：

+ COMMERCIAL INVOICE IN 3 COPIES
+ PACKING LIST IN 3MCOPIES
+ 2/3ORIGINAL CLEAN SHIPPED ON BOARD B/L，MADE OUT TO ORDER，MARKED "FREIGHT PREPAID" AND NOTIFY APPLICANT
+ GSP CERTIFICATE OF ORIGIN FORM A，CERTIFYING GOODS OF ORIGIN IN CHINA，ISSUDE BY COMPETENT AUTHORITIES
+ INSURANCE POLICY/CERTIFICATE COVERING RISKS FPA OF PICC. INCLUDING WAREHOUSE TO WAREHOUSE CLAUSE，FOR AT LEAST 130 PCT OF CIF-VALUE.
+ SHIPPING ADVICES MUST BE SENT TO APPLICANT WITHIN 2 DAYS AFTER SHIPPMENT ADVISING NUMBER OF PACKAGES，GROSS & NET WEIGHT，VESSEL NAME，BILL OF LADING NO. AND DATE，CONTRACT NO.，VALUE.

Addition Cond.	47A：

1. 1/3 ORIGINAL B/L MUST BE SENT DIRECTRY TO APPLICANT IN 3 DAYS AFTER B/L DATE AND SENT BY FAX.
2. QUANTITY 3 PCT MORE OR LESS ALLOWED.
3. ALL DOCUMENTS MUST BE MADE OUT IN

ENGLISH LANGUAGE.

4. ALL DOCUNENTS MUST BEAR OUR LET-
TER OF CREDIT NUMBER.

5. DISCREPANCY FEE OF UED 80. 00（OR E-
QUIVALENT）WILL BE PROCEEDS OF ANY
DRAWING IF DOCUMENTS ARE PRESENT-
ED WITH DISCREPANCY（IES）UNDER THIS
DOCUMENTARY CREDIT. NOT WITH STAND-
ING ANY INSTRUCTIONS TO THE CON-
TRARY, THIS CHARGE SHALL BE FOR THE
ACCOUNT OF BENEFICIARY.

Details of Charges 71B：ALL BANK CHARGES EXCLUDING ISSUING
BANKS ARE FOR ACCOUNT OF BENEFICIA-
RY

Presentation Period 48：DOCUMENTS TO BE PRESENTED WITHIN 15
DAYS FROM SHIPMENT DATE.

Confirmation ＊49：WITHOUT

Instructions 78：

DISREPANT DOCUMENTS, IF ACCEPTABLE, WILL BE SUB-
JECT TO A DISCREPANCY HANDLING FEE OF USD 50. 00
OR EQUIVALENT WHICH WILL BE FOR ACCOUNT OF
BENEFICIARY. ON RECEIPT OF DOCUMENTS IN CON-
FORMITY WITH THE TERMS OF THIS CREDIT, WE WILL
BE DULY HONOURED ON PRESENTATION IF THE DRAFT
（S）ACCEPTED BY APPLICNT.

Send To Rec. Info. 72：THIS CREDIT IS ISSUED SUBJECT TO 2007 RE-
VISION, I. C. C. PUBLICATIONS NO. 600

单 据 篇

一、商务单据的制作与审核

(一) 根据材料审核发票,指出单据错误并修改

售 货 合 同
SALES CONTRACT

NO: 2008KG02350

DATE: DEC. 28, 2008

THE SELLERS:

SUCCESS DEVELOPMENT TRADING LTD

39/FL, FLATF, TIANHE FLAZA

SHANGHAI, CHINA

THE BUYERS:

JYSK AB

FOERETA 6 S-23237 ARLOEV

SWEDEN

THIS SALES CONTRACT IS MADE BY AND BETWEEN THE SELLER AND THE BUYER, WHEREBY THE SELLER AGREE TO SELL AND THE BUYER AGREE TO BUY THE UNDER-MENTIONED GOODS ACCORDING TO THE TERMS AND CONDITIONS STIPULATED BELOW:

(9) 货号、品名及规格 NAME OF COMMODITY AND SPECIFICATIONS	(10) 数量 QUANTITY	(11) 单价 UNIT PRICE	(12) 金额 AMOUNT
LEATHER GLOVE ART 3900300 ART 3901400	 8 400 PCS 15 520 PCS	CIF GOTHENBURG USD 1.25/PC USD 1.02/PC	 USD 10 500.00 USD 15 830.40
AS PER S/C NO. 2008KG02350 AND JYSK ORDER 4500341081	TOTAL AMOUNT:		USD 26 330.40

装运港: LOADING IN CHARGE: CHINESE PORT

目的港: FOR TRANSPORT TO: GOTHENBURG, SWEDEN

转运: TRANSHIPMENT: ALLOWED

分批装运: PARTIAL SHIPMENT: ALLOWED

装运期限：THE LATEST DATE OF SHIPMENT：FEB. 28，2009

保险：　　INSURANCE：BE EFFECTED BY THE SELLERS FOR 110％ IN-VOICE VALUE，COVERING F. P. A RISKS AS PER PICC CLAUSE.

付款方式：PAYMENT：BY IRREVOCABLE L/C，IN FAVOR OF THE SELLER，TO BE AVAILABLE BY SIGHT DRAFT；REACHING THE SELLERS 30DAYS BEFORE THE SHIPMENT. REMAIN VALID FOR NEGOTIATION IN CHINA UNTIL THE 15TH DAYS AFTER THE FORE-SAID TIME OF SHIPMENT，ALL COMMIOSSION AND OUTSIDE SWE-DEN ARE FOR ACCOUNT OF THE SELLERS.

仲裁：　　ARBITRATION：ALL DISPUTE ARISING FROM THE EXE-CUTION OR IN CONNECTION WITH THIS CONTRACT SHALL BE AMICABLY SETTLED THROUGH NEGOTIATION IN CASE OF NO SETTLEMENT CAN BE REACHED THROUGH NEGOTIATION THE CASE SHALL THEN BE SUBMITED TO THE CHINA INTERNATION-AL ECONOMIC & TRADE ARBITRATION COMMISION. IN SHANG-HAI(OR IN BEIJING) FOR ARBITRATION. THE ARBITRAL AWAED IS FINAL AND BINDING UPON BOTH PARTIES FOR SETTLING THE DISPUTES. THE FEE，FOR ARBITRATION SHALL BE BORNE BY THE LOSING PARTY UNLESS OTHERWISE AWARDED.

THE SELLER　　　　　　　　　　　　　　　　THE BUYER

　　SUCCUSS DEVELOPMENT TRADING LTD　　　　JYSK AB

ISSUE OF A DOCUMENTARY CREDIT

TO　　　　　　　　　　　　HANGSENG BANK LTD. SHANGHAI BRANCH

FROM　　　　　　　　　　　NORDEA BANK，SWEDEN

MT700

SEQUENCE OF TOTAL	27：	1/1
FROM OF DA	40A：	REVOCABLE
DC NO.	20：	667-01-3042855
DATE OF ISSUE	31C：	090114
APPLICABLE RULES	40E：	UCP LATEST VERSION
EXPIRYDATE AND PLACE	31D：	DATE：MAR. 15，2009 PLACE：SWEDEN
APPLICANT	50：	JYSK AB

FOERETA　6　S-23237　ARLOEV SWEDEN

BEBEFICIARY	59：SUCCESS DEVELOPMENT TRADING LTD. 39/FL，FLAT F TIANHEP-LAZA SHANGHAI，CHINA
AMOUNT	32B：USD 26 330. 40
AVAILABLE WITH/BY	41A：ANY BANK BY NEGOTIATION
DRAFT AT…	42C：AT 30 DAYS SIGHT
DRAWEE	42A：ISSUING BANK
PARTIAL SHIPMENT	43P：ALLOWED
TRANSHIPMENT	43T：NOT ALLOWED
LOADING IN CHARGE	44 A:CHINESE PORTS
FOR TRANSPORT TO	44B：GOTHENBURG，SWEDEN
LATEST DATE OF SHIPMENT	44C：FEB. 08，2009
DESCRIPTION OF GOODS	45A：LEATHER GLOVE

AS PER S/C NO. 2008KG02350 AND JYSK ORDER 4500341081

8 400 PCS ART 3900300 USD 1. 25/PC

15 520 PCS ART 3901400 USD 1. 20/PC

CIF SHANGHAI（INCOTERMS 2000）

DOCUMENTS REQUIRED　46A：1 SIGNED ORIGINAL COMMERCIAL

INVOICE AND 5 COPIES

PACKING LIST IN 2 COPIES

FULL SET OF CLEAN ON BOARD MARINE BILLS OF LADING，MADE OUT TO ORDER OF ISSING BANK，MARKED "FREIGHT PREPAID" AND NOTIFY APPLICANT（AS INDICATED ABOVE）；MENTIONING L/C NO.

GSP CERTIFICATE OF ORIGIN FORM A，CERTIFYING GOODS OF ORIGIN IN CHINA，ISSUED

BY COMPETENT AUTHORITIES
INSURANCE POLICY/CERTIFI-
CATE COVERING ALL RISKS OF
PICC, INCLUDING WAREHOUSE
TO WAREHOUSE CLAUSE UP
TO FINAL DESTINATION AT
GOTHENBURG, FOPR AT LEAST
120 PCT OF CIF VALUE，SHOW-
ING CLAIMS PAYABLE IF ANY IN
SWEDEN.

ADDITIONAL CONDITIONS　　47A：ALL DOCUMENTS MUST BE IS-
SUED IN ENGLISH
MULTIMODAL TRANSPORT DOCU-
MENTS ACCEPTABLE EVIDENC-
ING SHIPMENT CLEAN ON BOARD
ON A NAMED VESSEL
BILL OF LADING MUST SHOW
CONTAINER NUMBER
P/L（PACKING LIST）MUST BE
SPECIFIED PER ART NO AND
CONTAINER NO.

DETAILS OF CHARGES　　71B：ALL COMMISSION AND CHARG-
ES OUTSIDE SWEDEN ARE FOR
ACCOUNT OF BENEFICIARY OUR
CHARGES WILL BE DEDUCTED/
CLAIMED AT THE TIME OF PAY-
MENT，NEGOTIATION OR EXPI-
RY.

PRESENTATION PERIOD　　48：DOCUMENTS TO BE PRESENTED
WITHIN 5 DAYS AFTER THE
DATE OF SHIPMENT，BUT WITHIN
THE VALIDITY OF THE CREDIT.

CONFIRMATION INSTRUCTIONS 79：ON RECEIPT OF MALL ADVICE OF
NEGOTIATION, WE SHALL COV-

ER AS PER INSTRUCTIONS RE-CEIVED.

THIS CREDIT IS SUBJECT TO UCP(2007 REVISON)，ICC PUUBL NO. 600

补充资料：NET WEIGHT：3. 00KGS/CTN, GROSS WEIGHT：5. 00 KGS/CTN, MEASUREMENT：（50 * 20 * 20）CM/CTN, PACKING：20 PCS/CTN；产品为完全自产品，于 2 月 20 日备妥，在上海港装 2 月 26 日 MOON V. 252 航次出运，贸易方式为一般贸易，2 月 19 日制作发票（号码为 Cg2003118），唛头为：JYSK/GOTHENBURG/VOS. 1-1196. FORM A 号码为 SH2506655111；提单号码为 TTCUSH6593255；保单号为 2008SH25066

成功发展贸易有限公司
SUCCESS DEVELOPMENT TRADING LTD.
39/FL，FLAT F，TIANHE PLAZA SHANGHAI，CHINA
COMMERCIAL INVOICE

TEL：0086-21-65658933
FAX：0086-21-65658932

INV. NO.：CG2003118
DATE：FEB. 19，2009
S/C NO.：2008KG02350
L/C NO.：667-01-3042855

TO：
　JYSK AB
　FOERETA 6 S-23237 ARLOEV SWEDEN
FROM：CHINESE PORT　TO：GOTHENBURG　　　BY：SEA

MARKS&.NOS.	DESCRIPTION OF GOODS	QUANTITY	UNIT PRICE	AMOUNT
JYSK/GOTHENBURG/NOS. 1-1196	LEATHER GLOVE ART 3900300 ART 3901400	8 400 PCS 15 520 PCS	USD 1. 25/PC USD 1. 02/PC	USD 10 500. 00 USD 15 830. 40 USD 26 330. 40

TOTAL AMOUNT：U. S. DOLLARS TWENTY SIX THOUSAND THREE HUNDRED AND THIRTY AND CENTS FOURTY ONLY.

审核结果如下：

SUCCESS DEVELOPMENTTRADING LTD.

（二）根据信用证以及相关资料缮制以下单据

信用证　MT S700 Issue of a Documentary Credit

User Header	Service code	103：
	Bank. Priority	113：
	Message User Ref.	108：
	Infor. Form C1	115：

27： Sequence of total
1/1
40A： Form of Documentary Credit
IRREVOCABLE
20： Documentary Credit Number
00001LCC0603814
31C： Date of Issue
12-APR-2007
40E： UCP LATEST VERSION
31D： Date and Place of Expiry
21-JUN-2007 IN GUANGZHOU
51A： Applicant Bank
BNP PARIBAS
ZI DE LA PILATERIE
59442 WASQUEHAL FRANCE
50： Applicant
DIRAMODE
3 RUE DU DUREMONT

BP 21,59531 NEUVILLE EN FERRAIN FRANCE

59：Beneficiary

GUANGDONG FENG QING TRADING CO.

NO. 31 ZHONG SHAN ROAD GUANGZHOU. CHINA

32B：Currency Code，Amount

USD 80 000. 00

39A：Percentage Credit Amount Tolerance

05/05

41A：Available With…By…

ANY BANK BY NEGOTIATION

42C：Draft at…

SIGHT

42A：Drawee

BNP PARIBAS

ZI DE LA PILATERIE

59442 WASQUEHAL FRANCE

43P：Partial Shipment

NOT ALLOWED

43T：Transshipment

NOT ALLOWED

44A：Loading on Board/Dispatch/Taking in Charge at/from…

GUANG ZHOU PORT

44B：For Transportation to…

DUNKIRK FRANCE

44C：Latest Date of Shipment

30-MAY-2007

45A：Description of Goods and/or Services

ORDER NO. 113851：LADIES DRESS

10 000 PCS AT USD 8. 00 CIF DUNKIRK INCLUDING 3% COMMIS-

SION

46A：Documents Required

+　COMMERCIAL INVOICE IN 4 FOLDS DULY SIGNED AND STAMPED，

BEARING DOCUMENTARY CREDIT NUMBER.

+　PACKING LIST IN FIVE FOLD.

+ CERTIFICATE OF ORIGIN
+ 3/3 ORIGINAL BILL OF LADING MADE OUT TO ORDER OF SHIP-PER AND ENDORSED IN BLANK NOTIFY EXPEDITORS INTER-NATIONAL-BAT L-ROUTE DES FAMARDS-59818 LESQUIN FRANCE MARKED FREIGHT PREPAID.
+ INSURANCE POLICY/CERTIFICATE COVERING ALL RISKS AND WAR RISK FOR 110% OF INVOICE VALUE INCLUDING W/W CLAUSE. CLAIMS AS PER CIC, IF ANY, PAYABLE AT PORT OF DESTINATION IN THE CURRENCY OF THE DRAFT.
+ SHIPPER MUST CABLE ADVISING BUYER SHIPMENT PARTICU-LARS IN BRIEF IMMEDIATELY AFTER SHIPMENT. COPY OF CA-BLE/FAX SHOULD BE PART OF NEGOTIATING DOCUMENTS.
+ ONE COPY OF SIGNED INVOICE AND ONE NON-NEGOTIABLE B/L TO BE SENT TO BUYER BY SPECIAL COURIER 5 DAYS BEFORE THE SHIPPING DATE. A CERTIFICATE OF THESE EFFECTS SHOULD BE PRESENTED TO THE NEGOTIATING BANK AS PART OF DOCUMENTS NEEDED.

47A: Additional Conditions
+ ALL DOCUMENTS MUST MENTIONING THIS L/C NO. AND S/C NO.
+ 3% COMMISSION SHOULD BE DEDUCTED FROM TOTAL AMOUNT OF THE COMMERCIAL INVOICE.
+ MORE OR LESS 5 PERCENT IN QUANTITY AND CREDIT AMOUNT ACCEPTABLE
+ A FEE OF USD 50.00 OR ITS EQUIVALENT WILL BE DEDUCTED FROM THE PROCEEDS OF EACH SET OF DISCREPANT DOCU-MENTS, WHICH REQUIRE OUR OBTAINING ACCEPTANCE FROM APPLICANT.
+ AN EXTRA COPY OF INVOICE AND TRANSPORT DOCUMENTS, IF ANY, FOR L/C ISSUING BANK'S FILE ARE REQUIRED.

71B: Charges
ALL BANKING CHARGES OUTSIDE OPENING BANK ARE FOR THE ACCOUNT OF BENEFICIARY.

48: Period of Presentation
DOCUMENTS TO BE PRESENTED WITHIN 21 DAYS AFTER

SHIPMENT DATE BUT WITHIN THE VALIDITY OF THE CREDIT.

49： Confirmation Instructions

WITHOUT

78： Instructions to the Paying/Accepting/Negotiating Bank

+ UPON RECEIPT OF DOCUMENTS CONFORMING TO THE TERMS AND

CONDITIONS OF THIS CREDIT, WE SHALL PAY THE PRO-CEEDS. AS DESIGNATED.

+ NEGOTIATING BANK MUST FORWARD ALL DOCUMENTS TO US IN ONE LOT BY COURIER SERVICE AT BENEFICIARY'S EXPENS-ES.

+ EXCEPT AS OTHERWISE STATED OR MODIFIED, THIS CREDIT IS SUBJECT TO THE *UCP 600*.

相关资料：

发票号码：07INC9988　　　　发票日期：MAY 5, 2007

船名：　FUXING V. 196　　　起运港：　GUANGZHOU

提单日期：MAY 20, 2007　　　提单号码：SIO5789666

包装情况：PACKED IN CARTONS OF 20 PCS EACH, 500 CARTONS TOTAL.

毛重：21 KGS/CARTON　净重：20 KGS/CARTON　体积：0.1M³/CARTON

唛头：DIRAMODE　　　　　H. S. 编码：6401.0058

　　　DUNKIRK

　　　C/NO. 1～500

合同号码：　SCGD2007001

原产地证日期：MAY 17, 2007

保险单日期：　MAY 18, 2007

I N V O I C E

NO. ....

TO：   **SHIPPED S. S.** ....

                 SHIPMENT DATE ....

                 DESTINATION ....

Marks & Nos.	Description of Goods	Amount

PACKING LIST

Commodity ....   Destination ....

Contract No. ....   Consignee ....

Means of
Transportation ....

Marks & Nos.

GUANGDONG FENG QING TRADING CO.
NO. 31 ZHONG SHAN ROAD GUANGZHOU, CHINA

FAX：+88-20-8331 5567

INVOICE NO.

                                DATE：

TO MESSRS：

SHIPPING ADVICE

(1) NAME OF COMMODITY：

(2) QUANTITY：

(3) INVOICE VALUE：

(4) NAME OF STEAMER：

(5) DATE OF SHIPMENT：

(6) CREDIT NO.：

(7) S/C NO.：

(8) PORT OF LOADING：

(9) PORT OF DISCHARGE：

(10) SHIPPING MARK：

（三）根据资料缮制发票

DOC. CREDIT NUMBER	*20：	540370
APPLICANT	*50：	ORCHID TRADING LTD.
		UNIT 513, CHINACHEM BLDG.,
		78 MODY ROAD, TST, KOWLOON,
		HONG KONG
BENEFICIARY	*59：	ZHEJIANG CLOTHING IMP. AND EXP.
		CO.,LTD.
		902 WULIN ROAD, HANGZHOU,
		CHINA
AMOUNT	*32B：	CURRENCY USD AMOUNT 18 188. 80
LOADING IN CHARGE	44A：	SHANGHAI CHINA
FOR TRANSPORT TO….	44B：	ROTTERDAM
LASTEST SHIPMENT DATE	44C：	080430
DESCRIPT. OF GOODS	45A：	LADIES WEARS

STYLE NO.	DESCRIPTION	QTY.	UNIT PRICE
1484020	ROUNDNECK	1 568 PCS	USD 5. 40/PC
1484521	JACKET	1 568 PCS	USD 6. 20/PC

CIF ROTTERDAM AS PER S/C NO. B04ED121.

MODE OF SHIPMENT： BY SEA

DOCUMENTS REQUIRED 46A：

　　＋　SIGNED COMMERCIAL INVOICE IN QUADRUPLI-CATE SHOWING SEPARATELY THE L/C NO., ST-YLE NO..

发票号码：04DL0F015　　　　发票日期：2008 年 4 月 22 日

圆领衫：　ROUNDNECK, 1 568 PCS, 14 PCS/箱，共 112 箱

拉链衫：　JACKET,　　1 568 PCS, 14 PCS/箱，共 112 箱

唛头：　　ORCHID

　　　　　B04ED121

　　　　　ROTTERDAM

　　　　　C/NO. 1-224

Issuer			
	商 业 发 票 **COMMERCIAL INVOICE**		
To			
	No.	Date	
Transport details	S/C No.	L/C No.	
	Terms of payment		

Marks and numbers	Number and kind of packages Description of goods	Quantity	Unit price	Amount

（四）根据信用证缮制下列单据

From：VOLKSBANK SCHORNDORF，HAMBURG，GERMANY
To：BANK OF CHINA，HEBEI BRANCH

Form of Doc. Credit	＊40A：	IRREVOCABLE
Doc. Credit Number	＊20：	08-4-1520
Date of Issue	31C：	080201
APPLICABLE RULES	40E：	UCP LATEST VERSION
Expiry	＊31D：	DATE：080415 IN THE COUNTRY OF BENEFICIARY
Applicant	＊50：	LUCKY VICTORY INTERNATIONAL STUTTGART STIR. 5, D-84618, SCHORNDORF, GERMANY
Beneficiary	＊59：	HEBEI MACHINERY IMP. AND EXP. CORP（GROUP） 720 DONGFENG ROAD, SHIJIAZHUANG, CHINA
Amount	＊32B：	Currency USD Amount 57 600. 00
Pos. /Neg. Tol.（％）	39A：	5/5
Available with/by	＊41A：	ANY BANK BY NEGOTIATION
Draft at…	42C：	DRAFTS AT 30 DAYS SIGHT

FOR FULL INVOICE VALUE

Drawee	42A：	VOLKSBANK SCHORNDORF HAMBURG, GERMANY
Partial Shipments	43P：	ALLOWED
Transshipment	43T：	ALLOWED
Loading in Charge	44A：	TIANJIN
For Transport to	44B：	HAMBURG
Latest Date of Ship.	44C：	080331
Descript. of Goods	45A：	

STAINLESS STEEL SPADE HEAD,
ART. NO. S569, 4 800 PCS, USD 5. 60 PER PC.,
ART. NO. F671, 3 200 PCS, USD 9. 60 PER PC.,
AS PER S/C NO. 08HM256 DATED JAN. 01, 2008.

CIF HAMBURG

Documents required 46A：

+　SIGNED COMMERCIAL INVOICE IN TRIPLICATE.

+　FULL SET OF CLEAN ON BOARD OCEAN BILLS OF LADING MADE OUT TO ORDER OF SHIPPER, MARKED "FREIGHT PREPAID" AND NOTIFY APPLICANT.

+　GSP CERTIFICATE OF ORIGIN FORM A

+　PACKING LIST IN TRIPLICATE.

+　INSURANCE POLICY COVERING RISKS AS PER INSTITUTE CARGO CLAUSE（A）INCLUDING WAREHOUSE TO WAREHOUSE CLAUSE UP TO FINAL DESTINATION AT SCHORNDORF, FOR 110 PCT OF THE CIF VALUE, MARKED PREMIUM PAID, SHOWING CLAIM PAYABLE IN GERMANY.

Additional Cond. 47A：j

1. A HANDING FEE OF USD 80.00 WILL BE DEDUCTED IF DISCREPANCY DOCUMENTS PRESENTED.

2. ALL DOCUMENTS MUST BE IN ENGLISH.

3. ALL DOCUMENTS INDICATING THIS L/C NUMBER.

Presentation Period 48：

DOCUMENTS TO BE PRESENTED WITHIN 15 DAYS AFTER THE DATE OF SHIPMENT, BUT WITHIN THE VALIDITY OF THE CREDIT.

Details of Charges 71B：

ALL BANKING CHARGES AND EXPENSES OUTSIDE THE ISSUING BANK ARE FOR BENEFICIARY'S ACCOUNT.

补充资料：

100PCS/CTN　80CTNS　G. W. 6 300 KGS　N. W. 6 000 KGS　MEAS. 18CBM

ISSUER	COMMERCIAL INVOICE		
	NO.		DATE
TO			
TRANSPORT DETAILS	S/C NO.		L/C NO.
	TERMS OF PAYMENT		

Marks& Numbers	Description of goods	Quantity	Unit Price	Amount

SAY TOTAL:

ISSUER					
		PACKING LIST			
TO					
		INVOICE NO.	DATE		
Marks& Numbers	Number and kind of package Description of goods	N. W.	G. W.	MEASUREMENT	

（五）阅读信用证及相关资料并制作单据

LETTER OF CREDIT

BASIC HEADER F 01 BKCHCNBJA5×× 9828 707783

＋BANK OF NOVA SCOTIA，TORONTO，CANADA

：MT：700 ——ISSUE A DOCUMENTARY CREDIT——

FORM OF CREDIT	40A：	IRREVOCABLE
DOC. CREDIT NUMBER	20：	078230CDI1117LC
DATE OF ISSUE	31C：	070118
APPLICABLE RULES	40E：	UCP LATEST VERSION
DATE AND PLACE OF EXPIRY	31D：	070310
APPLICANT	50：	WENSCO FOODS LTD., RUA DE GREENLAND STREET, 68-A 1260-297 WELL D. COQUIT-LAM,B. C. CANADA
BENEFICIARY	59：	HUNAN CEREALS, OILS & FOODSTUFFS IMPORT & EXPORT CORPO-RATION 38 WUYI RD., CHANGSHA CHINA
CURRENCY CODE AND AMOUNT	32B：	USD 10 830. 00
AVAILABLE WITH…BY…	41A：	ANY BANK IN CHINA BY NE-GOCIATION
DRAFT AT	42C：	DRAFT AT 45 DAYS AFTER B/L DATE FOR FUL INVOICE VALUE
DRAWEE	42A：	DRAWN ON US AND THE ADD：550 WEST GEORGIA ST., PO BOX 172 TORONTO, CAN-ADA
PARTIAL SHIPMENT	43P：	PROHIBIED
TRANSSHIPMENT	43T：	PERMITTIED
LODING/DISPATCH/TAKING/	44A：	MAIN CHINESE PORT

FROM

FOR TRANSPOTATION TO　　44B：　　VANCOUVER B. C.

LATEST DATE OF SHIPMENT　　44C：　　070301

DESCRIPTION OF GOODS/　　45A：　　"TROPIC ISLE CANNED MAN-

SERVICE　　　　　　　　　　　　DARIN ORIANGES LS-WHOLE

　　　　　　　　　　　　　　　　SEGMENTS" AS PER P/I NO.

　　　　　　　　　　　　　　　　CF07018 CIF VANCOUVER B. C.

DOCS REQUIERD：　　46A：

+ MANUALLY SIGNED COMMERCIAL INVOICE ONE ORINAL
  AND FOUR COPIES,
  CERTIFYING GOODS ARE OF CHINESE ORIGIN AND INDI-
  CATEING P/I NO.

+ FULL SET(3/3) OF CLEAN ON BOARD OCEAN BILLS OF LAD-
  ING, MADE OUT TO ORDER OF SHIPPER, BLANK INDORSED
  NOTIFYING APPLICANT, STATING FREIGHT PREPAID OR
  COLLECT.

+ PACKING LIST IN TRIPLICATE

+ NEGOCIABLE INSURANCE POLICY/CERTIFICATE, BLANK INDOR-
  SED, COVERING GOODS FOR THE INVOICE VALUE PLUS
  10% AGAINST THE RISKS OF ICC(A) AND ICC (CARGO).

+ SHIPPING ADVICE SHOULD SENT BY FAX TO APPLICANT
  INFORMING VESSEL'S NAME AND VOY. NO., GR. WT, MEAS,
  PACKING, TOTAL AMOUNT AND ETD.

+ G. S. P FORM A IN 1 ORIGINAL AND 2 COPIES, INDICATING
  ORIGIN CRITERION "W".

ADDITIONAL CONDITIONS：　　47A：　　+ A DESCREPANCY FEE OF
　　　　　　　　　　　　　　　　　　U. S. D 50. 00 FOR BENEFI-
　　　　　　　　　　　　　　　　　　CIARY'S ACCOUNT

　　　　　　　　　　　　　　　　　+ ONE COMPELE SET OF
　　　　　　　　　　　　　　　　　　DOCS TO BE SENT TO US
　　　　　　　　　　　　　　　　　　BY COURIER IN ONE
　　　　　　　　　　　　　　　　　　LOT.

　　　　　　　　　　　　　　　　　+ ALL DOCS MUST NOT IN-
　　　　　　　　　　　　　　　　　　DICATED L/C NO. EX-

CEPT INVOICE & DRAFT.

CHARGES　　　　　　　71B： ALL BANKING CHARGES OUT OF OUR COUNTER ARE FOR BENEFICIARY'S ACCOUNT

PERIOD FOR PRESENTATIONS 48： 15 DAYS AFTER SHIPMENT AND NOT EXCEEDING L/C EXPIRY

TRAILER　　　　MAC： 9FE41FBC　　CHK： 56783 EE6A448　NNNN

补充资料：

(1) QUANTITY： 950 CARTONS

(2) PACKING： IN PLASTIC BAGS OF 2. 84 KGS EACH THEN SIX BAGS IN A CARTON.

(3) UNIT PRICE： U. S. D 11. 40 PER CARTON

(4) TOTAL AMOUNT： U. S. D 10 830. 00

(5) SHIPPING PER S. S "DEWEI V. 213" FROM HUANGPU TO VANCOUVER B. C., B/L NO. 6180

(6) MARKS： W. F. L. /VANCOUVER/C/NO.： 1-UP

(7) B/L DATE： 070220

(8) ETD： 070221

(9) GROSS WEIGHT： 17138KGS　NET WEIGHT： 16188 KGS MEAS： 18. 365 M³

(10) NEGOCIATING BANK： BANK OF CHINA, HUNAN BRANCH

(11) S/C NO： P. O. 2007-018　INV. DATE： 070201　INV. NO.： CFF-016

(12) H. S. CODE： 8560. 3900

(13) CARRIER： ABC CO., LTD, FOR THE AGENT, COSCO AS THE CARRIER

业务员姓名：张三

(14) REFERENCE NO.： 1283890096

1. 下面是一张已经填好的箱单，请根据上面的 L/C 和补充资料将错误修改在空白处。

```
                          PACKING LIST
S/C NO.：P. O. 2007-018                      SHIPPING MARK：
INVOICE NO.：CFF-016                               N/M
L/C NO.：__078230CDI1117LC

C/NOS.   NOS&KIND OF PKGS   QTY(BAGS)   G. W. (KGS)   N. W. (KGS)   MEAS. (M³)
         TROPIC ISLE CANED MANDARIN ORIANGES LS-WHOLE SEGMENTS        950CTNS
                          5 760        17 138        16 188          183. 65

TOTAL                     5 760        17 138        16 188          183. 65

TOTAL AMOUNT：SAY US DOLLARS TEN THOUSAND EIGHT HUNDRED AND THIRTY ONLY.
```

HUNAN CEREALS, OILS &·FOODSTUFFS
IMPORT &· EXPORT CORPORATION

装箱单缮制错误的地方有：

2. 填制下列单据：

COMMERCIAL INVOICE

TO：   INVOICE NO.：

                                 DATE：

                                 S/C NO.：

                                 L/C NO.：

FROM：   TO：

MARKS&·NOS.	DESCRIPTIONS OF GOODS	QUANTITY (CTNS)	UNIT PRICE (USD/CTN)	AMOUNT
TOTAL AMOUNT：				

TOTAL NUMBER OF PACKAGE：

（六）根据信用证缮制发票和装箱单

题目名称	制作议付单证
基本要求	上海市对外贸易公司于 2000 年 11 月 29 日将货物装运后，即准备议付单据向交通银行上海分行交单。请根据提供的信用证的内容制作信用证指定的议付单证。

信用证

LETTER OF CREDIT

Basic Header appl ID：F APDU Id：01 LT　　Addr：OCMMCNSH××××
Session：8533 Sequence：142087

Application Header Input/Output：0　　　　　　Msg Type：700
Input Time：1622　　　　　Input Date：001103
Sender LT：BKKBTHBKE×××
BANGKOK BANK PUBLIC CO-
MPANY LIMITED BANCKOK
Input Session：5177 ISN：800333　Output Date：001103
Output Time：2033　　　　　Priority：N

Sequence Total ＊27：　1/1
Form Doc Credit ＊40A：　IRREVOCABLE
Doc Credit Num ＊20：　BKKB1103043
Date of Issue 31C：　001103
Applicable Rules 40E：　UCP LATEST VERSION
Date/Place Exp ＊31D：　Date 010114 Place BENEFICIARIES' COUNTRY
Applicant ＊50：　MOUN CO., LTD
NO. 443, 249 ROAD
BANGKOK THAILAND
Beneficiary ＊59　　/
SHANGHAI FOREIGN TRADE CORP.
SHANGHAI, CHINA
Curr Code，Amt ＊32B：　Code USD Amount 18 000,
Avail With By ＊41D：　ANY BANK IN
CHINA

		BY NEGOTIATION
Drafts At	42C：	SIGHT IN DUPLICATE INDICATING THIS L/C NUMBER
Drawee	43D：	//
		ISSUING BANK
Partial Shipmts	43P：	NOT ALLOWED
Transshipment	43T：	ALLOWED
Loading on Brd	44A：	
		CHINA MAIN FORT，CHINA
	44B：	
		BANGKOK，THAILAND
Latest Shipment	44C：	001220
Goods Descript.	45A：	2 000 KGS. ISONIAZID BP98
		PACKED IN 50 KGS/DRUM
		AT USD 9.00 PER KG CFR BANGKOK
Docs Required	46A：	

DOCUMENTS REQUIRED：

+　COMMERCIAL INVOICE IN ONE ORIGI-
NAL PLUS 5 COPIES INDICATING
F. O. B. VALUE，FREIGHT CHARGES SEPA-
RATELY AND THIS L/C NUMBER，
ALL OF WHICH MUST BE MANUALLY SIGNED.

+　FULL SET OF 3/3 CLEAN ON BOARD
OCEAN BILLS OF LADING AND TWO
NON-NEGOTIABLE，COPIES MADE OUT TO
ORDER OF BANGKOK BANK
PUBLIC COMPANY LIMITED，BANGKOK
MARKED FREIGHT PREPAID AND
NOTIFY APPLICANT AND INDICATING
THIS L/C NUMBER.

+　PACKING LIST IN ONE ORIGINAL PLUS 5
COPIES，ALL OF WHICH MUST BE
MANUALLY SIGNED.

dd. Conditions　　47A：

ADDITIONAL CONDITION：

A DISCREPANCY FEE OF USD 50.00 WILL BE IMPOSED ON EACH SET OF DOCUMENTS PRESENTED FOR NEGOTIATION UNDER THIS L/C WITH DISCREPANCY. THE FEE WILL BE DEDUCTED FROM THE BILL AMOUNT.

Charges   71B: ALL BANK CHARGES OUTSIDE THAILAND INCLUDING REIMBURSING BANK COMMISSION AND DISCREPANCY FEE (IF ANY) ARE FOR BENEFICIARIES' ACCOUNT.

Confirmat Instr   *49:   WITHOUT

Reimburs. Bank   53D: //
BANGKOK BANK PUBLIC COMPANY LIMITED, NEW YORK BRANCH ON T/T BASIS

Ins Paying bank   78:
DOCUMENTS TO BE DESPATCHED IN ONE LOT BY COURIER.
ALL CORRESPONDENCE TO BE SENT TO/ BANGKOK BANK PUBLIC COMPANY
LIMITED HEAD OFFICE, 333 SILOM ROAD, BANGKOK 10 500, THAILAND.

Send Rec Info   72:   REIMBURSEMENT IS SUBJECT TO ICC URR 525

Trailer MAC   :
CHK   :
DLM   :

-- End of Message --

补充资料：

运费共 1 500 美元   G. W. 2 300 KGS   N. W. 2 000 KGS

SHANGHAI FOREIGN TRADE CORP.
SHANGHAI, CHINA
COMMERCIAL INVOICE

To：_____　　　　　Invoice No.：_____

　　　　　　　　　　　　　　　　　　　Invoice Date：_____

　　　　　　　　　　　　　　　　　　　S/C No.：_____

　　　　　　　　　　　　　　　　　　　S/C Date：_____

From：_____　　To：_____

Letter of Credit No.：_____　　Issued By：_____

Marks and Numbers	Number and kind of package Description of goods	Quantity	Unit Price	Amount
		TOTAL：		

SAY TOTAL：

SHANGHAI FOREIGN TRADE CORP.
SHANGHAI, CHINA
PACKING LIST

To：_____　　　　　Invoice No.：_____

　　　　　　　　　　　　　　　　　　　Invoice Date：_____

　　　　　　　　　　　　　　　　　　　S/C No.：_____

　　　　　　　　　　　　　　　　　　　S/C Date：_____

From：_____　　To：_____

Letter of Credit No.：　　　　　　Date of Shipment：

Marks and Numbers	Number and kind of package Description of goods	Quantity	Package	G. W.	N. W.	Meas.
			TOTAL：			

SAY TOTAL：

（七）依据销售合同和信用证以及有关资料缮制商业发票、装箱单

ABC TEXTILES IMPORT AND EXPORT CORPORATION
127 ZHONGSHAN RD. E. 1 SHANGHAI R. P. OF CHINA
SALES CONFIRMATION

TO: MESSRS TOMSON TEXTILES INC.

3384 VINCENT ST.　　　　　　　　　　NO. 23CA1006

DOWNSVIEW, ONTARIO　　　　　　DATE: 20080306

M3J, 2J4, CANADA

ARTICLE NO. COMMODITY & SPECIFICATION QUANTITY UNIT PRICE AMOUNT

ART. NO.　　　TRUERAN DYED JEAN

77111　　　　　POLYESTES 65%, COTTON 35%

20×20, 94×60, 112/114 cm,

40 M AND UP ALLOWING 15% 27. 432 M

AND UP IN IRREGULAR CUTS

MAKES UP: FULL WIDTH ROLLER ON TUBES

　　　　　OF 1. 5 INCHES IN DIAMETER

PACKING: IN SEAWORTHY CARTONS

COL.	M.	CIF USD/M	TORONTO USD
RED	4 000	1.56	6 240. 00
SILVER	3 000	1.32	3 960. 00
FIESTA	4 000	1.56	6 240. 00
DKNAVY	3 000	1.62	4 860. 00
WINE	2 200	1.62	3 564. 00
ELEPHANT	3 000	1.44	4 320. 00
BLACK	4 800	1.62	7 776. 00
TOTAL:	24 000		36 960. 00

SHIPMENT: BEF. APR. 20TH 2008

WITH PARTIAL SHIPMENT & TRANSHIPMENT TO BE ALLOWED.

DESTINATION: TORONTO

PAYMENT: BY 100% IRREVOCABLE L/C AVAILAVLE BY DRAFT AT

30 DAYS SIGHT，TO BE OPENED IN SELLERS FAVOUR 15 DAYS BEFORE THE MONTH OF SHIPMENT，L/C TO REMAIN VALID IN CHINA FOR A PERIOD OF 15 DAYS AFTER THE LAST SHIPMENT DATE.

ABC 纺织品进出口公司

信用证

DOCUMENTARY CREDIT

ZCZC AHS302 CPUA520 S9203261058120RN025414394

P3 SHSOC

ICRA

TO：10306 26BKCHCNBJASH102514

FM：15005 25CIBCCATTF×××05905

CIBBCCATTF×××

* CANADIAN INPERIAL BANK OF COMMERCE

* TORONTO

MT：701 02

27： SEQENCE OF TOTAL：1/1

40A：FORM OF DOC. CREDIT：IRREVOCABLE

20： DOC. CREDIT NUMBER：T-017641

31C：DATE OF ISSUE：20080325

40E：UCP LATEST VERSION

31D：EXPIRY：DATE：20080505

PLACE：THE PEOPLES REP. OF CHINA

50： APPLICANT：TOMSCN TEXTJLES INC.

3384 VINCENT ST

DOWNSVIEW. ONTARIO

M3J. 2J4 CANADA

59： BENEFICIARY：ABC TEXILES IMPORT AND EXPORT CORPORATION

127 ZHONGSHAN RD. E. 1

SHANGHAI P. R. OF CHINA

32B：AMOUT：CURRENCY：USD　　AMOUT：36 960. 00

39A：POS/NEG TOL(%)：05/05

41-： AVAILABLE WITH/BY：AVAILABLE WITH ANY BANK IN CHINA

NEGOTIATION

42C：DRAFTS AT—：30DAYS AFTER SIGHT

42_：DRAWEE：CIBE—TORONTO TRADE FINANCE CENTRE，TORONTO

43P：PARTIAL SHIPMENTS：PERMITTED

43T：TRANSSHIPPMENT：PERMITTED

44A：LOADING IN CHARGE：CHINA

44B：FOR TRANSPORT TO：TORONTO

44C：LATEST DATE OF SHIP：20080420

45A：SHIPMENT OF GOODS：MERCHANDISE AS PER S/CNO. 23CA1006
CIF TORONTO

46A：DOCUMENTS REQUIRED：

- COMMERCIAL INVOICE IN QUADRUPLICATE
- CERTIFICATE OF ORIGIN
- FULL SET CLEAN ON BOARD BILLS OF LADING TO SHIPPER'S ORDER BLANK ENDORSED MARKED "FREIGHT PREPAID TO TORONTO" NOTIFY APPLICANT (SHOWING FULL NAME AND ADDRESS) AND INDICATING FREIGHT CHARGED.
- NEGOTIBLE INSURANCE POLICY OR CERTIFICATE ISSUED BY PEOPLES INSURANCE COMPANY OF CHINA INCORPORATING THEIR OCEAN MARINE CARGO CLAUSES (ALL RISKS) AND WAR RISKS FOR 110 PERCENT OF CIF INVOICE VALUE，WITH CLAIMS PAYABLE IN CANADA INDICATING INSURANCE CHARGES.
- DETAILED PACKING LIST IN TRIPLICATE
- EXPORT LICENSE
- COPY OF INSURANCE CHARGES
- COPY OF FREIGHT CHARGES

47A：ADDITIONAL COND：

THE NUMBER AND THE DATE OF THIS CREDIT AND THE NAME OF OUR BANK MUST BE QUOTED ON ALL DRAFTS REQUIRED

AN ADDITIONAL FEE OF USD 50. 00 OR EQUIVALENT WILL BE DEDUCTED FROM THE PROCEEDS PAID UNDER ANY DRAWING WHERE DOCUMENTS PRESENTED ARE FOUND NOT TO BE IN STRICT CONFORMITY WITH THE TERMS OF THIS CREDIT.

71B：DETAILS OF CHARGES：

ALL BANKING CHARGES OUTSIDE CANADA INCLUDING AD-VISING COMMISSION ARE FOR ACCOUNT OF BENIFICIARY AND MUST BE CLAIMED AT THE TIME OF ADVISING.

48：PRESENTATION PERIOD：

NOT LATER THAN 15DAYS AFTER THE DATE OF ISSUANCE OF THE SHIPPING DOCUMENTS BUT WITHIN THE VALIDITY OF THE CREDIT.

49：CONFIRMATION：WITHOUT

78：INSTRUCTIONS：

UPON OUR RECEIPT OF DOCUMENTS IN ORDER WE WILL RE-MIT IN ACCORDANCE WITH NEGOTIATING BANK'S INSTRUC-TIONS AT MATURITY.

外销出仓通知单(代提货单)

合约：23CA1006

发货仓库：永新 　　　　2008 年 4 月 4 日 　　　　发票号码：D2C4193

原进仓单 货号	货名及规格	件号	毛重/净重	件数	数量	尺码
号 码 77111	20×20, 94×60,		125/117		400 M	117×14×25cm
848607 TO204-75	114cm×40m 以上					
	RED	1-10		10	4 000 M	
	SILVER	11-17		7	2 800 M	
染色棉涤斜纹布	FIESTA	18-27		10	4 000 M	
	DK. NAVY	28-34		7	2 800 M	
	WINE	35-39		5	2 000 M	
TOMSON						
23CA1006	ELEPHANT	40-46		7	2 800 M	
TORONTO	BLACK	47-58		12	4 800 M	
NO. 1-60	SILVER	59		1	200 M	
	DK. NAVY				200 M	
	WINE	60		1	200 M	
	ELEPHANT				200 M	

合计：60 纸箱 　　　　24 000 M

开单员：

SUPPLEMENT：

1. VESSEL'S NAME：MILD VICTORY 　　V. 864
2. OCEAN FREIGHT：USD 1 532. 52
3. H. S. CODE：5513，3200
4. INSURANCE AGENT：TOPLIS HARDING CANADA INC.

1234 ISLINGTO AVENUE

SUITE 840，TORONTO ONTARIO

M8X，IY9，CANADA

5. INSURANCE CHARGES：USD 215.48

6. QUOTA YEAR：2002

7. CATEGORY PACKING：24A

8. EXPORT PACKING：USD 259.20

9. EXPORT LICENCE LINE 11："M"

ABC 纺织品进出口有限公司

ABC TEXTILES IMP. & EXP. CORPORATION

127ZHONGSHAN RD. E. 1 SHANGHAI P. R. OF CHINA

商 业 发 票

COMMERCIAL INVOICE

Messers：

INVOICE NO	:_____
INVOICE DATE	:_____
L/C NO.	:_____
L/C DATE	:_____
S/C NO.	:_____

Exporter：

Transport details：　　　　　　**Terms of payment**：

MARKS AND NUMBERS	DESCRIPTION OF GOODS	QUANTITY	UNIT PRICE	AMOUNT

TOTAL AMOUNT IN WORDS：

TOTAL GROSS WEIGHT：

TOTAL NUMBER OF PACKAGE

ABC 纺织品进出口有限公司
ABC TEXTILES IMP. & EXP. CORPORATION
127ZHONGSHAN RD. E. 1 SHANGHAI P. R. OF CHINA

装　箱　单
PACKING LIST

Exporter：

DATE：＿＿＿＿＿＿

INVOICE

NO.：＿＿＿＿＿＿

S/C　　　　NO.：

＿＿＿＿＿＿

BUYER

TRANSPORT DETAILS：

C/NOS.	NOS& KINDS OF PACKS	ITEM	QTY.	G. W.	N. W.	MEAS.

（STAMP）

（八）根据信用证、合同和补充资料的内容缮制商业发票

合同

SHANGHAI IMPORT & EXPORT TRADE CORPORATION.
1321 ZHONGSHAN ROAD SHANGHAI, CHINA
SALES CONTRACT

TEL：021-65788877

FAX：021-65788876

S/C NO：HX050264

DATE：JAN. 1，2005

TO：TKAMLA CORPORATION

　　6-7KAWARA MACH

　　OSAKA，JAPAN

　　DEAR SIRS,

WE HEREBY CONFIRM HAVING SOLD TO YOU THE FOLLOWING GOODS ON TERMS AND CONDITIONS AS SPECIFIED BELOW：

MARKS &.NO	DESCRIPTION	QUANTITY	UNIT PRICE	AMOUNT
T.C	COTTON SHIRT		CIF OSAKA	
OSAKA	ART NO. H666	500 PCS	USD 5. 50	USD 2 750. 00
C/NO. 1-250	ART NO. HX88	500 PCS	USD 4. 50	USD 2 250. 00
	ART NO. HE21	500 PCS	USD 4. 80	USD 2 400. 00
	ART NO. HA56	500 PCS	USD 5. 20	USD 2 600. 00
	ART NO. HH46	500 PCS	USD 5. 00	USD 2 500. 00
TOTAL：		2 500 PCS		USD 12 500. 00

PAGKING：IN 250 CARTONS

SHIPMENT FROM SHANGHAI TO OSAKA

PARTIAL SHIPMENT NOT ALLOWED AND TRANSHIPMENT AL-LOWED

PAYMENT：L/C AT SIGHT

INSURANCE POLICY FOR 110 PCT OF THE INVOICE VALUE COVERING ALL RISKS AND WAR RISK AS PER PICC.

　　TIME OF SHIPMENT：LATEST DATE OF SHIPMENT

　　MAR. 16，2005

THE BUYERS　　　　　　　　　　　　THE SELLERS
TKAMLA CORPORATION　　　　SHANGHAI IMPORT & EXPORT
　　　　　　　　　　　　　　　　　　　　　TRADE CORP.
　　　　高田四郎　　　　　　　　　　　　丁莉

信用证

FROM：FUJI BANK LTD
1013，SAKULA COTOLIKINGZA MACHI
TOKYO，JAPAN
TO：BANK OF CHINA SHANGHAI BRANCH

SEQUENCE OF TOTAL	*27：	1/1
FORM OF DOC,CREDIT	*40A：	REVOCABLE
DOC. CREDIT NUMBER	*20：	33416852
DATE OF ISSUE	*31C：	JAN. 12，2005
APPLICABLE RULES	40E：	UCP LATEST VERSION
DATE AND PLACE OF EXPIRY	*31D：	DATE MAR 17TH,2005 IN CHINA
APPLICANT	*50：	TKAMLA CORPORATION 6-7，KAWARA MACH OSAKA，JAPAN
BENEFICIARY	*59：	SHANGHAI IMPORT & EXPORT TRADE CORPORATION 1321 ZHONGSHAN ROAD SHANGHAI，CHINA
AMOUNT	*32B：	CURRENCY USD AMOUNT 12 500.00
AVAILABLE WITH…BY…	*41A：	ANY BANK IN CHINA BY NEGOTIATION
DRAFTS AT…	*42C：	DRAFTS AT SIGHT FOR FULL INVOICE COST
DRAWEE	*42A：	FUJI BANK LTD
PARTIAL SHIPMENTS	*43P：	NOT ALLOWED

TRANSHIPMENT	* 43T:	ALLOWED
LOADING ON BOARD	* 44A:	SHANGHAI, CHINA
FOR TRANSPORTATION TO...	* 44B:	OSAKA, JAPAN
LATEST DATE OF SHIPMENT	* 44C:	MAR. 16，2005
DESCRIPTION OF GOODS	* 45A:	COTTON SHIRT

ART NO. H666 500 PCS

USD5. 50/PC

ART NO. HX88 500 PCS

USD4. 50/PC

ART NO. HE21 500 PCS

USD4. 80/PC

ART NO. HA56 500 PCS

USD5. 20/PC

ART NO. HH46 500 PCS

USD5. 00/PC

CIF OSAKA

DOCUMENTS REQUIRED　　　　* 46A:

+ COMMERCIAL INVOICE IN DUPLICATE

+ PACKING LIST IN DUPLICATE

+ 3/3 CLEAN ON BOARD OCEAN BILLS OF LADING MADE OUT TO ORDER AND BLANK EN-DORSED MARKED "FREIGHT PREPAID" NOTIFY APPLI-CANT

+ CERTIFICATE OF ORIGIN

PERIOD FOR PRESENTATION　　* 48: DOCUMENTS MUST BE PR-ESENTED WITHIN 15 DAYS AFTER THE DATE OF SHIPMENT BUT WITHIN THE VALIDI-TY

OF THE CREDIT

CONFIRMATION INSTRUCTION　　*49：WITHOUT

CHARGES　　　　　　　　　　　　*71B：ALL BANKING CHARGES
OUTSIDE JAPAN ARE FOR
ACCOUNT OF THE
BENEFICIARY

SENDER TO RECEIVER INFO　*72：THIS CREDIT IS SUBJECT
TO THE UNIFORM CUS-
TOMS AND PRACTICE
FOR DOCUMETARY CREDIT,
2007 REVI-SION ICC PUBLCA-
TION NO. 600

补充资料：
(1) INVOICE NO. XH056671
(2) INVOICE DATE：FEB. 01，2005
(3) PACKING：
PACKED IN 250 CARTONS OF 10 PCS
PACKED IN TWO 20'CONTAINER(NO. TEXU2263999；TEXU2264000)
G. W：20. 5 KGS/CTN，N. W. 20 KGS/CTN
MESUREMENT：0. 456 M^3
(4) VESSEL：NANGXING V. 068
(5) B/L NO. COCS0511861
(6) B/L DATE：FEB. 26，2005，(SHIPPED ON BORAD)
(7) 承运人接收货物地在石家庄(SHI JIA ZHUANG)
铁路运输(BY RAIL)至上海装船
(8) 承运人货运代理：WAN HAI SHIPPING CO. (LI MING)
(9) H. S. Code：551. 000
(10) Certificate No. QDCD118　出证日期：2005 年 2 月 20 日

商业发票

SHANGHAI IMPORT & EXPORT TRADE CORPORATION.
1321 ZHONGSHAN ROAD SHANGHAI, CHINA
COMMERCIAL INVOICE

TEL：021-65788877   INV NO：_____

FAX：021-65788876   DATE _____

                                              S/C NO.：_____

TO：

FROM _____   TO _____

DRAWN UNDER _____   L/C NO. _____

MARKS & NO	DESCRIPTION OF GOODS	QUANTITY	U/PRICE	AMOUNT

TOTAL AMOUNT：

SHANGHAI IMPORT & EXPORT TRADE CORPORATION
李明

（九）根据信用证以及相关资料缮制发票和装箱单

信用证

FM/THE CITY BANK LIMITED, BANGABANDHU AVENUE BRANCH, DHAKA, BANGLADESH.

TO/THE BANK OF CHINA, SHAANXI BRANCH, 233 JIE FANG ROAD, XIAN, CHINA.

TEST NO. 2-334 DATED 2008, MARCH, 3 FOR USD 40 800

BENEFICIARY/M/S. CHINA SHAANXI TEXTILE IMPORT N EXPORT CORPORATION.

　　　　　NO. A-113 BEIKOU JIANGUO ROAD, XIAN, CHINA.

OPENER/M/S. F. K. TRADING, 26, AHSANULLAH ROAD, NAWAB BARI, DHAKA-1100, BANGLADESH.

AT THE REQUEST OF OPENER WE HEREBY ESTABLISH OUR IR-REVOCABLE DOCUMENTARY

CREDIT NO. 01080099-C DATED 2008, MARCH, 03 IN BENEFICIARY'S FAVOUR FOR THE AMOUNT

OF USD 40 800/= (US DOLLAR FORTY THOUSAND EIGHT HUN-DRED) ONLY. CFR CHITTAGONG BY STEAMER.

AVAILABLE BY BENEFICIARY'S DRAFT ON OPENING BANK AT SIGHT FOR FULL INVOICE VALUE OF SHIPMENT PURPORING TO BE/-RAW MATERIALS FOR TEXTILE INDUSTRIES

"TAYEN PAGDOA" BRAND 60 000 LBS GREY TR40S/1YARN ON COVES, POLYESTER 65, VISOSE 35. ART NO. TR40S/1. AT RATE OF USD 0. 68 PER LB. AS PER INDENT NO. DI/34 DT 2008-23-02 OF M/S.

DIAMOND INTERNATIONAL, 21, RAJAR, DEWRI, DHAKA-1100 BAN-GLADESH ANDSUPPLIER'S SALES CONFRACT NO. 08STRY040 AC-COMPANIED BY THE FOLLOWINGDOCUMENTS/—

A) BENEFICIARY'S SIGNED INVOICES IN EIGHT COPIES CERTIFY-ING MERCHANDISE TO BE OF CHINESE ORIGIN. INVOICE EX-CEEDING THIS CREDIT AMOUNT NOT ACCEPTABLE.

B) FULL SET OF CLEAN SHIPPED ON BOARD BILL OF LADING DRAWN OR ENDORSED TO THE ORDER OF CITY BANK LIMITED SHOWING FREIGHT PREPAID N MARKED NOTIFY OPENERS

AND US GIVING FULL NAME N ADDRESS.

C) A COPY OF SHIPMENT ADVICE TO BE SENT TO INSURANCE COMPANY. INSURANCE COVERED BY OPENNERS. ALL SHIPMENTS UNDER THIS CREDIT MUST BE ADVISED BY BENEFICIARY IMMEDIATELY AFTER SHIPMENT DIRECT TO M/S. BANGLADESH GENERAL INSURANCE CO. LTD. 42, DILKUSHA C/A DHAKA, DHAKA-1100, BANGLAESH AND TO THE OPENNER REFERRING TO COVER NOTE NO. BGIC/DA/MC-446/03/08 DT 03-03-08 GIVING FULL DETAILS OF SHIPMENT.

SHIPMENT FROM ANY CHINESE PORT TO CHITTAGONG PORT BY STEAMER.

BILL OF LADING MUST BE DATED NOT BEFORE THE DATE OF THIS CREDIT AND NOT LATER THAN 2008, MAY, 25. BILL OF EXCHANGE MUST BE NEGOTIATED WITHIN 15 DAYS FROM THE DATE OF SHIPMENT BUT NOT LATER THAN 2008, JUNE, 3.

OTHER TERMS AND CONDITIONS/—

1. GOODS DESTINED FOR BANGLADESH BY ISRAELI FLAG CARRIER NOT ALLOWED.

2. H. S. CODE 5509. 11 SHOULD BE APPEARED IN ALL INVOICES.

3. DRAFT MUST BE MARKED "DRAWN UNDER THE CITI BANK LIMITED, BANGABANDHU AVENUE BRANCH, DHAKA CREDIT NO. 01080099-C".

4. BENEFICIARY MUST CERTIFY ON THE INVOICES THAT THE SPECIFICATION, QUANTITY, QUALITY, PACKING, MARKING, RATES AND ALL OTHER DETAILS OF THE GOODS SHIPPED ARE STRICTLY IN ACCORDANCE WITH THE TERMS AND CONDITIONS OF THE CREDIT AS STATED ABOVE QUOTING INDENTORS NAME, ADDRESS, INDENT NUMBER N DATE, INDENTING REGISTRATION NO. B2611 AND BANGLADESH BANK'S PERMISSION NO. EC/DA/INV/729/261/79.

5. PACKING LIST IN SIX COPIES REQUIRED.

6. PACKING/IN CARTONS 100LBS PER CARTON SEA WORTHY EXPORT STANDARD.

7. ALL FOREIGN BANK CHARGES OUTSIDE BANGLADESH ARE ON

BENEFICIARY'S ACCOUNT INCLUDING REIMEURSMENT CHARGE.

8. ONE SET OF NON—NEGOTIABLE SHIPPING DOCUMENTS TO BE SENT TO THE OPENER DIRECT THROUGH AIR MAIL.

9. THE GOODS MUST BE SHIPPED IN A CONTAINER VESSEL (2×40′ FCL).

10. COMBINED LAND AND SEA BILL OF LADING ACCEPTABLE.

WE HEREBY AGREE WITH DRAWERS ENDORSERS AND BONAFIDE HOLDERS OF THE DRAFTS DRAWN UNDER AND IN COMPLIANCE WITH THE TERMS OF THIS CREDIT THAT THE SAME SHALL BE DULY HONOUED ON DUE PRESENTATION. THIS CREDIT IS SUBJECT TO UNIFORM CUSTOMS AND PRACTICE FOR DOCUMENTARY CREDITS (2007 REVISION) INTERNATIONAL CHAMBER OF COMMERCE PUBLICATION NO. 600.

INSTRCTIONS FOR THE NEGOTIATING BANK/—

1. AMOUNT OF DRFT NEGOTIATED SHOULD BE ENDORSED ON THE REVERSE SIDE OF THE CREDIT.

2. SIX COPIES OF INVOICES TO BE SENT WITH ORIGINAL SET OF DOCUMENTS BY FIRST CLASS AIRMAIL AND TWO COPIES OF INVOICES WITH DUOLICATED BY SUBSEQUENT' AIR MAIL.

3. IN REIMBURSEMENT PLEASE DRAW AS PER OUR ARRANGEMENT ON OUR HEAD OFFICE ACCOUNT NUMBER 00708354 WITH AMERICAN EXPRESS BANK LIMITED NEWYORK AGENCY, P. O. BOX 830, NEWYORK, N. Y. 10008 U. S. A. ACCOMPANIED BY A CERTIFICATE OF COMPLIANCE OF CREDIT TERMS.

PLEASE ACKNOWLEDGE RECEIPT BY AIRMAIL.

RGS

CITYAVENUE, DHAKA.

制单资料：

货号	毛重	净重	尺码
TR40S/1	49.5 KGS/CTN	45.4 KGS/CTN	0.1833 M³/CTN

发票号： SHAANXITEX08/03/A

发票日期： 2008,APRIL,15

合同日期： 2008,FEBURARY,25.

装运港： XIANGGANG CHINA

船名,航次： JINXING V. 788
提单号： COS0816787
提单日期： 2008,APRIL,25
装运标志： F. K.
CHITTAGONG
NOS1-UP

集装箱箱号及封号:COSU7854436/1234567

COMMERCIAL INVOICE		
1) SEELER	3) INVOICE NO.	4) INVOICE DATE
	5) L/C NO.	6) DATE
	7) ISSUED BY	
2) BUYER	8) CONTRACT NO.	9) DATE
	10) FROM	11) TO
	12) SHIPPED BY	13) PRICE TERM
14) MARKS 15) DESCRIPTION OF GOODS 16) QTY. 17) UNIT PRICE 18) AMOUNT		
TOTAL AMOUNT IN WORDS: TOTAL GROSS WEIGHT: TOTAL NUMBER OF PACKAGE:		
19) ISSUED BY		
20) SIGNATURE		

PACKING LIST		
1) SEELER	3) INVOICE NO.	4) INVOICE DATE
	5) FROM	6) TO
	7) TOTAL PACKAGES (IN WORDS)	
2) BUYER	8) MARKS & NOS.	

9) C/NOS,　10) NOS. & KINDS OF PKGS.　11) ITEM　　12) QTY.　　13) G. W.
14) N. W.　15) MEAS(M³)

16) ISSUED BY

17) SIGNATURE

（十）根据下列所提供资料和信用证有关信息缮制单据

1. 有关资料如下：G. W.：14 077. 00 KGS, N. W.：12 584. 00 KGS, MEAS：35 CBM, 包装件数：3298 卷（ROLLS），所有货物被装进 2×20′ CONTAINER，CONTAINER NO.：TSTU157504, TSTU156417, 提单号码：SHANK00710, 船名：DANUBHUM/S009。货物 H. S. 编码：5407. 1010。其他条件未知的，按照惯例自行定义。

2. 信用证如下所示：
209 07BKCHCNBJ95B BANK OF CHINA, SUZHOU BRANCH
409 07BKCHHKHH×××　BANK OF CHINA, HONGKONG BRANCH
MT700 O BKCHCNBJ95B××××
21：SEQUENCE OF TOTAL：1/1
40A：FORM OF DOC：IRREVOCABLE

20：DOCUMENT CREDIT NO：HK1112234
31C：DATE OF ISSUE：080101
40E：UCP LATEST VERSION
31D：DATE AND PLACE OF EXPIRY：080431，IN CHINA
50：APPLICANT：YOU DA TRADE CO.，LTD.，
     101 QUEENS ROAD CENTRAL，HONGKONG
     TEL：852-28566666
59：BENEFICIARY：KUNSHAN HUACHENG WEAVING AND DYEING
     CO.，LTD
     HUANGLONG RD.，LIUJIA ZHEN，SUZHOU，
     JIANGSU，CHINA
     TEL：86-520-7671386
32B：AMOUNT：USD 33 680.00
41A：AVAILABLE WITH…BY…
ANY BANK BY NEGOTIATION
42C：DRAFTS AT：SIGHT
42A：DRAWEE：OURSELVES
43P：PARTIAL SHIPMENT：NOT ALLOWED
43T：TRANSSHIPMENT：NOT ALLOWED
44A：LOADING ON BOARD/DISPATCH/TAKING IN CHARGE
AT/FROM：SHANGHAI
44B：FOR TRANSPORTATION TO：HONGKONG
44C：LATEST DATE：080415
45A：DESCRIPTION OF GOODS AND/OR SERVICES
DESCRIPTION QUANTITY UNIT PRICE AMOUNT
100PCT NYLON 100 000 YARDS USD 0.3368/YD USD 33 680.00
FABRICS
DETAILS AS PER CONTRACT NO.99WS061 DATED DEC.10，2007
PRICE TERM：CIF HONGKONG
SHIPPING MARK：
     YOU DA
     HONGKONG
     R/NO.：1-up
46A：DOCUMENTS REQUIRED：

1. SINGED COMMERCIAL INVOICE IN 5 FOLDS INDICATING L/C NO. AND CONTRACT NO. 99WS061.
2. FULL SET (3/3) OF CLEAN ON BOARD MARINE BILLS OF LADING MADE OUT TO ORDER AND BLANK ENDORSED, MARKED "FREIGHT PREPAID" AND NOTIFY THE APPLICANT.
3. INSURANCE POLICY OR CERTIFICATE IN 2 FOLDS FOR 110 PCT OF THE INVOICE VALUE INDICATING CLAIM PAYABLE AT DESTINATION COVERING OCEAN TRANSPORTATION ALL RISKS AND WAR RISKS AS PER ICC CLAUSES.
4. PACKING LIST IN 3 FOLDS INDICATING GROSS AND NET WEIGHT OF EACH PACKAGE.
5. CERTIFICATE OF ORIGIN IN 3 FOLDS.
6. BENEFICIARY'S LETTER MUST BE FAX TO THE APPLICANT ADVISING GOODS NAME, CONTRACT NO., L/C NO., NAME OF VESSEL, AND DATE OF SHIPMENT.

47A: ADDITIONAL CONDITIONS:
　　　+　ON DECK SHIPMENT IS NOT ALLOWED.
　　　+　ALL DOCUMENT MUST BE MANUALLY SIGNED.

48: PERIOD FOR PRESENTATION:
DOCUMENTS MUST BE PRESENTED WITHIN 15 DAYS AFTER THE DATE OF SHIPMENT BUT WITHIN THE VALIDITY OF THE CREDIT.

49: CONFIRMATION: WITHOUT

72: SPECIAL INSTRUCTIONS:
ALL DOCUMENT MUST BE SEND TO THE ISSUING BANK IN ONE LOT THROUGH THE NEGOTIATING BANK BY REGISTERED AIRMAIL.
UPON RECEIPT THE DOCUMENTS CONFORMITY WITH THE L/C'S CONDITIONS, WE SHALL PAY AS PER YOUR INSTRUCTIONS.

发票

KUNSHAN HUACHENG WEAVING AND DYEING CO.,LTD
HUANGLONG RD., LIUJIA ZHEN, SUZHOU,JIANGSU, CHINA

COMMERCIAL INVOICE

TO:		INVOICE NO.:	
		INVOICE DATE:	
		S/C NO.:	
		S/C DATE:	
FROM:		TO:	
LETTER OF CREDIT NO.:		ISSUED BY:	

MARKS AND NUMBERS	DESCRIPTION OF GOODS	QUANTITY	UNIT PRICE	AMOUNT
TOTAL:				

装箱单

KUNSHAN HUACHENG WEAVING AND DYEING CO.,LTD
HUANGLONG RD., LIUJIA ZHEN, SUZHOU,JIANGSU, CHINA

PACKING LIST

TO:		INVOICE NO.:	
		INVOICE DATE:	
		S/C NO.:	
		S/C DATE:	
FROM:		TO:	
LETTER OF CREDIT NO.:		ISSUED BY:	

MARKS AND NUMBERS	DESCRIPTION OF GOODS	QUANTITY	PACKAGE	G.W.	N.W.	MEAS.
TOTAL:						

SAY

受益人证明

KUNSHAN HUACHENG WEAVING AND DYEING CO.,LTD

HUANGLONG RD., LIUJIA ZHEN, SUZHOU,JIANGSU, CHINA

BENIFICIARY'S LETTER

MESSERS:

DEAR SIRS:
  RE: CONTRACT NO.:
    L/C NO.:

    WE HEREBY INFORM YOU THAT THE GOODS UNDER THE ABOVE MENTIONED CREDIT HAVE BEEN SHIPPED. THE DETAILS OF THE SHIPMENT ARE AS FOLLOWS:
    COMMODITY:
    QUANTITY:
    TOTAL AMOUNT:
    OCEAN VESSEL:
    PORT OF LOADING:
    PORT OF DESTINATION:
    DATE OF SHIPMENT

（十一）根据信用证审核相关单据，找出不符点

信用证

RECEIVED FROM：CHOHKRSE

CHO HUNG BANK

SEOUL

100 757 SEOUL

KOREA，REPUBLIC OF

DESTINATION：ABOCCNBJA110

AGRICULTURAL BANK OF CHINA，THE

HANGZHOU（ZHEJIANG BRANCH）

MESSAGE TYPE：700 ISSUE OF A DOCUMENTARY CREDIT

DATE：　　　7 MAR 2006

27：SEQUENCE OF TOTAL

1/1

40A：FORM OF DOCUMENTARY CREDIT

IRREVOCABLE

20：DOCUMENTARY CREDIT NUMBER

CUZ4825017

31C：DATE OF ISSUE

060605

40E：UCP LATEST VERSION

31D：DATE OF EXPIRY，PLACE OF EXPIRY

060715 AT NEGOTIATION BANK

50：APPLICANT

GENOSA TRADING CO.，LTD

NO. 251 KING ROAD

SEOUL，KOREA.

59：BENEFICIARY

ZHEJIANG HUAXING CHEMICAL TRADING CO.，LTD

NO. 32 DINGHAI ROAD

HANGZHOU CHINA

32B：AMOUNT

USD 35 500

41A：AVAILABLE WITH…BY…

ANY BANK
BY NEGOTIATION

42C：DRAFTS AT…
AT SIGHT

42A：DRAWEE
CHO HUNG BANK，SEOUL

43P：PARTIAL SHIPMENTS
PROHIBITED

43T：TRANSSHIPMENT
PROHIBITED

44A：LOADING ON BOARD/DISPATCH/TAKING IN CHARGE
SHANGHAI，CHINA

44B：FOR TRANSPORTATION TO…
PUSAN，KOREA

44C：LATEST DATE OF SHIPMENT
060631

45A：DESCRIPTION OF GOODS AND/OR SERVICES
HCFC BLEND-A FIRE EXTINGUISHER 5 000 KGS
CIF PUSAN PORT AT USD 7.10/KG
AS PER S/C NO. HX0159 AND P/I NO. HX060418

46A：DOCUMENTS REQUIRED
　+　SIGNED COMMERCIAL INVOICE IN QUINTUPLICATE
　+　FULL SET OF CLEAN ON BOARD OCEAN BILLS OF LADING
　　　MADE OUT TO THE ORDER OF CHO HUNG BANK MARKED
　　　"FREIGHT PREPAID"AND NOTIFY ACCOUNTEE
　+　INSURANCE POLICY，CERTIFICAT OR DECLARATION IN
　　　DUPLICATE，ENDORSED IN BLANK FOR 110 PCT OF THE
　　　INVOICE COST. INSURANCE POLICY，CERTIFICATE OR
　　　DECLARATION MUST EXPRESSLY STIPULATE THAT
　　　CLAIMS ARE PAYABLE IN THE CURRENCY OF THE CRED-
　　　IT AND MUST ALSO INDICATE A CLAIMS SETTLING
　　　AGENT IN KOREA INSURANCE MUST INCLUDE：I. C. C.
　　　ALL RISK
　+　PACKING LIST IN DUPLICATE

47A： ADDITIONAL CONDITIONS

UPON RECEIPT OF YOUR DOCUMENTS IN GOOD ORDER，WE WILL REMIT THE PROCEEDS TO THE ACCOUNT DESIGNATED BY NEGOTIATION.

71B： CHARGE

ALL BANKING COMMISSIONS AND CHARGES，INCLUDING RE-IMBURSEMENT CHARGES AND POSTAGE OUTSIDE KOREA ARE FOR ACCOUNT OF BENEFICIARY.

48： PERIOD FOR PRESENTATION

DOCUMENTS MUST BE PRESENTED WITHIN 15 DAYS AFTER THE DATE OF SHIPMENT

49： CONFIRMATION INSTRUCTIONS

WITHOUT

78： INSTRNS TO PAYING/ACCEPTING/NEGOTIATING BANK

THE AMOUNT OF EACH NEGOTIATION(DRAFT)MUST BE EN-DORSED ON THE REVERSE OF THIS CREDIT BY THE NEGOTI-ATING BANK. ALL DOCUMENTS MUST BE FORWARDED DI-RECTLY BY COURIER SERVICE IN ONE LOT TO CHO HUNG BANK H. O.,(INT'L OPERATIONS DIVISION) 14,1-KA,NAMDAMUN-RO,CHUNG-KU,SEOUL 100-757,KOREA.

IF DOCUMENTS ARE PRESENTED WITH DISRCREPANCIES, A DIS-CREPANCY FEE OF USD 60. 00 OR EQUIVALENT SHOULD（WILL）BE DEDUCTED FROM THE REIMBURSMENT CLAIM（THE PRO-CEEDS）. THIS FEE SHOULD BE CHARGED TO THE BENEFICIA-RY.

57A： "ADVISE THROUGH"BANK

PLS ADVISE THRU YR HANGZHOU BRANCH

INT'L DEPT.

72： SENDER TO RECEIVER INFORMATION

THIS CREDIT IS SUBJECT TO I. C. C. PUBLIC NO. 600(2007 REVI-SION)

相关资料：

合同号码：HX0159　船名：TIAN SHUN V. 329N　INV NO.：LT5067

装船日期：2006.6.20　集装箱号码：WSDU2066730/129531　1×20′

包装：5 CYLINDERS　　总毛重：7 654 KGS　　总净重：5 000 KGS　　总体积：7.0 CBM

商业发票：in 4 copies

ISSUER： ZHEJIANG HUAXING CHEMICAL TRADING CO.,LTD NO.32 DINGHAI ROAD HANGZHOU CHINA	**COMMERCIAL INVOICE**	
TO： GENOSA TRADING CO.,LTD NO.251 KING ROAD SEOUL,KOREA.	NO： LT5067	DATE： 20,JULY,2006
TRANSPORT DETAILS： SHIPPING TERMS：CIF PUSAN PORT LOADING ON BOARD：SHANGHAI PORT, CHINA FOR TRANSPORTATION TO：PUSAN PORT, KOREA	S/C NO： HX0159	L/C NO： CUZ4825017
	TERMS OF PAYMENT： L/C AT SIGHT	

MARKS AND NUMBERS	DESCRIPTION OF GOODS	QUANTITY	UNIT PRICE	AMOUNT
N/M	HCFC BLEND-A FIRE EXTINGUISHER	CFR PUSAN 5 000 KGS	USD 7.10/KG	USD 35 500.00

　　TOTAL：SAY UNITED STATES DOLLARS THIRTY FIVE THOUSAND FIVE HUNDRED ONLY.

ZHEJIANG HUAXING CHEMICAL TRADING CO.,LTD

林敬德

装箱单 in 2 copies

ISSUER： ZHEJIANG HUAXING CHEMICAL TRADING CO.，LTD NO. 32 DINGHAI ROAD HANGZHOU CHINA	PACKING LIST	
TO： GENOSA TRADING CO.，LTD NO. 251 KING ROAD SEOUL，KOREA.	INVOICE NO： HX0159	DATE： 3，JUN，2006

MARKS AND NUMBERS	DESCRIPTION OF GOODS	PACKAGE	GROSS WEIGHT	NET WEIGHT	MEASUR- EMENT
N/M	HCFC BLEND-A FIRE EXTINGUISHER	5 CYLINDERS	7 654 KGS	5 000 KGS	7．00 CBM

ZHEJIANG HUAXING CHEMICAL TRADING CO.，LTD

林敬德

错误之处：

（十二）根据信用证的内容和相关资料制作信用证指定的议付发票和装箱单

发票号码： SH25586
发票日期： 2008-4-20
单位毛重： 15.40 KGS/CTN
单位净重： 13.00 KGS/CTN
单位尺码： 60×40×50 CM/CTN
船名： DAFENG V3336
提单号码： SH223545
提单日期： 2008-5-15

信用证

	ISSUE OF A DOCUMENTARY CREDIT
ISSUING BANK	THE ROYAL BANK. TOKYO
SEQUENCE OF TOTAL	1/1
FORM OF DOC. CREDIT	IRREVOCABLE
DOC. CREDIT NUMBER	JST-AB12
DATE OF ISSUE	20080405
EXPIRY	DATE 20080615 PLACE CHINA
APPLICANT	WAV GENEAL TRADING CO.,OSAKA, JAPAN
BENEFICIARY	DESUN TRADING CO,LTD
	224 JINLIN ROAD,NANJING,CHINA
AMOUNT	CURRENCY USD AMOUNT 10 300.00
AVAILABLE WITH/BY	BANK OF CHINA BY NEGOTIATION
DRAFTS AT...	DRAFTS AT SIGHT FOR FULL INVOICE VALUE
DRAWEE	THE ROYAL BANK,TOKYO
PARTIAL SHIPMTS	ALLOWED
TRANSSHIPMENT	ALLOWED
LOADING IN CHARGE	NANJING PORT
FOR TRANSPIRT TO...	OSAKA,JAPAN
LATEST SHIPMENT	20080531
GOODS DESCRIPT.	

LADIES GARMENTS AS PER S/C NO. SHL553
PACKING：10 PCS/CTN

ART NO.	QUANTITY	UNIT PRICE
STYLE NO. ROCOCO	1 000 PCS	USD 5.50
STYLE NO. ROMANTICO	1 000 PCS	USD 4.80

CIF OSAKA
SHIPPING MARK：ITOCHU/OSAKA/NO. 1-200

续表

DOCS REQUIRED	
	* 3/3 SET OF ORIGINAL CLEAN ON BOARD OCEAN BILLS OF LADING MADE OUT TO ORDER OF SHIPPER AND BLANK ENDORSED AND MARKED "FREIGHT PREPAID" NOTIFY APPLICANT(WITH FULL NAME AND ADDRESS). * ORIGINAL SIGNED COMMERCIAL INVOICE IN 5 FOLD. * INSURANCE POLICY OR CERTIFICATE IN 2 FOLD ENDORSED IN BLANK, FOR 110 PCT OF THE INVOICE VALUE COVERING THE INSTITUTE CARGO CLAUSES (A), THE INSTITUTE WAR CLAUSES, INSURANCE CLAIMS TO BE PAYABLE IN JAPAN IN THE CURRENCY OF THE DRAFTS. * CERTIFICATE OF ORIGIN GSP FORM A IN 1 ORIGINAL AND 1 COPY. * PACKING LIST IN 5 FOLD.
ADDITIONAL COND	1. T. T. REIMBURSEMENT IS PROHIBITED 2. THE GOODS TO BE PACKED IN EXPIRT STRONG COLORED CARTONS. 3. SHIPPING MARKS: ITOCHU 　　　　　　　　OSAKA 　　　　　　　　NO. 1-200
DETAILS OF CHARGES	ALL BANKING CHARGES OUTSIDE JAPAN INCLUDING REIMBURSEMENT COMMISSION, ARE FOR ACCOUNT OF BENEFICIARY.
PRESENTATION PERIOD	DOCUMENTS TO BE PRESENTED WITHIN 10 DAYS AFTER THE DATE OF SHIPMENT, BUT WITHIN THE VALIDITY OF THE CREDIT.
CONFIRMATION	WITHOUT
INSTRUCTIONS	THE NEGOTIATION BANK MUST FORWARD THE DRAFTS AND ALL DOCUMENTS BY REGISTERED AIRMAIL DIRECT TO U. S. IN TWO CONSECUTIVE LOTS, UPON RECEIPT OF THE DRAFTS AND DOCUMENTS IN ORDER, WE WILL REMIT THE PROCEEDS AS INSTRUCTED BY THE NEGOTIATING BANK.

世格国际贸易有限公司
DESUN TRADING CO.,LTD.

224 JINLIN ROAD, NANJING, CHINA
TEL：025-4715004 025-4715619   FAX：4691619
COMMERCIAL INVOICE

To：

Invoice No.：_____

Invoice Date：_____

S/C No.：_____

From：_____   To：_____

Letter of Credit No.：

Marks and Numbers	Number and kind of package Description of goods	Quantity	Unit Price	Amount

TOTAL：

SAY TOTAL：

世格国际贸易有限公司
DESUN TRADING CO.,LTD.

224 JINLIN ROAD,NANJING,CHINA
TEL：025-4715004 025-4715619　FAX：4691619

PACKING LIST

To：

Invoice No.：＿＿＿＿＿＿＿＿

Invoice Date：＿＿＿＿＿＿＿

S/C No.：＿＿＿＿＿＿＿＿

From：＿＿＿＿＿＿＿＿＿＿＿＿＿＿　To：＿＿＿＿＿＿＿＿＿＿

Letter of Credit No.：＿＿＿＿＿＿＿＿　Date of Shipment：＿＿＿＿＿

Marks and Numbers	Number and kind of package Description of goods	Quantity	Package	G. W.	N. W.	Meas.

TOTAL：

SAY TOTAL：

（十三）根据托收指示书和合同缮制发票、装箱单、装船通知和受益人证明

INSTRUCTION FOR COLLECTION

TO：HUBEI TWIN HORSE TRADE CO.,LTD.　　DATE：MAY. 10，2000

CONTRACT NO. HW003　AMOUNT：USD 60 000. 00

DRAWEE：HANWA CO. LTD. KYOTO，JAPAN.

COLLECTING BANK：ASASHI BANK. CHIYODAKU 1-CHOME.
　　　　　　　　　KYOTO，JAPAN.

TRADE TERMS：CIF YOKOHAMA.　　　　PAYMNET：D/P AT SIGHT

DOCUMENTS REQUIRED：

1. SIGNED COMMERCIAL INVOICE IN 3 COPIES.

2. DETAILED PACKING LIST IN 3 COPIES.

3. GSP FORM A——1/1.

4. CERTIFICATES OF QUANTITY,QUALITY & WEIGHT——1/1.

5. INSURANCE POLICY IN 2 COPIES.

6. COPY OF SHIPPING ADVICE.

7. CERTIFICATE PROVING THAT ONE SET OF NON-NEGOTIABLE
   SHIPPING DOCU. HAS BEEN SENT DIRECTLY TO HANWA CO.
   LTD 24 HOURS AFTER THE SHIPMENT IS EFFECTED.

8. FULL SET CLEAN ON BOARD B/L MADE OUT TO ORDER AND
   BLANK ENDORSED MARKED FREIGHT PREPAID AND NOTIFY
   HANWA CO.,LTD H. K. TEL/FAX：008522678556

THIS COLLECTING INSTRUCTION IS SUBJECT TO URC 522.

售 货 合 同
Sales Contract

编　号(No.)：<u>HW003</u>
日　期(Date)：<u>MAY 1, 2006</u>
签约地点(Signed at)：<u>KYOTO</u>

HUBEI TWIN HORSE

卖方(Seller)：<u>TRADE CO.,LTD.</u>　　　买方(Buyer)：<u>HANWA CO., LTD.</u>
地址(Address)：<u>1ST XUDONG ROAD,</u>　　地址(Address)：_____
<u>WUCHANG, 430077, WUHAN, CHINA。</u>　_____
电话(Tel)：_____　　　电话(Tel)：_____
传真(Fax)：_____　　　传真(Fax)：_____
电子邮箱(E-mail)：_____　　　电子邮箱(E-mail)：_____

买卖双方经协商同意按下列条款成交：

The undersigned Seller and Buyer have agreed to close the following transactions according to the terms and conditions set forth as below：

1. 货物名称(Name)	规格(Specifications)	质量(Quality)
FASTENERS 2000M.	JIS FASTENERS	BLACK TREATED

2. 数量(Quantity)：100 MT

3. 单价及价格条款 (Unit Price and Terms of Delivery)：CIF YOKOHAMA, JAPAN.

［除非另有规定，"FOB"、"CFR"和"CIF"均应依照国际商会制定的《2000年国际贸易术语解释通则》(INCOTERMS 2000)办理。］

The terms FOB, CFR, or CIF shall be subject to the International Rules for the Interpretation of Trade Terms (INCOTERMS 2000) provided by International Chamber of Commerce (ICC) unless otherwise stipulated herein.

4. 总价 (Total Amount)：USD 600 000.00

5. 允许溢短装(More or Less)：_____5_____ %

6. 装运期限(Time of Shipment)：END OF MAY, 2006.

7. 付款条件(Terms of Payment)：D/P AT SIGHT.

8. 包装(Packing)：IN WOODEN CASE OF 25 KG EACH. /GROSS WT 26 KG.

9. 保险（Insurance）：

　　按发票金额的 _____ ％投保 _____ 险，由 _____ 负责投保。Covering ALL Risks for _____ 110% of Invoice Value to be effected by the _SELLERS_.

10. 品质/数量异议（Quality/Quantity discrepancy）：

　　如买方提出索赔，凡属品质异议须于货到目的口岸之日起 30 天内提出，凡属数量异议须于货到目的口岸之日起 15 天内提出，对所装货物所提任何异议于保险公司、轮船公司、其他有关运输机构或邮递机构所负责者，卖方不负任何责任。

　　In case of quality discrepancy, claim should be filed by the Buyer within 30 days after the arrival of the goods at port of destination, while for quantity discrepancy, claim should be filed by the Buyer within 15 days after the arrival of the goods at port of destination. It is understood that the Seller shall not be liable for any discrepancy of the goods shipped due to causes for which the Insurance Company, Shipping Company, other Transportation Organization/or Post Office are liable.

11. 由于发生人力不可抗拒的原因，致使本合约不能履行，部分或全部商品延误交货，卖方概不负责。本合同所指的不可抗力系指不可干预、不能避免且不能克服的客观情况。

　　The Seller shall not be held responsible for failure or delay in delivery of the entire lot or a portion of the goods under this Sales Contract in consequence of any Force Majeure incidents which might occur. Force Majeure as referred to in this contract means unforeseeable, unavoidable and insurmountable objective conditions.

12. 仲裁（Arbitration）：

　　凡因本合同引起的或与本合同有关的任何争议，如果协商不能解决，应提交中国国际经济贸易仲裁委员会华南分会，按照申请仲裁时该会实施的仲裁规则进行仲裁。仲裁裁决是终局的，对双方均有约束力。

　　Any dispute arising from or in connection with the Sales Contract shall be settled through friendly negotiation. In case no settlement can be reached, the dispute shall then be submitted to China International Economic and Trade Arbitration Commission（CIETAC）, South China Sub-Commission for arbitration in accordance with its rules in effect at the time of applying for arbitration. The arbitral award is final and binding upon both parties.

13. 通知（Notices）：

所有通知用＿＿＿＿文写成，并按照如下地址用传真/电子邮件/快件送达给各方。如果地址有变更，一方应在变更后＿＿＿＿日内书面通知另一方。

All notice shall be written in ＿＿＿＿ and served to both parties by fax/e-mail/courier according to the following addresses. If any changes of the addresses occur, one party shall inform the other party of the change of address within ＿＿＿＿ days after the change.

14. 本合同为中英文两种文本，两种文本具有同等效力。本合同一式 ＿＿＿＿份。自双方签字（盖章）之日起生效。

This Contract is executed in two counterparts each in Chinese and English, each of which shall be deemed equally authentic. This Contract is in ＿＿＿ copies effective since being signed/sealed by both parties.

The Seller:
卖方签字：马少华
有关资料：
发票号码：HW003
提单号码：KGES5825691
船名：BUTTERFLY V. 089
装箱情况：100 吨/4000 木箱
净重：25 KG/箱　　毛重：26 KG/箱
封志号：CUSO600341—5
生产厂家：武汉汽车标准件有限公司

The Buyer:
买方签字：山下岛本
发票日期：2006 年 5 月 15 日
提单日期：2006 年 5 月 20 日
保险单号：04-2988956
集装箱号：SOCU6689721-5（5×20'）
总尺码：156 CUBIC METRE
出口日期/申报日期：2006 年 5 月 19 日
生产地：武汉市洪山区

COMMERCIAL INVOICE——自制

PACKING LIST——自制

COPY OF SHIPPING ADVICE.

CERTIFICATE

(十四) 根据信用证及相关资料缮制发票和装箱单

信用证

ISSUING BANK: CYPRUS POPULAR BANK LTD, LARNAKA

ADVISING BANK: BANK OF CHINA, SHANGHAI BRANCH.

SEQUENCE OF TOTAL	*27:	1/1
FORM OF DOC. CREDIT	*40A:	IRREVOCABLE
DOC. CREDIT NUMBER	*20:	186/04/10014
DATE OF ISSUE	31C:	080105
APPLICABLE RULES	40E:	UCP LATEST VERSION
EXPIRY	*31D:	DATE 080229 PLACE CHINA
APPLICANT	*50:	LAIKI PERAGORA ORPHANIDES LTD., 020 STRATIGOU TIMAGIA AVE.,6046, LARNAKA,CYPRUS
BENEFICIARY	*59:	SHANGHAI GARDEN PRODUCTS IMP. AND EXP. CO., LTD. 27 ZHONGSHAN DONGYI ROAD, SHANGHAI, CHINA
AMOUNT	*32B:	CURRENCY USD AMOUNT 6 115.00
POS. /NEG. TOL. (%)	39A:	05/05
AVAILABLE WITH/BY	*41A:	ANY BANK BY NEGOTIATION
DRAFT AT...	42C:	AT SIGHT
DRAWEE	*42A:	LIKICY2N×××

* CYPRUS POPULAR BANK LTD, LARNAKA

PARTIAL SHIPMENT	43P:	ALLOWED
TRANSSHIPMENT	43T:	ALLOWED
LOADING IN CHARGE	44A:	SHANGHAI PORT
FOR TRANSPORT TO....	44B:	LIMASSOL PORT
LATEST DATE OF SHIP.	44C:	080214
DESCRIPT. OF GOODS	45A:	WOODEN FLOWER STANDS AND WOODEN FLOWER POTS

AS PER S/C NO. E03FD121. 350 PCS AND 600 PCS,CFR LIMASSOL INCOTERMS 2000

DOCUMENTS REQUIRED 46A:

+ COMMERCIAL INVOICE IN QUADRUPLICATE ALL STAMPED AND SIGNED BY BENEFICIARY CERTIFYING THAT THE GOODS ARE OF CHINESE ORIGIN.

+ FULL SET OF CLEAN ON BOARD BILL OF LADING MADE OUT TO ORDER OF SHIPPER AND BLANK ENDORSED, MARKED FREIGHT PREPAID AND NOTIFY APPLICANT.

+ PACKING LIST IN TRIPLICATE SHOWING PACKING DETAILS SUCH AS CARTON NO AND CONTENTS OF EACH CARTON.

+ CERTIFICATE STAMPED AND SIGNED BY BENEFICIARY STATING THAT THE ORIGIAL INVOICE AND PACKING LIST HAVE BEEN DISPATCHED TO THE APPLICANT BY COURIER SERVISE 2 DAYS BEFORE SHIPMENT.

ADDITIONAL COND. 47A：

+ EACH PACKING UNIT BEARS AN INDELIBLE MARK INDI-CATING THE COUNTRY OF ORIGIN OF THE GOODS. PACK-ING LIST TO CERTIFY THIS.

+ INSURANCE IS BEING ARRANGED BY THE BUYER.

+ A USD 50.00 DISCREPANCY FEE, FOR BENEFICIARY'S AC-COUNT, WILL BE DEDUCTED FROM THE REIMBURSEMENT CLAIM FOR EACH PRESENTATION OF DISCREPANT DOCU-MENTS UNDER THIS CREDIT.

+ THIS CREDIT IS SUBJECT TO THE U. C. P. FOR DOCUMEN-TARY CREDITS（2007 REVISION）I. C. C., PUBLICATION NO. 600.

DETAILS OF CHARGES　71B：　ALL BANK CHARGES OUTSIDE CY-PRUS ARE FOR THE ACCOUNT OF THE BENEFICIARY.

PRESENTATION PERIOD　48：　WITHIN 15 DAYS AFTER THE DATE OF SHIPMENT BUT WITHIN THE VALIDITY OF THE CREDIT.

CONFIRMATION　　＊49：　WITHOUT

INSTRUCTION　　78：　ON RECEIPT OF DOCUMENTS CON-FIRMING TO THE TERMS OF THIS DOCUMENTARY CREDIT, WE UN-

DERTAKE TO REIMBURSE YOU IN THE CURRENCY OF THE CREDIT IN ACCORDANCE WITH YOUR IN-STRUCTIONS, WHICH SHOULD IN-CLUDE YOUR UID NUMBER AND THE ABA CODE OF THE RECEIVING BANK.

相关资料：

发票号码：04SHGD3029   发票日期：2008 年 2 月 9 日   提单号码：SHYZ042234

提单日期：2008 年 2 月 12 日   集装箱号码：FSCU3214999   集装箱封号：1295312

1×20′FCL，CY/CY   船名：LT USODIMARE   航次：V. 021W

木花架，WOODEN FLOWER STANDS， H. S. CODE：44219090. 90，

QUANTITY：350 PCS，USD 8. 90/PC，2 PCS/箱，共 175 箱。

纸箱尺码：66×22×48cms，毛重：11 KGS/箱，净重：9 KGS/箱。

木花桶，WOODEN FLOWER POTS， H. S. CODE：44219090. 90，

QUANTITY：600 PCS，USD 5. 00/PC，4 PCS/箱，共 150 箱。

纸箱尺码：42×42×45cms，

毛重：15KGS/箱，净重：13 KGS/箱。

唛头：L. P. O. L.

　　DC NO. 186/04/10014

MADE IN CHINA

NO. 1-325

发票

COMMERCIAL INVOICE

TO:		INVOICE NO.:	
		INVOICE DATE:	
		S/C NO.:	
		S/C DATE:	

| FROM: | | TO: | |
| LETTER OF CREDIT NO.: | | ISSUED BY: | |

MARKS AND NUMBERS	DESCRIPTION OF GOODS	QUANTITY	UNIT PRICE	AMOUNT
TOTAL:				

装箱单

PACKING LIST

TO:		INVOICE NO.:	
		INVOICE DATE:	
		S/C NO.:	
		S/C DATE:	
FROM:		TO:	
LETTER OF CREDIT NO.:		ISSUED BY:	

MARKS AND NUMBERS	DESCRIPTION OF GOODS	QUANTITY	PACKAGE	G. W.	N. W.	MEAS.
TOTAL:						

SAY

（十五）按照下列信用证回答问题并制作发票

信用证

MT700——ISSUE OF A DOCUMENTARY CREDIT——

SEQUENCE OF TOTAL	27：	1/1
FORM OF DOCUMENTARY CREDIT	40A：	IRREVOCABLE TRANSFERABLE
DOCUMENTARY CREDIT NUMBER	20：	LCF776FV333324
DATE OF ISSUE	31C：	081119
APPLICABLE RULES	40E：	UCP LATEST VERSION
DATE AND PLACE OF EXPIRY	31D：	090115 IN OUR COUNTER
APPLICANT	50：	HOPE TRADING EST.,

P. O. BOX 0000 DAMMAN 31491, SAUDI ARABIA

BENEFICIARY	59：	JINHAI IMP. & EXP. GROUP CORP. NO. 233, TAIPING ROAD, QINGDAO, CHINA
CURRENCY CODE, AMOUNT	32B：	USD 46 693. 68
PERCENTAGE CREDIT AMT TOL.	39A：	05/05
AVAILABLE WITH…BY…	41A：	ADVISING BANK BY NEGOTIATION
DRAFTS AT…	42C：	AT SIGHT FOR 100 PCT OF THE INVOICE VALUE
DRAWEE	42A：	DRAWN ON US
PARTIAL SHIPMENT	43P：	NOT ALLOWED
TRANSHIPMENT	43T：	ALLOWED
LOADING/DISPATCH/ TAKING IN CHARGE/FM	44A：	ANY CHINESE PORT
FOR TRANSPORTATION TO…	44B：	DAMMAN PORT, SAUDI ARABIA
LATEST DATE OF SHIPMENT	44C：	081231

DESCRIPTION OF 45A：
GOODS/SERVICES

      FROZEN CHICKEN BREAST MEAT，A GRADE，

      PACKING：1KG X 12/CARTON，

      UNIT PRICE：USD 1 945. 57/MT

      QUANTITY：24 MTS

      AS PER S/C NO. 564676 DATED NOV. 10，2008

DOCUMENTS REQUIRED：46A：

1. MANUALLY SIGNED COMMERCIAL INVOICE IN 5 COPIES.

2. 2/3 CLEAN ON BOARD OCEAN BILLS OF LADING INCLUDING 2 NON-NEGOTIABLE COPIES MADE OUT TO ORDER AND BLANK ENDORSED, MARKED "FREIGHT PREPAID" NOTIFY-ING APPLICANT.

3. PACKING LIST IN 3 COPIES

4. A COPY OF BENEFICIARY'S SHIPPING ADVICE ADVISING NAME OF VESSEL, DATE OF SAILING, B/L NUMBER, INVOICE VALUE AND QUANTITY OF GOODS 48 HOURS AFTER SHIP-MENT EFFECT, REQUIRED.

5. CERTIFICATE OF ORIGIN FORM A ISSUED BY CIQ

ADDITIONAL CONTITIONS 47A：

1. A DISCREPANCY FEE OF USD 54 000 OR ITS EQUIVALLENT WILL BE DEDUCTED FROM THE PROCEEDS IF DOCUMENTS ARE PRESENTED WITH DISCREPANCY(IES).

2. 1/3 ORIGINAL B/L MUST SENT TO THE APPLICANT DIRECT-LY AFTER SHIPPMENT.

CHARGES 71B： ALL BANKING CHARGES OUTSIDE THE OPENING BANK ARE FOR BENEFICIARY'S ACCOUNT

CONFIRMATION 49： WITHOUT
INSTRUCTION

REIMBURSEMENT BANK 53A： CITIBANK, N. A., NEW YORK

INSTR. TO PAY/ACPT/ 78：
NGG BANK

1. ALL DOCUMENTS ARE TO BE FORWARDED TO BANQUE SA-
   UDI FRANSI, EASTERN REGIONAL MANAGEMENT, KING
   ABDUL AZIZ STREET, P. O. BOX 397, ALKHOBAR 31952, SAU-
   DI ARABIA, TEL（03）8871111, FAX（03）8821855, SWIFT：
   BSERSARIAEST. IN TWO CONSECUTIVE LOTS.
2. UPON RECEIPT OF ALL DOCUEMNTS IN ORDER, WE WILL
   DULY HONOUR/ACCEPT THE DRAFTS AND EFFECT THE
   PAYMENT AS INSTRUCTED AT MATURITY.

ADVISE THROUGH BANK 57A： BANK OF CHINA, SHANDONG BR.

SENDER TO RECEIVER INFO 72：

THIS LC IS SUBJECT TO UCP 2007 ICC PUB. NO. 600.

制单明细表：

数量：24MTS, N. W.：12 KG/CTN, G. W.：14 KG/CTN,

MEASUREMENT：48＊30＊41CM。

提单签发：CHINA OCEAN SHIPPING（GROUP）CO. 王彬,

B/L DATE：2008 年 12 月 20 日,在青岛装上 PRETTY V. 116 船,

集装箱号：FBZU876551/FBZU876552/FBZU876553/FBZU876554/FBZU876555/

FBZU876556/FBZU876557/FBZU876558,发票号：JH57868,B/L 号：BL3888,

产地证号码：8767544,H. S. CODE：5674. 8374

回答下列问题（根据信用证）：

    1. 信用证的有效期_____,装运期_____,交单期_____。

    2. 如装运日为 12 月 20 日,则最迟的交单日是_____。

    3. 该封信用证是什么类型的信用证：_____、_____、_____、_____ 的跟单信用证。

    4. 该封信用证项下外贸交易的成交条件是：_____

    5. 该封信用证所需提单的抬头人是_____

    6. 信用证的开证费由_____支付,议付费由_____支付,通知费由_____支付。

    7. 开证行在审单时如发现单单不符,有三个不符点,则开证行将收取不符点费用_____。

    8. 本信用证有一处不合理的需要修改的地方,请找出并修改：_____ 应改为_____

    9. 请分析该信用证是否存在风险？_____

原因何在？如何处理？_____

COMMERCIAL INVOICE

SELLER	INVOICE NO.	INVOICE DATE
	L/C NO.	DATE
BUYER	CONTRACT NO.	DATE
	FROM	TO
	SHIPPED BY	PRICE TERM

MARKS	DES. OF GOODS	QTY. UNIT PRICE	AMOUNT

ISSUED BY

SIGNATURE

（十六）按以下材料缮制商业发票

ISSUING BANK：TOKYO BANK LTD., TOKYO

L/C NO.：9426

DATE OF ISSUE：070615

APPLICANT：SAKA INTERNATIONAL FOOD CO.

26 TORIMI-CHO NISHI-PU, NAGOYA 546, JAPAN

BENEFICIARY：NINGBO NATIVE PRODUCTS CO. NO. 115 DONGFENG ROAD, NINGBO, CHINA

LOADING IN CHARGE：NINGBO, CHINA

FOR TRANSPORTION TO：NAGOYA, JAPAN

DESCRIPTION OF GOODS：20M/T FRESH BAMBOO SHOOTS AT CIF NAGOYA USD 1 080. 00 PER M/T AND 30 M/T FRESH ASPARAGUS AT CIF NAGOYA USD 1 600. 00 PER M/T AS PER CONTRACT NO. NP94051

DOCUMENTS REQUIRED：

+   COMMERCIAL INVOICE IN TRIPLICATE AND CERTIFY THAT THE GOODS ARE OF CHINESE ORIGIN.

...

SHIPPING MARKS：NO. MARKS

制作发票的日期：2007 年 6 月 19 日

发票

COMMERCIAL INVOICE

TO：		INVOICE NO.：	
		INVOICE DATE：	
		S/C NO.：	
		S/C DATE：	
FROM：		TO：	
LETTER OF CREDIT NO.：		ISSUED BY：	

MARKS AND NUMBERS	DESCRIPTION OF GOODS	QUANTITY	UNIT PRICE	AMOUNT
TOTAL：				

（十七）按以下材料缮制装箱单

ISSUING BANK：THE HONGKONG AND SHANGHAI BANKING COR-
PORATION，HONGKONG

L/C NO.：CMD 20808

APPLICANT：HONGKONG ABC COMPANY
NO. 18 BUILDING BROADSTONE STREET，
HONGKONG，CHINA

BENEFICIARY：NINGBO SHANYA IMP&. EXP CO.
NO. 12 ZHISHAN ROAD，NINGBO

COVERING：FROZEN SOYABEANS 10M/T CIF HONGKONG USD 920. 00
PER M/T FROM NINGBO TO HONGKONG

PACKING：IN SEAWORTHY CARTONS SIZE IS 30CM ＊ 30CM ＊ 40CM/
CTN

NET WIGHT：20 KGS PER CARTON

GROSS WEIGHT：21 KGS PER CARTON

INVOICE NO.：SY22

INVOCE DATE：APR. 15，2008

CONTRACT NO.：SYA2000663

PACKING LIST

TO:		INVOICE NO.:	
		INVOICE DATE:	
		S/C NO.:	
		S/C DATE:	
FROM:		TO:	
LETTER OF CREDIT NO.:		ISSUED BY:	

MARKS AND NUMBERS	DESCRIPTION OF GOODS	QUANTITY	PACKAGE	G. W.	N. W.	MEAS.
TOTAL:						

SAY

（十八）单选题

1. 空运货物保险中,按"仓至仓"条款的规定,货物运抵目的港后没有进入指定仓库,( )天内保单仍然有效。
   A. 30　　　　　B. 60　　　　　C. 90　　　　　D. 120

2. 出口商委托货代向船运公司办理租船订舱,出口商须填写( )。
   A. 海运货物运输合同　　　　B. 海运货物委托书
   C. 海运单　　　　　　　　　D. 装货单

3. 如果信用证规定 DRAFT AT 15 DAYS FROM B/L DATE,一套提单上有两个装船批注,批注中的日期分别是 JAN.3, 2009 和 JAN.7, 2009,则汇票的到期日应为( )。
   A. JAN. 21, 2009　　　　　B. JAN. 22, 2009
   C. JAN. 17, 2009　　　　　D. JAN. 18, 2009

4. 根据《UCP 600》,无需注明承运人身份和名称的运输单据是( )。
   A. 海运提单　　　　　　　　B. 航空货运单

C. 公路运单   D. 租船合约提单

5. L/C 规定"LOADING ON BOARD：NANJING FOR TRANSPORT TO：BUSAN"

提交"FULL SET OF MARINE BILL OF LADING"，禁止转运

提单显示 PORT OF LOADING：NANJING

ON BOARD OCEAN VESSEL FREEDOM V. 123 AT NANJING

PORT OF DISCHARGE：BUSAN

ON BOARD OCEAN VESSEL YANGZIJIANG V. 345 AT BUSAN FOR TRANSPORTATION TO FINAL DESTINATION：INCHON

以下陈述正确的是（   ）。

A. 提单可以接受，因为在整个航程中未发生转运

B. 提单可接受，因为在信用证规定的装货港和卸货港未发生转运

C. 提单有不符点，因为整个航程发生了转运

D. 提单有不符点，因为最终目的地和信用证不符

6. DOCUMENTS REQUIRED：INSURANCE POLICY COVERING OCEAN TRANSPORTATION ALL RISKS AS PER I. C. C. AND I. O. P. FOR 110 PCT OF INVOICE CLAIMS PAYABLE AT NEW YORK 保单上记载（   ）。

A. COVERING OCEAN TRANSPORTATION ALL RISKS AS PER I. C. C. AND I. O. P.

B. COVERING OCEAN TRANSPORTATION ALL RISKS AS PER I. C. C. AND I. O. P. SUBJECT TO 5 PCT FRANCHISE

C. COVERING OCEAN TRANSPORTATION ALL RISKS AS PER I. C. C. AND I. O. P. SUBJECT TO USD 1 000 EXCESS DEDUCTION

D. COVERING OCEAN TRANSPORTATION ALL RISKS AS PER I. C. C. AND EXCLUDING IRRESPECTIVE OF PENCENTAGE

7. DOCUMENTS REQUIRED：INSURANCE POLICY COVERING OCEAN TRANSPORTATION ALL RISKS AS PER I. C. C. FOR 110 PCT OF INVOICE CLAIMS PAYABLE AT DESTINATION.

提单显示装运港为上海，转运港为 MIAMI，卸货港为 NEW YORK

保单上记载（   ）。

A. COVERING OCEAN TRANSPORTATION ALL RISKS AS PER C. I. C. AND I. O. P. COVERING RISKS FROM SHANGHAI TO NEW YORK CLAIMS PAYABLE AT NEW YORK

B. COVERING OCEAN TRANSPORTATION ALL RISKS AS PER I. C. C.

       SUBJECT TO 5 PCT FRANCHISE COVERING RISKS FROM SHANGHAI TO MIAMI CLAIMS PAYABLE AT NEW YORK

C. COVERING OCEAN TRANSPORTATION ALL RISKS AS PER I. C. C. SUBJECT TO USD 1 000 EXCESS DEDUCTION COVERING RISKS FROM SHANGHAI TO NEW YORKCLAIMS PAYABLE AT NEW YORK

D. COVERING OCEAN TRANSPORTATION ALL RISKS AS PER P. I. C. C. CLAUSE COVERING RISKS FROM SHANGHAI TONEW YORK CLAIMS PAYABLE AT NEW YORK

8. 联合国贸发会议中,专门从事研究单据简化工作的独立机构是(　　)。

  A. "简化贸易程序特别项目"　　　　B. "国际贸易程序简化措施"

  C. "贸易单证中的代码位置"　　　　D. "套合式国际贸易发票设计样式"

9. 提单上装船日期批注符合《UCP 600》规定的是(　　)。

  A. GOODS DELIVERED TO SHIPPING COMPANY FOR SHIPMENT ON MAY 28, 2008

  B. GOODS SHALL BE SHIPPED ON BOARD ON JUNE 1ST,2008

  C. GOODS SHIPPED ON BOARD ON JUNE 3RD, 2008

  D. GOODS SHALL BE SHIPPED ON JUNE 4TH, 2008

10. 信用证规定货物从中国港口运至美国港口,不允许分批,提交正本海运提单,最迟装期为 2008 年 8 月 8 日。同时提交两套提单。

  第一套提单:

  PORT OF LODAING :SHANGHAI　　OCEAN VESSEL:FREEDOM V. 123

  PORT OF DISCHARGE: NEW YORK ON BOARD DATE : AUG. 7,2008

  第二套提单:

  PORT OF LODAING:GUANGZHOU　　OCEAN VESSEL:FREEDOM V. 123

  PORT OF DISCHARGE: NEW YORK　　ON BOARD DATE: AUG. 8, 2008

  根据《UCP 600》,以下关于提单陈述,正确的是(　　)。

  A. 分批装运,理由是提交了两套提单

  B. 分批装运,理由是两套提单的装运港和装船日期不同

  C. 未产生分批装运,理由是两套提单的目的地相同

  D. 未产生分批装运,理由是两套提单同时提交且装运船只、航程及目的地相同

11. 在托收和汇付方式下,商业发票的抬头人一般是(　　)。

  A. 进口地银行　　　　　　　　　　B. 合同买方

  C. 出口地银行　　　　　　　　　　D. 合同卖方

12. 提单与保险单背书后可以转让,它们转让的是( )。

　　A. 都是物权　　　　　　　　　B. 都是权益

　　C. 前者是物权,后者是权益　　D. 既不是物权也不是权益

13. 创造"套合一致"单据形式的国家是( )。

　　A. 美国　　　　　　　　　　　B. 英国

　　C. 瑞典　　　　　　　　　　　D. 日本

14. 集装箱运输条件下,托运人向承运人换取集装箱提单的凭证是( )。

　　A. Mate's Receipt　　　　　　B. Dock Receipt

　　C. Cargo Receipt　　　　　　 D. Shipping Order

15. 发票价值中含有佣金或折扣,保险单上的保险金额( )。

　　A. 应按毛额计算

　　B. 应按净额计算

　　C. 含有佣金按毛额计算、含有折扣按净额计算

　　D. 含有佣金按净额计算、含有折扣按毛额计算

16. 国外来证要求投保海洋运输货物平安险,包括破碎险和转船险。由于货物从起运港直达目的港,中途无须转船,在这种情况下,受益人( )。

　　A. 无须投保转船险

　　B. 仍应投保转船险

　　C. 如合同无规定,可以不投保转船险

　　D. 既可投保,也可不投保

17. 根据《UCP 600》,商业发票的抬头人应填写( )。

　　A. 受益人　　　　　　　　　　B. 开证行

　　C. 通知行　　　　　　　　　　D. 开证申请人

18. 以下属于副本单据的是( )。

　　A. 打字机打的单据　　　　　　B. 复印出来再手签

　　C. 复印件　　　　　　　　　　D. 出具(或复印)在原始函电用纸上

19. 航空运单( )。

　　A. 代表物权,经背书可转让

　　B. 代表物权,但不能转让

　　C. 不代表物权,也不能凭以向承运人提货

　　D. 不代表物权,但可以作为提货凭证

20. 对港铁路货物运输,发货人凭以向银行结汇的运输单据为( )。

　　A. 铁路运单正本　　　　　　　B. 铁路运单副本

　　C. 承运货物收据　　　　　　　D. 到货通知

21. 在有关单据的制作时间上，下列表述中不正确的是（　　）。

    A. 保险单的出单日早于提单日　　B. 发票日期早于信用证开证日

    C. 提单日早于商检证书签发日　　D. 汇票日期早于信用证到期日

22. 买卖双方以 D/P 远期 T/R 条件成交签约，货到目的港后，买方凭 T/R 向代收行借单提货，如果事后收不回货款，则（　　）。

    A. 代收行应负责向卖方偿付

    B. 由卖方自行负担货款损失

    C. 由卖方与代收行协商共同负担损失

    D. 由卖方先于代收行负担损失

23. 空运方式下，收货人凭（　　）提货。

    A. 给托运人的空运单正本　　　　B. 给收货人的空运单正本

    C. 用于记账的空运单正本　　　　D. 航空公司的到货通知

24. 我国是《万国邮政公约》的签约国之一，根据这一公约的规定，进出境邮递物品的"报税单"和"绿色标签"应随同物品通过（　　）或当事人呈递给海关。

    A. 报关企业　　　　　　　　　　B. 国际货运代理公司

    C. 邮政企业或快递公司　　　　　D. 收货人/发货人

25. 如果信用证的提单条款里要求"MADE OUT TO ORDERER"则提单的 consignee 一栏应该填（　　）。

    A. TO ORDERER　　　　　　　　B. TO ORDER

    C. 开证申请人名址　　　　　　　D. 受益人名址

26. 信用证的 50 域中有开证申请人的电话，但实际上却是个空号（开证申请人在开证时笔误造成的），信用证中的提单要求 notify applicant，那么根据《UCP 600》，下列哪个选项叙述正确？（　　）

    A. 实际缮制提单时被通知人栏无需填列该电话号码

    B. 实际缮制提单时被通知人栏只需把正确号码填列即可（虽然其他可以错，但被通知人一栏必须正确）

    C. 实际缮制发票时抬头人栏无需填列电话号码

    D. 实际缮制发票时抬头人栏必需填列该电话号码，否则将被银行视为存在不符

27. 根据 ISBP，更正和修改不必经过证实的单据是（　　）。

    A. 发票　　　　　　　　　　　　B. 提单

    C. 保险单据　　　　　　　　　　D. 原产地证明

28. 远期票据的持有人将未到期的票据提早向银行兑现，银行扣除贴现息后，把

票款净值付给票据持有人,这种业务称为( )。

　A. 出口押汇　　　　　　　　　B. 贴现

　C. 议付　　　　　　　　　　　D. 结汇

29. 由于航空货运单所填内容不准确、不完全,致使承运人或其他人遭受损失,
　　( )负有责任。

　A. 托运人　　　　　　　　　　B. 承运人

　C. 代理人　　　　　　　　　　D. 机场服务人员

30. 办理出口退税不需要提供的单据是( )。

　A. 已认证的采购出口货物的增值专用发票

　B. 运输单据

　C. 盖有海关验讫的出口货物报关单(出口退税联)

　D. 盖有核销单,办完核销手续的出口收汇核销单

31. 下列单据中,只有( )才可用来结汇。

　A. 大副收据　　　　　　　　　B. 铁路运单副本

　C. 场站收据副联　　　　　　　D. 铁路运单正本

32. 以下关于海运提单制作描述错误的是( )。

　A. 提单必须表面上看来显示承运人名称

　B. 提单必须用装船批注来表明货物已在信用证规定的装运港装载上具名
　　船只

　C. 可以由船长或其代理人签发提单

　D. 信用证规定"运输行提单可以接受"时,提单可以由运输行以运输行的身
　　份签发

33. L/C 仅仅要求"INVOICE",则( )不可以接受。

　A. 商业发票　　　　　　　　　B. 海关发票

　C. 形式发票　　　　　　　　　D. 领事发票

34. 如果信用证没有明确要求,以下单据中( )不必须注明日期。

　A. 汇票　　　　　　　　　　　B. 运输单据

　C. 发票　　　　　　　　　　　D. 保险单据

35. 根据《UCP 600》的规定如果信用证没有要求,以下( )不必予以签署。

　A. 汇票　　　　　　　　　　　B. 证明

　C. 保险单据　　　　　　　　　D. 装箱单

36. 以下关于发票制作描述错误的是( )。

　A. 发票必须表明装运货物的价值

　B. 发票必须显示信用证要求的折扣或扣减

   C. 发票不能显示信用证未规定的与付款或折扣等有关的扣减额

   D. 除非信用证要求，发票无需签字

（十九）多选题

1. 空运费一般按普通货物最低运费计算，但对于指定商品运费的运用，一般规律为（   ）。

   A. 指定商品运价优先于普通货物运价

   B. 等级运价优先于普通货物运价

   C. 某重量分界点运价高于实际重量普通运价

   D. 优先使用公布直达运价

2. 根据《UCP 600》，关于保险单陈述正确的（   ）。

   A. 除非另有规定，保单货币必须采用信用证货币

   B. 信用证规定投保 USUAL RISKS 银行将不对未经投保的任何险种负责

   C. 如信用证未免赔率或免赔额，银行将不接受注明免赔率和免赔额约束的保险单据

   D. 信用证要求投保 ALL RISKS，则注明投保 INSTITUTE CARGO CLAUSE(A)的保险单据将不被银行接受

3. 单证管理的重要意义是（   ）。

   A. 为完成履约提供保证

   B. 为统计分析提供原始数据

   C. 为查询和处理业务差错事故提供材料

   D. 标志着某一笔交易的开始

   E. 以上均正确

4. 制作受益人证明等附属单据时，必须注意（   ）。

   A. 单据名称和出具人签署符合信用证要求

   B. 单据内容应符合信用证要求，并与其他单据相关内容不矛盾

   C. 应该至少提供一份正本

   D. 应注明出单日

5. 关于形式发票，下列说法正确的是（   ）。

   A. 形式发票不是一种正式发票

   B. 能用于托收和议付，正式成交后无需另外重新缮制商业发票

   C. 形式发票与商业发票的关系密切，信用证在货物描述后面常有"按照某月某日之形式发票"等条款

   D. 假如来证附有形式发票，则形式发票构成信用证的组成部分，制单时要按

　　　形式发票内容全部打上

　　E. 形式发票就是一种正式发票

6. 在国际货物运输保险中,英国伦敦保险协会 ICC 六种险别,(　　)是可以单独投保的。

　　A. ICC 恶意损害险　　　　　　B. ICC(A)

　　C. ICC(B)　　　　　　　　　　D. ICC(C)

　　E. ICC 战争险、罢工险

7. 因租船订舱和装运而产生的单据是(　　)。

　　A. 托运单　　　　　　　　　　B. 装货单

　　C. 收货单　　　　　　　　　　D. 海运提单

　　E. 发票

8. 商业发票是国际货物买卖中的核心单据,其作用表现为(　　)。

　　A. 交接货物的依据　　　　　　B. 登记入账的依据

　　C. 报关纳税的依据　　　　　　D. 专卖合同的证明

　　E. 有时可替代汇票进行货款结算

9. 在使用提单的正常情况下,收货人要取得提货的权利,必须(　　)。

　　A. 将全套提单交回承运人　　　B. 将任一份正本提单交回承运人

　　C. 提单必须正确背书　　　　　D. 付清应支付的费用

　　E. 出具保函

10. 提单中 Shipper 一栏内通常可以记载(　　)。

　　A. 与承运人订立合同的人

　　B. 代表他人与承运人订立合同的人

　　C. 将货物交给承运人的人

　　D. 承运人

　　E. 与托运人订立合同的人

11. 下列哪些单据是《UCP 600》述及的运输单据?(　　)

　　A. 航空运单　　　　　　　　　B. 提单

　　C. 电放提单　　　　　　　　　D. 海运单

12. 根据《UCP 600》的规定,在出口业务中,卖方可以凭以结汇的装运单据有(　　)。

　　A. 海运提单　　　　　　　　　B. 不可转让海运单

　　C. 租船提单　　　　　　　　　D. 收货单

　　E. 空运单　　　　　　　　　　F. 报关单

　　G. 内河运单

13. 信用证规定"SHIPMENT TO BE EFFECTED ON OR ABOUT AUGUST 25，2006；DOCUMENTS REQUIRED：AWB CONSIGNED TO THE APPLICANT"没有其他特别要求，空运单显示正确的是（　　）。

A. ISSUING DATE：AUG. 30，2006，FLIGHT DATE：AUG. 31，2006

B. ISSUING DATE：AUG. 18，2006，FLIGHT DATE：AUG. 25，2006

C. ISSUING DATE：AUG. 18，2006，FLIGHT DATE：AUG. 19，2006

D. ISSUING DATE：AUG. 20，2006，FLIGHT DATE：AUG. 31，2006

（二十）判断题

（　　）1. 运输包装上的标志就是运输标志，也就是通常所说的唛头。

（　　）2. 航空运单的货物运价细目，当一票货物中如含有两种或两种以上不同运价类别计费的货物应分别填写，每填一项另起一行，如果含有危险品，则该危险货物应列在第一项。

（　　）3. 装箱单或重量单的签发日期既可等于或迟于发票日期，也可早于发票签发日期。

（　　）4. 海上货运保险单的转让与其他财产保险单的转让一样，必须征得保险公司的同意。

（　　）5. 托运单的收货人栏目应填写买卖合同的买方名称及地址。

（　　）6. 航空公司一般不接受货运代理人关于"危险货物"的间接运输。

（　　）7. 提单的签发人通常应为托运人。

（　　）8. 不可转让海运单除了单据上写明的收货人外，他人不能提货。

（　　）9. 托收项下，提单收货人一栏打 TO ORDER OF ×××　BANK，应事先获得该银行的同意。

（　　）10. 货物装船后，托运人凭船公司的装货单换取已装船提单。

（　　）11. 出口交易中采用 D/P 方式，出口人投保了"卖方利益险"，货物安全到达目的港，但遭到进口人的拒付，出口人即可凭保险单向保险公司索赔。

（　　）12. 不清洁提单是指承运人在签发提单时，对货物的包装等状况加注不良批注的提单。

（　　）13. 提单的收货人栏在填写"To order of shipper"内容情况下，提单应经背书才能转让。

（　　）14. 联运提单的签发人对运输全程负责。

（　　）15. 具有物权凭证作用的单据只有提单。

（　　）16. 票据法规定，背书人对票据所负的责任与出票人相同，但对其后手没有担保责任。

( ) 17. 票据是一种流通证券，所有票据都可经过背书转让。

( ) 18. 在托收业务中，如果委托人没有指定代收行，托收行可自行选择代收行。

( ) 19. 票据的转让必须通知债务人方为有效。

( ) 20. shipment before 15th April 我公司提单签发日期4月15日，是可以的。

( ) 21. L/C 规定装运期为 after 15th April, 2009 until 30th, April, 2009, 我实际提单日期为 15th April, 2009 或 30th April, 2009, 这是可以的。

( ) 22. L/C 在 FOB 条件下，要求提单在运费条款中注明：freight payable as per charter party 是可以的。

( ) 23. 提单上批注"short shipped one bale"，构成不清洁提单。

二、官方单据的制作与审核

(一) 保险单制作

售 货 合 同
SALES CONTRACT

NO.: 2008KG02350

DATE: DEC. 28, 2008

THE SELLERS: THE BUYERS:

SUCCESS DEVELOPMENT TRADING LTD   JYSK AB

39/FL, FLATF, TIANHE FLAZA   FOERETA 6 S-23237 ARLOEV

SWEDEN

SHANGHAI, CHINA

THIS SALES CONTRACT IS MADE BY AND BETWEEN THE SELLER AND THE BUYER, WHEREBY THE SELLER AGREE TO SELL AND THE BUYER AGREE TO BUY THE UNDER-MENTIONED GOODS ACCORDING TO THE TERMS AND CONDITIONS STIPULATED BELOW:

(13)货号、品名及规格 NAME OF COMMODITY AND SPECIFICATIONS	(14)数量 QUANTITY	(15)单价 UNIT PRICE	(16)金额 AMOUNT
LEATHER GLOVE ART 3900300 ART 3901400	 8 400 PCS 15 520 PCS	CIF GOTHENBURG USD 1.25/PC USD 1.02/PC	 USD 10 500.00 USD 15 830.40
AS PER S/C NO 2008KG02350 AND JYSK ORDER 4500341081	TOTAL AMOUNT:		USD 26 330.40

装运港: LOADING IN CHARGE: CHINESE PORT

目的港: FOR TRANSPORT TO: GOTHENBURG, SWEDEN

转运: TRANSHIPMENT: ALLOWED

分批装运: PARTIAL SHIPMENT: ALLOWED

装运期限: THE LATEST DATE OF SHIPMENT: FEB. 28, 2009

保险: INSURANCE: BE EFFECTED BY THE SELLERS FOR 110% INVOICE VALUE, COVERING F. P. A RISKS AS PER PICC CLAUSE.

付款方式： PAYMENT：BY IRREVOCABLE L/C，IN FAVOR OF THE SELLER，TO BE AVAILABLE BY SIGHT DRAFT；REACHING THE SELLERS 30DAYS BEFORE THE SHIPMENT. REMAIN VALID FOR NEGOTIATION IN CHINA UNTIL THE 15TH DAYS AFTER THE FORE-SAID TIME OF SHIPMENT，ALL COMMIOSSION AND OUTSIDE SWEDEN ARE FOR ACCOUNT OF THE SELLERS.

仲裁： ARBITRATION：ALL DISPUTE ARISING FROM THE EXE-CUTION OR IN CONNECTION WITH THIS CONTRACT SHALL BE AMICABLY SETTLED THROUGH NEGOTIATION IN CASE OF NO SETTLEMENT CAN BE REACHED THROUGH NEGOTIATION THE CASE SHALL THEN BE SUBMITED TO THE CHINA INTERNATION-AL ECONOMIC & TRADE ARBITRATION COMMISION. IN SHANG-HAI(OR IN BEIJING) FOR ARBITRATION. THE ARBITRAL AWAED IS FINAL AND BINDING UPON BOTH PARTIES FOR SETTLING THE DISPUTES. THE FEE，FOR ARBITRATION SHALL BE BORNE BY THE LOSING PARTY UNLESS OTHERWISE AWARDED.

信用证

THE SELLER   THE BUYER
    SUCCUSS DEVELOPMENT TRADING LTD   JYSK AB

                    ISSUE OF A DOCUMENTARY CREDIT

TO   HANGSENG BANK LTD. SHANGHAI BRANCH
FROM   NORDEA BANK，SWEDEN
MT 700
SEQUENCE OF TOTAL   27： 1/1
FROM OF DA   40A：REVOCABLE
DC NO.   20： 667-01-3042855
DATE OF ISSUE   31C：090114
APPLICABLE RULES   40E：UCP LATEST VERSION
EXPIRYDATE AND   31D：DATE：MAR. 15，2009 PLACE：SWE-
PLACE   DEN
APPLICANT   50： JYSK AB
                         FOERETA 6 S-23237 ARLOEV SWEDEN

BEBEFICIARY	59：	SUCCESS DEVELOPMENT TRADING LTD. 39/FL，FLAT F TIANHEPLAZA SHANGHAI，CHINA
AMOUNT	32B：	USD 26 330. 40
AVAILABLE WITH/BY	41A：	ANY BANK BY NEGOTIATION
DRAFT AT…	42C：	AT 30 DAYS SIGHT
DRAWEE	42A：	ISSUING BANK
PARTIAL SHIPMENT	43P：	ALLOWED
TRANSHIPMENT	43T：	NOT ALLOWED
LOADING IN CHARGE	44A：	CHINESE PORTS
FOR TRANSPORT TO	44B：	GOTHENBURG，SWEDEN
LATEST DATE OF SHIPMENT	44C：	FEB. 08，2009
DESCRIPTION OF GOODS	45A：	LEATHER GLOVE AS PER S/C NO 2008KG02350 AND JYSK ORDER 4500341081 8 400 PCS ART 3900300 USD 1. 25/PC 15 520 PCS ART 3901400 USD 1. 20/PC CIF SHANGHAI (INCOTERMS 2000)
DOCUMENTS REQUIRED	46A：	1 SIGNED ORIGINAL COMMERCIAL INVOICE AND 5 COPIES PACKING LIST IN 2 COPIES FULL SET OF CLEAN ON BOARD MARINE BILLS OF LADING, MADE OUT TO ORDER OF ISSING BANK, MARKED "FREIGHT PREPAID" AND NOTIFY APPLICANT (AS INDICAT-ED ABOVE); MENTIONING L/C NO. GSP CERTIFICATE OF ORIGIN FORM A, CERTIFYING GOODS OF ORIGIN IN CHINA, ISSUED BY COMPETENT AUTHORITIES INSURANCE POLICY/CERTIFICATE COVERING ALL RISKS OF PICC, IN-

CLUDING WAREHOUSE TO WARE-
HOUSE CLAUSE UP TO FINAL DES-
TINATION AT GOTHENBURG, FOPR
AT LEAST 120 PCT OF CIF VALUE,
SHOWING CLAIMS PAYABLE IF ANY
IN SWEDEN.

ADDITIONAL CONDITIONS. 47A: ALL DOCUMENTS MUST BE ISSUED
IN ENGLISH
MULTIMODAL TRANSPORT DOCU-
MENTS ACCEPTABLE EVIDENCING
SHIPMENT CLEAN ON BOARD ON A
NAMED VESSEL BILL OF LADING
MUST SHOW CONTAINER NUMBER
P/L(PACKING LIST) MUST BE SPEC-
IFIED PER ART NO AND CONTAIN-
ER NO.

DETAILS OF CHARGES 71B: ALL COMMISSION AND CHARGES OUT-
SIDE SWEDEN ARE FOR ACCOUNT
OF BENEFICIARY OUR CHARGES
WILL BE DEDUCTED/CLAIMED AT
THE TIME OF PAYMENT, NEGOTIA-
TION OR EXPIRY.

PRESENTATION PERIOD 48: DOCUMENTS TO BE PRESENTED WIT-
HIN 5 DAYS AFTER THE DATE OF
SHIPMENT, BUT WITHIN THE VA-
LIDITY OF THE CREDIT.

CONFIRMATION 79: ON RECEIPT OF MALL ADVICE OF
INSTRUCTIONS NEGOTIATION, WE SHALL COVER
AS PER INSTRUCTIONS RECEIVED.

THIS CREDIT IS SUBJECT TO UCP(2007 REVISON), ICC PUUBL NO. 600
补充资料：NET WEIGHT：3.00 KGS/CTN, GROSS WEIGHT：5.00 KGS/
CTN, MEASUREMENT：（50 * 20 * 20）CM/CTN, PACKING：20 PCS/
CTN；产品为完全自产品，于2月20日备妥，在上海港装2月26日MOON
V.252航次出运，贸易方式为一般贸易，2月19日制作发票（号码为Cg2003118），唛头为：JYSK/GOTHENBURG/VOS. 1-1196. FORM A 号码为：SH2506655111；
提单号码为：TTCUSH6593255；保单号为：2003SH25066。

（二）根据信用证以及相关资料缮制结汇单据

信用证

MT S700 Issue of a Documentary Credit

User Header	Service code	103：
	Bank. Priority	113：
	Message User Ref.	108：
	Infor. Form C1	115：

28： Sequence of total
　　1/1

40A： Form of Documentary Credit
　　IRREVOCABLE

20： Documentary Credit Number
　　00001LCC0603814

31C： Date of Issue
　　12-APR-2007

40E： UCP LATEST VERSION

31D： Date and Place of Expiry
　　21-JUN-2007 IN GUANGZHOU

51A： Applicant Bank
　　BNP PARIBAS
　　ZI DE LA PILATERIE
　　59442 WASQUEHAL FRANCE

50： Applicant
　　DIRAMODE
　　3 RUE DU DUREMONT
　　BP 21, 59531 NEUVILLE EN FERRAIN FRANCE

59： Beneficiary
　　GUANGDONG FENG QING TRADING CO.
　　NO. 31 ZHONG SHAN ROAD, GUANZHOU, CHINA

32B： Currency Code, Amount
　　USD 80 000. 00

39A：Percentage Credit Amount Tolerance
05/05

41A：Available With…By…
ANY BANK BY NEGOTIATION

42C：Draft at…
SIGHT

42A：Drawee
BNP PARIBAS
ZI DE LA PILATERIE
59442 WASQUEHAL FRANCE

43P：Partial Shipment
NOT ALLOWED

43T：Transshipment
NOT ALLOWED

44A：Loading on Board/Dispatch/Taking in Charge at/from…
GUANG ZHOU PORT

44B：For Transportation to…
DUNKIRK FRANCE

44C：Latest Date of Shipment
30-MAY-2007

45A：Description of Goods and/or Services
ORDER NO. 113851：LADIES DRESS
10 000 PCS AT USD 8. 00 CIF DUNKIRK INCLUDING 3% COMMIS-
SION

46A：Documents Required
+ COMMERCIAL INVOICE IN 4 FOLDS DULY SIGNED AND STAMPED，
   BEARING DOCUMENTARY CREDIT NUMBER.
+ PACKING LIST IN FIVE FOLD.
+ CERTIFICATE OF ORIGIN
+ 3/3 ORIGINAL BILL OF LADING MADE OUT TO ORDER OF SHIP-
   PER AND ENDORSED IN BLANK NOTIFY EXPEDITORS INTER-
   NATIONAL-BAT L-ROUTE DES FAMARDS-59818 LESQUIN
   FRANCE MARKED FREIGHT PREPAID.
+ INSURANCE POLICY/CERTIFICATE COVERING ALL RISKS AND

WAR RISK FOR 110% OF INVOICE VALUE INCLUDING W/W CLAUSE. CLAIMS AS PER CIC, IF ANY, PAYABLE AT PORT OF DESTINATION IN THE CURRENCY OF THE DRAFT.

+ SHIPPER MUST CABLE ADVISING BUYER SHIPMENT PARTICU-LARS IN BRIEF IMMEDIATELY AFTER SHIPMENT. COPY OF CA-BLE/FAX SHOULD BE PART OF NEGOTIATING DOCUMENTS.

+ ONE COPY OF SIGNED INVOICE AND ONE NON-NEGOTIABLE B/L TO BE SENT TO BUYER BY SPECIAL COURIER 5 DAYS BEFORE THE SHIPPING DATE. A CERTIFICATE OF THESE EFFECTS SHOULD BE PRESENTED TO THE NEGOTIATING BANK AS PART OF DOCUMENTS NEEDED.

47A: Additional Conditions

+ ALL DOCUMENTS MUST MENTIONING THIS L/C NO. AND S/C NO.

+ 3% COMMISSION SHOULD BE DEDUCTED FROM TOTAL AMOUNT OF THE COMMERCIAL INVOICE.

+ MORE OR LESS 5 PERCENT IN QUANTITY AND CREDIT AMOUNT ACCEPTABLE

+ A FEE OF USD 50.00 OR ITS EQUIVALENT WILL BE DEDUCTED FROM THE PROCEEDS OF EACH SET OF DISCREPANT DOCU-MENTS, WHICH REQUIRE OUR OBTAINING ACCEPTANCE FROM APPLICANT.

+ AN EXTRA COPY OF INVOICE AND TRANSPORT DOCUMENTS, IF ANY, FOR L/C ISSUING BANK'S FILE ARE REQUIRED.

71B: Charges

ALL BANKING CHARGES OUTSIDE OPENING BANK ARE FOR THE ACCOUNT OF BENEFICIARY.

48: Period of Presentation

DOCUMENTS TO BE PRESENTED WITHIN 21 DAYS AFTER SHIP-MENT DATE BUT WITHIN THE VALIDITY OF THE CREDIT.

49: Confirmation Instructions

WITHOUT

78: Instructions to the Paying/Accepting/Negotiating Bank

+ UPON RECEIPT OF DOCUMENTS CONFORMING TO THE TERMS

AND CONDITIONS OF THIS CREDIT, WE SHALL PAY THE PRO-
CEEDS. AS DESIGNATED.

+ NEGOTIATING BANK MUST FORWARD ALL DOCUMENTS TO US IN
ONE LOT BY COURIER SERVICE AT BENEFICIARY'S EXPENSES.

+ EXCEPT AS OTHERWISE STATED OR MODIFIED, THIS CREDIT
IS SUBJECT TO THE *UCP 600*.

相关资料：

发票号码：07INC9988　　　　　发票日期：MAY5，2007

船名：　FUXING V. 196　　　起运港：　GUANGZHOU

提单日期：MAY 20，2007　　　提单号码：SIO5789666

包装情况：PACKED IN CARTONS OF 20 PCS EACH, 500CARTONS TOTAL.

毛重：21 KGS/CARTON　净重：20 KGS/CARTON　体积：0.1 M³/CARTON

唛头：DIRAMODE　　　　H. S. 编码：6401. 0058

　　DUNKIRK

　　C/NO. 1～500

合同号码：　SCGD2007001

原产地证日期：MAY 17，2007

保险单日期：　MAY 18，2007

Shipper	B/L No.:
Consignee or Order	**Bill of Lading**
Notify Address	**Original**
Pre-carriage by　　Place of Receipt	
Ocean Vessel　　Port of Loading	

Port of Discharge	Place of delivery	Freight Payable at	Number of Original B/L

Marks & Numbers	No. and kind of package, description of goods	G. W. kgs	M m³

Freight and Charges	
	Place and date of issue
	Singed for or on behalf of the Maste

Original

1. Exporter	Certificate No.
2. Consignee	**CERTIFICATE OF ORIGIN** **OF** **THE PEOPLE'S REPUBLIC OF CHINA**
3. Means of transport and route	5. For certifying authority use only
4. Country/region of destination	

6. Marks and numbers	7. Number and kind of packages; description of goods	8. H. S. Code	9. Quantity	10. Number and date of invoices

11. Declaration by the exporter	12. Certification
The undersigned hereby declares that the above details and statements are correct, that all the goods were produced in China and that they comply with the Rules of the People's Republic of China	It is hereby certified that the declaration by the export is Correct.
Place and date, signature and stamp of authorized signatory	Place and date, signature of authorized signatory

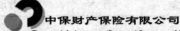

中保财产保险有限公司
The people's insurance (Property) Company of China, Ltd
No.of Original, one

发票号码
Invoice No.

保险单号次
Policy No

海 洋 货 物 运 输 保 险 单
MARINE CARGO TRANSPORTATION INSURANCE POLICY

被保险人

Insured:

中保财产保险有限公司(以下简称本公司)根据被保险人的要求，及其所缴付约定的保险费，按照本保险单承保险别和背面所载条款与下列条款承保下述货物运输保险，特签发本保险单。

This POLICY OF Insurance witnesses that The People's Insurance（Property）Company of China, Ltd.（hereinafter called "The Company"），at the request of the Insured and in consideration of the agreed premium paid by the Insured, undertakes to insure the under-mentioned goods in transportation subject to the conditions of this Policy as per the Clauses printed overleaf and other special clauses attached hereon.

保险货物项目 Descriptions of Goods	包装 单位 数量 Packing Unit Quantity	保险金额 Amount Insured

承保险别：
Conditions

货物标记
Marks of Goods

总保险金额
Total Amount Insured:

保 费   运输工具   开航日期
Premium: as arranged   Per conveyance S. S.   Slg. On or abt.

起运港   目的港
From   To

所保货物，如发生本保险单项下可能引起索赔的损失或损坏,应立即通知本公司下属代理人查勘，如有索赔，应向本公司提交保险单正本(本保险单共有　份正本)及有关文件，如一份正本已用于索赔,其余正本则自动失效。

In the event of loss or damage which may result in a claim under this Policy, immediate notice must be given to the Company's Agent as mentioned hereunder. Claims, if any, one of the Original Policy which has been issued in　Original(s) together with the relevant documents shall be surrendered to the Company, If one of the Original Policy has been accomplished, the others to be void.

中保财产保险有限公司
THEPEOPLESINSURANCE (PROPERTY) COMPANY OF CHINA LTD.

赔付地点
Claim payable at

日期   在
Date   at

地址
Address

（三）根据资料缮制提单

ISSUING BANK：NATIONAL BANK，NAGOYA NO. 145 FIRST ROAD NAGOYA，JAPAN

L/C NO.：E-06777

ISSUING DATE：JAN. 15，2008

BENEFIGIARY：ZHEJIANG DONGFANG FOOD CO.，LTD.

NO. 124 QINGCHUN ROAD HANGZHOU，CHINA

APPLICANT：JEANS CO. NAGOYA

NO. 111 AVENUE，NAGOYA，JAPAN

SHIPMENT：FROM NINGBO TO NAGOYA，NOT LATER THAN JAN. 25TH，2008

PARTIAL SHIPMENT：ALLOWED

TRANSSHIPMENT：ALLOWED

COVERING：3000 CANS CANNED MEAT

SHIPPING MARKS：N/M

THE GOODS ARE PACKED IN 210 CASES

GROSS WEIGHT：3 300 KGS

MEASUREMENT：76. 43 M^3

OCEAN VASEEL：YURONG VOY. NO. E244

DOCUMENTS REQUIRED：

FULL SET OF CLEAN ON BOARD OCEAN BILLS OF LADING MADE OUT TO ORDER OF ISSUING BANK AND BLANK ENDORSED MARKED FREIGHT PREPAID AND NOTIFY ISSUING BANK

其他制单材料：

货物装运日期：2008-01-22

Shipper	B/L NO

中国远洋运输(集团)总公司

CHINA OCEAN SHIPPING (GROUP)CO.

Consignee	
Notify Party	

Combined Transport BILL OF LADING

Pre-carriage by	Place of receipt

Ocean Vessel Voy No.	Port of Loading

Port of Discharge	Place of Delivery	Final Destination

Marks & nos container Seal no.	No. of Containers or P'kgs	Kind of Packages; Description of Goods	Gross Weight	Measurement

TOTAL NUMBER OF CONTAINERS OR PACKAGES(IN WORDS)

FREIGHT & CHARGES	Revenue Tons	Rate	Per	Prepaid	Collect
Ex Rate	Prepaid at	Payable at		Place and date of Issue	
	Total Prepaid	No. Of Original B(S)/L		Signed for the Carrier	

（四）根据信用证缮制保险单

From：VOLKSBANK SCHORNDORF，HAMBURG，GERMANY

To：BANK OF CHINA，HEBEI BRANCH

Form of Doc. Credit *40A：IRREVOCABLE

Doc. Credit Number *20：08-4-1520

Date of Issue 31C：080201

APPLICABLE RULES 40E：UCP LATEST VERSION

Expiry *31D：DATE：080415 IN THE COUNTRY OF BENE-FICIARY

Applicant *50：LUCKY VICTORY INTERNATIONAL STUTTGART STIR. 5,

		D-84618, SCHORNDORF, GERMANY
Beneficiary	* 59:	HEBEI MACHINERY IMP. AND EXP. CORP
		(GROUP)
		720 DONGFENG ROAD, SHIJIAZHUANG,
		CHINA
Amount	* 32B:	Currency USD Amount 57 600.00
Pos. /Neg. Tol. (%)	39A:	5/5
Available with/by	* 41A:	ANY BANK BY NEGOTIATION
Draft at…	42C:	DRAFTS AT 30 DAYS SIGHT

FOR FULL INVOICE VALUE

Drawee	42A:	VOLKSBANK SCHORNDORF
		HAMBURG, GERMANY
Partial Shipments	43P:	ALLOWED
Transshipment	43T:	ALLOWED
Loading in Charge	44A:	TIANJIN
For Transport to	44B:	HAMBURG
Latest Date of Ship.	44C:	080331
Descript. of Goods	45A:	

STAINLESS STEEL SPADE HEAD,

ART. NO. S569, 4 800 PCS, USD 5.60 PER PC.,

ART. NO. F671, 3 200 PCS, USD 9.60 PER PC.,

AS PER S/C NO. 08HM256 DATED JAN. 01, 2008

CIF HAMBURG

Documents required　46A:

+　SIGNED COMMERCIAL INVOICE IN TRIPLICATE.

+　FULL SET OF CLEAN ON BOARD OCEAN BILLS OF LADING
MADE OUT TO ORDER OF SHIPPER, MARKED "FREIGHT PREPAID"
AND NOTIFY APPLICANT.

+　GSP CERTIFICATE OF ORIGIN FORM A

+　PACKING LIST IN TRIPLICATE.

+　INSURANCE POLICY COVERING RISKS AS PER INSTITUTE
CARGO CLAUSE(A) INCLUDING WAREHOUSE TO WARE-
HOUSE CLAUSE UP TO FINAL DESTINATION AT SCHORN-
DORF, FOR 110 PCT OF THE CIF VALUE, MARKED PREMI-

UM PAID, SHOWING CLAIM PAYABLE IN GERMANY.

Additional Cond. 47A：

1. A HANDING FEE OF USD 80. 00 WILL BE DEDUCTED IF DIS-CREPANCY DOCUMENTS PRESENTED.

2. ALL DOCUMENTS MUST BE IN ENGLISH.

3. ALL DOCUMENTS INDICATING THIS L/C NUMBER.

Presentation Period 48：

DOCUMENTS TO BE PRESENTED WITHIN 15 DAYS AFTER THE DATE OF SHIPMENT, BUT WITHIN THE VALIDITY OF THE CREDIT.

Details of Charges 71B：

ALL BANKING CHARGES AND EXPENSES OUTSIDE THE ISSU-ING BANK ARE FOR BENEFICIARY'S ACCOUNT.

有关资料：

发票号码： 08HM248

提单号码： CANEI29-30554   提单日期：2008 年 03 月 20 日

船名：   HUAFENG V. 872W   装运港： 天津港

海运费：   USD 1 500. 00,

外包装尺码：(65CM×18CM×12CM)/CTN

ART NO	QUANTITY	PACKAGE	G. W.	N. W.
S569	4 800 PCS	10 PCS/CTN	7. 60 KGS/CTN	7. 20 KGS/CTN
F671	3 200 PCS	20 PCS/CTN	14 KGS/CTN	13 KGS/CTN

唛头：

LUCKY

08HM256

HAMBURG

NO. 1-UP

中国人民保险公司河南省分公司

The People's Company of China Henan Branch

总公司设于北京　一九四九年创立

Head Office Beijing Established in 1949

货物运输保险单　　ORINGINAL

CARGO TRANSPORTATION INSURANCE POLICY

INVOICE NO.　　　　　　　　POLICY NO.

L/C NO.

INSURED：

中国人民保险公司（以下简称本公司）根据被保险人的要求，由被保险人向本公司缴付约定的保险费，按照本保险单承保险别和背面所载条款与下列特别条款承保下述货物运输保险，特立本保险单。

THIS POLICY OF INSURANCE WITNESSES THAT THE PIOPLE'S INSURANCE COMPANY OF CHINA(HEREINAFTER CALLED "THE COMPANY")AT THE REQUEST OF THE INSURED AND IN CONSIDERATION OF THE AGREED PREMIUM PAID TO THE COMPANY BY THE INSURED, UNDERTAKES TO INSURE THE UNDERMENTIONED GOODS INTRANSPORTATION SUBJECT TO THE CONDITONS OF THIS POLICY AS PER THE CLAUSES PRINTED OVERLEAF AND OTHER SPECIAL CLAUSES ATTACHED HEREON.

标记 MARKS & NOS	包装及数量 QUANTITY	保险货物项目 DESCRIPTION OF GOODS	保险金额 AMOUNT INSURED

总保险金额：

TOTAL AMOUNT INSURED

保费：　　　　　　　　费率：　　　　　　　　装载运输工具：

PREMIUM：AS ARRANGED RATE：AS ARRANGED PER CONVEYANCE S. S.

开航日期　　　　　　　自　　　　　　　　　　至

SLG. ON OR ABT.　　　FROM　　　　　　　　TO

承保险别：

CONDITONS

所保货物，如发生本保险单项下可能引起赔偿的损失或损坏，应立即通知本公司下属代理人查勘。如有索赔，应向本公司提交保险单正本（本保险单共有正本　份）及有关文件。如一份正本已用于索赔，其余正本自动失效。

IN THE EVENT OF LOSS OR DAMAGE WHICH MAY RESULT IN A CLAIM UNDER THIS POLICY, IMMEDIATE NOTICE MUST BE GIVEN TO THE COMPANY'S AGENT AS MENTIONED HEREUNDER. IN THE EVENT OF CLAIMS, IF ANY, ONE OF THE ORIGINAL POLICY WHICH HAS BEEN ISSUED IN ORIGINAL(S) WITH THE RELEVANT DOCUMENTS SHALL BE SURRENDERED TO THE COMPANY. IF ONE OF THE ORIGINAL POLICY HAS BEEN ACCOLPLISHED, THE OTHERS SHALL BE VOID.

赔款偿付地

CLAIM PAYABLE AT：　　　　　　　中国人民保险公司河南省分公司

出单日期　　　　　　　　　　　THE PIEPLE'S INSURANCE COMPANY OF

ISSUING DATE：　　　　　　　　CHINA, HENAN BRANCH

（五）根据信用证制作下列单据

LETTER OF CREDIT

BASIC HEADER F 01 BKCHCNBJA5×× 9828 707783

＋BANK OF NOVA SCOTIA，TORONTO，CANADA

:MT: 700 ·············· ISSUE A DOCUMENTARY CREDIT ··············

FORM OF CREDIT | 40A： | IRREVOCABLE

DOC. CREDIT NUMBER | 20： | 078230CDI1117LC

DATE OF ISSUE | 31C： | 070118

APPLICABLE RULES | 40E： | UCP LATEST VERSION

DATE AND PLACE OF | 31D： | 070310
EXPIRY

APPLICANT | 50： | WENSCO FOODS LTD.,
RUA DE GREENLAND STREET，68-A
1260-297 WELL D. COQUITLAM，B. C.
CANADA

BENEFICIARY | 59： | HUNAN CEREALS, OILS & FOOD-
STUFFS IMPORT & EXPORT
CORPORATION
38 WUYI RD., CHANGSHA CHINA

CURRENCY CODE AND | 32B： | USD 10 830. 00
AMOUNT AVAILABLE | 41A： | ANY BANK IN CHINA BY NEGOCI-
WITH…BY… | | ATION

DRAFT AT | 42C： | DRAFT AT 45 DAYS AFTER B/L DATE
FOR FUL INVOICE VALUE

DRAWEE | 42A： | DRAWN ON US AND THE ADD: 550
WEST GEORGIA ST., PO BOX 172
TORONTO, CANADA

PARTIAL SHIPMENT | 43P： | PROHIBIED

TRANSSHIPMENT | 43T： | PERMITTIED

LODING/DISPATCH/ | 44A： | MAIN CHINESE PORT
TAKING/FROM

FOR TRANSPOTATION   44B：   VANCOUVER B. C.
TO

LATEST DATE OF   44C：   070301
SHIPMENT

DESCRIPTION OF   45A：   "TROPIC ISLE CANNED MANDARIN
GOODS/SERVICE   ORIANGES LS-WHOLE SEGMENTS"
AS PER P/I NO. CF07018 CIF VAN-
COUVER B. C.

DOCS REQUIERD：   46A：

+   MANUALLY SIGNED COMMERCIAL INVOICE ONE ORINAL
AND FOUR COPIES, CERTIFYING GOODS ARE OF CHINESE
ORIGIN AND INDICATEING P/I NO.

+   FULL SET（3/3）OF CLEAN ON BOARD OCEAN BILLS OF
LADING, MADE OUT TO ORDER OF SHIPPER, BLANK IN-
DORSED NOTIFYING APPLICANT, STATING FREIGHT PRE-
PAID OR COLLECT.

+   PACKING LIST IN TRIPLICATE

+   NEGOCIABLE INSURANCE POLICY/CERTIFICATE, BLANK
INDORSED, COVERING GOODS FOR THE INVOICE VALUE
PLUS 10% AGAINST THE RISKS OF ICC(A) AND ICC (CAR-
GO).

+   SHIPPING ADVICE SHOULD SENT BY FAX TO APPLICANT
INFORMING VESSEL'S NAME AND VOY. NO., GR. WT, MEAS,
PACKING, TOTAL AMOUNT AND ETD.

+   G. S. P FORM A IN 1 ORIGINAL AND 2 COPIES, INDICATING
ORIGIN CRITERION "W".

ADDITIONAL   47A：   +   A DESCREPANCY FEE OF U. S. D
CONDITIONS：   50. 00 FOR BENEFICIARY'S AC-
COUNT

+   ONE COMPELE SET OF DOCS TO
BE SENT TO US BY COURIER IN
ONE LOT.

+ ALL DOCS MUST NOT INDICAT-
ED L/C NO. EXCEPT INVOICE &
DRAFT.

CHARGES   71B： ALL BANKING CHARGES OUT OF
OUR COUNTER ARE FOR BENEFI-
CIARY'S ACCOUNT

PERIOD FOR PRESENT- 48： 15 DAYS AFTER SHIPMENT AND
ATIONS   NOT EXCEEDING L/C EXPIRY

TRAILER   MAC：9FE41FBC   CHK：56783 EE6A448   NNNN

补充资料：

1. QUANTITY：950 CARTONS

2. PACKING：IN PLASTIC BAGS OF 2. 84 KGS EACH THEN SIX
BAGS IN A CARTON.

3. UNIT PRICE：U. S. D 11. 40 PER CARTON

4. TOTAL AMOUNT：U. S. D 10 830. 00

5. SHIPPING PER S. S "DEWEI V. 213" FROM HUANGPU TO VAN-
COUVER B. C.，B/L NO. 6180

6. MARKS：W. F. L. /VANCOUVER/   C/NO.：1-UP

7. B/L DATE：070220

8. ETD：070310

9. GROSS WEIGHT：17138 KGS   NET WEIGHT：16188 KGS
MEAS：18. 365 M³

10. NEGOCIATING BANK：BANK OF CHINA，HUNAN BRANCH

11. S/C NO：P. O. 2007-018   INV. DATE：070201   INV. NO.：CFF-016

12. H. S. CODE：8560. 3900

13. CARRIER：   ABC CO.，LTD, FOR THE AGENT, COSCO AS
THE CARRIER
业务员姓名:张三

14. REFERENCE NO.：1283890096

Shipper	B/L No.
Consignee or order	中国对外贸易运输总公司 CHINA NATIONAL FOREIGN TRADE TRANSPORTATION CORP. 直运或转船提单 BILL OF LADING DIRECT OR WITH TRANSHIPMENT
Notify address	SHIPPED on board in apparent good order and condition（unless otherwise indicated）the goods or packages specified herein and to be discharged at the mentioned port of discharge or as near thereto as the vessel may safely get and be always afloat. 　　In WITNESS whereof the number of original Bills of Lading stated below has been signed one of them being accomplished，the other(s) to be void.

Pre-carriage by	Port of loading	
Vessel	Port of transshipment	
Port of discharge	Final destination	

Container，seal No. or Marks and Nos.	Number and kinds of packages	Description of goods	Gross weight (kgs.)	Measurement(m)

Freight and charges	REGARDING TRANSHIPMENT INFORMATION PLEASE CONTACT

Ex. rate	Prepaid at	Freight payable at	Place and date of issue
	Total Prepaid	Number of original Bs/L	Signed for or on behalf of the Master as Agent

SUBJECT TO THE TERMS AND CONDITIONS ON BACK 93A NO. 0241877

ORIGINAL

1. Goods consigned from (Exporter's business name, address, country)	Reference No. GENERALIZED SYSTEM OF PREFERENCES
2. Goods consigned to (Consignee's name, address, country)	Issued in .... (country) See Notes overleaf
3. Means of transport and route (as far as known)	4. For official use

5. Item num-ber
6. Marks and numbers of packages
7. Number and kind of packages; description of goods
8. Origin criterion (see Notes overleaf)
9. Gross weight or other quantity
10. Number and date of invoices

11. Certification It is hereby certified, on the basis of control carried out, that the declaration by the exporter is correct. .... Place and date, signature and stamp of certifying authority	12. Declaration by the exporter The undersigned hereby declares that the above details and statements are correct, that all the goods were produced in .... (country) and that they comply with the origin requirements specified for those goods in the Generalized System of Preferences for goods exported to .... Place and date, signature and stamp of authorized signatory

（六）根据信用证改正下列单据中你认为填错的日期或出单人

LETTER OF CREDIT

BASIC HEADER F 01 BKCHCNBJA5×× 9828 707783
+BANK OF NOVA SCOTIA, TORONTO, CANADA
:MT: 700 ·············· ISSUE A DOCUMENTARY CREDIT ···············

FORM OF CREDIT	40A:	IRREVOCABLE
DOC. CREDIT NUMBER	20:	078230CDI1117LC
DATE OF ISSUE	31C:	070425
APPLICABLE RULES	40E:	UCP LATEST VERSION
DATE AND PLACE OF EXPIRY	31D:	070615
APPLICANT	50:	WENSCO FOODS LTD., RUA DE GREEN-LAND STREET, 68-A 1260-297 WELL D. COQUITLAM, B. C. CANADA
BENEFICIARY	59:	HUNAN CEREALS, OILS & FOODSTUFFS IMPORT & EXPORT CORPORATION 38 WUYI RD., CHANGSHA CHINA
CURRENCY CODE AND AMOUNT	32B:	USD 10 830. 00
AVAILABLE WITH…BY…	41A:	ANY BANK IN CHINA BY NEGOCIA-TION
DRAFT AT	42C:	DRAFT AT 45 DAYS AFTER B/L DATE FOR FUL INVOICE VALUE
DRAWEE	42A:	DRAWN ON US AND THE ADD: 550 WEST GEORGIA ST., PO BOX 172 TO-RONTO, CANADA
PARTIAL SHIPMENT	43P:	PROHIBIED
TRANSSHIPMENT	43T:	PERMITTIED
LODING/DISPATCH/ TAKING/FROM	44A:	MAIN CHINESE PORT
FOR TRANSPOTATION TO	44B:	VANCOUVER B. C.

LATEST DATE OF SHIPMENT	44C:	070531
DESCRIPTION OF GOODS/SERVICE	45A:	"TROPIC ISLE CANNED MANDARIN ORIANGES LS-WHOLE SEGMENTS" AS PER P/I NO. CF07018 CIF VANCOUVER B. C.
DOCS REQUIERD:	46A:	

+ MANUALLY SIGNED COMMERCIAL INVOICE ONE ORINAL AND FOUR COPIES, CERTIFYING GOODS ARE OF CHINESE ORIGIN AND INDICATEING P/I NO.

+ FULL SET(3/3) OF CLEAN ON BOARD OCEAN BILLS OF LADING, MADE OUT TO ORDER OF SHIPPER, BLANK INDORSED NOTIFYING APPLICANT, STATING FREIGHT PREPAID OR COLLECT.

+ PACKING LIST IN TRIPLICATE

+ NEGOCIABLE INSURANCE POLICY/CERTIFICATE, BLANK INDORSED, COVERING GOODS FOR THE INVOICE VALUE PLUS 10% AGAINST THE RISKS OF ICC(A) AND ICC(CARGO).

+ SHIPPING ADVICE SHOULD SENT BY FAX TO APPLICANT INFORMING VESSEL'S NAME AND VOY. NO., GR. WT, MEAS, PACKING, TOTAL AMOUNT AND ETD.

+ G. S. P FORM A IN 1 ORIGINAL AND 2 COPIES, INDICATING ORIGIN CRITERION "W".

ADDITIONAL CONDITIONS:	47A:	+ A DESCREPANCY FEE OF U. S. D 50. 00 FOR BENEFICIARY'S ACCOUNT
		+ ONE COMPELE SET OF DOCS TO BE SENT TO US BY COURIER IN ONE LOT.
		+ ALL DOCS MUST NOT INDICATED L/C NO. EXCEPT INVOICE & DRAFT.
CHARGES	71B:	ALL BANKING CHARGES OUT OF OUR COUNTER ARE FOR BENEFICIARY'S ACCOUNT

PERIOD FOR PRESENT-　48：　15 DAYS AFTER SHIPMENT AND
ATIONS　　　　　　　　　　NOT EXCEEDING L/C EXPIRY

TRAILER　　　MAC：9FE41FBC　　CHK：56783 EE6A448　NNNN

已知资料：

　　已装船日期：MAY. 28，2007

　　最迟装运期：MAY. 30，2007

　　信用证效期：JUNE. 15，2007　信用证开证日期：APR. 10，2007

　　交易术语：CIF LONDON

单据名称	出单日期	出单机构
出口许可证	4 月 12 日	出口方
形式发票	4 月 08 日	进口方
商业发票	5 月 29 日	出口方
装箱单	5 月 29 日	货运代理
G. S. P FORM A	5 月 27 日	C. C. P. I. T
熏蒸证书	5 月 29 日	商务部
报关单	5 月 26 日	中国海关
保险单	5 月 30 日	出口方
受益人证明	6 月 02 日	出口方
汇票	5 月 27 日	出口方
备运提单	5 月 29 日	出口方

（七）根据信用证缮制提单

LETTER OF CREDIT

....

Basic Header	appl ID：F APDU Id：01 LT Addr：OCMMCNSH×××× Session：8533 Sequence：142087	
Application Header	Input/Output：0	Msg Type：700
	Input Time：1622	Input Date：001103
	Sender LT：BKKBTHBKE××× BANGKOK BANK PUBLIC COMPANY LIMITED BANCKOK	
	Input Session：5177	Output Date：001103
	ISN：800333	
	Output Time：2033	Priority：N
Sequence Total	*27：	1/1
Form Doc Credit	*40A：	IRREVOCABLE
Doc Credit Num	*20：	BKKB1103043
Date of Issue	31C：	001103
APPLICABLE Rules	40E：	UCP LATEST VERSION
Date/Place Exp	*31D：	Date 010114 Place BENEFICIARIES' COUNTRY
Applicant	*50：	MOUN CO., LTD NO. 443,249 ROAD BANGKOK THAILAND
Beneficiary	*59：	/ SHANGHAI FOREIGN TRADE CORP. SHANGHAI, CHINA
Curr Code，Amt	*32B：	Code USD Amount 18 000,
Avail With By	*41D：	ANY BANK IN CHINA BY NEGOTIATION
Drafts At	42C：	SIGHT IN DUPLICATE INDICATING THIS L/C NUMBER
Drawee	43D：	//

		ISSUING BANK
Partial Shipmts	43P:	NOT ALLOWED
Transshipment	43T:	ALLOWED
Loading on Brd	44A:	
		CHINA MAIN FORT, CHINA
	44B:	
		BANGKOK, THAILAND
Latest Shipment	44C:	001220
Goods Descript.	45A:	2 000 KGS. ISONIAZID BP98
		PACKED IN 50 KGS/DRUM
		AT USD 9. 00 PER KG CFR BANGKOK
Docs Required	46A:	

DOCUMENTS REQUIRED:

+ COMMERCIAL INVOICE IN ONE ORIG-INAL PLUS 5 COPIES INDICATING F. O. B. VALUE, FREIGHT CHARGES SEPARATELY AND THIS L/C NUM-BER, ALL OF WHICH MUST BE MAN-UALLY SIGNED.

+ FULL SET OF 3/3 CLEAN ON BOARD OCEAN BILLS OF LADING AND TWO NON-NEGOTIABLE, COPIES MADE OUT TO ORDER OF BANGKOK BANK PUBLIC COMPANY LIMITED, BANG-KOK MARKED FREIGHT PREPAID AND NOTIFY APPLICANT AND INDI-CATING THIS L/C NUMBER.

+ PACKING LIST IN ONE ORIGINAL PLUS 5 COPIES, ALL OF WHICH MUST BE MANUALLY SIGNED.

dd. Conditions 47A:

ADDITIONAL CONDITION:
A DISCREPANCY FEE OF USD 50. 00 WILL BE IMPOSED ON EACH SET OF DOCU-

MENTS PRESENTED FOR NEGOTIATION UNDER THIS L/C WITH DISCREPANCY. THE FEE WILL BE DEDUCTED FROM THE BILL AMOUNT.

Charges   71B: ALL BANK CHARGES OUTSIDE THAILAND INCLUDING REIMBURSING BANK COMMISSION AND DISCREPANCY FEE (IF ANY) ARE FOR BENEFICIARIES' ACCOUNT.

Confirmat Instr   *49:   WITHOUT

Reimburs. Bank   53D: //
BANGKOK BANK PUBLIC COMPANY LIMITED, NEW YORK BRANCH ON T/T BASIS

Ins Paying bank   78:
DOCUMENTS TO BE DESPATCHED IN ONE LOT BY COURIER.
ALL CORRESPONDENCE TO BE SENT TO/ BANGKOK BANK PUBLIC COMPANY LIMITED HEAD OFFICE, 333 SILOM ROAD, BANGKOK 10500, THAILAND.

Send Rec Info   72:   REIMBURSEMENT IS SUBJECT TO ICC URR 525

Trailer MAC   :

CHK   :

DLM   :

----------------------------------- End of Message -----------------------------------

1. Shipper Insert Name，Address and Phone	B/L No.	

2. Consignee Insert Name，Address and Phone

中远集装箱运输有限公司
COSCO CONTAINER LINES

TLX，33057 COSCO CN
FAX，+86(021) 6545 8984

ORIGINAL

Port-to-Port or Combined Transport

BILL OF LADING

RECEIVED in external apparent good order and condition except as other-

3. Notify Party Insert Name，Address and Phone

　　(It is agreed that no responsibility shall attach to the Carrier or his agents for failure to notify)

4. Combined Transport * Pre-carriage by	5. Combined Transport * Place of Receipt
6. Ocean Vessel Voy. No.	7. Port of Loading
8. Port of Discharge	9. Combined Transport * Place of Delivery

Marks &. Nos. Container/Seal No.	No. of Containers or Packages	Description of Goods (If Dangerous Goods, See Clause 20)	Gross Weight Kgs	Measurement
		Description of Contents for Shipper's Use Only (Not part of This B/L Contract)		

10. Total Number of containers and/or packages (in words)
　　Subject to Clause 7
　　Limitation

11. Freight &. Charges Declared Value Charge	Revenue Tons	Rate	Per	Prepaid	Collect

Ex. Rate：	Prepaid at	Payable at	Place and date of issue
	Total Prepaid	No. of Original B(s)/L	Signed for the Carrier, COSCO CONTAINER LINES

LADEN ON BOARD THE VESSEL

DATE　　　　BY

（八）依据销售合同和信用证以及相关资料缮制提单、产地证、保险单

ABC TEXTILES IMPORT AND EXPORT CORPORATION
127 ZHONGSHAN RD. E. 1 SHANGHAI R. P. OF CHINA
SALES CONFIRMATION

TO：MESSRS TOMSON TEXTILES INC.

3384 VINCENT ST.　　　　　　　　NO. 23CA1006

DOWNSVIEW，ONTARIO　　　　DATE：20080306

M3J，2J4，CANADA

ARTICLE NO. COMMODITY & SPECIFICATION QUANTITY UNIT PRICE AMOUNT

ART. NO.　　　　　TRUERAN DYED JEAN

77111　　　　　　　POLYESTES 65％，COTTON 35％

20×20，94×60，112/114cm，

40M AND UP ALLOWING 15％ 27. 432 M

AND UP IN IRREGULAR CUTS

MAKES UP：FULL WIDTH ROLLER ON TUBES

OF 1. 5 INCHES IN DIAMETER

PACKING：IN SEAWORTHY CARTONS

CIF TORONTO

COL.	M.	USD/M	USD
RED	4 000	1.56	6 240. 00
SILVER	3 000	1.32	3 960. 00
FIESTA	4 000	1.56	6 240. 00
DKNAVY	3 000	1.62	4 860. 00
WINE	2 200	1.62	3 564. 00
ELEPHANT	3 000	1.44	4 320. 00
BLACK	4 800	1.62	7 776. 00
TOTAL：	24 000		36 960. 00

SHIPMENT：BEF. APR. 20TH 2008

WITH PARTIAL SHIPMENT & TRANSHIPMENT TO BE ALLOWED.

DESTINATION：TORONTO

PAYMENT：BY 100％ IRREVOCABLE L/C AVAILAVLE BY DRAFT AT 30 DAYS SIGHT, TO BE OPENED IN SELLERS FAVOUR 15 DAYS BEFORE THE MONTH OF SHIPMENT, L/C TO REMAIN VALID IN CHINA FOR A PERIOD OF 15 DAYS AFTER THE LAST SHIPMENT DATE.

ABC 纺织品进出口公司

信用证

DOCUMENTARY CREDIT

ZCZC AHS302 CPUA520 S9203261058120RN025414394

P3 SHSOC ICRA

TO：10306 26BKCHCNBJASH102514

FM：15005 25CIBCCATTF×××05905

    CIBBCCATTF×××

     * CANADIAN INPERIAL BANK OF COMMERCE

     * TORONTO

MT： 701 02

27：   SEQENCE OF TOTAL：1/1

40A： FORM OF DOC. CREDIT：IRREVOCABLE

20：   DOC. CREDIT NUMBER：T-017641

31C： DATE OF ISSUE：20080325

40E： UCP LATEST VERSION

31D： EXPIRY：DATE：20080505

       PLACE：THE PEOPLES REP. OF CHINA

50：APPLICANT：TOMSCN TEXTJLES INC.

           3384 VINCENT ST

           DOWNSVIEW. ONTARIO

           M3J. 2J4 CANADA

59：BENEFICIARY：ABC TEXILES IMPORT AND EXPORT

             CORPORATION

             127 ZHONGSHAN RD. E. 1

             SHANGHAI P. R. OF CHINA

32B：AMOUT：CURRENCY：USD AMOUT：36 960. 00

39A：POS/NEG TOL（%）：05/05

41-：AVAILABLE WITH/BY：AVAILABLE WITH ANY BANK IN CHINA

                   NEGOTIATION

42C：DRAFTS AT—：30DAYS AFTER SIGHT

42_：DRAWEE：CIBE—TORONTO TRADE FINANCE CENTRE. TORONTO

43P：PARTIAL SHIPMENTS：PERMITTED

43T：TRANSSHIPPMENT：PERMITTED

44A：LOADING IN CHARGE：CHINA

44B：FOR TRANSPORT TO：TORONTO

44C：LATEST DATE OF SHIP：20080420

45A：SHIPMENT OF GOODS：MERCHANDISE AS PER S/CNO. 23CA1006

CIF TORONTO

46A：DOCUMENTS REQUIRED：

- COMMERCIAL INVOICE IN QUADRUPLICATE
- CERTIFICATE OF ORIGIN
- FULL SET CLEAN ON BOARD BILLS OF LADING TO SHIPPER'S ORDER BLANK ENDORSED MARKED "FREIGHT PREPAID TO TORONTO" NOTIFY APPLICANT (SHOWING FULL NAME AND ADDRESS) AND INDICATING FREIGHT CHARGED.
- NEGOTIBLE INSURANCE POLICY OR CERTIFICATE ISSUED BY PEOPLES INSURANCE COMPANY OF CHINA INCORPO- RATING THEIR OCEAN MARINE CARGO CLAUSES (ALL RISKS) AND WAR RISKS FOR 110 PERCENT OF CIF INVOICE VALUE, WITH CLAIMS PAYABLE IN CANADA INDICATING INSURANCE CHARGES.
- DETAILED PACKING LIST IN TRIPLICATE
- EXPORT LICENSE
- COPY OF INSURANCE CHARGES
- COPY OF FREIGHT CHARGES

47A：ADDITIONAL COND：

THE NUMBER AND THE DATE OF THIS CREDIT AND THE NAME OF OUR BANK MUST BE QUOTED ON ALL DRAFTS REQUIRED

AN ADDITIONAL FEE OF USD 50. 00 OR EQUIVALENT WILL BE DEDUCTED FROM THE PROCEEDS PAID UNDER ANY DRAW- ING WHERE DOCUMENTS PRESENTED ARE FOUND NOT TO BE IN STRICT CONFORMITY WITH THE TERMS OF THIS CREDIT.

71B：DETAILS OF CHARGES：

ALL BANKING CHARGES OUTSIDE CANADA INCLUDING AD- VISING COMMISSION ARE FOR ACCOUNT OF BENIFICIARY AND MUST BE CLAIMED AT THE TIME OF ADVISING.

48：PRESENTATION PERIOD：

NOT LATER THAN 15DAYS AFTER THE DATE OF ISSUANCE OF THE SHIPPING DOCUMENTS BUT WITHIN THE VALIDITY OF THE CREDIT.

49：CONFIRMATION：WITHOUT

78：INSTRUCTIONS：

UPON OUR RECEIPT OF DOCUMENTS IN ORDER WE WILL RE-MIT IN ACCORDANCE WITH NEGOTIATING BANK'S INSTRUC-TIONS AT MATURITY.

ORIGINAL

BILL OF LADING

Shipper	**COSCO**		
	B/L NO.		
CONSIGNEE	CHINA OCEANS SHIPPIGN COMPANY 总公司 HEAD OFFICE. 北京 BELJNG		
	CABLE： TALEX： **ORIGINAL**		
Notify			
Vessel Voy.			
Port of Loading	Port of Discharge	TRANSPORT THROUGH OR VIA：	
Nationality THE PEOPLE'S REPUBLIC OF CHINA	Freight Payable at		
Particular furnished by the Shipper			
Marks and Number	No. Of Packages	Description of Goods	Gross Weight	Measurement
Total Packages（in words）			
Freight and Changes	NO OF ORIGINAL B/L	PLACE AND DATE OF ISSUE Dated .... at	
LOADING ON BOARD THE VESSEL			
DATE BY	_____ SIGNED For the CARRIER		

中保财产保险有限公司

The people insurance (Property) Company of China, LTD.
PICC PROPERTY

发票号码   保险单号次
Invoice No.   Policy No.

海洋货物运输保险单
MARINE CARGO TRANSPORTATION INSURANCE POLICY

被保险人：
Insured：

中保财产保险有限公司(以下简称本公司)根据被保险人的要求，及其所缴付约定的保险费，按照本保险单承担险别和背面所载条款与下列特别条款承保下列货物运输保险，特签发本保险单。

This policy of Insurance witnesses that The People Insurance (Property) Company of China, Ltd. (hereinafter called the Company), at the request of the Insured and in consideration of the agreed premium paid by the Insured, undertakes to insure the under mentioned goods in transportation subject to the conditions of this Policy as per the Clauses printed overleaf and other special clauses attached hereon.

保险货物项目 Descriptions of Goods	包装 单位 数量 Packing Unit Quantity	保险金额 Amount Insured

承 保 险 别   货物标记
Conditions   Marks of Goods

COVERING ALL RISKS AND WAR RISKS AS PER OCEAN
MARINE CARGO CLAUSES (WAREHOUSE TO WAREHOUSE CLAUSE
IS INCLUDED) AND OCEAN MARINE CARGO WAR RISK
        CLAUSES OF THE PEOPLES INSURANCE COMPANY OF CHINA (1/1/1981)

总保险金额：
Total Amount Insured：

保险   载运输工具   开航日期
Premium   As arranged   Per. conveyance S. S   Sig. on or abt.

起运港目的港
From   To

所保货物，如发生本保险单项下可能引起索赔的损失或损坏，应立即通知本公司下属代理人查勘。如有索赔，应向本公司提交保险单正本(本保险单共有 2 份正本)及有关文件。如一份正本已用于索赔，其余正本则自动失效。

In the event of damage which may result in a claim under this Policy, immediate notice be given to the Company Agent as mentioned hereunder? Claims, if any, one of the Original Policy which has been issued in (15) 2 Original(s) together with the relevant documents shall be surrendered to be Company, if one of the Original Policy has been accomplished, the others to be IN void.

中保财产保险有限公司
THE PEOPLE INSURANCE (PROPERTY) COMPANY OF CHINA, LTD.

赔款偿付地点
Claim payable at

日期   (17)   在
Date   at

Address：地址：

1. Goods consigned from（Exporter's business name, address, country)	Reference No.
	GENERALIZED SYSTEM OF PREFERENCES
2. Goods consigned to（Consignee's name, address, country）	Issued in .... 　　　　　　　　　　（country） See Notes overleaf
3. Means of transport and route（as far as known）	4. For official use

5. Item number
6. Marks and numbers of packages
7. Number and kind of packages; description of goods
8. Origin criterion
9. Gross weight
10. Number and date of invoices

SAY TOTAL:

| 11. Certification
It is hereby certified, on the basis of control carried out, that the declaration by the exporter is correct.

....
Place and date, signature and stamp of certifying authority | 12. Declaration by the exporter
The undersigned hereby declares that the above details and statements are correct, that all the goods were produced in ....
　　　　　　　　　　（country）
and that they comply with the origin requirements specified for those goods in the Generalized System of Preferences for goods exported to

....
Place and date, signature and stamp of authorized signatory |

（九）根据信用证、合同和补充资料的内容缮制提单和产地证

合同

SHANGHAI IMPORT & EXPORT TRADE CORPORATION.
1321 ZHONGSHAN ROAD SHANGHAI, CHINA
SALES CONTRACT

TEL：021-65788877   S/C NO：HX050264

FAX：021-65788876   DATE：JAN. 1, 2005

TO：TKAMLA CORPORATION

　　　6-7KAWARA MACH

　　　OSAKA, JAPAN

DEAR SIRS,

WE HEREBY CONFIRM HAVING SOLD TO YOU THE FOLLOWING
GOODS ON TERMS AND CONDITIONS AS SPECIFIED BELOW：

MARKS &NO	DESCRIPTION	QUANTITY	UNIT PRICE	AMOUNT
T. C	COTTON SHIRT		CIF OSAKA	
OSAKA	ART NO. H666	500 PCS	USD 5. 50	USD 2 750. 00
C/NO. 1-250	ART NO. HX88	500 PCS	USD 4. 50	USD 2 250. 00
	ART NO. HE21	500 PCS	USD 4. 80	USD 2 400. 00
	ART NO. HA56	500 PCS	USD 5. 20	USD 2 600. 00
	ART NO. HH46	500 PCS	USD 5. 00	USD 2 500. 00
TOTAL：		2 500 PCS		USD 12 500. 00

PAGKING：IN 250 CARTONS

SHIPMENT FROM SHANGHAI TO OSAKA

PARTIAL SHIPMENT NOT ALLOWED AND TRANSHIPMENT ALLOWED

PAYMENT：L/C AT SIGHT

INSURANCE POLICY FOR 110 PCT OF THE INVOICE VALUE COVER-
ING ALL RISKS AND WAR RISK AS PER PICC.

TIME OF SHIPMENT：LATEST DATE OF SHIPMENT MAR. 16，2005

THE BUYERS   THE SELLERS

TKAMLA CORPORATION   SHANGHAI IMPORT & EXPORT TRADE CORP.

　　高田四郎　　　　　　　　　　　　　　　丁莉

信用证

FROM：FUJI BANK LTD

1013，SAKULA COTOLIKINGZA MACHI

TOKYO, JAPAN

TO：BANK OF CHINA SHANGHAI BRANCH

SEQUENCE OF TOTAL   ＊27： 1/1

FORM OF DOC, CREDIT   ＊40A：REVOCABLE

DOC. CREDIT NUMBER   ＊20： 33416852

DATE OF ISSUE   ＊31C：JAN. 12，2005

APPLICABLE RULES   40E： UCP LATEST VERSION

DATE AND PLACE OF EX- ＊31D：DATE MAR 17TH，2005 IN CHINA
PIRY

APPLICANT   ＊50： TKAMLA CORPORATION
                              6-7, KAWARA MACH
                              OSAKA，JAPAN

BENEFICIARY   ＊59：SHANGHAI IMPORT & EXPORT
                              TRADE CORPORATION
                              1321 ZHONGSHAN ROAD SHANG-
                              HAI, CHINA

AMOUNT   ＊32B：CURRENCY USD AMOUNT
                              12 500. 00

AVAILABLE WITH…BY…   ＊41A：ANY BANK IN CHINA BY NEGO-
                              TIATION

DRAFTS AT...   * 42C: DRAFTS AT SIGHT
                                               FOR FULL INVOICE COST

DRAWEE   * 42A: FUJI BANK LTD
PARTIAL SHIPMENTS   * 43P: NOT ALLOWED
TRANSHIPMENT   * 43T: NOT ALLOWED
LOADING ON BOARD   * 44A: SHANGHAI, CHINA
FOR TRANSPORTATION   * 44B: OSAKA, JAPAN
TO...
LATEST DATE OF SHIP-   * 44C: MAR. 16, 2005
MENT

DESCRIPTION OF GOODS   * 45A: COTTON SHIRT
                                               ART NO. H666 500 PCS USD 5.50/PC
                                               ART NO. HX88 500 PCS USD 4.50/PC
                                               ART NO. HE21 500 PCS USD 4.80/PC
                                               ART NO. HA56 500 PCS USD 5.20/PC
                                               ART NO. HH46 500 PCS USD 5.00/PC
                                               CIF OSAKA

DOCUMENTS REQUIRED   * 46A:
                                      + COMMERCIAL INVOICE IN DUPLICATE
                                      + PACKING LIST IN DUPLICATE
                                      + 3/3 CLEAN ON BOARD OCEAN BILLS
                                        OF LADING MADE OUT TO ORDER
                                        AND BLANK ENDORSED MARKED
                                        "FREIGHT PREPAID" NOTIFY AP-
                                        PLICANT
                                      + CERTIFICATE OF ORIGIN
PERIOD FOR PRESENTA-   * 48: DOCUMENTS MUST BE PRESENTED
TION   WITHIN 15 DAYS AFTER THE
                                             DATE OF SHIPMENT BUT WITHIN
                                             THE VALIDITY
                                             OF THE CREDIT

CONFIRMATION   *49：WITHOUT
INSTRUCTION

CHARGES   *71B：ALL BANKING CHARGES OUT-
                                SIDE JAPAN ARE FOR ACCOUNT
                                OF THE BENEFICIARY

SENDER TO RECEIVER INFO *72：THIS CREDIT IS SUBJECT TO THE
                                UNIFORM CUSTOMS AND PRAC-
                                TICE FOR DOCUMETARY CREDIT，
                                2007 REVI-SION ICC PUBLCATION
                                NO. 600

补充资料：
(1) INVOICE NO. XH056671
(2) INVOICE DATE：FEB. 01，2005
(3) PACKING：
    PACKED IN 250 CARTONS OF 10 PCS
    PACKED IN TWO 20'CONTAINER（NO. TEXU2263999；TEXU2264000）
    G. W.：20.5 KGS/CTN，N. W. 20 KGS/CTN
    MESUREMENT：0.456 M^3
(4) VESSEL：NANGXING V. 068
(5) B/L NO. COCS0511861
(6) B/L DATE：FEB. 26，2005，(SHIPPED ON BORAD)
(7) 承运人接收货物地在石家庄(SHI JIA ZHUANG)
    铁路运输(BY RAIL)至上海装船
(8) 承运人货运代理：WAN HAI SHIPPING CO. (LI MING)
(9) H. S. Code：551.000
(10) Certificate No. QDCD118
    出证日期：2005 年 2 月 20 日

提单

Shipper	B/L No.cocs0511861
.Consignee	中远集装箱运输有限公司 **COSCO CONTAINER LINES**
Notify Party	
	Port-to-Port or Combined Transport

Pre-carriage by	Place of Receipt	**BILL OF LADING**
Ocean Vessel Voy. No.	.Port of Loading	
.Port of Discharge	Place of Delivery	

Particulars Furnished by

Marks & Nos. Container / Seal No.	No. of Containers or Packages	Description of Goods (If Dangerous Goods, See Clause 20)	Gross Weight Kgs	Measurement
		Description of Contents for Shipper's Use Only (Not Part of This B/L Contract)		

.Total Number Of Containers and/or Packages (In Words)

Freight & Charge	Revenue Tons	Rate	Per	Prepaid	Collect

Ex.Rate:	Prepaid at	Payable at	Place and date of Issue
	Total Prepaid	No. of Original B(s)/L	Signed for the Carrier: COSCO CONTAINER LINES WAN HAI SHIPPING CO. *LI MING* AS AGENT FOR THE CARRIER

产地证

ORIGINAL

1. Exporter	Certificate No.
2. Consignee	**CERTIFICATE OF ORIGIN** **OF** **THE PEOPLE'S REPUBLIC OF CHINA**
3. Means of transport and route	5. For certifying authority use only
4. Country/region of destination	
6. Marks and numbers and date of packages 7. Number and kind of packages; description of goods 8. H. S. Code 9. Quantity 10. Number and date of Invoices	

11. Declaration by the exporter
    The undersigned hereby declares that the above details and statements are correct, that all the goods were produced in China and that they comply with the Rules of Origin of the People's Republic of China.
	12. Certification
	    It is hereby certified that the declaration by the exporter is correct.

Place and date, signature and stamp of authorized signatory	Place and date, signature and stamp of certifying authority

（十）根据信用证以及相关资料缮制提单

FM/THE CITY BANK LIMITED, BANGABANDHU AVENUE BRANCH, DHAKA, BANGLADESH.

TO/THE BANK OF CHINA, SHAANXI BRANCH, 233 JIE FANG ROAD,

XIAN, CHINA.

TEST NO. 2-334 DATED 2008, MARCH, 3 FOR USD 40 800

BENEFICIARY/M/S. CHINA SHAANXI TEXTILE IMPORT N EXPORT CORPORATION.

NO. A-113 BEIKOU JIANGUO ROAD, XIAN, CHINA.

OPENER/M/S. F. K. TRADING, 26, AHSANULLAH ROAD, NAWAB BARI, DHAKA-1100, BANGLADESH.

AT THE REQUEST OF OPENER WE HEREBY ESTABLISH OUR IR-REVOCABLE DOCUMENTARY

CREDIT NO. 01080099-C DATED 2008, MARCH, 03 IN BENEFICIARY'S FAVOUR FOR THE AMOUNT OF USD 40 800/=（US DOLLAR FORTY THOUSAND EIGHT HUNDRED） ONLY. CFR CHITTAGONG BY STEAMER.

AVAILABLE BY BENEFICIARY'S DRAFT ON OPENING BANK AT SIGHT FOR FULL INVOICE

VALUE OF SHIPMENT PURPORING TO BE/-RAW MATERIALS FOR TEXTILE INDUSTRIES

"TAYEN PAGDOA" BRAND 60 000 LBS GREY TR40S/1YARN ON COVES, POLYESTER 65, VISOSE 35. ART NO. TR40S/1. AT RATE OF USD 0. 68 PER LB. AS PER INDENT NO. DI/34 DT 2008-23-02 OF M/S. DIAMOND INTERNATIONAL, 21, RAJAR, DEWRI, DHAKA-1100 BANGLADESH AND SUPPLIER'S SALES CONFRACT NO. 08STRY040 AC-COMPANIED BY THE FOLLOWING DOCUMENTS/-

D) BENEFICIARY'S SIGNED INVOICES IN EIGHT COPIES CERTIFY-ING MERCHANDISE TO BE OF CHINESE ORIGIN. INVOICE EX-CEEDING THIS CREDIT AMOUNT NOT ACCEPTABLE.

E) FULL SET OF CLEAN SHIPPED ON BOARD BILL OF LADING DRAWN OR ENDORSED TO THE ORDER OF CITY BANK LIMITED SHOWING FREIGHT PREPAID N MARKED NOTIFY OPENERS AND US GIVING FULL NAME N ADDRESS.

F) A COPY OF SHIPMENT ADVICE TO BE SENT TO INSURANCE COMPANY. INSURANCE COVERED BY OPENNERS. ALL SHIP-MENTS UNDER THIS CREDIT MUST BE ADVISED BY BENEFICIA-RY IMMEDIATELY AFTER SHIPMENT DIRECT TO M/S. BAN-

GLADESH GENERAL INSURANCE CO. LTD. 42, DILKUSHA C/A DHAKA, DHAKA-1100, BANGLAESHAND TO THE OPENNER REFERRING TO COVER NOTE NO. BGIC/DA/MC-446/03/08 DT 03-03-08 GIVING FULL DETAILS OF SHIPMENT.

SHIPMENT FROM ANY CHINESE PORT TO CHITTAGONG PORT BY STEAMER.

BILL OF LADING MUST BE DATED NOT BEFORE THE DATE OF THIS CREDIT AND NOT LATER THAN 2008, MAY, 25. BILL OF EXCHANGE MUST BE NEGOTIATED WITHIN 15 DAYS FROM THE DATE OF SHIPMENT BUT NOT LATER THAN 2008, JUNE, 3. OTHER TERMS AND CONDITIONS/-

11. GOODS DESTINED FOR BANGLADESH BY ISRAELI FLAG CARRIER NOT ALLOWED.

12. H. S. CODE 5509. 11 SHOULD BE APPEARED IN ALL INVOICES.

13. DRAFT MUST BE MARKED "DRAWN UNDER THE CITI BANK LIMITED, BANGABANDHU AVENUE BRANCH, DHAKA CREDIT NO. 01080099-C".

14. BENEFICIARY MUST CERTIFY ON THE INVOICES THAT THE SPECIFICATION, QUANTITY, QUALITY, PACKING, MARKING, RATES AND ALL OTHER DETAILS OF THE GOODS SHIPPED ARE STRICTLY IN ACCORDANCE WITH THE TERMS AND CONDITIONS OF THE CREDIT AS STATED ABOVE QUOTING INDENTORS NAME, ADDRESS, INDENT NUMBER N DATE, INDENTING REGISTRATION NO. B2611 AND BANGLADESH BANK'S PERMISSION NO. EC/DA/INV/729/261/79.

15. PACKING LIST IN SIX COPIES REQUIRED.

16. PACKING/IN CARTONS 100LBS PER CARTON SEA WORTHY EXPORT STANDARD.

17. ALL FOREIGN BANK CHARGES OUTSIDE BANGLADESH ARE ON BENEFICIARY'S ACCOUNT INCLUDING REIMEURSMENT CHARGE.

18. ONE SET OF NON—NEGOTIABLE SHIPPING DOCUMENTS TO BE SENT TO THE OPENER DIRECT THROUGH AIR MAIL.

19. THE GOODS MUST BE SHIPPED IN A CONTAINER VESSEL (2×40'FCL).

20. COMBINED LAND AND SEA BILL OF LADING ACCEPTABLE.

WE HEREBY AGREE WITH DRAWERS ENDORSERS AND BONAFIDE HOLDERS OF THE DRAFTS DRAWN UNDER AND IN COMPLIANCE WITH THE TERMS OF THIS CREDIT THAT THE SAME SHALL BE DULY HONOUED ON DUE PRESENTATION. THIS CREDIT IS SUBJECT TO UNIFORM CUSTOMS AND PRACTICE FOR DOCUMENTARY CREDITS (2007 REVISION) INTERNATIONAL CHAMBER OF COMMERCE PUBLICATION NO. 600. INSTRCTIONS FOR THE NEGOTIATING BANK/-

4. AMOUNT OF DRFT NEGOTIATED SHOULD BE ENDORSED ON THE REVERSE SIDE OF THE CREDIT.

5. SIX COPIES OF INVOICES TO BE SENT WITH ORIGINAL SET OF DOCUMENTS BY FIRST CLASS AIRMAIL AND TWO COPIES OF INVOICES WITH DUOLICATED BY SUBSEQUENT' AIR MAIL.

6. IN REIMBURSEMENT PLEASE DRAW AS PER OUR ARRANGEMENT ON OUR HEAD OFFICE ACCOUNT NUMBER 00708354 WITH AMERICAN EXPRESS BANK LIMITED NEWYORK AGENCY, P. O. BOX 830, NEWYORK, N. Y. 10008 U. S. A. ACCOMPANIED BY A CERTIFICATE OF COMPLIANCE OF CREDIT TERMS.

PLEASE ACKNOWLEDGE RECEIPT BY AIRMAIL.

RGSCITYAVENUE, DHAKA.

制单资料：

货号	毛重	净重	尺码
TR40S/1	49. 5 KGS/CTN	45. 4 KGS/CTN	0. 1833 M^3/CTN

发票号： SHAANXITEX08/03/A

发票日期： 2008, APRIL, 15

合同日期： 2008, FEBURARY, 25.

装运港： XIANGGANG CHINA

船名, 航次： XINXING V. 788

提单号： COS0816787

提单日期： 2008, APRIL, 25

装运标志： F. K.

CHITTAGONG

NOS1-UP

集装箱箱号及封号：COSU7854436/1234567

BILL OF LADING	
1) SHIPPER	10) B/L NO. CARRIER：
2) CONSIGNEE	**C O S C O** 中国远洋运输(集团)总公司 **CHINA OCEAN SHIPPING (GROUP) CO.**
3) NOTIFY PARTY	
4) PLACE OF RECEIPT　5) OCEAN VESSEL	
6) VOYAGE NO.　7) PORT OF LOADING	ORIGINAL
8) PORT OF DISCHARGE　9) PLACE OF DELIVERY	Combined Transport BILL OF LADING

11) MARKS　12) NOS. & KINDS OF PKGS.　13) DESCRIPTION OF GOODS 14) G. W. (kg)　15) MEAS(m³)					
16)					
17) TOTAL NUMBER OF CONTAINERS 　OR PACKAGES (IN WORDS)					
FREIGHT & CHARGES	REVENUE TONS	RATE	PER	PREPAID	COLLECT
PREPAID AT	PAYABLE AT	21) PLACE AND DATE OFISSUE			
TOTAL PREPAID	18) NUMBER OF ORIG- INAL B(S)L				
LOADING OF BOARD THE VESSEL		22)			
19) DATE	20) BY				

（十一）根据所提供资料和信用证有关信息缮制单据产地证

1. 有关资料如下：G. W. ：14 077. 00 KGS, N. W. ：12 584. 00 KGS, MEAS：35 CBM, 包装件数：3 298 卷（ROLLS），所有货物被装进 2×20′ CONTAINER，CON- TAINER NO.：TSTU157504，TSTU156417，提单号码：SHANK00710，船名： DANUBHUM/S009。货物 H. S. 编码：5407. 1010。其他条件未知的，按照惯

例自行定义。

2. 信用证如下所示：

209 07BKCHCNBJ95B BANK OF CHINA, SUZHOU BRANCH

409 07BKCHHKHH×××BANK OF CHINA, HONGKONG BRANCH

MT700 O BKCHCNBJ95B××××

21：SEQUENCE OF TOTAL：1/1

40A：FORM OF DOC：IRREVOCABLE

20：DOCUMENT CREDIT NO：HK1112234

31C：DATE OF ISSUE：080315

40E：UCP LATEST VERSION

31D：DATE AND PLACE OF EXPIRY：080431，IN CHINA

50：APPLICANT：YOU DA TRADE CO.,LTD.,

101 QUEENS ROAD CENTRAL,HONGKONG

TEL：852-28566666

59：BENEFICIARY：KUNSHAN HUACHENG WEAVING AND DYE-ING CO.,LTD

HUANGLONG RD., LIUJIA ZHEN, SUZHOU, JIANGSU, CHINA

TEL：86-520-7671386

32B：AMOUNT：USD 33 680. 00

41A：AVAILABLE WITH…BY…

ANY BANK BY NEGOTIATION

42C：DRAFTS AT：SIGHT

42A：DRAWEE：OURSELVES

43P：PARTIAL SHIPMENT：NOT ALLOWED

43T：TRANSSHIPMENT：NOT ALLOWED

44A：LOADING ON BOARD/DISPATCH/TAKING IN CHARGE AT/ FROM：SHANGHAI

44B：FOR TRANSPORTATION TO：HONGKONG

44C：LATEST DATE：080415

45A：DESCRIPTION OF GOODS AND/OR SERVICES

DESCRIPTION   QUANTITY   UNIT PRICE   AMOUNT

100 PCT NYLON FABRICS 100 000 YARDS USD 0. 3368/YD USD 33 680. 00

DETAILS AS PER CONTRACT NO. 99WS061 DATED MAR. 10，2003

PRICE TERM：CIF HONGKONG

SHIPPING MARK：

YOU DA

HONGKONG

R/NO.：1-up

46A：DOCUMENTS REQUIRED：

1. SINGED COMMERCIAL INVOICE IN 5 FOLDS INDICATING L/C NO. AND CONTRACT NO. 99WS061.

2. FULL SET (3/3) OF CLEAN ON BOARD MARINE BILLS OF LADING MADE OUT TO ORDER AND BLANK ENDORSED, MARKED "FREIGHT PREPAID" AND NOTIFY THE APPLICANT.

3. INSURANCE POLICY OR CERTIFICATE IN 2 FOLDS FOR 110 PCT OF THE INVOICE VALUE INDICATING CLAIM PAYABLE AT DESTINATION COVERING OCEAN TRANSPORTATION ALL RISKS AND WAR RISKS AS PER ICC CLAUSES.

4. PACKING LIST IN 3 FOLDS INDICATING GROSS AND NET WEIGHT OF EACH PACKAGE.

5. CERTIFICATE OF ORIGIN IN 3 FOLDS.

6. BENEFICIARY'S LETTER MUST BE FAX TO THE APPLICANT ADVISING GOODS NAME, CONTRACT NO., L/C NO., NAME OF VESSEL, AND DATE OF SHIPMENT.

47A：ADDITIONAL CONDITIONS：

＋ ON DECK SHIPMENT IS NOT ALLOWED.

＋ ALL DOCUMENT MUST BE MANUALLY SIGNED.

48：PERIOD FOR PRESENTATION：

DOCUMENTS MUST BE PRESENTED WITHIN 15 DAYS AFTER THE DATE OF SHIPMENT BUT WITHIN THE VALIDITY OF THE CREDIT.

：49：CONFIRMATION：WITHOUT

：72：SPECIAL INSTRUCTIONS：

ALL DOCUMENT MUST BE SEND TO THE ISSUING BANK IN ONE LOT THROUGH THE NEGOTIATING BANK BY REGISTERED AIRMAIL.

UPON RECEIPT THE DOCUMENTS CONFORMITY WITH THE L/C'S CONDITIONS, WE SHALL PAY AS PER YOUR INSTRUCTIONS.

1. Exporter	Certificate No. 040377950
	CERTIFICATE OF ORIGIN
2. Consignee	**OF**
	THE PEOPLE'S REPUBLIC OF CHINA

3. Means of transport and route	5. For certifying authority use only
4. Country/region of destination	

6. Marks and numbers	7. Number and kind of packages; description of goods	8. H. S. code	9. Quantity	10. Number and date of invoices

11. Declaration by the exporter	12. Certification
The undersigned hereby declares that the above details and statements are correct; that all the goods were produced in china and that they comply with the rules of origin of the people's republic of china.	It is hereby certified that the declaration by the exporter is correct.
Place and date, signature and stamp of certifying authority	Place and date, signature and stamp of certifying authority

（十二）根据信用证审核相关单据，找出不符点

RECEIVED FROM: CHOHKRSE

                 CHO HUNG BANK

                 SEOUL

100 757 SEOUL

KOREA, REPUBLIC OF

DESTINATION: ABOCCNBJA110

AGRICULTURAL BANK OF CHINA, THE

HANGZHOU(ZHEJIANG BRANCH)

MESSAGE TYPE: 700 ISSUE OF A DOCUMENTARY CREDIT

DATE: 7 MAR, 2006

27: SEQUENCE OF TOTAL

1/1

40A: FORM OF DOCUMENTARY CREDIT

IRREVOCABLE

20: DOCUMENTARY CREDIT NUMBER

CUZ4825017

31C: DATE OF ISSUE

060605

40E: UCP LATEST VERSION

31D: DATE OF EXPIRY, PLACE OF EXPIRY

060715 AT NEGOTIATION BANK

50: APPLICANT

GENOSA TRADING CO., LTD

NO. 251 KING ROAD

SEOUL, KOREA.

59: BENEFICIARY

ZHEJIANG HUAXING CHEMICAL TRADING CO., LTD

NO. 32 DINGHAI ROAD

HANGZHOU CHINA

32B: AMOUNT

USD 35 500

41A: AVAILABLE WITH…BY…

ANY BANK

BY NEGOTIATION

42C: DRAFTS AT…

AT SIGHT

42A: DRAWEE

CHO HUNG BANK, SEOUL

43P: PARTIAL SHIPMENTS
PROHIBITED

43T: TRANSSHIPMENT
PROHIBITED

44A: LOADING ON BOARD/DISPATCH/TAKING IN CHARGE
SHANGHAI, CHINA

44B: FOR TRANSPORTATION TO…
PUSAN, KOREA

44C: LATEST DATE OF SHIPMENT
060631

45A: DESCRIPTION OF GOODS AND/OR SERVICES
HCFC BLEND-A FIRE EXTINGUISHER 5 000 KGS
CIF PUSAN PORT AT USD 7. 10/KG
AS PER S/C NO. HX0159 AND P/I NO. HX060418

46A: DOCUMENTS REQUIRED
+ SIGNED COMMERCIAL INVOICE IN QUINTUPLICATE
+ FULL SET OF CLEAN ON BOARD OCEAN BILLS OF LADING
MADE OUT TO THE ORDER OF CHO HUNG BANK MARKED
"FREIGHT PREPAID" AND NOTIFY ACCOUNTEE
+ INSURANCE POLICY, CERTIFICAT OR DECLARATION IN
DUPLICATE, ENDORSED IN BLANK FOR 110PCT OF THE
INVOICE COST. INSURANCE POLICY, CERTIFICATE OR
DECLARATION MUST EXPRESSLY STIPULATE THAT
CLAIMS ARE PAYABLE IN THE CURRENCY OF THE CRED-
IT AND MUST ALSO INDICATE A CLAIMS SETTLING
AGENT IN KOREA INSURANCE MUST INCLUDE: I. C. C.
ALL RISK
+ PACKING LIST IN DUPLICATE

47A: ADDITIONAL CONDITIONS
UPON RECEIPT OF YOUR DOCUMENTS IN GOOD ORDER, WE
WILL REMIT THE PROCEEDS TO THE ACCOUNT DESIGNATED
BY NEGOTIATION.

71B: CHARGE

ALL BANKING COMMISSIONS AND CHARGES, INCLUDING RE-IMBURSEMENT CHARGES AND POSTAGE OUTSIDE KOREA ARE FOR ACCOUNT OF BENEFICIARY.

48： PERIOD FOR PRESENTATION

DOCUMENTS MUST BE PRESENTED WITHIN 15 DAYS AFTER THE DATE OF SHIPMENT

49： CONFIRMATION INSTRUCTIONS

WITHOUT

78： INSTRNS TO PAYING/ACCEPTING/NEGOTIATING BANK

THE AMOUNT OF EACH NEGOTIATION(DRAFT)MUST BE EN-DORSED ON THE REVERSE OF THIS CREDIT BY THE NEGOTI-ATING BANK. ALL DOCUMENTS MUST BE FORWARDED DI-RECTLY BY COURIER SERVICE IN ONE LOT TO CHO HUNG BANK H. O., (INT'L OPERATIONS DIVISION) 14, 1-KA, NAMDAMUNRO, CHUNG-KU, SEOUL 100-757, KOREA.

IF DOCUMENTS ARE PRESENTED WITH DISRCREPANCIES, A DISCREPANCY FEE OF USD 60. 00 OR EQUIVALENT SHOULD(WILL) BE DEDUCTED FROM THE REIMBURSMENT CLAIM (THE PRO-CEEDS). THIS FEE SHOULD BE CHARGED TO THE BENEFICIA-RY.

57A： "ADVISE THROUGH"BANK

PLS ADVISE THRU YR HANGZHOU BRANCH

INT'L DEPT.

72： SENDER TO RECEIVER INFORMATION

THIS CREDIT IS SUBJECT TO I. C. C. PUBLIC NO. 600(2007 REVI-SION)

相关资料：

合同号码：HX0159　　船名：TIAN SHUN V. 329N　　INV NO.：LT5067

装船日期：2006. 6. 20　　集装箱号码：WSDU2066730/129531　1×20′

包装：5 CYLINDERS　　总毛重：7 654 KGS　　总净重：5 000 KGS

总体积：7. 0 CBM

海运提单 3/3

Shipper ZHEJIANG HUAXING CHEMICAL TRADING CO.,LTD NO. 32 DINGHAI ROAD HANGZHOU CHINA	B/L NO. SHYZ042234

Consignee CHO HUNG BANK	DE-WELL CONTAINER SHIPPING CO. LTD.

Notify Party GENOSA TRADING CO.,LTD NO. 251 KING ROAD SEOUL,KOREA	For delivery of goods please apply to: ABC Worldwide Logistics 5th Floor, No. 66, 999 RST Street, Limassol, Cyprus.

Pre-carriage by	Place of Receipt	Port of loading SHANGHAI,CHINA	Freight Payable at
Ocean Vessel	**Port of Discharge** PUSAN,KOREA	**Port of delivery** PUSAN,KOREA	**No. of Original B/L** 3/THREE

Marks and numbers	Number and kind of packages	Description of goods	Gross weight	Measurement
N/M	5 CYLINDERS SAY FIVE CYLINDERS ONLY.	HCFC BLEND-A FIRE EXTINGUISHER WSDU2066730/129531 1×20′ FCL CY-CY SHIPPED ON BOARD	5 000 KGS	7. 00 CBM

Feight And Charge FREIGHT TO COLLECT	SHIPPER'S LOAD COURT & SEAL

Freight details, charges, etc.	RECEIVED apparent good order and condition except as otherwise noted the total number of containers or other packages or units enumerated below (*) for transportation from the place of receipt to the place of delivery subject to the terms hereof. 　(Terms of Bill of Lading continued on the back here of)

Laden on board the date　　20 JUN, 2006 BY DE-WELL CONTAINER SHIPPING CO. LTD.	Place and date of issue　SHANGHAI　21 JUN, 2006 Signed by DE-WELL CONTAINER SHIPPING CO. LTD.
As carrier　程铁衣	As Carrier　　　　　　　　　　　　程铁衣

保险单 2/2

中国平安保险股份有限公司
PING AN INSURANCE COMPANY OF CHINA，LTD.
货 物 运 输 保 险 单
CARGO TRANPORTATION INSURANCE POLICY

被保险人：ZHEJIANG HUAXING CHEMICAL TRADING CO.，LTD
Insured

中国平安保险股份有限公司根据被保险人的要求及其所交付约定的保险费，按照本保险单背面所载条款与下列特别条款，承保下述货物运输保险，特立本保险单。

This Policy of Insurance witnesses that PING AN INSURANCE COMPANY OF CHINA，LTD.，at the request of the Insured and in consideration of the agreed premium paid by the Insured，undertakes to insure the undermentioned goods in transportation subject to the conditions of Policy as per the clauses printed overleaf and other special clauses attached hereon.

保单号 Policy No.　　1206007787	赔款偿付地点 Claim Payable at PUSAN
发票号 Invoice No. LT5067	
运输工具 per conveyance S. S.　　TIAN SHUN V. 329N	查勘代理人 Survey By：
起运日期 Slg. on or abt.　　AS PER B/L NO. SHYZ042234	INCOK LOSS & AVERAGE ADJUSTERS NO. 81 CHUNGANG-DONG 4GA
自　　　　　　　　　　至 From SHANGHAI，CHINA To PUSAN，KOREA	CHUNG-KU，PUSAN，KOREA TEL：＋82(51)4698377 FAX：＋82(51)4698366

保险金额
Amount Insured USD 35 500
　　　　　　　　　(SAY US DOLLARS THIRTY FIVE THOUSAND FIVE HUNDRED ONLY)

保险货物项目、标记、数量及包装： Description，Marks，Quantity & Packing of Goods： 5 CYLINDERS OF HCFC BLEND-A FIRE EXTINGUISHER	承保条件 Conditions： COVERING MARINE ALL RISKS AS PER INSTITUTE CARGO CLAUSES（A）DATED1/1/1982
签单日期 Date：JUN. 16，2006	

　　　　　　　　　　　　　　　For and on behalf of
　　　　　　　　　　　　　　PING AN INSURANCE COMPANY OF CHINA，LTD.
　　　　　　　　　　　　　　　　　　　李明骏

（十三）根据提供的信用证的内容和相关资料制作信用证指定的议付提单和产地证

发票号码：SH25586

发票日期：2008-4-20

单位毛重：15.40 KGS/CTN

单位净重：13.00 KGS/CTN

单位尺码：60×40×50 CM/CTN

船名：DAFENG V3336

提单号码：SH223545

提单日期：2008-5-15

信用证

ISSUE OF A DOCUMENTARY CREDIT	
ISSUING BANK	THE ROYAL BANK. TOKYO
SEQUENCE OF TOTAL	1/1
FORM OF DOC. CREDIT	IRREVOCABLE
DOC. CREDIT NUMBER	JST-AB12
DATE OF ISSUE	20080405
EXPIRY	DATE 20080615 PLACE CHINA
APPLICANT	WAV GENEAL RUA DE, 98-OSAKA, JAPAN
BENEFICIARY	DESUN TRADING CO., LTD
	224 JINLIN ROAD, NANJING, CHINA
AMOUNT	CURRENCY USD AMOUNT 10 300.00
AVAILABLE WITH/BY	BANK OF CHINA BY NEGOTIATION
DRAFTS AT...	DRAFTS AT SIGHT FOR FULL INVOICE VALUE
DRAWEE	THE ROYAL BANK, TOKYO
PARTIAL SHIPMTS	ALLOWED
TRANSSHIPMENT	ALLOWED
LOADING IN CHARGE	NANJING PORT
FOR TRANSPIRT TO...	OSAKA, JAPAN
LATEST SHIPMENT	20080531
GOODS DESCRIPT.	

续表

	LADIES GARMENTS AS PER S/C NO. SHL553
	PACKING: 10 PCS/CTN
	ART NO.　　　　　　　QUANTITY　　UNIT PRICE
	STYLE NO. ROCOCO　　1 000 PCS　　USD 5. 50
	STYLE NO. ROMANTICO　1 000 PCS　USD 4. 80
	CIF OSAKA
	SHIPPING MARK: ITOCHU/OSAKA/NO. 1-200
DOCS REQUIRED	* 3/3 SET OF ORIGINAL CLEAN ON BOARD OCEAN BILLS OF LADING MADE OUT TO ORDER OF SHIPPER AND BLANK ENDORSED AND MARKED "FREIGHT PREPAID" NOTIFY APPLICANT(WITH FULL NAME AND ADDRESS). * ORIGINAL SIGNED COMMERCIAL INVOICE IN 5 FOLD. * INSURANCE POLICY OR CERTIFICATE IN 2 FOLD ENDORSED IN BLANK, FOR 110 PCT OF THE INVOICE VALUE COVERING THE INSTITUTE CARGO CLAUSES (A), THE INSTITUTE WAR CLAUSES, INSURANCE CLAIMS TO BE PAYABLE IN JAPAN IN THE CURRENCY OF THE DRAFTS. * CERTIFICATE OF ORIGIN GSP FORM A IN 1 ORIGINAL AND 1 COPY. * PACKING LIST IN 5 FOLD.
ADDITIONAL COND	1. T. T. REIMBURSEMENT IS PROHIBITED 2. THE GOODS TO BE PACKED IN EXPIRT STRONG COLORED CARTONS. 3. SHIPPING MARKS: ITOCHU 　　　　　　　　　OSAKA 　　　　　　　　　NO. 1-200
DETAILS OF CHARGES	ALL BANKING CHARGES OUTSIDE JAPAN INCLUDING REIMBURSEMENT COMMISSION, ARE FOR ACCOUNT OF BENEFICIARY.
PRESENTATION PERIOD	DOCUMENTS TO BE PRESENTED WITHIN 10 DAYS AFTER THE DATE OF SHIPMENT, BUT WITHIN THE VALIDITY OF THE CREDIT.
CONFIRMATION	WITHOUT
INSTRUCTIONS	THE NEGOTIATION BANK MUST FORWARD THE DRAFTS AND ALL DOCUMENTS BY REGISTERED AIRMAIL DIRECT TO U. S. IN TWO CONSECUTIVE LOTS, UPON RECEIPT OF THE DRAFTS AND DOCUMENTS IN ORDER, WE WILL REMIT THE PROCEEDS AS INSTRUCTED BY THE NEGOTIATING BANK.

1. Shipper Insert Name, Address and Phone		B/L No.

中远集装箱运输有限公司
COSCO CONTAINER LINES

2. Consignee Insert Name, Address and Phone

3. Notify Party Insert Name, Address and Phone
(It is agreed that no responsibility shall attach to the Carrier or his agents for failure to notify)

TLX, 33057 COSCO CN
FAX, +86(021) 6545 8984

ORIGINAL

Port-to-Port or Combined Transport

BILL OF LADING

RECEIVED in external apparent good order and condition except as other-Wise noted. The total number of packages or unites stuffed in the container, the description of the goods and the weights shown in this Bill of Lading are furnished by the Merchants, and which the carrier has no reasonable means of checking and is not a part of this Bill of Lading contract. The carrier has Issued the number of Bills of Lading stated below, all of this tenor and date. One of the original Bills of Lading must be surrendered and endorsed or signed against the delivery of the shipment and whereupon any other original Bills of Lading shall be void. The Merchants agree to be bound by the terms and conditions of this Bill of Lading as if each had personally signed this Bill of Lading.

SEE clause 4 on the back of this Bill of Lading (Terms continued on the back hereof, please read carefully).

* Applicable Only When Document Used as a Combined Transport Bill of Lading.

4. Combined Transport * Pre-carriage by	5. Combined Transport * Place of Receipt
6. Ocean Vessel Voy. No.	7. Port of Loading
8. Port of Discharge	9. Combined Transport * Place of Delivery

Marks & Nos. Container/Seal No.	No. of Containers or Packages	Description of Goods (If Dangerous Goods, See Clause 20)	Gross Weight Kgs	Measurement
		Description of Contents for Shipper's Use Only (Not part of This B/L Contract)		

10. Total Number of containers and/or packages (in words)
Subject to Clause 7
Limitation

11. Freight & Charges Declared Value Charge	Revenue Tons	Rate	Per	Prepaid	Collect

Ex. Rate:	Prepaid at	Payable at	Place and date of issue
	Total Prepaid	No. of Original B(s)/L	Signed for the Carrier, COSCO CONTAINER LINES

ORIGINAL

1. Goods consigned from (Exporter's business name, address, country)	Reference No. GENERALIZED SYSTEM OF PREFERENCES
2. Goods consigned to (Consignee's name, address, country)	Issued in .... 　　　　　　(country) 　　　　　See Notes overleaf
3. Means of transport and route (as far as known)	4. For official use

5. Item number	6. Marks and numbers of packages	7. Number and kind of packages; description of goods	8. Origin criterion (see Notes overleaf)	9. Gross weight or other quantity	10. Number and date of invoices

11. Certification It is hereby certified, on the basis of control carried out, that the declaration by the exporter is correct.	12. Declaration by the exporter The undersigned hereby declares that the above details and statements are correct, that all the goods were produced in .... 　　　　　　　　　(country) and that they comply with the origin requirements specified for those goods in the Generalized System of Preferences for goods exported to ....

（十四）根据托收指示书和合同制作全套清关单证和全套结算单证

INSTRUCTION FOR COLLECTION

TO: HUBEI TWIN HORSE TRADE CO.,LTD.　　DATE: MAY. 10, 2000

CONTRACT NO. HW003 AMOUNT: USD 60 000. 00
DRAWEE: HANWA CO. LTD. KYOTO,JAPAN.
COLLECTING BANK: ASASHI BANK. CHIYODAKU 1-CHOME.
　　　　　　　　　KYOTO, JAPAN.
TRADE TERMS: CIF YOKOHAMA. PAYMNET: D/P AT SIGHT
DOCUMENTS REQUIRED:

1. SIGNED COMMERCIAL INVOICE IN 3 COPIES;
2. DETAILED PACKING LIST IN 3 COPIES;
3. GSP FORM A ···················· 1/1
4. CERTIFICATES OF QUANTITY,QUALITY & WEIGHT ··············· 1/1
5. INSURANCE POLICY IN 2 COPIES.
6. COPY OF SHIPPING ADVICE.
7. CERTIFICATE PROVING THAT ONE SET OF NON-NEGOTIABLE SHIPPING DOCU. HAS BEEN SENT DIRECTLY TO HANWA CO. LTD 24 HOURS AFTER THE SHIPMENT IS EFFECTED.
8. FULL SET CLEAN ON BOARD B/L MADE OUT TO ORDER AND BLANK ENDORSED MARKED FREIGHT PREPAID AND NOTIFY HANWA

　CO.,LTD H. K. TEL/FAX: 008522678556

THIS COLLECTING INSTRUCTION IS SUBJECT TO URC 522.

合同

售 货 合 同
Sales Contract

编　号(No.)：HW003
日　期(Date)：MAY 1, 2006
签约地点(Signed at)：KYOTO

HUBEI TWIN HORSE
卖方(Seller)：TRADE CO.,LTD.　　买方(Buyer)：HANWA CO., LTD.
地址(Address)：1ST XUDONG ROAD,　　地址(Address)：＿＿＿＿＿＿＿＿
WUCHANG,430077,WUHAN,CHINA。＿＿＿＿＿＿＿＿＿＿＿＿＿＿
电话(Tel)：＿＿＿＿＿＿＿＿　　电话(Tel)：＿＿＿＿＿＿＿＿
传真(Fax)：＿＿＿＿＿＿＿＿　　传真(Fax)：＿＿＿＿＿＿＿＿
电子邮箱(E-mail)：＿＿＿＿＿　　电子邮箱(E-mail)：＿＿＿＿＿

买卖双方经协商同意按下列条款成交：

The undersigned Seller and Buyer have agreed to close the following transactions according to the terms and conditions set forth as below：

1. 货物名称(Name)　　　规格(Specifications)　　质量(Quality)

FASTENERS	JIS FASTENERS	BLACK TREATED
2000 M.		

2. 数量(Quantity)：100 MT
3. 单价及价格条款 (Unit Price and Terms of Delivery)：CIF YOKOHAMA,
JAPAN.

〔除非另有规定，"FOB"、"CFR"和"CIF"均应依照国际商会制定的《2000 年国际贸易术语解释通则》(INCOTERMS 2000)办理。〕

The terms FOB,CFR,or CIF shall be subject to the International Rules for the Interpretation of Trade Terms (INCOTERMS 2000) provided by International Chamber of Commerce (ICC) unless otherwise stipulated herein.)

4. 总价 (Total Amount)：USD 600 000.00
5. 允许溢短装(More or Less)：　5 ＿＿＿%。
6. 装运期限(Time of Shipment)：END OF MAY, 2006.
7. 付款条件(Terms of Payment)：D/P AT SIGHT.

8. 包装（Packing）：IN WOODEN CASE OF 25 KG EACH. /GROSS WT 26 KG.

9. 保险（Insurance）：

按发票金额的 _____ %投保_____险，由_____负责投保。CoveringALL Risks for _____110% of Invoice Value to be effected by the SELLERS.

10. 品质/数量异议（Quality/Quantity discrepancy）：

如买方提出索赔，凡属品质异议须于货到目的口岸之日起 30 天内提出，凡属数量异议须于货到目的口岸之日起 15 天内提出，对所装货物所提任何异议于保险公司、轮船公司、其他有关运输机构或邮递机构所负责者，卖方不负任何责任。

In case of quality discrepancy, claim should be filed by the Buyer within 30 days after the arrival of the goods at port of destination, while for quantity discrepancy, claim should be filed by the Buyer within 15 days after the arrival of the goods at port of destination. It is understood that the Seller shall not be liable for any discrepancy of the goods shipped due to causes for which the Insurance Company, Shipping Company, other Transportation Organization/or Post Office are liable.

11. 由于发生人力不可抗拒的原因，致使本合约不能履行，部分或全部商品延误交货，卖方概不负责。本合同所指的不可抗力系指不可干预、不能避免且不能克服的客观情况。

The Seller shall not be held responsible for failure or delay in delivery of the entire lot or a portion of the goods under this Sales Contract in consequence of any Force Majeure incidents which might occur. Force Majeure as referred to in this contract means unforeseeable, unavoidable and insurmountable objective conditions.

12. 仲裁（Arbitration）：

凡因本合同引起的或与本合同有关的任何争议，如果协商不能解决，应提交中国国际经济贸易仲裁委员会华南分会，按照申请仲裁时该会实施的仲裁规则进行仲裁。仲裁裁决是终局的，对双方均有约束力。

Any dispute arising from or in connection with the Sales Contract shall be settled through friendly negotiation. In case no settlement can be reached, the dispute shall then be submitted to China International Economic and Trade Arbitration Commission (CIETAC), South China Sub-Commission for arbitration in accordance with its rules in effect at the time of applying for arbitration. The arbitral award is final and binding upon both parties.

13. 通知（Notices）：

所有通知用＿＿＿＿文写成，并按照如下地址用传真/电子邮件/快件送达给各方。如果地址有变更，一方应在变更后＿＿＿＿日内书面通知另一方。

All notice shall be written in ＿＿＿＿ and served to both parties by fax/e-mail/courier according to the following addresses. If any changes of the addresses occur, one party shall inform the other party of the change of address within ＿＿＿＿ days after the change.

14. 本合同为中英文两种文本，两种文本具有同等效力。本合同一式＿＿＿＿份。自双方签字（盖章）之日起生效。

This Contract is executed in two counterparts each in Chinese and English, each of which shall be deemed equally authentic. This Contract is in ＿＿＿＿ copies effective since being signed/sealed by both parties.

The Seller：　　　　　　　　　　**The Buyer：**
卖方签字：马少华　　　　　　　　　买方签字：山下岛本

有关资料：

发票号码：INV. HW003　　　　　　发票日期：2006 年 5 月 15 日
保险单号：04-2988956　　　　　　　提单号码：KGES5825691
提单日期：2006 年 5 月 20 日　　　　装运港：上海
船名：BUTTERFLY V. 089　　　　　集装箱号：SOCU6689721-5（5×20'）
装箱情况：100 吨/4 000 木箱
净重：25 KG/箱　　毛重：26 KG/箱　　总尺码：156 CUBIC METRE
封志号：CUSO600341-5　　　　　　出口日期：2006 年 5 月 20 日
申报日期：2006 年 5 月 19 日　　　　生产厂家：武汉汽车标准件有限公司
生产地：武汉市洪山区
产地证书号：HU-3748　　H. S. CODE 6201. 0922

SHIPPING NOTE

经营单位 （托运人）				公司编号		

提/ 运单 项目	发货人（SHIPPER）					
	收货人（CONSIGNEE）					
	通知人（NOTIFY ）					

运费（√） FREIGHT	预付（　　）或到付 （　　）PREPAID/COLLECT		提单 份数		寄送 地址	

起运港	目的港		可否转船		可否分批	

标记 唛码	包装 件数	中英文货名 DESCRIPTION	毛重 KG	尺码 CUB	成交条件（总价）	

声明事项		结算方式	
		代办项目	
		预配运输 工具名称	
		提/运单号	
		签名：	

中华人民共和国出口货物报关单

预录入编号　　　　　　　　海关编号

出口口岸	备案号		出口日期	申报日期
经营单位	运输方式		运输工具	提运单号
发货单位	贸易方式		征免性质	结汇方式
许可证号	抵运国（地区）		指运港	境内货源地
批准文号	成交方式	运费	保费	杂费
合同协议号	件数	包装种类	毛重	净重
集装箱号	随附单据			生产厂家

标记唛码及备注

项号	商品编号	商品名称、规格型号	数量及单位	最终目的国（地区）	单价	总价	币制	征免

税费征收情况

录入员　　录入单位	兹申明以上申报无讹并承担法律责任	海关审单批注及放行日期（签章）	
		审单	审价
报关员　　申报单位（签章） 　查验　　　放行		征税	统计
邮编　　电话　　填制日期			

出口收汇核销单 存根	出口收汇核销单	出口收汇核销单
（鄂）编号：315808954	（鄂）编号：315808954	（鄂）编号：315808954

出口单位：
单位代码：
出口币种汇总
收回方式
预计收款日期
报关日期
备注
此单报关有效期截止到

出口单位盖章

出口单位：
单位代码：

类别	币种金额	日期	盖章

海关签注栏

外汇局签注栏

出口单位盖章

出口单位：
单位代码：

货物名称	数量	币种总价

报关单编号：

外汇局签注栏：

年　月　日（盖章）

中华人民共和国出入境检验检疫
出境货物通关单

编号：3100034568729

1. 发货人			5. 标记及号码	
2. 收货人				
3. 合同/信用证号		4. 输往国家或地区		
6. 运输工具名称及号码		7. 发货日期	8. 集装箱规格及数量	
9. 货物名称及规格	10. H.S.编码	11. 申报总值	12. 数、重量、包装数量及种类	

13. 证明
上述货物业经检验检疫，请海关予以放行
本通关单有效期至　　年　月　日
签字

14. 备注

中华人民共和国出入境检验检疫
ENTRY-EXIT INSPECTION AND QUARNTINE
OF THE PEOPLE'S REPUBLIC OF CHINA

熏蒸/消毒证明书   编号 NO. 005988

FUMIGATION/DISINFECTION CERTIFICATE

发货人名称及地址
Name and address of consignor _____

收货人名称及地址
Name and address of consignee _____

品名   产地
Description of goods _____   Place of origin _____

报验数量   标记及号码
Quantity declared _____   Mark & no.

启运地
Place of dispatch _____

到达口岸
Port of destination _____

运输工具
Name of conveyance _____

ORIGINAL

1. Goods consigned from (Exporter's business name, address, country)	Reference No. GENERALIZED SYSTEM OF PREFERENCES Issued in .... (country) See Notes overleaf
2. Goods consigned to (Consignee's name, address, country)	

3. Means of transport and route (as far as known)	4. For official use

5. Item number	6. Marks and numbers of packages	7. Number and kind of packages; description of goods	8. Origin criterion (see Notes overleaf)	9. Gross weight or other quantity	10. Number and date of invoices

11. Certification It is hereby certified, on the basis of control carried out, that the declaration by the exporter is correct. Place and date, signature and stamp of certifying authority	12. Declaration by the exporter The undersigned hereby declares that the above details and statements are correct, that all the goods were produced in .... (country) and that they comply with the origin requirements specified for those goods in the Generalized System of Preferences for goods exported to .... Place and date, signature and stamp of authorized signatory

INSURANCE POLICY

PICC 中国人民保险公司湖北分公司

The People's Insurance Company of China，Shanghai Branch

货 物 运 输 保 险 单

CARGO TRANSPORTATION INSURANCE POLICY

发票号(INVOICE NO.)　　　　　　　　保单号次.

合同号(CONTRACT NO.)　　　　　　　POLICY NO

信用证号(L/C NO.)

被保险人：

Insured：

中国人民保险公司(以下简称本公司)根据被保险人的要求,由被保险人向本公司缴付约定的保险费,按照本保险单承保险别和背面所列条款与下列特别条款承保下述货物运输保险,特立本保险单。

THIS POLICY OF INSURANCE WITNESSES THAT THE PEOPLE'S INSURANCE COMPANY OF CHINA(HEREINAFTER CALLED THE COM-PANY) AT THE RQUEST OF THE INSURED AND IN CONSIDERATION OF THE AGREED PREMIUM PAID TO THE COMPANY BY THE INSURED.

UNDERTAKES TO INSURE THE UNDERMENTIONED GOODS IN TRAN-SPORTA-TION SUBJECT TO THE CONDITIONS OF THIS POLICY AS PER THE CLAUSES PRINTED OVERLEAF AND OTHER SPECIAL CLAUSES ATTA-CHED HEREIN.

标记 MARKS & NOS.	包装、数量及保险货物项目 PACKING,QUANTITY,DESCRIPTION OF GOODS	保险金额 AMOUNT INSURED

总保险金额

TOTAL AMOUNT INSURED：

保费　　　　　　启运日期

PREMIUM　　　　　DATEOFCOMMENCEMENT

装载运输工具　　　　　　　　　　自

PERCONVEYANCE：　　　　　　　FROM

经　　　　　　　　　　至

VIA　　　　　　　　　TO

承保险别：

CONDITIONS：

所保货物,如发生保险单项下可能引起索赔的损失或损坏,应立即通知本公司下属代理人查勘。如有索赔应向本公司提交保险单正本(共　　份正本)及有关文件。如一份正本已用于索赔,其余正本自动失效。

IN THE EVENT OF LOSS OR DAMAGE WHICH MAY RESULT IN A CLAIM UNDER THIS POLICY. IMMEDIATE NOTICE MUST BE GIVEN TO THE COMPANY'S A-GENT AS MENTIONED HEREUNDER. IN THE EVENT OF CALIMS IF ANY, ONE OF THE ORIGINAL POLICY WHICH HAS BEEN ISSUED IN　　ORIGINALS TO-GETHER WITH THE RELEVANT DOCUMENTS SHAL BE SURRENDERED TO THE COMNPANY. IF ONE OF THE ORIGINAL POLICY HAS BEEN ACCOMPLISHED, THE OTHERS SHALL BE VOID.

中国人民保险公司湖北分公司

The People's Insurance Company of China

Shanghai Branch

赔款偿付地点

CLAIM PAYABLE AT

出单日期

ISSUING DATE

Authorised Signature

地址：中国湖北武汉　　　　　　　　　　　电话：027 77889900

ADDRESS：WUHAN,HUBEI,CHINA.　　　　TEL：027 77889900

（十五）按照下列信用证制作海运提单、原产地证书

SEQUENCE OF TOTAL	27：	1/1
FORM OF DOCUMENTARY CREDIT	40A：	IRREVOCABLE TRANSFER-ABLE
DOCUMENTARY CREDIT NUMBER	20：	LCF776FV333324
DATE OF ISSUE	31C：	081119
APPLICABLE RULES	40E：	UCP LATEST VERSION
DATE AND PLACE OF EXPIRY	31D：	090115 IN OUR COUNTER
APPLICANT	50：	HOPE TRADING EST.,

P. O. BOX 0000 DAMMAN 31491，SAUDI ARABIA

BENEFICIARY	59：	JINHAI IMP. & EXP. GROUP CORP.
		NO. 233，TAIPING ROAD, QINGDAO, CHINA
CURRENCY CODE，AMOUNT	32B：	USD 46 693. 68
PERCENTAGE CREDIT AMT TOL.	39A：	05/05
AVAILABLE WITH…BY…	41A：	ADVISING BANK BY NEGOTIATION
DRAFTS AT…	42C：	AT SIGHT FOR 100 PCT OF THE INVOICE VALUE
DRAWEE	42A：	DRAWN ON US
PARTIAL SHIPMENT	43P：	NOT ALLOWED
TRANSHIPMENT	43T：	ALLOWED
LOADING/DISPATCH/TAKING IN CHARGE/FM	44A：	ANY CHINESE PORT
FOR TRANSPORTATION TO…	44B：	DAMMAN PORT，SAUDI ARABIA
LATEST DATE OF SHIPMENT	44C：	081231
DESCRIPTION OF GOODS/SERVICES	45A：	

FROZEN CHICKEN BREAST MEAT，A GRADE,

PACKING：1 KG X 12/CARTON,

UNIT PRICE：USD 1 945. 57/MT

QUANTITY：24 MTS

AS PER S/C NO. 564676 DATED NOV. 10，2008

DOCUMENTS REQUIRED：　　　　　46A：

6. MANUALLY SIGNED COMMERCIAL INVOICE IN 5 COPIES.

7. 2/3 CLEAN ON BOARD OCEAN BILLS OF LADING INCLUDING 2 NON-NEGOTIABLE COPIES MADE OUT TO ORDER AND BLANK ENDORSED, MARKED "FREIGHT PREPAID" NOTIFYING APPLICANT.

8. PACKING LIST IN 3 COPIES

9. A COPY OF BENEFICIARY'S SHIPPING ADVICE ADVISING NAME OF VESSEL，DATE OF SAILING，B/L NUMBER，INVOICE VALUE AND QUANTITY OF GOODS 48 HOURS AFTER SHIPMENT EFFECT，REQUIRED.

10. CERTIFICATE OF ORIGIN FORM A ISSUED BY CIQ

ADDITIONAL CONTITIONS　　　　　47A：

3. A DISCREPANCY FEE OF USD 54. 00 OR ITS EQUIVALLENT WILL BE DEDUCTED FROM THE PROCEEDS IF DOCUMENTS ARE PRESENTED WITH DISCREPANCY(IES).

4. 1/3 ORIGINAL B/L MUST SENT TO THE APPLICANT DIRECTLY AFTER SHIPPMENT.

CHARGES　　71B：ALL BANKING CHARGES OUTSIDE THE OPENING BANK ARE FOR BENEFICIARY'S ACCOUNT

CONFIRMATION INSTRUCTION　　　　49：WITHOUT

ADVISE THROUGH BANK　　　　　57A：BANK OF CHINA，SHANDONG BR.

REIMBURSEMENT BANK　　　　　53A：CITIBANK，N. A.，NEW YORK

INSTR. TO PAY/ACPT/NGG BANK　78：

3. ALL DOCUMENTS ARE TO BE FORWARDED TO BANQUE SAUDI FRANSI, EASTERN REGIONAL MANAGEMENT, KING ABDUL AZIZ STREET, P. O. BOX 397, ALKHOBAR 31952，SAUDI ARABIA, TEL(03) 8871111, FAX(03) 8821855, SWIFT：BSERSARIAEST. IN TWO CONSECUTIVE LOTS.

4. UPON RECEIPT OF ALL DOCUEMNTS IN ORDER, WE WILL DULY HONOUR/ACCEPT THE DRAFTS AND EFFECT THE

PAYMENT AS INSTRUCTED AT MATURITY.

SENDER TO RECEIVER INFO 　　　72：

　　THIS LC IS SUBJECT TO UCP 2007 ICC PUB. NO. 600.

制单明细表：

数量：24MTS, N. W.：12 KG/CTN, G. W.：14 KG/CTN, MEASUREMENT：48 * 30 * 41CM。

提单签发：CHINA OCEAN SHIPPING （GROUP） CO. 王彬，B/L DATE：2008 年 12 月 20 日，在青岛装上 PRETTY V. 116 船，集装箱号：FBZU876551/FBZU876552/FBZU876553/FBZU876554/FBZU876555/FBZU876556/FBZU876557/FBZU876558，发票号：JH57868，B/L 号：BL3888，产地证号码：8767544，H. S. CODE：5674. 8374

ORIGINAL

1. Exporter (full name and address)	Certificate No.
	CERTIFICATE OF ORIGIN
2. Consignee (full name, address, country)	**OF**
	THE PEOPLE'S REPUBLIC OF CHINA
3. Means of transport and route	5. For certifying authority use only
4. Destination port	

6. Marks and Numbers of packages	7. Description of goods; number and kind of packages	8. H. S. Code	9. Quantity or weight	10. Number and date of invoices

11. Declaration by the exporter	12. Certification
Place and date. signature and stamp of certifying authority	Place and date. signature and stamp of certifying authority

BILL OF LADING

1) SHIPPER	7) B/L NO.
2) CONSIGNEE	**CARRIER**　C O S C O
3) NOTIFY PARTY	中国远洋运输(集团)总公司

PRE-CARRIAGE	PLACE OF RECEIPT	CHINA OCEAN SHIPPING (GROUP) CO.
4) VESSEL VOY NO.	5) PORT OF LOADING	Combined Transport BILL OF LADING
6) PORT OF DISCHARGE	PLACE OF DELIVERY	

8) MARKS　9) NO. OF PACKAGE　10) DESCRIPTION OF GOODS　11) G. W. (kg)
12) MEAS(m³)

13) TOTAL NUMBER OF CONTAINERS
　　OR PACKAGES(IN WORDS)

FREIGHT & CHARGES	REVENUE TONS	RATE	PER	PREPAID	COLLECT
PREPAID AT	14)PAYABLE AT		15) PLACE AND DATE OF ISSUE		
TOTAL PREPAID	16)NUMBER OF ORIGINAL B(S)L		17) SIGNATURE		

（十六）单选题

1. 非一批一证的出口许可证有效期从发证之日起（　　）有效。
　　A. 一年　　　　B. 三个月　　　　C. 半年　　　　D. 30 天
2. 发生不可抗力事件后,我国通常由（　）出具证明文件。
　　A. 出口商　　　　　　　　B. 中国国际贸易促进委员会
　　C. 出入境商品检验检疫机构　　D. 出口商的上级主管部门
3. 根据海关规定,进口货物的进口日期是指（　　）。
　　A. 载货的运输工具申报的日期　　B. 向海关申报货物进口的日期

C. 申报货物准予提取的日期　　　D. 申报货物进入海关监管仓库的日期

4. 进口商在货物到达目的港后,应在运输工具进境之日起(　　)天内向海关申报。

A. 3 天　　　　B. 7 天　　　　C. 14 天　　　　D. 15 天

5. 出口报关单上对于"200 美元"的运费单价填报正确的是(　　)。

A. 110/200/1　　　　　　　　B. 303/200/3

C. 502/200/2　　　　　　　　D. 502/200/3

6. 出口 500 吨散装小麦,分装在同一条船上的 3 个货舱内。以下关于出口报关单上的"件数"和"包装种类"两个项目的正确填报应是(　　)。

A. 件数:500/包装种类:吨　　B. 件数:1/包装种类:船

C. 件数:3/包装种类:船舱　　D. 件数:1/包装种类:散装

7. 出口货物报关单上的批准文号一栏,应填写(　　)。

A. 合同编号　　　　　　　　B. 出口许可证编号

C. 信用证编号　　　　　　　D. 出口收汇核销单编号

8. 根据我国出入境检验检疫机构的规定,出境货物最迟应于报关或装运前(　　)办理检验检疫。

A. 7 天　　　　B. 14 天　　　　C. 21 天　　　　D. 30 天

9. 根据海关法规定,进口货物的报关期限为自运输工具申报进境之日起 14 天之内,进口货物的收货人或其代理人逾期申报的,由海关征收滞报金,滞报金的日征收额为进口货物完税价的(　　)。

A. 5%　　　　B. 0.5%　　　　C. 5‰　　　　D. 0.5‰

10. 北京某贸易公司一批进口货从美国波士顿装运经香港中转,运抵天津塘沽港报关进境。该公司填写进口报关时,应在装运港一栏中填报(　　)。

A. 香港　　　B. 天津　　　　C. 波士顿　　　　D. 塘沽港

11. 出口业务中,国外客户往往要出口方提供"GSP"产地证。在我国这种证书的签发机构是(　　)。

A. 商会　　　B. 行业公会　　　C. 贸促会　　　　D. 出入境检验检疫局

12. 出口企业于报关后(　　)天内,将出口报关单、出口收汇核销单、存根和发票交外汇管理局备案。

A. 180　　　　B. 90　　　　C. 100　　　　D. 120

13. 进口货物许可证的有效期一般是(　　)。

A. 6 个月　　B. 一年　　　　C. 3 个月　　　　D. 9 个月

14. 出口货物许可证的有效期一般是(　　)。

A. 6 个月　　B. 一年　　　　C. 3 个月　　　　D. 9 个月

15. 对列入《出入境检验检疫机构实施检验检疫的进出境商品目录》范围的进出口货物，海关凭（　　）验放。
   A.《报关单》　　　　　　　　　　B.《报检单》
   C.《出入境货物通关单》　　　　　D.《放行单》

16. 从中国出口货物到新西兰，提供下列哪种文件新西兰的进口商能享受到最优惠的关税待遇？
   A. 一般原产地证　　　　　　　　B. FORM 59A 格式的产地证
   C. FORM A 产证　　　　　　　　D. 中国-新西兰自由贸易区优惠原产地证

17. 纸质托运单十联单中，（　　）被电子托运单保留使用，此联在海关放行后，被海关盖上"放行章"，据此联，船公司才可以将货物装船。
   A. 第二联　船代留底　　　　　　B. 第五联　装货单
   C. 第七联　场站收据　　　　　　D. 第九联　配舱回单

18. 下列各种单证中，不属于申报人办理出口报关必备单证的是（　　）。
   A. 发票和箱单　　　　　　　　　B. 出口收汇核销单
   C. 装货单　　　　　　　　　　　D. 原产地证

19. DDD 包装厂从国外进口钢板，拟制成桶后在国内销售，进口许可证申请表贸易方式一栏中，该项进口货物的贸易性质应填（　　）。
   A. 进料加工　　　　　　　　　　B. 来料加工
   C. 一般贸易　　　　　　　　　　D. 许可证贸易

20. 以下应该填报在进口报关单"备注栏"（　　）。
   A.《机电产品进口登记表》编号　　B. 入境货物通关单
   C. 进口货物报关单　　　　　　　D. 进口许可证

21. 出口货物的发货人或其代理人除海关特准以外，应当根据规定在货物运抵海关监管区后，（　　）向海关申报。
   A. 装货前 24 小时内　　　　　　B. 装货的 24 小时以前
   C. 货运抵口岸 24 小时内　　　　D. 承载的运输工具起运的 24 小时前

22. 我国某进口商从新加坡购进澳大利亚生产的羊毛，用船运至香港再转车进入深圳。进口报关单上起运国和运抵国两栏正确的填报为（　　）。
   A. 澳大利亚/中国　　　　　　　B. 新加坡/中国
   C. 香港/中国　　　　　　　　　D. 新加坡/香港

（十七）多选题

1. 产地证明书通常用于不需要提交以下何种单据的国家和地区（　　）。
   A. 证实发票　　B. 领事发票　　C. 海关发票　　D. 联合发票

2. 下列何种单证属于报关基本单证(　　)。

    A. 商业发票　　　　　　　　B. 贸易合同

    C. 装箱单　　　　　　　　　D. 通关单

    E. 信用证

3. 根据我国《商检法》的规定,地方检验检疫局在进出口商品检验方面的基本任务是(　　)。

    A. 对所有商品进行检验检疫　　B. 实施法定检验

    C. 办理鉴定业务　　　　　　　D. 对进出口商品工作实施监督管理

4. 以下不可在进口报关单的"标记码及备注"栏填报的内容是(　　)。

    A.《进口加工登记手册》

    B.《进口付汇核销单》的编号

    C.《"NO MARK"》字样

    D.《进口商品检验检疫通关单》一份和编号

5. 以下关于报关单正确填报的选项为(　　)。

    A. 裸装货物在件数栏内填报为 1

    B. 毛重栏的计量单位为千克,货物不足 1 千克的填报为 1

    C. 净重栏的计量单位为千克,也可以填报计量单位为磅(折算为磅填报)

    D. 数量和单位栏的计量单位按照成交数量和单位填报,不必按照海关计量单位填

(十八) 判断题

(　　) 1. 列入《出入境检验检疫机构实施检验检疫的进出境商品目录》内的进口商品,海关在办理通关手续时需加验检验检疫机构签发的《入境货物通关单》。

(　　) 2. 普惠制原产地证明书 FORM A 一般使用英文填制,应进口商的要求,也可使用法文,除此之外,证明书不得使用其他文种。

(　　) 3. 买方对货物的检验权是强制性的,是接受货物的前提条件。

(　　) 4. 一般原产地证书可由检验检疫局或贸促会或商务部出具,不能由出口商或生产厂家出具。

(　　) 5. 普惠制产地证书上的原产地标准应按货物原料进口成分的实际情况分别按比例填制,"W"表示出口加拿大货物中的进口成分在 40% 以上。

(　　) 6. 海关发票是一种重要的结汇单证,它是由出口地海关制作,提供给出口方的。

(　　) 7. 出境货物最迟在出口报关或装运前 10 天报验,个别检验检疫周期长

的货物,应留有相应的检验检疫时间。

(　　)8. 出口报关单上备案号一栏,应填写加工贸易手册号、海关征免税证明或其他海关备案审批文件的编号。

(　　)9. 出口收汇核销单由国家外汇管理局统一印制,通常为出口商办理完出口退税后,才能办理出口收汇的核销。

(　　)10. 对外已签合同的进口货物,在显示器许可证有效期限内尚未进口的,则可到原发证机构申请进口许可证的展期。

(　　)11. 法定检验的商品仅指列入《实施检验检疫的进出口商品目录》中的商品。

三、金融单据的制作与审核

（一）根据信用证以及相关资料缮制汇票

1. MT S700 Issue of a Documentary Credit

User Header   Service code   103：

                        Bank. Priority   113：

                        Message User Ref. 108：

                        Infor. Form C1   115：

30： Sequence of total

     1/1

40A： Form of Documentary Credit

     IRREVOCABLE

20： Documentary Credit Number

     00001LCC0603814

31C： Date of Issue

     12-APR-2007

40E： UCP LATEST VERSION

31D： Date and Place of Expiry

     21-JUN-2007 IN GUANGZHOU

51A： Applicant Bank

     BNP PARIBAS

     ZI DE LA PILATERIE

     59442 WASQUEHAL FRANCE

50： Applicant

     DIRAMODE

     3 RUE DU DUREMONT

     BP 21,59531 NEUVILLE EN FERRAIN FRANCE

59： Beneficiary

     GUANGDONG FENG QING TRADING CO.

     NO. 31 ZHONG SHAN ROAD GUANGZHOU. CHINA

32B： Currency Code，Amount

     USD 80 000. 00

39A：Percentage Credit Amount Tolerance

05/05

41A：Available With…By…

ANY BANK BY NEGOTIATION

42C：Draft at…

SIGHT

42A：Drawee

BNP PARIBAS

ZI DE LA PILATERIE

59442 WASQUEHAL FRANCE

43P：Partial Shipment

NOT ALLOWED

43T：Transshipment

NOT ALLOWED

44A：Loading on Board/Dispatch/Taking in Charge at/from…

GUANG ZHOU PORT

44B：For Transportation to…

DUNKIRK FRANCE

44C：Latest Date of Shipment

30-MAY-2007

45A：Description of Goods and/or Services

ORDER NO. 113851：LADIES DRESS

10 000 PCS AT USD 8. 00 CIF DUNKIRK INCLUDING 3% COMMIS-
SION

46A：Documents Required

+　COMMERCIAL INVOICE IN 4 FOLDS DULY SIGNED AND STAMPED，
BEARING DOCUMENTARY CREDIT NUMBER.

+　PACKING LIST IN FIVE FOLD.

+　CERTIFICATE OF ORIGIN

+　3/3 ORIGINAL BILL OF LADING MADE OUT TO ORDER OF SHIP-
PER AND ENDORSED IN BLANK NOTIFY EXPEDITORS INTER-
NATIONAL-BAT L-ROUTE DES FAMARDS-59818 LESQUIN
FRANCE MARKED FREIGHT PREPAID.

+　INSURANCE POLICY/CERTIFICATE COVERING ALL RISKS AND

WAR RISK FOR 110% OF INVOICE VALUE INCLUDING W/W CLAUSE. CLAIMS AS PER CIC, IF ANY, PAYABLE AT PORT OF DESTINATION IN THE CURRENCY OF THE DRAFT.

+ SHIPPER MUST CABLE ADVISING BUYER SHIPMENT PARTICU-LARS IN BRIEF IMMEDIATELY AFTER SHIPMENT. COPY OF CA-BLE/FAX SHOULD BE PART OF NEGOTIATING DOCUMENTS.

+ ONE COPY OF SIGNED INVOICE AND ONE NON-NEGOTIABLE B/L TO BE SENT TO BUYER BY SPECIAL COURIER 5 DAYS BEFORE THE SHIPPING DATE. A CERTIFICATE OF THESE EFFECTS SHOULD BE PRESENTED TO THE NEGOTIATING BANK AS PART OF DOCUMENTS NEEDED.

47A: Additional Conditions

+ ALL DOCUMENTS MUST MENTIONING THIS L/C NO. AND S/C NO.

+ 3% COMMISSION SHOULD BE DEDUCTED FROM TOTAL AMOUNT OF THE COMMERCIAL INVOICE.

+ MORE OR LESS 5 PERCENT IN QUANTITY AND CREDIT AMOUNT ACCEPTABLE

+ A FEE OF USD 50.00 OR ITS EQUIVALENT WILL BE DEDUCTED FROM THE PROCEEDS OF EACH SET OF DISCREPANT DOCU-MENTS, WHICH REQUIRE OUR OBTAINING ACCEPTANCE FROM APPLICANT.

+ AN EXTRA COPY OF INVOICE AND TRANSPORT DOCUMENTS, IF ANY, FOR L/C ISSUING BANK'S FILE ARE REQUIRED.

71B: Charges
ALL BANKING CHARGES OUTSIDE OPENING BANK ARE FOR THE ACCOUNT OF BENEFICIARY.

48: Period of Presentation
DOCUMENTS TO BE PRESENTED WITHIN 21 DAYS AFTER SHIPMENT DATE BUT WITHIN THE VALIDITY OF THE CRED-IT.

49: Confirmation Instructions
WITHOUT

78: Instructions to the Paying/Accepting/Negotiating Bank

+ UPON RECEIPT OF DOCUMENTS CONFORMING TO THE TERMS

AND CONDITIONS OF THIS CREDIT，WE SHALL PAY THE PRO-
CEEDS. AS DESIGNATED.

+　NEGOTIATING BANK MUST FORWARD ALL DOCUMENTS TO US
IN ONE LOT BY COURIER SERVICE AT BENEFICIARY'S EXPENS-
ES.

+　EXCEPT AS OTHERWISE STATED OR MODIFIED，THIS CREDIT
IS SUBJECT TO THE *UCP 600*.

相关资料：
发票号码：07INC9988　　　　发票日期：MAY 5，2007
船名：　FUXING V. 196　　　起运港：　GUANGZHOU
提单日期：MAY 20，2007　　　提单号码：SIO5789666
包装情况：PACKED IN CARTONS OF 20PCS EACH，500 CARTONS TOTAL.
毛重：21 KGS/CARTON　净重：20 KGS/CARTON　体积：0.1 M³/CARTON
唛头：DIRAMODE　　　　H. S. 编码：6401.0058
　　　DUNKIRK
　　　C/NO. 1～500
合同号码：　SCGD2007001
原产地证日期：MAY. 17，2007
保险单日期：　MAY. 18，2007
议付行：中国银行广东分行　议付日期：2007 年 5 月 25 日

No.＿＿＿＿＿＿＿＿
Exchange for ＿＿＿＿＿＿＿＿＿＿＿＿，＿＿＿＿＿＿＿＿＿＿＿＿
　　　　　　At ＿＿＿＿＿＿＿＿sight of this **Second** of Exchange
(**First** of the same tenor and date unpaid)，pay to the Order of
＿＿＿＿＿＿＿＿＿＿＿＿＿＿＿＿＿＿＿＿＿＿＿＿＿＿＿ the sum of
＿＿＿＿＿＿＿＿＿＿＿＿＿＿＿＿＿＿＿＿＿＿＿＿＿＿＿＿＿＿＿

Drawn under ＿＿＿＿＿＿＿＿＿＿＿＿＿＿＿＿＿＿＿＿＿＿＿＿＿

＿＿＿＿＿＿＿＿＿＿＿＿＿＿＿＿＿＿＿＿＿＿＿＿＿＿＿＿＿＿＿
To ＿＿＿＿＿＿＿＿＿＿＿＿＿＿＿＿＿＿＿＿＿＿＿＿＿＿＿＿＿

2. FM/THE CITY BANK LIMITED, BANGABANDHU AVENUE BRANCH, DHAKA, BANGLADESH.

TO/THE BANK OF CHINA, SHAANXI BRANCH, 233 JIE FANG ROAD, XIAN, CHINA. TEST NO. 2-334 DATED 2008, MARCH, 3 FOR USD 40 800

BENEFICIARY/M/S. CHINA SHAANXI TEXTILE IMPORT N EXPORT CORPORATION.

NO. A-113 BEIKOU JIANGUO ROAD, XIAN, CHINA.

OPENER/M/S. F. K. TRADING, 26, AHSANULLAH ROAD, NAWAB BARI, DHAKA-1100, BANGLADESH.

AT THE REQUEST OF OPENER WE HEREBY ESTABLISH OUR IRREVOCABLE DOCUMENTARY

CREDIT NO. 01080099-C DATED 2008, MARCH, 03 IN BENEFICIARY'S FAVOUR FOR THE AMOUNT OF

USD40 800/= (US DOLLAR FORTY THOUSAND EIGHT HUNDRED) ONLY. CFR CHITTAGONG BY STEAMER.

AVAILABLE BY BENEFICIARY'S DRAFT ON OPENING BANK AT SIGHT FOR FULL INVOICE VALUE OF SHIPMENT PURPORING TO BE/-RAW MATERIALS FOR TEXTILE INDUSTRIES "TAYEN PAGDOA" BRAND 60 000 LBS GREY TR40S/1YARN ON COVES, POLYESTER 65, VISOSE 35.

ART NO. TR40S/1. AT RATE OF USD 0. 68 PER LB. AS PER INDENT NO. DI/34 DT 2008-23-02 OF M/S. DIAMOND INTERNATIONAL, 21, RAJAR, DEWRI, DHAKA-1100 BANGLADESH AND SUPPLIER'S SALES CONFRACT NO. 08STRY040 ACCOMPANIED BY THE FOLLOWING DOCUMENTS/-

G) BENEFICIARY'S SIGNED INVOICES IN EIGHT COPIES CERTIFYING MERCHANDISE TO BE OF CHINESE ORIGIN. INVOICE EXCEEDING THIS CREDIT AMOUNT NOT ACCEPTABLE.

H) FULL SET OF CLEAN SHIPPED ON BOARD BILL OF LADING DRAWN OR ENDORSED TO THE ORDER OF CITY BANK LIMITED SHOWING FREIGHT PREPAID N MARKED NOTIFY OPENERS AND US GIVING FULL NAME N ADDRESS.

l) A COPY OF SHIPMENT ADVICE TO BE SENT TO INSURANCE COM-
PANY. INSURANCE COVERED BY OPENNERS. ALL SHIPMENTS
UNDER THIS CREDIT MUST BE ADVISED BY BENEFICIARY
IMMEDIATELY AFTER SHIPMENT DIRECT TO M/S. BANGLADESH
GENERAL INSURANCE CO. LTD. 42, DILKUSHA C/A DHAKA, DHAKA-
1100, BANGLAESH AND TO THE OPENNER REFERRING TO COVER
NOTE NO. BGIC/DA/MC-446/03/08 DT 03-03-08 GIVING FULL DE-
TAILS OF SHIPMENT.

SHIPMENT FROM ANY CHINESE PORT TO CHITTAGONG PORT BY
STEAMER.

BILL OF LADING MUST BE DATED NOT BEFORE THE DATE OF THIS
CREDIT AND NOT LATER THAN 2008, MAY, 25. BILL OF EXCHANGE
MUST BE NEGOTIATED WITHIN 15 DAYS FROM THE DATE OF
SHIPMENT BUT NOT LATER THAN 2008, JUNE, 3.

OTHER TERMS AND CONDITIONS/-

21. GOODS DESTINED FOR BANGLADESH BY ISRAELI FLAG CARRI-
ER NOT ALLOWED.

22. H. S. CODE 5509. 11 SHOULD BE APPEARED IN ALL INVOICES.

23. DRAFT MUST BE MARKED "DRAWN UNDER THE CITI BANK
LIMITED, BANGABANDHU AVENUE BRANCH, DHAKA CREDIT
NO. 01080099-C".

24. BENEFICIARY MUST CERTIFY ON THE INVOICES THAT THE
SPECIFICATION, QUANTITY, QUALITY, PACKING, MARKING,
RATES AND ALL OTHER DETAILS OF THE GOODS SHIPPED
ARE STRICTLY IN ACCORDANCE WITH THE TERMS AND CON-
DITIONS OF THE CREDIT AS STATED ABOVE QUOTING INDEN-
TORS NAME, ADDRESS, INDENT NUMBER N DATE, INDENTING
REGISTRATION NO. B2611 AND BANGLADESH BANK'S PERMIS-
SION NO. EC/DA/INV/729/261/79.

25. PACKING LIST IN SIX COPIES REQUIRED.

26. PACKING/IN CARTONS 100LBS PER CARTON SEA WORTHY EX-
PORT STANDARD.

27. ALL FOREIGN BANK CHARGES OUTSIDE BANGLADESH ARE ON
BENEFICIARY'S ACCOUNT INCLUDING REIMEURSMENT CHARGE.

28. ONE SET OF NON—NEGOTIABLE SHIPPING DOCUMENTS TO BE SENT TO THE OPENER DIRECT THROUGH AIR MAIL.
29. THE GOODS MUST BE SHIPPED IN A CONTAINER VESSEL（2×40'FCL）.
30. COMBINED LAND AND SEA BILL OF LADING ACCEPTABLE.

WE HEREBY AGREE WITH DRAWERS ENDORSERS AND BONAFIDE HOLDERS OF THE DRAFTS DRAWN UNDER AND IN COMPLIANCE WITH THE TERMS OF THIS CREDIT THAT THE SAME SHALL BE DULY HONOUED ON DUE PRESENTATION. THIS CREDIT IS SUBJECT TO UNIFORM CUSTOMS AND PRACTICE FOR DOCUMENTARY CREDITS（2007 REVISION）INTERNATIONAL CHAMBER OF COMMERCE PUBLICATION NO. 600.

INSTRCTIONS FOR THE NEGOTIATING BANK/-

1. AMOUNT OF DRFT NEGOTIATED SHOULD BE ENDORSED ON THE REVERSE SIDE OF THE CREDIT.
2. SIX COPIES OF INVOICES TO BE SENT WITH ORIGINAL SET OF DOCUMENTS BY FIRST CLASS AIRMAIL AND TWO COPIES OF INVOICES WITH DUOLICATED BY SUBSEQUENT' AIR MAIL.
3. IN REIMBURSEMENT PLEASE DRAW AS PER OUR ARRANGEMENT ON OUR HEAD OFFICE ACCOUNT NUMBER 00708354 WITH AMERICAN EXPRESS BANK LIMITED NEWYORK AGENCY, P. O. BOX 830, NEWYORK, N. Y. 10008 U. S. A. ACCOMPANIED BY A CERTIFICATE OF COMPLIANCE OF CREDIT TERMS.

PLEASE ACKNOWLEDGE RECEIPT BY AIRMAIL.

制单资料：

货号	毛重	净重	尺码
TR40S/1	49.5 KGS/CTN	45.4 KGS/CTN	0.1833 M³/CTN

发票号： SHAANXITEX08/03/A
发票日期： 2008,APRIL,15
合同日期： 2008,FEBURARY,25.
装运港： XIANGGANG CHINA

Inv. No. ....

Exchange for ▓▓▓▓▓▓▓▓▓▓▓

At .... sight of this First of Exchange

(Second of the same tenor and date unpaid), pay to the Order of

_____ _____ the sum of

▓▓▓▓▓▓▓▓▓▓▓▓▓▓▓▓▓▓▓▓▓▓▓▓▓▓▓▓▓▓▓▓

Drawn under ....

....

To ....

....

（二）根据资料缮制汇票

ISSUING BANK: AUSTRALIA AND NEW ZEALAND BANKING GROUP LIMITED NORTH SHORE AREA 8 RAILWAY ST CHATSWO OD NSW2067

L/C NO. AND DATE: LC06067 NOV. 5, 2006

AMOUNT: USD 21 600. 00

APPLICANT: CHANG FENG INTERNATIONAL CO.

NORTH SHORE AREA 16 RAILWAY ST CHATSWO OD NEW2068

BENEFICIARY: NINGBO YITONG LEATHER CO., LTD.

WE OPEN A DOCUMENTARY CREDIT AVAILABLE BY NEGOTIA-TION AGAINST PRESENTATION OF THE DOCUMENTS DETAILED HEREIN AND OF BENEFICIARY'S DRAFTS IN DUPLICATE AT SIGHT DRAWN ON US.

THE DATE AND ADDRESS OF DRAFT: NOV. 25, 2006 NINGBO,CHINA

INVOICE NO.: BP0600636

No. ________

Exchange for ________ ________, ________

At ________ sight of this **Second** of Exchange (**First** of the same tenor and date unpaid), pay to the Order of ________ the sum of

____

Drawn under ________

____

To ________

（三）根据信用证缮制汇票

1. From：VOLKSBANK SCHORNDORF，HAMBURG，GERMANY

To：BANK OF CHINA，HEBEI BRANCH

Form of Doc. Credit	*40A：	IRREVOCABLE
Doc. Credit Number	*20：	08-4-1520
Date of Issue	31C：	080201
APPLICABLE RULES	40E：	UCP LATEST VERSION
Expiry	*31D：	DATE：080415 IN THE COUNTRY OF BENEFICIARY
Applicant	*50：	LUCKY VICTORY INTERNATIONAL STUTTGART STIR. 5, D-84618，SCHORNDORF，GERMANY
Beneficiary	*59：	HEBEI MACHINERY IMP. AND EXP. CORP（GROUP）720 DONGFENG ROAD, SHIJIAZHUANG，CHINA
Amount	*32B：	Currency USD Amount 57 600. 00
Pos. /Neg. Tol.（%）	39A：	5/5
Available with/by	*41A：	ANY BANK BY NEGOTIATION
Draft at…	42C：	DRAFTS AT 30 DAYS SIGHT

FOR FULL INVOICE VALUE

Drawee	42A：	VOLKSBANK SCHORNDORF HAMBURG，GERMANY
Partial Shipments	43P：	ALLOWED

Transshipment   43T：   ALLOWED
Loading in Charge   44A：   TIANJIN
For Transport to   44B：   HAMBURG
Latest Date of Ship.   44C：   080331
Descript. of Goods   45A：

STAINLESS STEEL SPADE HEAD,

ART. NO. S569, 4 800 PCS, USD 5. 60 PER PC.,

ART. NO. F671, 3 200 PCS, USD 9. 60 PER PC.,

AS PER S/C NO. 08HM256 DATED JAN. 01, 2008.

CIF HAMBURG

Documents required 46A：

+   SIGNED COMMERCIAL INVOICE IN TRIPLICATE.

+   FULL SET OF CLEAN ON BOARD OCEAN BILLS OF LADING
    MADE OUT TO ORDER OF SHIPPER, MARKED "FREIGHT PRE-
    PAID" AND NOTIFY APPLICANT.

+   GSP CERTIFICATE OF ORIGIN FORM A

+   PACKING LIST IN TRIPLICATE.

+   INSURANCE POLICY COVERING RISKS AS PER INSTITUTE CAR-
    GO CLAUSE（A）INCLUDING WAREHOUSE TO WAREHOUSE
    CLAUSE UP TO FINAL DESTINATION AT SCHORNDORF, FOR
    110 PCT OF THE CIF VALUE, MARKED PREMIUM PAID, SHOW-
    ING CLAIM PAYABLE IN GERMANY.

Additional Cond. 47A：

1. A HANDING FEE OF USD 80. 00 WILL BE DEDUCTED IF DIS-
   CREPANCY DOCUMENTS PRESENTED.

2. ALL DOCUMENTS MUST BE IN ENGLISH.

3. ALL DOCUMENTS INDICATING THIS L/C NUMBER.

Presentation Period 48：

DOCUMENTS TO BE PRESENTED WITHIN 15 DAYS AFTER THE
DATE OF SHIPMENT, BUT WITHIN THE VALIDITY OF THE CREDIT.

Details of Charges 71B：

ALL BANKING CHARGES AND EXPENSES OUTSIDE THE ISSU-
ING BANK ARE FOR BENEFICIARY'S ACCOUNT.

有关资料：

发票号码：08HM248

提单号码：CANEI29-30554　　　　　　提单日期：2008 年 03 月 20 日

船名：　　HUAFENG V. 872W　　　　装运港：　天津港

海运费：　USD 1 500.00

外包装尺码：（65CM×18CM×12CM）/CTN

ART NO	QUANTITY	PACKAGE	G. W.	N. W.
S569	4 800 PCS	10 PCS/CTN	7.60 KGS/CTN	7.20 KGS/CTN
F671	3 200 PCS	20 PCS/CTN	14 KGS/CTN	13 KGS/CTN

唛头：

LUCKY

08HM256

HAMBURG

NO. 1-UP

BILL OF EXCHAGE

NO.

Exchange for _____

AT _____ sight of this **FIRST** of Exchange（Second of Exchange being unpaid）

Pay to the order of _____ the sum of

_____

Drawn under _____

_____

_____

To _____

_____

_____

2.　　　　　　　　　LETTER OF CREDIT

BASIC HEADER F 01 BKCHCNBJA5×× 9828 707783

＋BANK OF NOVA SCOTIA, TORONTO, CANADA

:MT: 700 ············· ISSUE A DOCUMENTARY CREDIT ·············

FORM OF CREDIT　　　　　　40A：　IRREVOCABLE

DOC. CREDIT NUMBER　　　20：　078230CDI1117LC

DATE OF ISSUE   31C：   070118

APPLICABLE RULES   40E：   UCP LATEST VERSION

DATE AND PLACE OF EXPIRY   31D：   070310

APPLICANT   50：   WENSCO FOODS LTD.,
RUA DE GREENLAND STR-
EET,68-A 1260-297 WELL
D. COQUITLAM, B. C. CAN-
ADA

BENEFICIARY   59：   HUNAN CEREALS, OILS &
FOODSTUFFS IMPORT &
EXPORT CORPORATION
38 WUYI RD., CHANGSHA
CHINA

CURRENCY CODE AND AMOUNT   32B：   USD 10 830.00

AVAILABLE WITH…BY…   41A：   ANY BANK IN CHINA BY
NEGOCIATION

DRAFT AT   42C：   DRAFT AT 45 DAYS AFTER
B/L DATE FOR FUL IN-
VOICE VALUE

DRAWEE   42A：   DRAWN ON US AND THE
ADD：550 WEST GEORGIA
ST.,PO BOX 172 TORONTO,
CANADA

PARTIAL SHIPMENT   43P：   PROHIBIED

TRANSSHIPMENT   43T：   PERMITTIED

LODING/DISPATCH/TAKING/   44A：   MAIN CHINESE PORT
FROM

FOR TRANSPOTATION TO   44B：   VANCOUVER B. C.

LATEST DATE OF SHIPMENT   44C：   070301

DESCRIPTION OF GOODS/   45A：   "TROPIC ISLE CANNED MAN-
SERVICE   DARIN ORIANGES LS-WHOLE
SEGMENTS" AS PER P/I
NO. CF07018 CIF VANCOU-
VER B. C.

DOCS REQUIERD: 46A:
+   MANUALLY SIGNED COMMERCIAL INVOICE ONE ORINAL AND FOUR COPIES, CERTIFYING GOODS ARE OF CHINESE ORIGIN AND INDICATEING P/I NO.
+   FULL SET (3/3) OF CLEAN ON BOARD OCEAN BILLS OF LADING, MADE OUT TO ORDER OF SHIPPER, BLANK INDORSED NOTIFYING APPLICANT, STATING FREIGHT PREPAID OR COLLECT.
+   PACKING LIST IN TRIPLICATE
+   NEGOCIABLE INSURANCE POLICY/CERTIFICATE, BLANK INDORSED, COVERING GOODS FOR THE INVOICE VALUE PLUS 10% AGAINST THE RISKS OF ICC(A) AND ICC (CARGO).
+   SHIPPING ADVICE SHOULD SENT BY FAX TO APPLICANT INFORMING VESSEL'S NAME AND VOY. NO., GR. WT, MEAS, PACKING, TOTAL AMOUNT AND ETD.
+   G. S. P FORM A IN 1 ORIGINAL AND 2 COPIES, INDICATING ORIGIN CRITERION "W".

ADDITIONAL CONDITIONS: 47A:
+ A DESCREPANCY FEE OF U. S. D 50. 00 FOR BENEFICIARY'S ACCOUNT
+ ONE COMPELE SET OF DOCS TO BE SENT TO US BY COURIER IN ONE LOT.
+ ALL DOCS MUST NOT INDICATED L/C NO. EXCEPT INVOICE &. DRAFT.

CHARGES   71B: ALL BANKING CHARGES OUT OF OUR COUNTER ARE FOR BENEFICIARY'S ACCOUNT

PERIOD FOR PRESENTATIONS   48: 15 DAYS AFTER SHIPMENT AND NOT EXCEEDING L/C EXPIRY

TRAILER   MAC: 9FE41FBC   CHK: 56783 EE6A448   NNNN

补充资料:
1. QUANTITY: 950 CARTONS
2. PACKING: IN PLASTIC BAGS OF 2. 84 KGS EACH THEN SIX

BAGS IN A CARTON.

3. UNIT PRICE：U. S. D 11. 40 PER CARTON

4. TOTAL AMOUNT：U. S. D 10 830. 00

5. SHIPPING PER S. S "DEWEI V. 213" FROM HUANGPU TO VAN-COUVER B. C.，B/L NO. 6180

6. MARKS：W. F. L. /VANCOUVER/C/NO.：1-UP

7. B/L DATE：070220

8. ETD：070221

9. GROSS WEIGHT：17138KGS   NET WEIGHT：16 188 KGS
   MEAS：18 365 M^3

10. NEGOCIATING BANK：BANK OF CHINA，HUNAN BRANCH

11. S/C NO：P. O. 2007-018   INV. DATE：070201   INV. NO.：CFF-016

12. H. S. CODE：8560. 3900

13. CARRIER：ABC CO.，LTD，FOR THE AGENT，COSCO AS THE CARRIER

　　　　业务员姓名：张三

14. REFERENCE NO.：1283890096

BILL OF EXCHANGE

DRAWN UNDER .... 　　　　　　1

L/C NO.：...

DATED ....

NO .... EXCHANGE FOR .... CHANGSHA. CHINA ....

AT .... SIGHT OF THIS FIRST OF EXCHANGE（SECOND OF EXCHANGE BEING UNPAID）. PAY TO THE ORDER OF ....

THE SUM OF ....

TO：...

....

　　　　　　　　　　　　　　FOR：...........................

3. LETTER OF CREDIT

Basic Header 　appl ID：F APDU Id：01 LT 　　　Addr：OCMMCNSH××××
　　　　　　　 Session：8533 Sequence：142087

Application 　Input/Output：0 　　　　　　　 Msg Type：700

Header 　　　 Input Time：1622 　　　　　　 Input Date：001103
　　　　　　　 Sender LT：BKKBTHBKE×××

BANGKOK BANK PUBLIC
COMPANY LIMITED
BANCKOK

Input Session: 5177 ISN: 800333　　Output Date: 001103

Output Time: 2033　　　　　　　Priority: N

Sequence Total	*27:	1/1
Form Doc Credit	*40A:	IRREVOCABLE
Doc Credit Num	*20:	BKKB1103043
Date of Issue	31C:	001103
APPLICABLE Rules	40E:	UCP LATEST VERSION
Date/Place Exp	*31D:	Date 010114 Place BENEFICIARIES' COUNTRY
Applicant	*50:	MOUN CO., LTD NO. 443, 249 ROAD BANGKOK THAILAND
Beneficiary	*59:	/ SHANGHAI FOREIGN TRADE CORP. SHANGHAI, CHINA
Curr Code, Amt	*32B:	Code USD Amount 18 000
Avail With By	*41D:	ANY BANK IN CHINA BY NEGOTIATION
Drafts At	42C:	SIGHT IN DUPLICATE INDICATING THIS L/C NUMBER
Drawee	43D:	// ISSUING BANK
Partial Shipmts	43P:	NOT ALLOWED
Transshipment	43T:	ALLOWED
Loading on Brd	44A:	CHINA MAIN FORT, CHINA
	44B:	BANGKOK, THAILAND
Latest Shipment	44C:	001220

Goods Descript.	45A:	2 000 KGS. ISONIAZID BP98
		PACKED IN 50 KGS/DRUM
		AT USD 9. 00 PER KG CFR BANGKOK
Docs Required	46A:	

DOCUMENTS REQUIRED:

+ COMMERCIAL INVOICE IN ONE ORIGINAL PLUS 5 COPIES INDICATING

  F. O. B. VALUE, FREIGHT CHARGES SEPARATELY AND THIS L/C NUMBER, ALL OF WHICH MUST BE MANUALLY SIGNED.

+ FULL SET OF 3/3 CLEAN ON BOARD OCEAN BILLS OF LADING AND TWO NON-NEGOTIABLE, COPIES MADE OUT TO ORDER OF BANGKOK BANK PUBLIC COMPANY LIMITED, BANGKOK MARKED FREIGHT PREPAID AND

  NOTIFY APPLICANT AND INDICATING THIS L/C NUMBER.

+ PACKING LIST IN ONE ORIGINAL PLUS 5 COPIES, ALL OF WHICH MUST BE MANUALLY SIGNED.

dd. Conditions	47A:	

ADDITIONAL CONDITION:

A DISCREPANCY FEE OF USD 50. 00 WILL BE IMPOSED ON EACH SET OF DOCUMENTS PRESENTED FOR NEGOTIATION UNDER THIS L/C WITH DISCREPANCY. THE FEE WILL BE DEDUCTED FROM THE BILL AMOUNT.

Charges	71B:	ALL BANK CHARGES OUTSIDE
		THAILAND INCLUDING REIMBURSING

BANK COMMISSION AND DISCREPANCY FEE (IF ANY) ARE FOR BENEFICIARIES' ACCOUNT.

Confirmat Instr   ＊49：   WITHOUT

Reimburs. Bank   53D：   //

BANGKOK BANK PUBLIC COMPANY LIMITED, NEW YORK BRANCH ON T/T BASIS

Ins Paying bank   78：

DOCUMENTS TO BE DESPATCHED IN ONE LOT BY COURIER.

ALL CORRESPONDENCE TO BE SENT TO/BANGKOK BANK PUBLIC COMPANY LIMITED HEAD OFFICE, 333 SILOM ROAD, BANGKOK 10500, THAILAND.

Send Rec Info   72：   REIMBURSEMENT IS SUBJECT TO ICC URR 525

Trailer MAC   :

CHK   :

DLM   :

------------------ End of Message ------------------

BILL OF EXCHANGE

凭
Drawn Under

不可撤销信用证
Irrevocable   L/C No.

日期
Date

支取 Payable With interest @ ％ 按 息 付款

号码   汇票金额
No.   Exchange for

南京
Nanjing

见票
at

日后(本汇票之副本未付)付交
sight of this FIRST of Exchange (Second of Exchange

Being unpaid) Pay to the order of

金额
the sum of

此致
To

（四）依据销售合同和信用证以及相关资料缮制汇票

DOCUMENTARY　CREDIT

ZCZC AHS302 CPUA520 S9203261058120RN025414394

P3 SHSOC

ICRA

TO：10306 26BKCHCNBJASH102514

FM：15005 25CIBCCATTF×××05905

　　 CIBBCCATTF×××

　　 ＊CANADIAN INPERIAL BANK OF COMMERCE

　　 ＊TORONTO

MT：701 02

27：SEQENCE OF TOTAL：1/1

40A：FORM OF DOC. CREDIT：IRREVOCABLE

20：DOC. CREDIT NUMBER：T-017641

31C：DATE OF ISSUE：20080325

40E：UCP LATEST VERSION

31D：EXPIRY：DATE：20080505

　　　　　　 PLACE：THE PEOPLES REP. OF CHINA

50：APPLICANT：TOMSCN TEXTJLES INC.

　　　　　　 3384 VINCENT ST

　　　　　　 DOWNSVIEW. ONTARIO

　　　　　　 M3J. 2J4 CANADA

59：BENEFICIARY：ABC TEXILES IMPORT AND EXPORT CORPORA-

　　　　　　 TION

　　　　　　 127 ZHONGSHAN RD. E. 1

　　　　　　 SHANGHAI P. R. OF CHINA

32B：AMOUT：CURRENCY：USD　AMOUT：36 960. 00

39A：POS/NEG TOL（％）：05/05

41-：AVAILABLE WITH/BY：AVAILABLE WITH ANY BANK IN CHINA

　　　　　　 NEGOTIATION

42C：DRAFTS AT—：30DAYS AFTER SIGHT

42 _：DRAWEE：CIBE—TORONTO TRADE FINANCE CENTRE. TO-

　　 RONTO

43P：PARTIAL SHIPMENTS：PERMITTED

43T：TRANSSHIPPMENT：PERMITTED

44A：LOADING IN CHARGE：CHINA

44B：FOR TRANSPORT TO：TORONTO

44C：LATEST DATE OF SHIP：20080420

45A：SHIPMENT OF GOODS：MERCHANDISE AS PER S/C

　　　　　　　　　　NO. 23CA1006

　　　　　　　　　　CIF TORONTO

46A：DOCUMENTS REQUIRED：

- COMMERCIAL INVOICE IN QUADRUPLICATE
- CERTIFICATE OF ORIGIN
- FULL SET CLEAN ON BOARD BILLS OF LADING TO SHIPPER'S ORDER BLANK ENDORSED MARKED "FREIGHT PREPAID TO TORONTO" NOTIFY APPLICANT（SHOWING FULL NAME AND ADDRESS）AND INDICATING FREIGHT CHARGED.
- NEGOTIBLE INSURANCE POLICY OR CERTIFICATE ISSUED BY PEOPLES INSURANCE COMPANY OF CHINA INCORPORATING THEIR OCEAN MARINE CARGO CLAUSES（ALL RISKS）AND WAR RISKS FOR 110 PERCENT OF CIF INVOICE VALUE，WITH CLAIMS PAYABLE IN CANADA INDICATING INSURANCE CHARGES.
- DETAILED PACKING LIST IN TRIPLICATE
- EXPORT LICENSE
- COPY OF INSURANCE CHARGES
- COPY OF FREIGHT CHARGES

47A：ADDITIONAL COND：

THE NUMBER AND THE DATE OF THIS CREDIT AND THE NAME OF OUR BANK MUST BE QUOTED ON ALL DRAFTS REQUIRED

AN ADDITIONAL FEE OF USD 50. 00 OR EQUIVALENT WILL BE DEDUCTED FROM THE PROCEEDS PAID UNDER ANY DRAWING WHERE DOCUMENTS PRESENTED ARE FOUND NOT TO BE IN STRICT CONFORMITY WITH THE TERMS OF THIS CREDIT.

71B：DETAILS OF CHARGES：

ALL BANKING CHARGES OUTSIDE CANADA INCLUDING AD-VISING COMMISSION ARE FOR ACCOUNT OF BENIFICIARY AND MUST BE CLAIMED AT THE TIME OF ADVISING.

48：PRESENTATION PERIOD：

NOT LATER THAN 15DAYS AFTER THE DATE OF ISSUANCE OF THE SHIPPING DOCUMENTS BUT WITHIN THE VALIDITY OF THE CREDIT.

49：CONFIRMATION：WITHOUT

78：INSTRUCTIONS：

UPON OUR RECEIPT OF DOCUMENTS IN ORDER WE WILL RE-MIT IN ACCORDANCE WITH NEGOTIATING BANK'S INSTRUC-TIONS AT MATURITY.

外销出仓通知单(代提货单)

合约：23CA1006

发货仓库：永新　　　　　　　2008 年 4 月 4 日　　　　　　发票号码：D2C4193

原进仓单 号 码 848607	货号 77111 TO204-75	货名及规格 20×20，94×60，114cm×40m 以上	件号	毛重/净重 @125/117	件数	数量 @400M	尺码 @117×14×25cm
		RED	1-10		10	4 000 M	
		SILVER	11-17		7	2 800 M	
染色棉涤斜纹布		FIESTA	18-27		10	4 000 M	
		DK. NAVY	28-34		7	2 800M	
		WINE	35-39		5	2 000 M	
TOMSON							
23CA1006		ELEPHANT	40—46		7	2 800 M	
TORONTO		BLACK	47—58		12	4 800 M	
NO. 1-60		SILVER DK. NAVY }	59		1	{ 200 M 200M	
		WINE ELEPHANT } 60			1	{ 200M 200M	

合计：60 纸箱　24 000 M

SUPPLEMENT：

1. VESSEL'S NAME：MILD VICTORY V. 864

2. OCEAN FREIGHT：USD 1 532. 52

3. H. S. CODE：5513，3 200

4. INSURANCE AGENT：TOPLIS HARDING CANADA INC.

1234 ISLINGTO AVENUE

SUITE 840，TORONTO ONTARIO

M8X，IY9，CANADA

5. INSURANCE CHARGES：USD 215.48

6. QUOTA YEAR：2002

7. CATEGORY PACKING：24A

8. EXPORT PACKING：USD 259.20

9. EXPORT LICENCE LINE 11："M"

凭　　　------------------------------

Drawn under

信用证　　　第　　号

L/C　　　No.

日期　------　年　　月　　日

Dated

按　　　　息　------------------------　付款

Payable with interest @　　　　％ per annum

号码　------------------------　汇票金额　------------------------　中国　------　年　月　日

No.　　　　Exchange for　　　　China

见票　　　　　　　日后(本汇票之副本未付)付

At _____ sight of this **FIRST** of Exchange (Second of exchange being unpaid)

Pay to the order of　　　　　　　　　　或其指定人

金额

The sum of

此致

To

(五) 根据信用证和有关信息资料缮制汇票

1) 有关资料如下：G.W.：14 077.00 KGS,N.W.：12 584.00 KGS, MEAS：35 CBM, 包装件数：3 298 卷(ROLLS),所有货物被装进 2×20′ CONTAINER,CON-TAINER NO.：TSTU157504,TSTU156417, 提单号码：SHANK00710, 船名：DANUBHUM/S009。货物 H.S. 编码：5407.1010。其他条件未知的,按照惯例自行定义。

2) 信用证如下所示：

209 07BKCHCNBJ95B BANK OF CHINA，SUZHOU BRANCH

409 07BKCHHKHH×××　BANK OF CHINA, HONGKONG BRANCH
MT700 O BKCHCNBJ95B××××

21： SEQUENCE OF TOTAL：1/1

40A： FORM OF DOC：IRREVOCABLE

20： DOCUMENT CREDIT NO：HK1112234

31C：DATE OF ISSUE：080101

40E：UCP LATEST VERSION

31D：DATE AND PLACE OF EXPIRY：080431，IN CHINA

50： APPLICANT：YOU DA TRADE CO.,LTD.,
　　　　　　　 101 QUEENS ROAD CENTRAL，HONGKONG
　　　　　　　 TEL：852-28566666

59.： BENEFICIARY：KUNSHAN HUACHENG WEAVING AND DYE-
　　　　　　　 ING CO.,LTD
　　　　　　　 HUANGLONG RD.，LIUJIA ZHEN，SUZHOU，
　　　　　　　 JIANGSU，CHINA
　　　　　　　 TEL：86-520-7671386

32B：AMOUNT：USD 33 680.00

41A：AVAILABLE WITH…BY…
ANY BANK BY NEGOTIATION

42C：DRAFTS AT：SIGHT

42A：DRAWEE：OURSELVES

43P：PARTIAL SHIPMENT：NOT ALLOWED

43T：TRANSSHIPMENT：NOT ALLOWED

44A：LOADING ON BOARD/DISPATCH/TAKING IN CHARGE AT/
FROM：SHANGHAI

44B：FOR TRANSPORTATION TO：HONGKONG

44C：LATEST DATE：080415

45A：DESCRIPTION OF GOODS AND/OR SERVICES

DESCRIPTION	QUANTITY	UNIT PRICE	AMOUNT
100 PCT NYLON	100 000 YARDS	USD 0.3368/YD	USD 33 680.00
FABRICS			

DETAILS AS PER CONTRACT NO.99WS061 DATED MAY 10，2003
PRICE TERM：CIF HONGKONG
SHIPPING MARK：

YOU DA

HONGKONG

R/NO.：1-up

46A：DOCUMENTS REQUIRED：

13. SINGED COMMERCIAL INVOICE IN 5 FOLDS INDICATING L/C NO. AND CONTRACT NO. 99WS061.

14. FULL SET(3/3) OF CLEAN ON BOARD MARINE BILLS OF LADING MADE OUT TO ORDER AND BLANK ENDORSED, MARKED "FREIGHT PREPAID" AND NOTIFY THE APPLICANT.

15. INSURANCE POLICY OR CERTIFICATE IN 2 FOLDS FOR 110 PCT OF THE INVOICE VALUE INDICATING CLAIM PAYABLE AT DESTINATION COVERING OCEAN TRANSPORTATION ALL RISKS AND WAR RISKS AS PER ICC CLAUSES.

16. PACKING LIST IN 3 FOLDS INDICATING GROSS AND NET WEIGHT OF EACH PACKAGE.

17. CERTIFICATE OF ORIGIN IN 3 FOLDS.

18. BENEFICIARY'S LETTER MUST BE FAX TO THE APPLICANT ADVISING GOODS NAME, CONTRACT NO., L/C NO., NAME OF VESSEL, AND DATE OF SHIPMENT.

47A：ADDITIONAL CONDITIONS：

+ ON DECK SHIPMENT IS NOT ALLOWED.

+ ALL DOCUMENT MUST BE MANUALLY SIGNED.

48： PERIOD FOR PRESENTATION：

DOCUMENTS MUST BE PRESENTED WITHIN 15 DAYS AFTER THE DATE OF SHIPMENT BUT WITHIN THE VALIDITY OF THE CREDIT.

:49: CONFIRMATION：WITHOUT

:72: SPECIAL INSTRUCTIONS：

ALL DOCUMENT MUST BE SEND TO THE ISSUING BANK IN ONE LOT THROUGH THE NEGOTIATING BANK BY

REGISTERED AIRMAIL.

UPON RECEIPT THE DOCUMENTS CONFORMITY WITH THE L/C'S CONDITIONS, WE SHALL PAY AS PER YOUR INSTRUCTIONS.

BILL OF EXCHANGE

DRAWN UNDER

L/C NO .... DATED ....

PAYABLE WITH INSTERST @ .... ‰ PER ANMUM

NO: .... EXCHANGE FOR

AT .... SIGHT OF HIS FIRST OF EXCHANGE (SECOND

OF EXCHANGE BEING UNPAID) PAY TO THE ORDER OF

THE SUM OF

TO ....

（六）根据信用证和相关资料制作议付汇票

ISSUE OF A DOCUMENTARY CREDIT	
ISSUING BANK	THE ROYAL BANK. TOKYO
SEQUENCE OF TOTAL	1/1
FORM OF DOC. CREDIT	IRREVOCABLE
DOC. CREDIT NUMBER	JST-AB12
DATE OF ISSUE	20080405
EXPIRY	DATE 20080615 PLACE CHINA
APPLICANT	WAV GENEAL TRADING CO.,OSAKA, JAPAN
BENEFICIARY	DESUN TRADING CO,LTD
	224 JINLIN ROAD,NANJING,CHINA
AMOUNT	CURRENCY USD AMOUNT 10 300. 00
AVAILABLE WITH/BY	BANK OF CHINA BY NEGOTIATION
DRAFTS AT...	DRAFTS AT SIGHT FOR FULL INVOICE VALUE
DRAWEE	THE ROYAL BANK,TOKYO
PARTIAL SHIPMTS	ALLOWED
TRANSSHIPMENT	ALLOWED
LOADING IN CHARGE	NANJING PORT
FOR TRANSPIRT TO...	OSAKA,JAPAN
LATEST SHIPMENT	20080531
GOODS DESCRIPT.	

LADIES GARMENTS AS PER S/C NO. SHL553

PACKING: 10 PCS/CTN

ART NO.	QUANTITY	UNIT PRICE
STYLE NO. ROCOCO	1 000 PCS	USD 5. 50
STYLE NO. ROMANTICO	1 000 PCS	USD 4. 80

CIF OSAKA

SHIPPING MARK: ITOCHU/OSAKA/NO. 1-200

DOCS REQUIRED	
	* 3/3 SET OF ORIGINAL CLEAN ON BOARD OCEAN BILLS OF LADING MADE OUT TO ORDER OF SHIPPER AND BLANK ENDORSED AND MARKED "FREIGHT PREPAID" NOTIFY APPLICANT(WITH FULL NAME AND ADDRESS). * ORIGINAL SIGNED COMMERCIAL INVOICE IN 5 FOLD. * INSURANCE POLICY OR CERTIFICATE IN 2 FOLD ENDORSED IN BLANK, FOR 110 PCT OF THE INVOICE VALUE COVERING THE INSTITUTE CARGO CLAUSES (A), THE INSTITUTE WAR CLAUSES, INSURANCE CLAIMS TO BE PAYABLE IN JAPAN IN THE CURRENCY OF THE DRAFTS. * CERTIFICATE OF ORIGIN GSP FORM A IN 1 ORIGINAL AND 1 COPY. * PACKING LIST IN 5 FOLD.
ADDITIONAL COND	1. T. T. REIMBURSEMENT IS PROHIBITED 2. THE GOODS TO BE PACKED IN EXPIRT STRONG COLORED CARTONS. 3. SHIPPING MARKS: ITOCHU OSAKA NO. 1-200
DETAILS OF CHARGES	ALL BANKING CHARGES OUTSIDE JAPAN INCLUDING REIMBURSEMENT COMMISSION, ARE FOR ACCOUNT OF BENEFICIARY.
PRESENTATION PERIOD	DOCUMENTS TO BE PRESENTED WITHIN 10 DAYS AFTER THE DATE OF SHIPMENT, BUT WITHIN THE VALIDITY OF THE CREDIT.
CONFIRMATION	WITHOUT
INSTRUCTIONS	THE NEGOTIATION BANK MUST FORWARD THE DRAFTS AND ALL DOCUMENTS BY REGISTERED AIRMAIL DIRECT TO U. S. IN TWO CONSECUTIVE LOTS, UPON RECEIPT OF THE DRAFTS AND DOCUMENTS IN ORDER, WE WILL REMIT THE PROCEEDS AS INSTRUCTED BY THE NEGOTIATING BANK.

BILL OF EXCHANGE

凭
Drawn Under

不可撤销信用证
Irrevocable   L/C No.

日期
Date   支取 Payable With interest @   ％   按   息   付款
号码   汇票金额   ═══════════════════ 南京
No.   Exchange for   ═══════════════════ Nanjing
                                见票   日后（本汇票之副本未付）付交
                                at   sight of this FIRST of Exchange （Second of Exchange

Being unpaid）Pay to the order of

金额   ═══════════════════════════════════════
the sum of ═══════════════════════════════════════

此致
To

（七）按照信用证制作汇票

BILL OF EXCHANGE ISSUING BANK：CYPRUS POPULAR BANK LTD，
LARNAKA
ADVISING BANK：BANK OF CHINA，SHANGHAI BRANCH．
SEQUENCE OF TOTAL   ＊27：1/1
FORM OF DOC. CREDIT   ＊40A：IRREVOCABLE
DOC. CREDIT NUMBER   ＊20： 186/04/10014
DATE OF ISSUE   31C： 080105
APPLICABLE RULES   40E： UCP LATEST VERSION
EXPIRY   ＊31D：DATE 080229 PLACE CHINA
APPLICANT   ＊50： LAIKI PERAGORA ORPHANIDES LTD．，
                            020 STRATIGOU TIMAGIA AVE．，
                            6046，LARNAKA，CYPRUS
BENEFICIARY   ＊59： SHANGHAI GARDEN PRODUCTS IMP．
                            AND EXP．CO．，LTD．27 ZHONGSHAN
                            DONGYI ROAD，SHANGHAI，CHINA
AMOUNT   ＊32B：CURRENCY USD AMOUNT 6 115．00
POS．/NEG．TOL．（％）   39A： 05/05
AVAILABLE WITH/BY   ＊41A：ANY BANK BY NEGOTIATION
DRAFT AT…   42C： AT SIGHT

DRAWEE　　　　　　　* 42A：LIKICY2N×××

* CYPRUS POPULAR BANK LTD, LARNAKA

PARTIAL SHIPMENT　　43P：　ALLOWED

TRANSSHIPMENT　　　43T：　ALLOWED

LOADING IN CHARGE　44A：　SHANGHAI PORT

FOR TRANSPORT TO…　44B：　LIMASSOL PORT

LATEST DATE OF SHIP.　44C：　080214

DESCRIPT. OF GOODS　　45A：　WOODEN FLOWER STANDS AND WOOD-
　　　　　　　　　　　　　　　EN FLOWER POTS AS PER S/C
　　　　　　　　　　　　　　　NO. E03FD121.
　　　　　　　　　　　　　　　CFR LIMASSOL PORT, INCOTERMS
　　　　　　　　　　　　　　　2000

DOCUMENTS REQUIRED 46A：

+ COMMERCIAL INVOICE IN QUADRUPLICATE ALL STAMPED AND SIGNED BY BENEFICIARY CERTIFYING THAT THE GOODS ARE OF CHINESE ORIGIN.

+ FULL SET OF CLEAN ON BOARD BILL OF LADING MADE OUT TO ORDER OF SHIPPER AND BLANK ENDORSED, MARKED FREIGHT PREPAID AND NOTIFY APPLICANT.

+ PACKING LIST IN TRIPLICATE SHOWING PACKING DETAILS SUCH AS CARTON NO. AND CONTENTS OF EACH CARTON.

+ CERTIFICATE STAMPED AND SIGNED BY BENEFICIARY STATING THAT THE ORIGIAL INVOICE AND PACKING LIST HAVE BEEN DISPATCHED TO THE APPLICANT BY COURIER SERVISE 2 DAYS BEFORE SHIPMENT.

ADDITIONAL COND. 47A：

+ EACH PACKING UNIT BEARS AN INDELIBLE MARK INDICATING THE COUNTRY OF ORIGIN OF THE GOODS. PACKING LIST TO CERTIFY THIS.

+ INSURANCE IS BEING ARRANGED BY THE BUYER.

+ A USD 50.00 DISCREPANCY FEE, FOR BENEFICIARY'S ACCOUNT, WILL BE DEDUCTED FROM THE REIMBURSEMENT CLAIM FOR EACH PRESENTATION OF DISCREPANT DOCUMENTS UNDER THIS CREDIT.

+　THIS CREDIT IS SUBJECT TO THE U. C. P. FOR DOCUMEN-
TARY CREDITS（2007 REVISION）I. C. C., PUBLICATION
NO. 600.

DETAILS OF CHARGES 71B：ALL BANK CHARGES OUTSIDE CYPRUS
ARE FOR THE ACCOUNT OF THE BEN-
EFICIARY.

PRESENTATION PERIOD 48：WITHIN 15 DAYS AFTER THE DATE OF
SHIPMENT BUT WITHIN THE VALIDI-
TY OF THE CREDIT.

CONFIRMATION ＊49：WITHOUT

INSTRUCTION 78：ON RECEIPT OF DOCUMENTS CON-
FIRMING TO THE TERMS OF THIS
DOCUMENTARY CREDIT, WE UNDER-
TAKE TO REIMBURSE YOU IN THE
CURRENCY OF THE CREDIT IN AC-
CORDANCE WITH YOUR INSTRUC-
TIONS, WHICH SHOULD INCLUDE
YOUR UID NUMBER AND THE ABA
CODE OF THE RECEIVING BANK.

相关资料：

发票号码：04SHGD3029　　发票日期：2008 年 2 月 9 日　　提单号码：SHYZ042234

提单日期：2008 年 2 月 12 日　集装箱号码：FSCU3214999　集装箱封号：1295312

1×20′FCL，CY/CY　　　　船名：LT USODIMARE　　　航次：V. 021W

木花架，WOODEN FLOWER STANDS, H. S. CODE：44219090. 90，

QUANTITY：350 PCS，USD 8. 90/PC，2 PCS/箱，共 175 箱。

纸箱尺码：66×22×48 cms，毛重：11 KGS/箱，净重：9 KGS/箱。

木花桶，WOODEN FLOWER POTS, H. S. CODE：44219090. 90，

QUANTITY：600 PCS，USD 5. 00/PC，4 PCS/箱，共 150 箱。

纸箱尺码：42×42×45cms，毛重：15 KGS/箱，净重：13 KGS/箱。

唛头：

L. P. O. L.

DC NO. 186/04/10014

MADE IN CHINA

NO. 1-325

凭 Drawn under		信用证 L/C NO.

日期　　　　　　支取　　　　　　　　　　按　　　息　　　付款
Dated　　　　　　Payable with interest　　@　　　　　　　%

号码　　　　汇票金额　　　　　　　　　　上海
NO　　　　　Exchange for　　　　　　　Shanghai　　　　20

见票　　　　日后（本汇票之正本未付）付交　　　　　　金额
At　　　　　　　　　　sight of this **SECOND** of Exchange（First of Exchange being unpaid）Pay to the order of　　　　　　　　the sum of

款已付讫
Value received

此致：
To

（八）根据信用证要求制作全套结汇单证

+　MIDLAND BANK PLC
+　LONDON
SEQUENCE OF TOTAL　　　　　　27：1/1
FORM OF DOCUMENTARY CREDIT　40A：IRREVOCABLE TRANSFERA-
　　　　　　　　　　　　　　　　　　BLE
DOCUMENTARY CREDIT NUMBER　20：CR2594/183865
DATE OF ISSUE　　　　　　　　31C：071107
APPLICABLE RULES　　　　　　　40E：UCP LATEST VERSION
DATE AND PLACE OF EXPIRY　　31D：080227 IN CHINA
APPLICANT　　　　　　　　　　50：W/W TEXTILES
　　　　　　　　　　　　　　　　　P. O. BOX 9
　　　　　　　　　　　　　　　　　CEMEERY ROAD
　　　　　　　　　　　　　　　　　LONDON

U. K.

BENEFICARY 　　　　　　　　 59： QINGDAO BRIGHT CO. LTD.
66， SHANDONG ROAD, QING-
DAO, CHINA

CURRENCY CODE, AMOUNT 　 32B： USD 265 540. 00

AVAILABLE WITH ... BY ... 　　 41A： BANK OF CHINA, SHANDONG
BRANCH BY NEGOTIATION

DRAFT AT 　　　　　　　　　 42C： SIGHT

DRAWEE 　　　　　　　　　　 42A： DRAWN ON US FOR FULL
INVOICE VALUE

PARTIAL SHIPMENT 　　　　　 43P： ALLOWED

TRANSSHIPMENT 　　　　　　 43T： ALLOWED

LOADING/DISPTCH/TAKING/FROM 44A： QINGDAO PORT

FOR TRANSPORTATION TO 　　 44B： LONDON， U. K

LATEST DATE OF SHIPMENT 　 44C： 080206

DESCRPT OF GOODS/SERVICES 　 45A：

　　+　837 MEN'S RAIN JACKET 5 200 PCS AT THE UNIT PRICE OF
USD 28. 60 EQUAL TO USD 148 720. 00

　　+　840 LADIES' RAIN JACKET 4 400 PCS AT THE UNIT PRICE OF
USD 26. 55 EQUAL TO USD 116 820. 00

AS PER SALES CONFIRMATION NO. 27SGB062018 DTD OCT. 24/
2007 TOTAL CREDIT AMOUNT USD 265 540. 00

DELIVER TERMS FOB QINGDAO PORT

DOCUMENTS REQUIRED 　　　 46A：

1. FULL SET CLEAN ON BOARD COMBINED BILL OF LADING
PLUS TWO NOT NEGOTABLE COPIES ISSUED TO ORDER AND
BLANK ENDORSED, MARKED FREIGHT COLLECT AND NOTI-
FY APPLICANT'S FULL NAME AND ADDRESS.

2. CERTIFICATE OF ORIGIN IN ONE ORIGINAL AND ONE COPY
ISSUED BY QUALIFIED AUTHORITIES.
CERTIFICATE OF ORIGIN SHOWING THIRD PARTY AS EX-
PORTER IS ACCEPTABLE

3. DATED AND HANDSIGNED COMMERCIAL INVOICE IN FIVE
ORIGINALS STATING THAT GOODS ARE FOR QUANTITY,

QUALITY AND PRICE IN CONFORMITY WITH S/C
NO. 27SGB062018 DATED OCT. 24/2007

参考资料：

1. COMMODITY：RAIN JACKET
2. QUANTITY：9 600 PCS
3. PACKING：ONE PC IN A PLASTIC BAG，ONE HUNDRED BAGS
   TO A CARTON
4. VESSEL："MAYOR" V. 26　B/L NO. GB211
5. SHIPPING MARK：

   W/W
   LONDON
   NO. 1-96

6. GR. WT：2 400 KGS　　　NET WT：2 208 KGS
7. INVOICE NO. QB12
8. MEASUREMENT：96 000 M³　　H. S. CODE 87596215

（九）根据信用证和其他资料制作全套结汇单据

1. 信用证

BASIC HEADER　0700 1126090311　　　CREBIT22A×××7189 372738
　　　　　　　　　　　　　　　　　　　090311 1826 N
　　　　　　　　　　　　　　　　　　　＊CREDIT0 BERGAMASCO
　　　　　　　　　　　　　　　　　　　S. P. A. (BANCO
　　　　　　　　　　　　　　　　　　　＊POPOLARE GROUP)
　　　　　　　　　　　　　　　　　　　＊BERGAMO
　　　　　　　　　　　　　　　　　　　＊(HEAD OFFICE)

USER HEADER　SERVICE CODE　　　103：
　　　　　　　　BANK PRIORITY　　113：
　　　　　　　　MSG USER REF.　　 1108：3090311003650700
　　　　　　　　INFO. FROM CI　　 115：
SEQUENCE OF TOTAL　　　＊27：1/1
FORM OF DOC. CREDIT　　＊40A：IRREVOCABLE
DOC. CREDIT NUMBER　　 ＊20：32390CI006500700
DATE OF ISSUE　　　　　31C：090311

APPLICABLE RULES　　　　＊40E：UCP LATEST VERSION
　　　　　　　　　　　　　　　/

EXPIRY　　　　　　　　　＊31D：DATE 090503 PLACE CHINA

APPLICANT　　　　　　　＊50：　××××CO SRL
　　　　　　　　　　　　　　VIA VENTIQUATTRO ×××××，35
　　　　　　　　　　　　　　20099 ×××××××××-ITALY

BENEFICAARY　　　　　　＊59：　HEBEI ×××× TRADING CO.,
　　　　　　　　　　　　　　LTD. BLDG. NO. ××××× STREET
　　　　　　　　　　　　　　SHIJIAZHUANG，HEBEI，CHINA

AMOUNT　　　　　　　　＊32B：CURRENCY SUD AMOUNT 169 150

MAX. CREDIT AMOUNT　　39B：　NOT EXCEEDING

AVAILABLE WITH/BY　　　＊41A：ANY BANK
　　　　　　　　　　　　　　BY NEGOTIATION

PARTIAL SHIPMENTS　　　43P：　NOT PERMITTED

TRANSHIPMENT　　　　　43T：　NOT PERMITTED

PORT OF LOADING/AIRPORT 44E：　XINGANG PORT，CHINA
OF DEPARTURE

PORT OF DISCHARGE/AIRPORT
OF DESTINATION　　　　　44F：　LA SPEZIA PORT，ITALY

LATEST DATE OF SHIP.　　44C：　090418

DESCRIPT. OF GOODS　　　45A：

　　　　　　　　　　　　　　85.000 PCS MICROFIBER TRAVEL BAG-SIZE 50×70
　　　　　　　　　　　　　　×20 CM BLACK AND WHITE EACH FOLDED IN
　　　　　　　　　　　　　　SINGLE POLIBAG AT USD 1.99/PC
　　　　　　　　　　　　　　AS PER PROFORMA INVOICE NO. 09HM1042 DAT-
　　　　　　　　　　　　　　ED MAR. 9, 2009 DELIVER TERMS：FOB XINGANG
　　　　　　　　　　　　　　PORT，CHINA

DOCUMENTS REQUIRED　46A：

　　　　　　　　　　　　　　1) SIGNED COMMERCIAL INVOICE IN TRIPLICATE
　　　　　　　　　　　　　　2) PACKING LIST IN TRIPLICATE
　　　　　　　　　　　　　　3) FULL SET(3/3) ORIGIANL OF CLEAN ON BOARD
　　　　　　　　　　　　　　BILL OF LADING ISSUED BY JAS FORWARDING-
　　　　　　　　　　　　　　XINGANG, TO THE ORDER AND BLANK EN-
　　　　　　　　　　　　　　DORSED, MARKED FREIGHT COLLECT AND

NOTIFY：

A. ××××CO SRI

VIA XXIV MAGGIO, 35-SESTO SAN GIOVANNI
(MI) ITALY

B. JAS SPA

VIA SANZIO, 6/8 SEGRATE (MI) ITALY

ADDITIONAL COND.　　47A：

+ SHIPMENT TO BE EFFECTED IN 2×40/HQ/
FCL PLUS 1×20/FCL

+ PLEASE DO NOT SEND ANY DRAFT IN DRAW-
ING OF THE DOCUMENTARY CREDIT
(IF PRESENTED, WILL BE RETURNED AND
OUR CHARGES EUR. 30 OR EQUIVALENT,
WILL BE DEDUCTED FROM OUR PAYMENT)

+ ALL DOCUMENTS TO BE ISSUED IN ENG-
LISH LANGUAGE

+ A DISCREPANCY FEE OF EUR 70 OR EQUIVA-
LENT WILL BE DEDUCTED FROM THE REIM-
VURSEMENT CLAIM (PROCEEDS), FOR EACH
PRESENTATION OF DISCREPANT DOCUMENTS
UNDER THIS CREDIT. NOTWITHSTANDING
ANY INSTRUCTIONS TO THE CONTRARY,
THIS CHARGE WILL BE FOR BENEFICIARY'S
ACCOUNT.

+ PLEASE NOTE THAT NO ANSWER WILL BE
GIVEN TO THE TRACERS ADDRESSED TO
OURSELVES FROM COLLECTING AGENT
BANKS

DETAILS OF CHARGES　　71B：　ALL BANKING CHARGES AND COM-
MISSIONS OUTSIDE ITALY ARE FOR
BENEFICIARY'S ACCOUNT, INCLU-
DING OUR TT CHARGES

PRESENTATION PERIOD　48：　15DAYS

CONFIRMATION　　　　＊49：　WITHOUT

INSTRUCTIONS   78：

    +   UPON RECEIPT OF COMPLIED DOCUMENTS AT OUR COUNTERS WE WILL CREDIT REEEMITTING BANK ACCORDING TO THEIR INSTRUCTIONS

    +   DOCUMENTS TO BE SENT BY SPECIAO COURIER（ONLY DHL OR FED. EXP.）

TO：

CREDITO BERGAMASCO UFFICIO MERCI LARGO PORTA NUOVA，224122 BERGAMO BG ITALY

SEND. TO REC. INFO.   72：   REGARDS SP

ORDER IS〈MAC：〉〈PAC：〉〈ENC：〉〈CHK：〉〈TNG：〉〈PDE：〉

MAC：B1890E36

CHK：19FF4E78A028

2. 其他资料

(1) INVOICE NO.：09HD1042   HS CODE 98547584   Certificate No. 154879658

POLICY NO. 5874589658

(2) S/C NO.：09HM1042   即期支付

(3) DETAILS OF PACKAGING：PACKED IN CARTONS

ONE PC IN A POLYBAG，30 PCS IN A CTN TOTAL：2 833 PCS

ONE PC IN A POLYBAG，10 PCS IN A CTN TOTAL：10 PCS

G. W.：42 500. 50 KGS

N. W.：39 666. 50 KGS

MEA.：191 907 M^3

(4) SHIPPING MARK：×××× IMPORT

SESTO DAN GIOVANNI

RCS MEDIA GROUP

BORSA

(5) CONTAINER NUMBER AND SEAL NO.

BMOU4106754/40'HQ

CS5031766

HJCU7896930/40'HQ

CS5031777

SENU4246407/40'GP

CS5031778

(6) VESSEL NAME：HANJIN AMSTERDAM　VOYAGE NO.：0056W

（十）根据信用证及有关业务资料缮制全部结汇单据

DOCUMENTARY CREDIT

40A：FORM OF DOC. CREDIT：IRREVOCABLE

20C：DOC. CREDIT NO. DCMTN55123

31C：DATE OF ISSUE：050212

31D：PLACE/DATE OF EXPIRY：050409 IN CHINA

ISSUING BANK：THE NORINCHUK BANK TOKYO

APPLICANT：NICHIMEN CORPORATION

2-2 NAKANOSHIMA 3-CHOME, KITA-KU,

NAGOYA，632-8620，JAPAN

BENEFICIARY：JIANGXI INTERNATIONAL IMP. & EXP. CORP.

8TH FLOOR FOREIGN TRADE BUILDING

200 ZHANQIAN ROAD, NANCHANG, CHINA

41A：AVAILABLE WITH ANY BANK BY NEGOTIATION

32B：AMOUNT：USD 64 000. 00

42C：DRAFT AT SIGHT FOR 100 PCT OF INVOICE VALUE

42A：DRAWEE：ISSUING BANK

PARTIAL SHIPMENT AND TRANSSHIPMENT ALLOWED

44A：LOADING PORT：SHANGHAI

44B：FOR TRANSPORATION TO：NAGOYA，JAPAN

44C：LATEST SHIPMENT DATE：MARCH. 20，2005

45A：DESCRIPTION OF GOODS：

100 PCT COTTON GREIGE PRINT CLOTH

ART. NO. 3042 FIRST QUALITY

SIZE：30×30 68×68 50" EXPORT PACKING IN SEAWORTHY BALES

TOTAL QUANTITY：ABOUT 200 000 YDS

PRICE/YD USD 0. 32 CIF NAGOYA

AS PER CONTRACT NO. J515

46A：DUCUMENT REQUIRED

+ SIGNED COMMERCIAL INVOICE IN 5 COPIES
+ PACKING LIST IN 2 ORIGINAL AND 1 COPY
+ FULL SET OF CLEAN ON BOARD OCEAN BILL OF LADING MADE OUT TO ORDER AND BLANK ENDORSED AND MARKED FREIGHT PREPAID AND NOTIFY APPLICANT. BILL OF LADING MUST SHOW THAT EXACT OCEAN FREIGHT AMOUNT PAID BY BENEFICIARY TO THE STEAMSHIP CO.
+ CERTIFICATE OF ORIGIN G. S. P. FORM A IN 2 COPIES.
+ MARINE INSURANCE POLICY OR CERTIFICATE IN DUPLICATE MADE OUT TO ORDER AND BLANK ENDORSED FOR 110 PCT OF INVOICE VALUE INCLUDING: OCEAN MARINE CARGO CLAUSEA(ALL RISKS), OCEAN MARIEN CRIGO WAR RISK CLAUSES OF THE P. I. C. C. (SUBJECT TO C. I. C.), MARKED PREMIUM PAID CLAIMS ARE TO BE PAYABLE IN JAPAN IN THE CURRENCY OF THE DRAFTS
+ BENEFICIARY'S CERTIFICATE STATING THAT ONE COMPLETE SET OF NON-NEGOTIABLE SHIPPING DOCUMENTS HAVE BEEN AIRMAILED TO THE APPLICANT IMMEDIATELY AFTER SHIPMENT.
+ SHIPPING ADVICE FROM BENIFICIARY SHOWING THAT CONTRACT NO. B/L NO. /DATE, VESSEL NAME, DESTINATION, NET WEIGHT, MEASUREMENT AND QUANTITY WITH BALE NUMBERS HAVE BEEN BY CABLE TO THE APPLICANT WITHIN 2 DAYS AFTER SHIPMENT.

47A: ADDITIONAL CLAUSES:
+ ALL DOCUMENTS MUST BEAR THE L/C NO.
+ DOCUMENT MUST BE PRESENTED WITHIN 15 DAYS AFTER SHIPMENT.

有关补充资料：

1. 发票号：05AO-P001　　　　日期：2005 年 3 月 10 日
2. 包装明细：布包（IN BALE）

件号	货号	包装率	每包毛重	每包净重	每包尺码
1-166	3042	1 200 YDS/BALE	141 KGS	139 KGS	95×68×50

3. 出运数量：199 200 YDS　　H. S. CODE 96528745

4. 船名：MSC SARAH V. 6A　B/L NO. DMDF2390　Certificate No. 12587965258
CONTAINER NO. MSCU4201437　装运日期：2005. 3. 20
承运人代理：CHINA NATIONAL FOREIGN TRADE TRANSPORT
CORPORATION
承运人：COSCO CONTAINER LINES

5. SHIPPING MARK：J-515
NAGOYA
PKG. NO. 1-166

6. 保险单号：SH058812
查勘代理：THE PEOPLE'S INSURANCE OSAKA BRANCH
98 LSKL MACH NAGOYA JAPAN
TEL：028-543657

7. 汇票日期：自定
议付行：中行南昌分行

（十一）根据资料信息制单

（1）发票号为：TSW15，Certificate No. CQS5147 H. S. CODE95021245　托运
日期为：AUG. 17，2007
船名：XNGBAO V. 0716　　　　POLICY NO. 1528794625879 B/L
NO. OUS45879521635

（2）该批商品有关数据如下：MEAS＝7. 2 CBM.　UNIT PMCE＝USD 18. 00
ART NO. 176：12 CRATES，NW＝8. 480 KG，GW＝8 800 KG
ART NO. 178：12 CRATES.　NW＝8. 480 KG，GW＝8 800 KG

（3）运输路线：FROM SHANG HAI TO HAMBURG TRANSIT TO BERN，
SWITZER LAND

以下是信用证资料：

FROM：STANDARD CHARTERED BANK，LONDON

TO：BANK OF CHINA JIANGSU

AT THE START OF ANY TELEXED REPLAY PLEASE QUOTE（QQQ' CR）

DATE：23，JUNE，2007

700 ISSUED OF L/C

15：　TEST 1050

27：　MESSAGE SEQENCE 1/1

40A：FORM OF L/C：IRREVOCABLE

20：L/C NO.：327984XY 070623

31C：ISSUE DATE 23，JUNE，2007

40E：UCP LATEST VERSION

31D：EXPIRY DATE/PLACE：070920 IN COUNTRY OF BENEFICIARY

50：APPLICANT：ALEXANDER FRASERE AND SON LTD

FRAKLAND MOORE HOUSE，185/187 HIGH ROAD，BERN．SWITZER
LAND

59：BENEFICIARY：CHINA NATIONAL METALS AND MINERALS
EXP AND IMP CORP.，JIANGSU．201 ZHUJIANG ROAD，NAN
JING，JIANGSU，CHINA

32B：L/CAMOUNT：USD 11 252.16

39：AMOUNT SPECIFICATION：CIF BERN

41A：AVAILABLE WITH/BY：ANY BANK BY NEGOTIATION

42：DRAFTS AT：SIGHT

DRAWN ON：OURSELVES

43P：PARTIAL SHIPMENT：NOT ALLOWED

43T：TRANSSHIPMENT：ALLOWED

44：TRANSPORT DETAILS：FROM CHINESE PORT WHEN NOT
LATER THAN 25th AUG.2007 TO BERN，SWITZERLAND

45A：DESCRIPTION OF GOODS：AS PER APPLICANT ORDER NO. PTC5
POLISHED MARBLE TILES，30.5×30.5×1 CM．（PLUS OR MI-
NUS0.3 MM）

ARTNO.176：312.56 SQM

ARTNO.178：312.56 SQM

TOTAL：625.12 SQM AS PER S/C SPGS45

46A：DOCUMENTS REQUIRED.

——OMMERCIAL INVOICES IN SIX COPIES QUOTING ORDER NO.
MADE OUT IN NAME OF CONSIGNEE SHOWING THE CIF VALUE
OF THE GOODS.

——PACKING LIST IN 6 COPIES

——CERTIFICATE OF ORIGIN FORM A IN 6 COPIES

——ALL RISKS AND WAR RISKS INSURANCE POLICIES OR CERTIFI-
CATE IN DUPLICATE ENDORSED IN BLANK FOR NOT LESS
THAN THE FULL CIF VALUE PIUS 10 PERCENT OF THE SHIP-

MENT IN THE CURRENCY OF THE CREDIT. TRANSSHIPMENT RISKS TO BE COVERED IF TRANSSHIPMENT EFFECTED.

——COMPLETE SET OF NOT LESS THAN 3 ORIGINAL CLEAN ON BOARD OCEAN BILLS OF LADING MADE OUT TO ORDER MARKED FREIGHT PAID. NOTIFY PETRICO INTERNATIONAL TRADING CORP., 1110 SHEPPARD AVENUE EAST SUITE 406 BERN, SWITZERLAND.

——BENEFICIARYS CERTIFICATE IN REQUIRED EVIDENCING THAT ONE COMPLETE SET OF NON-NEGOTIABLE SHIPPING DOCUMENTS HAVE BEEN SENT BY AIRMAIL TO BOTH THE CONSIGNEE AND ALEXANDER FRASER AND SON LTD, NOT LATER THAN DATE OF PERSENTATIONG OF NEGOTIABLE DOCUMENTS.

——BENEFICIARYS SIGNED STATEMENT THAT MERCHANDISE PACKED IN WOODEN CRATES WITH PLASTIC FOAM BOX.

47A: CONDITIONS: BILL OF LADING TO EVIDENCE GOODS SHIPPED IN A 20 FEET CONTAINER. CONSIGNEE—RICO INTERNATIONAL TRADING CORPORATION 1110 SHEPPARD AVENUE EAST SUITE 406 BERN,SWITZERLAND

71B: CHARGES: ALL BANK CHARGES AIRSING OUTSIDE THE UNITED KINGDOM ARE FOR THE BENEFIGICIARYS ACCOUNT.

48: PERSENTATION PERIOD: DOCUMENTS TO BE PRESENTED WITHIN15 DAYS AFTER THE DATE OF ISSUANCE OF THE SHIPPING-DOCUMENTS BUT WITHIN THE VALIDITY OF THE CREDIT.

49: CONFIRMATION INSTRUCTIONS: WITHOUT.

78: INSTRUCTIONS: IN REIMBURSEMENT WE SHALL COVER YOU UPON RECERPT OF DOCUMENTS IN ORDER. NEGOTIATING BANK IS TO DISPATCH ALL DOCUMENTS YO US BY REGISTERED AIRMAIL IN ONE COVER.

THIS CREDIT IS SUBJECT TO UNIFORM CUSTOMS AND PRACTICE FOR DOCUMENTARY CREDITS (2007 REVISION) INTERNATIONAL CHAMBER OF COMMERCE PUBLICATION 600. THIS TELECOMMUNICATION REPRESENTS THE OPERATIVE INSTRUMENT AND NO MAIL CONFIRMATION WILL BE ISSUED.

72: BANK TO BANK INFO: FOR BANK OF CHINA JIANGSU BR.

（十二）单选题

1. 承兑是指汇票付款人承诺对远期汇票承担到期付款责任的行为。我国票据法规定，自收到提示承兑汇票之日起（   ）日内付款人必须做出承兑。

   A. 3　　　　　　B. 4　　　　　　C. 5　　　　　　D. 6

2. 由出口商签发的要求银行在一定时间内付款的汇票不可能是（   ）。

   A. 商业汇票　　B. 银行汇票　　C. 远期汇票　　D. 即期汇票

3. 支票的主票据行为是（   ）。

   A. 出票　　　　B. 背书　　　　C. 提示　　　　D. 付款

4. 某公司持有一张经银行承兑的期限为 90 天的银行承兑汇票，票面金额为 500 万美元，为提前取得资金，该公司找某银行要求贴现，当时的贴现率为 10%，每笔贴现手续费 150 美元，求该公司贴现后可取得多少资金（   ）。

   A. 4 487 850 美元　　　　　　　　B. 4 478 850 美元

   C. 4 874 850 美元　　　　　　　　D. 4 784 850 美元

5. 在其他条件相同的前提下，（   ）的远期汇票对收款人最为有利。

   A. 出票后 30 天后付款　　　　　　B. 提单签发日后 30 天付款

   C. 见票后 30 天付款　　　　　　　D. 货到目的港后 30 天付款

6. 承兑是（   ）对远期汇票表示承担到期付款责任的行为。

   A. 付款人　　B. 收款人　　　　C. 出口人　　　　D. 议付银行

7. 信用证若未注明汇票的付款人，根据《UCP 600》，汇票的付款人应是（   ）。

   A. 开证申请人　　B. 开证行　　　C. 议付行　　　D. 出口人

8. 汇付方式主要包括信汇、电汇和票汇三种（   ）。

   A. 汇付方式属商业信用，银行只是提供服务

   B. 信汇、电汇属商业信用，票汇因为使用银行汇票，所以属银行信用

   C. 信汇属商业信用，电汇和票汇属银行信用

   D. 汇付方式属银行信用

9. 根据 ISBP，某信用证所使用的汇票的到期日为"10 DAYS FROM MARCH 1"，则该汇票的到期日是（   ）。

   A. 3 月 11 日　　　　　　　　　　B. 3 月 12 日

   C. 3 月 10 日　　　　　　　　　　D. 以承兑日期为准

10. 一张商业汇票见票日为 2011 年 1 月 31 日，见票后 1 个月付款，则到期日为（   ）。

    A. 2 月 28 日　　B. 3 月 1 日　　C. 3 月 2 日　　　D. 3 月 3 日

11. 凡做成限制性背书的汇票，只能由（   ）取款。

A. 其他被背书人   B. 指定的被背书人

C. 银行   D. 买方

12. 我国票据法规定,即期汇票持票人对出票人和承兑人的追索权,应在出票日起算（　　）内行使。

A. 3个月   B. 6个月   C. 1年   D. 2年

13. 在使用票汇付款方式时,汇出行应汇款人的申请,向其分行或代理行所开立的票据是（　　）。

A. 商业汇票   B. 本票

C. 银行即期汇票   D. 银行远期汇票

14. 本票和汇票的区别中表述错误的是（　　）。

A. 本票有两个当事人,而汇票有三个当事人

B. 本票的付款是有条件的,而汇票的付款是无条件的

C. 本票的出票人即是付款人,远期本票无须办理承兑手续;而远期汇票则要办理承兑手续

D. 本票在任何情况下,出票人都是绝对的主债务人;而汇票的出票人在承兑前是主债务人,在承兑后,承兑人是主债务人

（十三）多选题

1. 《日内瓦统一法》和我国《票据法》都规定的汇票付款期限是（　　）。

A. at sight/on demand/on presentation

B. at a fixed date

C. at a fixed period after date

D. at a fixed period after sight

E. Deferred payment

2. 善意持票人应具备的条件是（　　）。

A. 善意取得票据   B. 票据需合格且未过期

C. 曾遭拒付出   D. 必须给付对价

3. 信用证规定 DRAFT AT 30 DAYS FROM B/L DATE,提单上显示的签发日为 2009 年 1 月 6 日,装船批注中的日期分别是 JAN. 3, 2009,则汇票期限填制正确的是（　　）。

A. AT 30 DAYS FROM B/L DATE

B. AT 30 DAYS FROM B/L DATE JAN. 3, 2009

C. AT 30 DAYS FROM JAN. 3, 2009

D. DATE: JAN. 3, 2009 AT 30 DAYS FROM DATE

E. AT FEB. 2，2009

4. 根据《中华人民共和国票据法》,汇票上必须记载的事项包括（　　）。

    A. 确定的金额　　　　　　　　　B. 出票日期

    C. 付款人姓名　　　　　　　　　D. 汇票编号

    E. 付款项目

5. 本票与汇票的区别在于（　　）。

    A. 前者是无条件的支付承诺,后者是无条件支付命令

    B. 前者是当事人为两个,后者则有三个

    C. 前者在使用过程中有承兑,后者则无须承兑

    D. 前者的主债务人不会变化,后者则会因承兑而变化

    E. 汇票有即期与远期之分,本票则只有远期

6. 常见的规定远期汇票起算日期的方法有（　　）。

    A. 自出票日起算　　　　　　　　B. 自开证日起算

    C. 自收证日起算　　　　　　　　D. 自提单日起算

    E. 自见票日起算

7. 远期汇票使用的一般程序有（　　）。

    A. 承兑　　B. 贴现　　C. 提示　　D. 付款　　E. 背书

8. 票据的性质有（　　）。

    A. 有价性　　B. 要式性　　C. 流通性　　D. 命令性　　E. 条件性

9. 下列属于汇票和本票的区别的有（　　）。

    A. 当事人　　　　B. 份数　　　　C. 承兑与否　　　　D. 证券性质

    E. 出票人的债务人身份

10. 信用证的汇票期限为:30 days after B/L date,如果实际的提单日是2008年4月5日,当天交单,则在提示的汇票中,如下表示期限一栏正确的是在"at sight"中把"sight"划掉并填上（　　）。

    A. 30 days after B/L date　　　　B. 30 days after date

    C. 30 days after 2008-04-05　　　D. 2008-05-05

（十四）判断题

（　　）1. 本票的出票人可以是单独一个人,也可以允许由两个或更多的出票人一起签发。

（　　）2. 远期汇票只有经过承兑才能转让。

（　　）3. 如果汇票上加注"按某号信用证开立"、"按某合同装运某货物",则构成支付的附加条件,该汇票无效。

（　　）4. 即期议付信用证条件下，议付行 ABC 银行提交的汇票收款人规定为：TO ORDER OF ABC BANK，但对汇票未做背书，则应视为不合格汇票。

（　　）5. 追索（Recourse）：是指汇票等票据遭到拒付时，持票人要求其前手背书人、出票人、承兑人或其他的汇票人清偿汇票金额及有关费用的行为。

（　　）6. 一张商业汇票上的收款人是："仅付给 ABC 有限公司"（Pay to ABC Co.，Ltd. Only)，这种汇票不能转让。

（　　）7. D/A 方式下既可以使用即期汇票也可以使用远期汇票，但只能是商业汇票。

（　　）8. 持票人将汇票提交付款人要求承兑或付款的行为，称之为"承兑"。

（　　）9. 票据上的付款日期不肯定或有条件的付款日期视为无效汇票。

（　　）10. 承兑附有条件的被认为是拒付承兑。

（　　）11. 汇票、提单和保险单的抬头人通常各是付款人、收货人、被保险人。

（　　）12. 所有的汇票都可以背书转让，特殊的可以连续背书，多次转让。

（十五）问答题

A 公司出口一笔货物，提单日期为 5 月 21 日通过中国银行办理 D/A30days after sight 支付方式的托收手续。6 月 1 日单到国外代收行，代收行当天即向付款人提示汇票。付款人应于何日付款？何日取得单据（不计优惠期）？

综 合 篇

综合练习一

（一）根据合同审核信用证，并填写审单记录

SALES CONFIRMATION

NO：20406

DATE：AUG. 5，2009

SELLER：TIANJIN SEWING MACHINE IMP. & EXP. CORPORATION.

BUYER：ABC COMPANY, P. O. BOX NO. 123. KUWAIT.

COMMODITY AND SPECIFICATIONS：

SPRING FLOWER BRAND SEWING MACHINE JA-1 3-DRAWER' FOLD-ING COVER

QUANTITY：5 000 SETS, 5% MORE OR LESS AT SELLER'S OPTION

PACKING：IN CARTONS OF ONE SET EACH

UNIT PRICE：USD 58. 00 PER SET CFRC3% KUWAIT

TOTAL VALUE：USD 290 000. 00 （U. S. DOLLARS TWO HUNDRED NINTY THOUSAND ONLY）

TIME OF SHIPMENT：DURING OCT. /NOV, 2009 IN TWO EQUAL MONTHLY LOTS, FROM TIANJIN TO KU-WAIT, ALLOWING TRANSSHIPMENT.

INSURANCE：TO BE COVERED BY THE BUYER

TERMS OF PAYMENT：BY IRREVOCABLE SIGHT LETTER OF CREDIT TO REACH THE SELLER 15 DAYS BEFORE THE MONTH OF SHIPMENT AND REMAIN VALID FOR NEGOTIATION IN CHINA UNTIL THE 15TH DAYS AFTER DATE OF SHIPMENT.

REMARKS：THIS CONTRACT IS CONCLUDED THROUGH AGENT-ABDULLA COMPANY, KUWAIT.

IRREVOCABLE DOCUMENTARY CREDIT

No. 101465

SEP. 2nd 2009

TO: BANK OF CHINA TIANJIN BRANCH

FROM: THE COMMERCIAL BANK OF KUWAIT, KUWAIT

WE OPEN IRREVOCABLE DOCUMENTARY CREDIT NO. 101465

BENEFICIARY: TIANJIN SEWING MACHINE IMPORT AND EXPORT
CORPORATION

APPLICANT: ABC COMPANY. P. O. BOX NO. 123 KUWAIT

AMOUNT: USD 290 000. 00 (US DOLLARS TWO HUNDRED AND NIN-
TY THOUSAND ONLY)

THIS CREDIT IS AVAILABLE BY BENEFICIARY'S DRAFT AT 30 DAYS AF-
TER SIGHT FOR 100% OF INVOICE VALUE DRAWN ON THE COMMER-
CIAL BANK OF KUWAIT, NEW YORK BRANCH, NEWYORK. U. S. A.

ACCOMPANIED BY THE FOLLOWING DOCUMENTS:

1. SIGNED COMMERCIAL INVOICE IN 3 COPIES.

2. FULL SET OF CLEAN ON BOARD BILL OF LADING MADE OUT TO
   ORDER AND NOTIFY APPLICANT.

3. INSURANCE POLICY IN DUPLICATE COPIES FOR 120% OF IN-
   VOICE VALUE COVERING ALL RISKS AND WAR RISK SUBJECT
   TO CIC DATED JAN. 1ST, 1981.

4. CERTIFICATE OF ORIGIN IN DUPLICATE ISSUED BY CHINA IN-
   TERNATIONAL CHAMBER OF COMMERCE OR OTHER GOVERN-
   MENT AUTHORITIES.

5. INSPECTION CERTIFICATE OF QUALITY ISSUED BY APPLICANT.

5 000 SETS SPRING FOLWER BRAND SEWING MACHINE JA-103
DRAWERS FOLDING COVER AT USD 58. 00 PER SET CFR KUWAIT AS
PER S/C NO. 95406 DATED AUG. 5TH, 2009.

LATEST SHIPMENT: OCT. 31ST, 2009 FROM BEIJING TO KUWAIT.

PARTIAL SHIPMENTS: ALLOWED

TRANSSHIPMENT: PROHIBITED

THE GOODS SHALL BE CONTAINERIZED

DOCUMENTS MUST BE PRESENTED WITHIN 15 DAYS AFTER THE

DATE OF ISSUANCE OF THE B/L, BUT WITHIN THE VALIDITY OF THE CREDIT.

THE COMMERCIAL BANK OF KUWAIT

信用证审核结果

信用证号	
合 同 号	
审证结果	

（二）根据交易信息及信用证制作结汇单据及托收项下的汇票

金属铬合同贸易背景

这是天津市进出口公司与美国 COMETALS 公司签订的出售 200 吨金属铬的一笔业务。以 USD 35 550.00/MT CIF BALTIMORE 价格成交，90％以即期不可撤销信用证结算，另外 10％以 D/P 即期结算。

货物由天津检验检疫局 2009 年 11 月 21 日检验合格出证，运往天津新港出口。

货物的基本情况如下：

合同号：	JZIE041101
发票日期：	2009 年 11 月 22 日
净重：	40 公吨
每钢桶重：	3 公斤
装运期：	2009 年 11 月 28 日
船名/航次：	BLUE SKY V.312E
提单号：	BS04112823
体积：	30 立方米
集装箱号/封号：	20′ CBHU0611758/25783 CY/CY
	20′ CBHU2765381/25784 CY/CY

保险索赔代理： ABCD THE UNITED STATES

议付行：　　　　CHINA CONSTRUCTION BANK,TIANJIN BRANCH

H. S. CODE：81122100

MSG TYPE：　　　700（ISSUE OF A DOCUMENTARY CREDIT）

APPLICANT HEADER：CHASUS33D×××N 1555 192579 030328 0458 N

　　　　　　　　　＊JPMORCAN CHASE BANK

　　　　　　　　　＊NEW YORK,NY

SEQUENCE TOTAL	＊27：	1/2
FORM OF DOCUMENTARY CREDIT	＊40A：	IRREVOCABLE
LETTER OF CREDIT NUMBER	＊20：	C-788520
DATE OF ISSUE	31C：	090112
APPLICABLE RULES	40E：	UCP LATEST VERSION
DATE AND PLACE OF EXPIRY	＊31D：	DATE 091210 PLACE IN CHINA
APPLICANT	＊50：	COMETALS
		222 BRIDGE PLAZA SOUTH FORT LEE, NJ 07024
BENEFICIARY	＊59：	TIANJIN IMPORT AND EXPORT CORPORATION NO. 29， JIEFANG ROAD TIANJIN,CHINA
CURRENCY CODE,AMOUNT	＊32B：	CURRENCY USD AMOUNT 7 110 000. 00
AVAILABLE WITH…BY…	＊41A：	ANY BANK BY NEGOTIATION
DRAFTS AT	42C：	SIGHT FOR 90 PCT OF INVOICE VALUE
DRAWEE	42A：	JPMORCAN CHASE BANK, NY, USA
PARTIAL SHIPMENTS	43P：	PERMITTED
TRANSHIPMENT	43T：	PERMITTED
SHIPPING ON BOARD/DISPATCH/LOADING IN CHARGE AT/FROM CHINESE MAIN PORT	44A：	
TRANSPORTATION TO	44B：	BALTIMORE,MD
LATEST DATE OF SHIPMENT	44C：	091130

PERIOD FOR PRESENTATION 48：

DOCUMENTS MUST BE PRESENTED WITHIN 15 DAYS AFTER SHIPPMENT BUT WITHIN THE VALIDITY OF THE LETTER OF CREDIT.

CONFIMATION INSTRUCTIONS ＊49： WITHOUT

INSTRUCTIONS TO THE PAYING/ACCEPTING/NEGOTIATING BANK：78

1. ALL DOCUMENTS MUST BE FORWARDED TO US IN ONE AIR-MAIL TO THE JPMORCAN CHASE BANK.

2. A DISCREPANT DOCUMENT FEE OF USD 75.00 BE DEDUCTED FROM PROCEEDS IF DOCUMENTS WITH DISCREPANCIES ARE ACCEPTED.

3. UPON RECEIPT OF ALL DOCUMENTS AND DRAFT IN CON-FORMITY WITH THE TERMS AND CONDITIONS OF THIS CREDIT，WE SHALL REMIT THE PROCEEDS TO THE BANK DESIGNATED BY YOU.

"ADVISING THROUGH" BANK 57 D：

BANK OF CHINA, TIANJIN BR.

NO. 25 SEC 5 JIEFANG RD HEXI DIST TIANJIN CHINA

MSG TYPE：700(ISSUE OF A DOCUMENTARY CREDIT)

APPLICANT HEADER：CHASUS33D×××N 1555 192579 030328 0458 N

＊JPMORCAN CHASE BANK

＊NEW YORK，NY

SEQUENCE TOTAL ＊27： 2/2

LETTER OF CREDIT NUMBER ＊20： C-788520

DESCRIPTION OF GOODS OR SERVICES： 45A：

200 METRIC TONS CHROMIUM METAL FROM MAIN CHINESE PORT TO BALTIMORE，MD AT USD 35 550.00 PER METRIC TON

GOODS ARE SUPPLIED IN STEEL DRUMS OF 250 KGS NET EACH ON FUMIGATED WOODEN PALLETS，IN SEAWORTHY OCEAN CONTAINERS

SHIPPING TERMS：CIF BALTIMORE

DOCUMENTS REQUIRED： 46A：

++ SIGNED COMMERCIAL INVOICE IN 6 COPIES BEARING THE FOLLOWING
   CLAUSE: WE CERTIFY THAT THE CONTENTS OF THIS INVOICE IS TRUE AND CORRECT

++ ORIGINAL PACKING LIST IN 3 COPIES INDICATING QUANTITY/GROSS AND NET WEIGHT OF EACH PACKAGE AND CERTIFY THAT EACH EXPORT PACKAGE CARRIES A "MADE IN CHINA" LABEL.

++ CERTIFICATE OF ORIGIN GSP FORM A IN 2 COPIES

++ CERTIFICATE OF WEIGHT IN DUPLICATE ISSUED BY CIQ.

++ INSURANCE POLICY IN TRIPLICATE FOR 110 PERCENT OF THE INVOICE VALUE SHOWING CLAIMS SETTING AGENT AT DESTINATION PORT AND THAT CLAMIS ARE PAYABLE IN THE CURRENCR OF THE DRAFT, COVERING ALL RISKS, WAR RISKS AND S. R. C. C.

++ 3/3 OF SIGNED CLEAN ON BOARD OCEAN BILLS OF LADING MADE OUT TO ORDER OF SHIPPER, NOTIFYING JOHN S. CONNOR, INC. INDICATIING OUR LETTER OF CREDIT NUMBER AND MARKED "FREIGHT PREPAID"

++ BENEF'S CERTIFICATE CERTIFYING THAT ONE SET OF NON-NEGOTIABLE B/L TOGETHER WITH INVOICE AND PACKING LIST HAS BEEN SENT TO APPLICANT BY DHL BY BENEFICIARY WITHIN 24 HOURS AFTER SHIPMENT.

ADDITIONAL INSTRUCTIONS: 47A:

1. THIS L/C IS NON TRANSFERABLE
2. BOTH QUANTITY AND AMOUNT 10 PERCENT MORE OR LESS ARE ALLOWED.
3. ALL DOCUMENT MUST INDICATE THIS CREDIT NUMBER
4. SHIPPING MARKS ON EACH DRUM:
   CHROMIUM METAL/PC-14228/COMETALS/MADE IN CHINA
5. BENEFICIARY'S STATEMENT INDICATES THAT A COPY OF SHIPPING ADVICE DESPATCHED TO THE ACCOUNTEE IMMEDIATELY AFTER SHIPMENT.

CHARGES   71B:

ALL BANKING CHARGES OUTSIDE THE OPENNING BANK ARE
FOR BENEFICIARY'S ACCOUNT.

REIMBURSING BANK　53A：

　　　　PNBPUS3NNYC
　　　　CORESTATES BANK INTERNATIONAL
　　　　NEW YORK，NY
　　　　180 MAIDEN LANE

综合练习二

(一) 根据成交资料审核信用证,列明不符点,并说明应如何修改

成交资料:

IMPORTER: PACIFIC IMPORT AND EXPORT COMPANY

    5/F., FLAT B, SHUN PONT COMM. BLDG.

    5-11 THOMSON ROAD, WANCHAI,

    HONG KONG

EXPORTER: TIANJIN TIANMEI TRADING COMPANY

    NO. 47, CHANGJIANG RD.,

    TIANJIN, P. R. CHINA

COMMODITY: ART. 41GH87 FISH MEAL IN GUNNY BAGS
GROSS FOR NET

CONTRACT AMOUNT: USD 17 250. 00 CFR LAE, PAPUA NEW GUINEA
WITH 5% MORE OR LESS ALLOWED

CONTRACT DATE: 10/Oct/09

QUANTITY: 23 M/T WITH 5% MORE OR LESS AT SELLER'S
OPTION

SHIPMENT: DURING DEC, 2009

PAYMENT: SIGHT LC REACH THE SELLER BEFORE 3-NOV-
09

信用证:

Union Bank of Hong Kong Ltd.

122-126 QUEEN'S ROAD CENTRAL, HONG KONG TEL: 25343333

FAX：（*852*）*28051183*
TELEX：*73264 UNIBK HX*
CABLE：*BANKUNION*
SWIEFT：*UBHKHKHH*

IRREVOCABLE DOCUMENTARY
CREDIT NO.：HLC972859SP
OPERATIVE CREDIT INSTRUMENT
CONFIRMING OUR PREADVICE BY
SWIFT OF****

PLACE AND DATE OF ISSUE：
HONGKONG 30 OCT，2009
DATE AND PLACE OF EXPIRY：
15 JAN 2010 AT THE COUNTER OF
ISSUING BANK

APPLICANT：
PACIFIC IMPORT AND EXPORT
COMPANY 5/F.，FLAT B，SHUN
PONT COMM. BLDG.
5-11 THOMSON ROAD，WANCHAI，
HONG KONG

BENEFICIARY：
TIANJIN TIANMEI TRADING
COMPANY NO. 47，CHANGJIANG
RD.，
TIANJIN，P. R. CHINA

ADVISING BANK：
BANK OF CHINA
TIANJIN BR
CHINA

AMOUNT：
USD 17 250.00
SAY US DOLLARS SEVENTEEN
THOUSAND

THIS CREDIT IS AVAILABLE WITH ANY BANK BY NEGOTIATION
AGAINST PRESENTATION OF YOUR DRAFT（S）AT SIGHT DRAWN
ON UNION BANK OF HK LTD HONG KONG BEARING THE CLAUSE
"DRAWN UNDER DOCUMENTARY CREDIT NO. HLC972859SP OF
UNION BANK OF HONG KONG LTD.，HONG KONG DATED 3 OCT
2009" ACCOMPANIED BY THE FOLLOWING DOCUMENTS：

1. SIGNED COMMERCIAL INVOICE IN 4 COPIES SHOWING THE
   DATE & NUMBER OF SALES CONFIRMATION AS 10 OCT，2009
   AND NO. TYDAC036.
2. FULL SET（3/3）OF CLEAN ON BOARD MARING BILL（S）OF LAD-

ING MADE OUT TO ORDER, BLANK ENDORSED, MARKED FREIGHT PREPAID AND NOTIFY APPLICANT.

3. CERTIFIED COPY OF BENEFICIARY'S FAX ADDRESSED TO THE APPLICANT (FAX NO. 852-38650236 OR 852-35290086) ADVISING AMOUNT, ART NO., QUANTITY, VESSEL'S NAME, B/L NO., EACH MEASUREMENT OF RACH BAG, TOTAL PACKAGES MEAS-UREMENT, H. K. SHIPPING AGENT'S NAME AND TELEPHONE NO., DEPARTURE DATE WITHIN 3 DAYS AFTER SHIPMENT EF-FECTED AND ALSO MENTIONING APPLICANT'S REF NO. SP910

4. PACKING LIST IN 4 COPIES.

5. INSURANCE POLICY COVERING ICC (A) CLAUSE IN 2 COPIES

COVERING:

23 M/T FISH MEAL ART. 41GH78 AS PER S/C NO. TYPAC036 CFR LAE, PAPUA NEW GUINEA

OTHER CONDITIONS:

5% IN QUANTITY IS ALLOWED

BILLS OF LADING MUST SHOW THAT GOODS ARE SHIPPED IN 20' CONTAINER.

SHIPMENT FROM ANY CHINESE PORT TO LAE, PAPUA NEW GUINEA
NOT LATER THAN 30 DEC, 2009

PARTIAL SHIPMENTS ALLOWED. TRANSHIPMENT ALLOWED

DOCUMENTS MUST BE PRESENTED WITHIN 2 DAYS AFTER THE DATE OF SHIPMENT BUT WITHIN THE VALIDITY OF THE CREDIT AND SENT TO US BY REGISTERED AIRMAIL IN ONE COVER

ALL BANKING CHARGES INCLUDING NEGOTIATION INTEREST AND ADVISING CHARGES OUTSIDE HONG KONG ARE FOR ACCOUNT OF BENEFICIARY.

REIMBURSEMENT INSTRUCTIONS:

UPON RECEIPT OF THE DOCUMENTS WHICH CONPORM TO THE TERMS AND CONDITIONS OF THIS CREDIT, WE SHALL REMIT THE PROCEEDS TO THE NEGOTIATING BANK ACCORDING TO THEIR INSTRUCTIONS.

NOTWITHSTANDING ANY TERMS AND CONDITIONS IN THIS CREDIT, AN ADDITIONAL HANDLING FEE OF USD33.-WHICH IS BORNE BY THE BENEFICIARY, WILL BE DEDUCTED FROM THE DRAWING(S) FOR EACH SET OF DISCREPANT DOCUMENTS PRESENTED THEREUNDER.

WE HEREBY ISSUE THIS DOCUMENTARY CREDIT IN YOUR FAVOUR.

IF THIS CREDIT IS AVAILABLE BY NEGOTIATION EACH PRESENTATION MUST BE NOTED ON THE REVERSE OF THIS ADVICE BY THE BANK WHERE THE CREDIT IS AVAILABLE.

FOR AND ON BEHALF OF
UNION BANK OF HONG KONG LTD.

（二）单据制作

天津蓝鸟进出口公司与美国商人达成一笔台灯交易，买方通过美国银行洛杉矶分行开来信用证（见下页），试根据下列出口货物明细填制汇票和装箱单并审核发票和海运班轮提单。（请将审单意见用中文——列明在审核单据的下方）

货物明细单

货号	数量	计量单位	单价 (US$)	包装种类	装箱 方式	毛重 (KGS)	净重 (KGS)	长 (CM)	宽 (CM)	高 (CM)
JIE-452	500	PIECE	69.80	CARTONS	2	10	8	60	40	30
HEQ-349	200	PIECE	55.90	CARTONS	2	10	8	60	40	30
VPU-875	200	PIECE	66.80	CARTONS	2	12	10	60	40	30
PNC-684	300	PIECE	70.20	CARTONS	2	12	10	55	45	40

承运船名：	ASIAN GLORY
航次：	V.03
发票号码：	LK-LTIV7923
发票日期：	22-Dec-09
保险代理：	HUASHUN INSURANCE CO. 12TH FL., UERCY PLAZA
	LOS ANGELES, U.S.A.
提单号码：	CSO09201
装船日期：	30-Dec-09
保单号码：	ZB017659
产地证号：	OR034838
汇票号码：	LK-LTIV7923
H.S.编码：	90028953
承运人目的港代理：	COSCO LOS ANGELES OFFICE
	307 22FL STONE TOWER BUILDING
	TEL:001-4590-3832　　FAX:001-4590-3864
合同号码：	LK-LTSC0738
合同日期：	8-Nov-09
汇票日期：	31-Dec-09

制作汇票及装箱单，并审核发票和提单。

AMERICAN BANK, LOS ANGELES BRANCH

340 ROUHA STREET

LOS ANGELES, U. S. A

DATE 15-Nov-2009 Cable advised by preliminary on: Issued at: LOS ANGELES

IRREVOCABLE DOCUMENTARY	OUR NO.	ADVISING BANK NO.
LETTER OF CREDTT	LT-LKLC9375	

ADVISING BANK	APPLICANT
THE BANK OF CHINA TIANJIN BR. 623 YANG GAO ROAD, TAIDA, TIANJIN, CHINA	LIEANE TRADING CORP. UNIT87 FAREAST BUILDING LOS ANGELES, U. S. A

BENEFICIARY	AMOUNT US$ 80 500. 00 (SAY U. S DOLLARS EIGHTY THOUSAND FIVE HUNDRED ONLY)
TIANJIN BLUEBIRD IMPORT & EXPORT CORP. NO. 249 SANGUAN ROAD, TIANJIN CHINA	**EXPIRY** 15-Jan-10 TIANJIN CHINA

GENTLEMEN: YOU ARE AUTHORIZED TO VALUE ON US
BY DRAWIG DRAFTS AT ＊＊＊＊＊＊＊＊＊＊＊＊ SIGHT FO 100％ OF INVOICE VALUE
ACCOMPANIED BY THE FOLLOWING DOCUMENTS:

1. SIGNED COMMERCIAL INVOICE IN 3 COPIES.
2. PACKING LIST IN 2 COPIES SHOWING G. W., N. W. AND MEASUREMENT OF EACHT-TEM.
3. CERTIFICATE OF ORIGIN IN DUPLICATE.
4. FULL SET OF 3/3 CLEAN ON BOARD OCEAN BILLS OF LADING MADE OUT TO OR-DER OF SHIPPER AND END ORSED IN BLANK MARKED FREIGHT PREPAID NOTI-FY APPLICANT WTTH FULL NAME AND ADDRESS AND ALSO SHOW THE NAME AND TELEHONE NUMBER OF THE DELIVERY AGENT AT DESTTNATION.
5. MARINE INSURANCE POLICY IN DUPLICATE ENDORSED IN BLANK FOR 110％ OF INVOICE VALUE AGAINST ALL RISKS & WAR RISK SUBJECT TO P. I. C. C. DATED 1/1/1981 SHOWING THE NAME AND ADDRESS OF THE INSURANCE AGENT AT DESTINATIION WITH
CLAIMS PAYABLE AT DESTINA TION IN THE SAME CURRENCY OF THE DRAFTS
6. BENEFICIARY'S CERTIFICATE ACCOMPANIED WITH THE RELATIVE FAX COPY CERTIFYING THAT ALL SHIPPING DETAILS HAVE BEEN FACSIMILED TO APPLICANT WITHIN 2 DAYS AFTER SHIPMENT EFFECTED.

SHIPPING TERMS: CIFLOS ANGELES	SHIPPING MARK: LIEANE LK-LTSC0738
COVERING: N & A BRAND LAMPS AS PER S/C LK-LTSC0738	LOS ANGELES NO. 1-UP

续表

THE AMOUNT OF ANY DRAFT DRAWN UNDER THIS CREDIT MUST BE ENDORSED ON THE REVERSE OF THE
ORIGINAL CREDIT. ALL ORAFTS MUST BE MARKED DRAWN UNDER THIS DOCUMENTARY CREDIT AND BEARING
ITS NUMBER AND DATE.

FROM: TIANJIN TO: LOS ANGELES	PARTIAL SHIPMENTS: UNPERMITIED TRANSSHIPMENT: PERMITIED	LATEST DATE OF SHIPMENT: 30-Dec-09

SPECIAL INSTRUCTIONS:

ALL CHARGES OUTSIDE OPENING BANK ARE FOR ACCOUNT OF BENEFICIARY

ALL DOCUMENTS PRESENTED FOR NEGOTIATION SHALL BEAR THE NO. OF THIS CREDIT AND THE NAME OF ISSUING BANK.

Drafts and documents to be presented for negotiation not later than 15 days after the bill of lading date

Except so far as otherwise expressly stated, this documentary credit is subject to the "Uniform Custom and Practice for Documentary Credits" 1993 Revision International Chamber of Commerce Publication No. 500

WE HEREBY AGREE WITH THE DRAWERS ENDORSERS AND BONA-FIDE HOLDERS OF DRAFTS DRAWN UNDER AND IN-COMPLIANCE WITH THE TERMS OF THIS CREDIT THAT SUCH DRAFTS WILL BE DULY HONORED ON DUE PRESENTATION TO THE DRAWEE IF NEGOTIATED ON OR BEFORE THE EXPIRY DATE.	ADVISING BANK NOTIFICATION THE BANK OF CHINA, TIANJIN BR. 623 YANG GAO ROAD, TAIDA.
David Calven Authorized Signature	TIANJIN 陈 洁 18-Nov-09 Place, date, name and signature of the advising bank

COMMERCIAL INVOICE

1) SELLER LANKE IMPORT & EXPORT CORP NO. 249 SANGUAN ROAD, SHANGHAI CHINA	3) INVOICE NO. LK-LTIV7923	4) INVOICE DATE 22-Dec-00
	5) LIC NO. LT-LKLC9375	6) DATE 15-Nov-00
	7) ISSUED BY AMERICAN BANK, LOS ANGELES BRANCH	
2) BUYER LIEANE TRADING CORP UNIT87 FAREAST BUILDING LOS ANGELES, U. S. A.	8) CONTRACT NO. LK-LTSC0738	9) DATE 8-Nov-00
	10) FROM SHANGHAI	11) TO NEW YORK
	12) SHIPPED BY ASIAN GLOR V. 03	13) PRICE TERM CIF LOS ANGELES

14) MARKS   15) OESCRIPTION OF GOODS   16) QUANTITY(SET)   17) UNIT PRICE
18) AMOUNT(US$)

	N&A BRANDLAMPS			
	ART. NO.	SET	CIF NEW YORK	
LIEANE	JIE-452	500	US$ 69. 80	34 900. 00
LK-LTSC0738	HEQ-349	200	US$ 55. 90	11 180. 00
NEW YORK	VPU-875	200	US$ 66. 80	13 360. 00
NO. 1-600	PNC-684	300	US$ 70. 20	21 060. 00
			TOTAL US$:80 500. 00	

L/C NO. LT-LKLC9375   15-Nov-00
ISSUING BANK：AMERICAN BANK，LOS ANGELES BRANCH

BILL OF LADING   1-C

1) SHIPPER LANFE IMPORT & EXPORT CORP NO. 249 SANGUAN ROAD, SHANGHAI CHINA	10) BVL NO.
2) CONSIGNEE ORDER OF APPLICANT	**COSCO** 中国远洋运输(集团)总公司 CHINA OCEAN SHIPPING (GROUP) CO. CABLE:COSCO BEIJING TLX:210740 CPC CN
3) NOTIFY PARTY LIEANE TRADING CORP UNIT87 FAREAST BUILDING LOS ANGELES, U. S. A.	*ORIGINAL*

4) PLACE OF RECEIPT	5) OCEAN VESSEL ASIAN GLORY	
6) VOYAGE NO. V. 03	7) PORT OF LOADING LOS ANGELES	**Combined Transport BILL OF LADING**
8) PORT OF DISCHARGE SHANGHAI	9) PLACE OF DELIVERY	

11) MARKS & NOS. 13) DESCRIPTION OF GOODS	12) NOS & KNDS OF PKGS.	14) G. W. (kg)	15) MEAS(m³)
LIEANE LK-LTSC0738 NEW YORK NO. 1-600	N & A BRAND LAMPS 600 CARTONS		
		6 500	47 250

L/C NO. LT-LKLC9375 15-Nov-00
ISSUING BANK:AMERICAN BANK, LOS ANGELES BRANCH

CONTAINER NO.
UEMQ 3 490

FREIGHT PREPAID

16) TOTAL NUMBER OF CONTAINERS   SAY SIX HUNDRED CARTONS ONLY
    OR PACKAGES(IN WORDS)

FREIGHT & CHARGES	REVENUE TONS	RATE	PER	PREPAID	COLLECT
PREPAID AT	PAYABLEAT		17) PLACE AND DATE OF ISSUE SHANGHAI 30-Dec-2000		
TOTAL PREPAID	18) UNMBER OF ORIGINAL B(S)L THREE				
LOADIMG ON BOARD THE VESSEL			21) 倪 永 海 *COSCO Shanghai hipping Co., Ltd.* *As Agent For the Camier:* **CHINA OCEAN SHIPPING(GROUP)COMPANY**		
19) DATE 30-Dec-2000	20) BY COSCO Shanghai Shipping Co., Ltd. 倪 永 海				

ENDORSEMENT:LANKE IMPORT & EXPORT CORP.
　　万 念 辉

3copies

参考答案

信用证篇

一、认知信用证

(一) 信用证中英文条款互译

1. 一整套已装船的清洁提单,指示性抬头、空白背书,并注明买方详细地址,运输从中国到汉堡,运费已付。
2. 卖方出据以买方为抬头的正本已签字商业发票,至少3份复件,并且在发票上注明商品的名称、原产地国以及其他相关信息。
3. 我们向这张汇票的出票人、背书人以及善意持票人承诺,在信用证的有效期内提交符合要求的全套单据,我行则会无条件兑现该汇票。
4. 受益人需要在装船后5天内用电传的方式通知史密斯先生关于信用证号、数量、载货船只等相关信息,且交单议付时该通知的复印件也需要一并提交。
5. The buyer should open the relevant sight irrevocable L/C to the buyer 40 days before the month of shipment, document to be presented within 21 days in China, but still within the validity of the credit.
6. From shanghai to Hong Kong before JAN. 31st, 2009, transhipment and partial shipment are not allowed.
7. To be cover by the seller for 110% of invoice value against All RISK and WAR RISKS as per Ocean Marine Transportation of PICC dated 1981. 1. 1.
8. pieces to a box, 20 boxes to a carton, total 200 cartons.

(二) 问答题

1. 本信用证的附加条款中提出了哪几点要求?
   答:(1) 所提交的单据中如果有不符点,则每套不符点的单据将扣除80美元。

    （2）所有单据均用英文缮制。

    （3）所有单据上均须载明信用证的号码。

2. 在此信用证业务结汇时，受益人应向银行提交哪些单据？

    答：所需提交的单据有发票、海运提单、保险单、原产地证书和装箱单。

3. 此信用证对于分批装运、转船及装运期的要求是什么？

    答：允许分批装运和转船。装运期为不晚于 2008 年 3 月底。

4. 此信用证对提单缮制的要求有哪些规定？

    答：提单的抬头为凭托运人指定，标明运费已付，并且载明开证申请人的详细地址。

（三）单选题

1～5　BBCCB	6～10　ACBDA	11～15　CBBDD
16～20　BCBAC	21～25　DCAAC	26～30　DCDCA
31～35　ACCDD	36～40　BBAAB	41～45　AACAD
46～50　BAACA	51～55　BBAAD	56～60　CCBCB

（四）多选题

1. ACD	2. BCDE	3. ABD	4. ABDE	5. ABD
6. ABC	7. AD	8. ACD	9. ACD	10. ACE
11. ABC	12. ABC	13. BD	14. ABCD	15. BCD
16. ABC	17. ABCE	18. ABCD	19. BCD	20. ABCDE
21. CDE	22. ACDE	23. ABC		

（五）判断题

1. F	2. T	3. F	4. F	5. F	6. F	7. F	8. F	9. F	10. F
11. T	12. F	13. F	14. F	15. F	16. F	17. F	18. T	19. F	20. F
21. F	22. F	23. T	24. T	25. F	26. F	27. T	28. T	29. F	30. F
31. F	32. F	33. F	34. F	35. T	36. F	37. F	38. T	39. F	40. T
41. F	42. T	43. T	44. F	45. F	46. T	47. T	48. F	49. F	50. F
51. F									

二、开立信用证

（一）依据合同，按照业务规范自行填制信用证开证申请书

Beneficiary(full name, address) DESUN TRADING CO.,LTD. HUARONG MANSION RM2901 NO. 85 GUAN-JIAQIAO, NANJING 210005，CHINA	L/C No. Ex Card No. Contract No.：NEO2009026

	Date and place of expiry： MAY 15th,2009 in China

Partial shipments (×) allowed ( )not allowed	Transhipment (×)allowed ( ) not allowed	( )Issue by airmail ( ) With brief advice by teletransmission ( )Issue by express delivery (×)Issue by teletransmission（which shall be the operative instrument

Loading on board/dispatch/ taking in charge at/from SHANGHAI PORT, CHINA Not later than Apr. 30，2009 For transportation to DAMMAM PORT，SAUDI ARABIA	Amount：(both in figures and words)： USD 30 000. 00 SAY USD THIRTY THOUSAND ONLY.

Description of goods： 300 PCS OF SHANGHAI COUNTRY BICYCLE. ART SH28 INCH USD 100 CFR DAMMAM PORT，SAUDI ARABIA	Credit available with ( )by sight payment ( ) by acceptance (×) by negotiation ( ) by deferred payment at against the documents detailed herein (×) and beneficiary's draft for 100% of invoice value
	( )FOB ( ) CFR (×) CIF ( ) or other terms

Documents required：(marked with ×)
1. (×) Signed commercial invoice in 3 copies indicating L/ C No. and Contract No. _____
2. (×) Full set of clean on board Bills of Lading made out to ____ and blank endorsed,marked "freight [ ] prepaid/ [ ] to collect[ ] showing freight amount" notifying the applicant
3. ( ) Air Waybills showing "freight [ ]prepaid/ [ ] to collect indicating freight amount" and consigned to
4. ( ) Insurance Policy/Certificate in 3 copies for 110% of the invoice value showing claims payable in China in currency of the draft, blank endorsed, covering [ ] Ocean Marine Transportation /[ ] Air Transportation /[ ] Over Land Transportation，All Risks，War Risks.
5. (×) Packing list / Weight Memo in 3 copies indicating Contract No. NEO2001026
6. (×) Certificate of Quantity/ Weight in 3 copies issued by [ ] manufacturer /[ ] Seller /[×] independent surveyor at the loading port，indicating the actual surveyed quantity / weight of shipped goods as well as the packing condition.

7. （×）Certificate of Quality in 3 copies issued by ［　］manufacturer /［×］public recognized surveyor

8. （×）Beneficiary's Certified copy of fax dispatched to the applicant within 2 days after shipment advising the contract number, name of commodity, quantity, invoice value, bill of loading, bill of loading date, the ETA date and shipping Co.

9. （×）Beneficiary's Certificate certifying that extra copies of the documents have been dispatched to the ［×］applicant/［　］

10. （×）Certificate of Origin in 3 copies certifying.

11. （　）Other documents, if any：

　　Additional instruction：（marked with ×）

1. （×）All banking charges outside the opening bank are for beneficiary's account.

2. （×）Documents must be presented within 21 days after the date of issuance of the transport documents but within the validity of this credit.

3. （×）Third party as shipper is not acceptable, Short Form / Blank B/l is not acceptable.

4. （　）Both quantity and amount ％ more or less are allowed.

5. （×）All documents to be forwarded in one lot by express unless otherwise stated above.

6. （　）Other terms, if any：

（二）依据销售合同填写信用证开证申请书

Applicant MESSRS TOMSON TEXTILES INC. 3384 VINCENT ST. M3J, 2J4, CANADA DOWNSVIEW, ONTARIO	Beneficiary (full name, address and tel. etc.) ABC TEXTILES IMPORT AND EXPORT CORPORATION 127 ZHONGSHAN RD. E. 1 SHANGHAI R. P. OF CHINA
Partial shipments （×）allowed （　）not allowed　　Transshipment （×）allowed （　）not allowed	issued by （×）teletransmission （　）express delivery
Loading on board/dispatch/ taking in charge at/ from：ANY PORT Not later than　APR. 20TH, 2008 For transportation to：TORONTO	Contract No.：23CA1006 Credit Amount (both in figures and words)： 　　USD 36 960. 00 US DOLLARS THIRTY-SIX THOUSAND NINE HUNDRED AND SIXTY ONLY. Trade Term：（　）FOB（　）CFR（　）CIF（×） Others：
Description of goods： ART. NO. 7711 TRUERAN DYED JEAN AS PER S/C NO. 23CA1006	Date and place of expiry： MAY 5, 2008 in China
	Credit available with （　）by sight payment （　）by acceptance （×）by negotiation （　）by deferred payment at against the documents detailed herein （×）by 30 days after sight

Documents required：（marked with ×）

1. （×）Signed commercial invoice in copies indicating L/C No. and Contract No.

2. （×）Full set of clean on board Bills of Lading made out ［ ］to order/［ ］to the order of shipper and blank endorsed，marked "freight ［ ］prepaid/［ ］to collect showing freight amount" notifying ［ ］the applicant/［ ］

3. （ ）Air Waybills showing "freight ［ ］prepaid/［ ］to collect indicating freight amount" and consigned to

4. （×）Insurance Policy/Certificate in 3 copies for 110% of the invoice value showing claims payable in Canada in currency of the draft，blank endorsed，covering （［×］Ocean Marine Transportation / ［ ］Air Transportation /［ ］Over Land Transportation）All Risks，War Risks. /［ ］

5. （×）Packing list / Weight Memo in 3 copies indicating

6. （×）Certificate of Quantity/ Weight in 3 copies issued by ［ ］manufacturer /［ ］Seller /［×］independent surveyor at the loading port，indicating the actual surveyed quantity / weight of shipped goods as well as the packing condition.

7. （×）Certificate of Quality in 3 copies issued by ［ ］manufacturer /［×］public recognized surveyor /［ ］

8. （×）Beneficiary's Certified copy of fax dispatched to the applicant within 2 days after shipment advising the contract number，name of commodity，quantity，invoice value，bill of loading，bill of loading date，the ETA date and shipping Co.

9. （×）Export license.

10. （×）Certificate of Origin in copies certifying.

11. （ ）Other documents，if any：

Additional instruction：（marked with ×）

1. （×）All banking charges outside the opening bank are for beneficiary's account.

2. （×）Documents must be presented within 15 days after the date of issuance of the transport documents but within the validity of this credit.

3. （×）Third party as shipper is not acceptable，Short Form / Blank B/l is not acceptable.

4. （ ）Both quantity and amount % more or less are allowed.

5. （×）All documents to be forwarded in one lot by express unless otherwise stated above.

6. （ ）Other terms，if any：

For banks use only	我公司承担本申请书背面所列责任及承诺,并保证按照办理。
Seal and / or Signature checked by（ ）	
L/C Margin % checked by（ ）	（申请人名称及印鉴章）
Credit Facility checked by（ ）	
Ent（ ）Ver（ ）App（ ）	RMB A/C No.
Date：	
	USD or（ ）A/C No.
	联系人：　　　　　电话：

（三）根据下面给出的条件填写开证申请书

Beneficiary (full name and address)： XYZ COMPANY NO. 203 LIDIA HOTEL OFFICE 1546-49, DONG-GU, BUSAN, KOREA		Applicant (full name and address)： ABC COMPANY NO. 529, QUIANG ROAD, TIANJIN, CHINA
Partial shipment （ ）allowed （×）not allowed	Transshipment： （ ） allowed （×） not allowed	Latest date of shipment： 　JULY 15，2008 Place and date of expiry：JULY 25，2008 in China
Loading on board/dispatch/taking in charge From：BUSAN To：XINGANG PORT, TIANJIN, CHINA Price term：FOB BUSAN USD 210/MT		Amount (Both in figures and words)： USD 12 600. 00 SAY US DOLLAR TWELF THOUSAND SIX HUNDRED ONLY.

Credit available with （ ）＿＿＿＿＿＿＿＿＿＿＿＿＿＿＿

（×）by negotiation/ （ ）by acceptance with beneficiary's draft for ＿＿100＿＿ % of the invoice value at ＊＊＊＊＊＊＊＊ sight on issuing bank.

（×）by sight payment/ （ ）by deferred payment at ＿＿＿＿＿＿＿＿＿＿＿＿ days

Against the documents detailed herein

Commodity： GOLD ROLLED STEEL SHEET IN COIL. SPECIFICATIONS：JIS G3141 SPCC-SD	Shipping mark： ST NO. 1-UP

Documents required：

1. （×）Signed commercial invoice in ＿＿＿＿THREE＿＿＿＿ folds indicating L/C no. and contract no.

2. （×）Full set (3/3) of clean on board ocean bills of lading made out to order and blank endorsed marked "（ ）freight prepaid/（×）to collect" notify the applicant.

3. （ ）Air waybill consigned to the applicant notify the applicant marked "freight （ ）to collect/ （ ）prepaid".

4. （ ）Insurance policy/certificate in ＿＿＿＿＿＿ folds for 110% of the invoice value, showing claims pay in china in the currency of the draft, blank endorsed covering （ ）ocean marine transportation / （ ）air transportation / （ ）overland transportation all risks, war risks as per ＿＿＿＿＿ clause.

5. （×）Packing list in ＿＿＿THREE＿＿＿ folds indicating quantity / gross and net weights.

6. （×）Certificate of origin in ＿＿＿TWO＿＿＿ folds.

7. （ ）Certificate of quantity in ＿＿＿＿＿＿ folds.

8. （ ）Certificate of quality in ＿＿＿＿＿＿ folds issued by （ ）manufacturer/ （ ）beneficiary.

9. （×）Beneficiary's certified copy of telex/fax dispatched to the applicant within ＿＿＿ONE＿＿＿ day after shipment advising goods name, （×）name of vessel / （ ）flight no. date, quantity. Weight and value of shipment.

10. （ ）Beneficiary's certificate certifying that （ ）one set of non-negotiable documents/ （ ）one set of non-negotiable documents (including 1/3 original b/l) has been dispatched to the applicant directly by courier/speed post.

11. Other documents, if any：

Additional instructions：

1. (×) All banking charges outside the issuing bank are for beneficiary's account.

2. (×) Documents must be presented within 1 days after the date of shipment but within the validity of the credit

3. ( ) Both quantity and amount ____% more or less are allowed

4. (×) All documents must be sent to issuing bank by courier/speed post in one lot.

5. ( ) Other terms, if any

(四) 根据提供的合同填写开证申请书

IRREVOCABLE DOCUMENTARY CREDIT APPLICATION

TO: BANK OF CHINA SHANTOU BRANCH		Date: 2007-11-12	
□Issue by airmail　(×)teletransmission □Issue by express delivery □(which shall be the operative instrument)		Credit No. SHTD 937449 Date and place of expiry　JAN. 15, 2008 in China	
Applicant MAURICIO DEPORTS INTERNATIONALS. A. RM 1008-1011 CONVENTION PLAZA, 101 HARBOR ROAD, COLON,R. P.		Beneficiary (Full name and address) SHANTOU GARMENTS IMPORT &. EXPORT COMPANY ZHONGSHAN ROAD 106, SHANTOU China	
Advising Bank BANK OF CHINA SHANTOU BRANCH		Amount USD 200 000. 00 Say Us Dollars Two Hundred Thousand Only	
Partial shipments (×)allowed □not allowed	Transshipment (×) allowed □not allowed	Credit available with 　BANK OF CHINA SHANTOU BRANCH By □payment　　□acceptance	
Loading on board/dispatch/taking in charge at/ from Shanghai not later than　The end of December 2007 For transportation to: COLON		(×) negotiation against the documents detailed herein ☒and beneficiary's draft(s) for ___100___ % of invoice value	
□FOB　　□CFR　　(×) CIF □or other terms		At ___30 DAYS after___ sight drawn on	

Documents required: (marked with ×)

1. (×) Signed commercial invoice in　THREE　copies

2. (×) Full set of clean on board Bills of Lading made out to order and blank endorsed, marked "freight [×] to collect / [ ]prepaid [ ] showing freight amount"notifying MAURICIO DEPORTS INTERN ATIONAL S. A. RM1008－1011CONVENTIONPLAZA, 101HARBORROAD, COLON, R. P.

( ) Airway bills/cargo receipt/copy of railway bills issued by showing "freight [ ] to collect/[ ] prepaid [ ] indicating freight amount" and consigned to _____.

3. （×）Insurance Policy/Certificate in TWO copies for 110% of the invoice value showing claims payable in ___China___ in currency of the draft, blank endorsed, covering All Risks, War Risks and

4. （×）Packing List/Weight Memo in ___THREE___ copies

5. （ ）Certificate of Quantity/Weight in copies issued by _____.

6. （ ）Certificate of Quality in copies issued by 〔 〕manufacturer/〔 〕public recognized survey-or _____.

7. （×）Certificate of Origin in ___ONE___ copies.

8. （ ）Beneficiary's certified copy of fax / telex dispatched to the applicant within days after ship-ment advising L/C No., name of vessel, date of shipment, name, quantity, weight and value of goods.

Other documents, if any

Description of goods：

2 000 PCS LADIES SHIRTS AS PER NO. YD-MDSC9811

QUANTITY：2 000 PCS

PRICE TERM：CIF COLON USD 10.00 PER PEC

Additional instructions：

1. （×）All banking charges outside the opening bank are for beneficiary's account.

2. （×）Documents must be presented within ___15___ days after date of issuance of the transport documents but within the validity
of this credit.

3. （×）Third party as shipper is not acceptable, Short Form/Blank back B/L is not acceptable.

4. （ ）Both quantity and credit amount _____% more or less are allowed.

5. （×）All documents must be sent to issuing bank by courier/speed post in one lot.

（ ）Other terms, if any

（五）单选题

C

（六）多选题

1. ABC 2. ABDE

（七）判断题

1. T 2. F 3. F 4. T 5. T 6. F 7. F

三、审核信用证

（一）根据合同审核信用证

1. 审核结果如下：

经审核 667-01-3042855 号信用证有如下错误，请修改

（1）信用证的种类应该改为 IRREVOCABLE.

（2）信用证的到期地点应该改为 CHINA

（3）汇票的种类应该为即期汇票，请将"30 DAYS"去掉。

（4）货描中 ART 3900300 的单价请改为 USD 1.02/PC。

（5）应该允许转船，请将 NOT 去掉。

（6）货描中 CIF 后应该跟目的港，请将 SHANGHAI 改为 GOTHENBURG

（7）保险条款中投保险别改为 PFA，投保金额应该为发票金额的 110％而不是 120％

（8）交单日应为装船完毕后的 15 天内，而非 5 天内。

2. 审核结果如下：

经审核信用证有如下错误，请修改

（1）信用证的到期地点应该为 CHINA，而非 LINZ。

（2）开证申请人的公司名称有误，请将 GARDEN 改为 GARTEN。

（3）受益人公司名称和合同不完全一致，请将 IMP. & EXP. 改为 IMPORT & EXPORT。

（4）信用证的总金额与合同不符，请将金额改为 22 485.40。

（5）请删除信用证中的溢短装条款。

（6）41A 栏处应规定卖方所在地的银行，应选择该行在中国的分行。

（7）信用证应该允许分批装运，请将 NOT 去掉。

（8）最迟装运期有误，请改为 060601。

（9）货描中引用的合同号与合同实际号码不一致，请改为 NO. 205001。

（10）要求提交的装箱单应由买方签字以及开证行的许可，此为软条款，应当删除。

3. 审核结果如下：

经审核信用证有如下错误，请修改

（1）信用证中金额大小写不一致，请将大写中的 EIGHTEEN 改为 EIGHTY。

（2）信用证的到期地点应该在卖方所在地，请将 IN APPLICANT COUNTRY 改为 IN BENEFICIARY COUNTRY。

（3）保险金额应该为发票金额的110％,而非130％,参照的是 OCEAN MA-
RINE CARGO OF P. I. C. C. DATE 1/1/1981,而非信用证上所载。

（4）货描中 DS1511 对应的数量是 542 而非 544,DS5120 对应的数量是 254
而非 245。

（5）目的港应该为 TORONTO ,而非 VANCOUVER。

（6）应该允许分批装运和转运。

4. 审核结果如下:

经审核信用证有如下错误,请修改

（1）信用证中应该允许分批装运。

（2）装运港应该改为 DALIAN。

（3）货描中货物型号应该为 STYLE NO. A101 和 STYLE NO. A102。

（4）发票的抬头应该为 BBB TRADING CO.。

（5）保险条款中投保金额应该为发票金额的110％而非130％,投保险别为
PFA,而非 ALL RISKS。

（6）交单日期应为提单日后60天,而非15天。

5. 审核结果如下:

经审核信用证有如下错误,请修改:

（1）受益人公司名称与合同不符,请将 IMPORT AND EXPORT 改为 IMP.
& EXP.。

（2）汇票的种类为即期汇票,请将 30 DAYS AFTER 删除。

（3）开证不是纽约分行,请修改。

（4）删除保险条款。

（5）需要体检买方出具的质检证书,此为软条款,请删除。

（6）最迟装运期应该为 NOV. 30th, 2008

（7）应该允许转运。

(二)对照合同,请指出六处信用证与合同不符的地方

审核结果如下:

经审核信用证有如下错误,请修改

（1）开证申请人公司名称错误,请改为 Hong Kong Food Company。

（2）信用证的总金额与合同不一致,请改为 125 000（SAY ONE HUNDRED
TWENTY FIVE THOUSAND ONLY）。

（3）提单里应该表明"FREIGHT PREPAID"。

（4）请删除保险条款。

（5）目的港应该为 VANCOURE 而非 Montreal。

（6）罐头的规格应该为 340gram per tin，而非 430gram per tin

（三）单选题

1. B 2. C 3. B

（四）多选题

1. AD 2. ABD 3. ABCD 4. ABD 5. BDE

（五）判断题

1. T 2. F 3. F 4. F 5. F 6. F

四、信用证改证函的书写

（一）Please check the L/C with the contract below and then write a letter to ask for the amendment to the L/C

Dear Sirs,

While we thank you for your L/C No. 112235，we regret to say that we have found some discrepancies after examining it carefully. You are requested to make the following amendments：

1. The amount both in figures and in words should respectively read"GBP 14550(Say British Pounds Fourteen Thousand Five Hundred And Fifty Only).

2. "From Copenhagen to China port"should read "From China port to Copenhagen".

3. The Bill of Lading should be marked "Freight Prepaid"instead of "Freight Collect".

4. Delete the clause "Partial shipments and transshipment prohibited".

   Please make the necessary amendment as soon as possible.

（二）根据下列合同审核信用证，指出不符点并草拟改证函

Dear Sirs,

While we thank you for your L/C, we regret to say that we have found some discrepancies after examining it carefully. You are requested to make the following amendments：

1. Partial shipments should not be allowed.

2. The date of shipment should be July 30，2006 instead of 2006. 6. 30

　　Please make the necessary amendment as soon as possible.

Yours faithfully，

（三）审证并草拟改证函

1. Dear Sirs，

While we thank you for your L/C，we regret to say that we have found some discrepancies after examining it carefully. You are requested to make the following amendments：

（1）"Draft at 30 days sight"should be "Draft at sight".

（2）"Partial shipment permitted"should be "Partial shipment not allowed".

（3）"S/C No. GL25013"should be "S/C No. GD25013".

（4）Presentation period should within 15days.

Please make the necessary amendment as soon as possible.

Yours faithfully，

2. Dear Sirs，

While we thank you for your L/C，we regret to say that we have found some discrepancies after examining it carefully. You are requested to make the following amendments：

（1）"Partial shipments not allowed"should be "Partial shipment allowed".

（2）"Port of Loading from Shanghai" should be"Port of Loading from Dalian".

（3）"Covering All Risks"should be "Covering F. P. A. Risk".

　　Please make the necessary amendment as soon as possible.

Yours faithfully，

3. Dear Sirs，

While we thank you for your L/C，we regret to say that we have found some discrepancies after examining it carefully. You are requested to make the following amendments：

（1）The amount both in figures and in words should respectively read"HKD 900 000"（Say HongKong Dollars Nine Hundred Thousand Only）instead of HONGKONG DOLLARS TWO HUNDRED THREE THOUSAND ONLY.

（2）"Freight Collect"should be "Freight Prepaid".

(3) "Insurance Policy for invoice value plus 50%"should be "Plus 10%".

(4) "All Risks and War Risks should be W. P. A and War Risks"

(5) "65% Poly ester, 35% Cotton"should be "100% Cotton".

(6) "From China to Port KELANG"should be "From Nanjing to Port Singapore".

(7) Delete the clause "Partial shipment are allowed. Transhipment prohibitted".

Please make the necessary amendment as soon as possible.

Yours faithfully,

4. Dear Sirs,

While we thank you for your L/C, we regret to say that we have found some discrepancies after examining it carefully. You are requested to make the following amendments:

(1) "Revocable L/C"should be "Irrevocable L/C".

(2) The amount in figures should read"USD 25 650"instead of "USD 256 500".

(3) "L/C available by NanYang Commercial Bank"should be "L/C available by Bank of China, Shanghai".

(4) "Draft at 20 days sight"should be "Draft at sight".

(5) "Transhipment prohibited"should be "Transhipment allowed".

(6) "the port of destination should be Hongkong"

(7) "Freight Collect"should be "Freight Prepaid".

(8) "Insurance clause should be All Risks and War Risks".

(9) "Confirmation without"should be "Confirmation with"

　　Please make the necessary amendment as soon as possible.

Yours faithfully,

(四)根据合同审核信用证

Dear Sirs,

While we thank you for your L/C, we regret to say that we have found some discrepancies after examining it carefully. You are requested to make the following amendments:

1. "Revocable L/C"should be "Irrevocable L/C".

2. "Draft at 30 days sight"should be "Draft at sight".

3. "Transhipment not allowed" should be "Transhipment allowed".

4. "Latest Date of shipment"should be "FRB. 28, 2009".

5. "Presentation period should to be presented within 15/21 days after the

date of shipment".

Please make the necessary amendment as soon as possible.

Yours faithfully,

（五）审证并改证

Dear Sirs,

While we thank you for your L/C, we regret to say that we have found some discrepancies after examining it carefully. You are requested to make the following amendments:

1. "Draft at 45 days sight"should be "Draft at sight".
2. "Port of Loading should be Shanghai Port".
3. "S/C No. 800678"should read "S/C No. JXIND4006".
4. "Covering Risks F. P. A"should be "Covering F. P. A. and War Risk".

Please make the necessary amendment as soon as possible.

Yours faithfully,

单　据　篇

一、商务单据的制作与审核

（一）根据材料审核发票，指出单据错误并修改

信用证审核结果如下：

1. 信用证中信用证的性质是可撤销（REVOCABLE）的，与合同不一致，应改为不可撤销（IRREVOCABLE）。
2. 信用证中的到期地点是在瑞典，与合同不一致，应改为中国。
3. 信用证中汇票的付款期限是见票后 30 天付款，与合同不一致，应改为即期付款。
4. 信用证中转船是不允许，与合同不一致，应改为允许。
5. 信用证中最迟装运期是 FEB. 08，2009，与合同不一致，应改为 FEB. 28，2009。
6. 信用证中 ART 3901400 的货物的价格是 USD 1. 20/PC，应改为 USD 1. 02/PC。
7. 信用证中贸易术语是 CIF SHANGHAI，应改为 CIF GOTHENBURG。

8. 信用证中保险险别是一切险（ALL RISKS），与合同不一致，应改为平安险（F. P. A RISKS）。

9. 信用证中投保为发票价值的 120％，与合同不一致，应改为发票价值的 110％。

10. 信用证中交单期为装运日期后的 5 天内交单，与合同不一致，应改为 15 天。

11. 信用证中规定信用证适用的惯例是《UCP 500》，应改为《UCP 600》，1993 REVISON 应改为 2007 REVISON.

发票错误之处：

1. 商业发票中的装运港为 CHINESE PORTS，应改为 SHANGHAI PORT, CHINA。

2. 商业发票中单价部分缺少贸易术语，应加上 CIF GOTHENBURG。

3. 商业发票中的唛头描写不标准，应改为 JYSK

GOTHENBURG

VOS. 1-1196

4. 商业发票中数量 QUANTITY 部分应该加总，应为 23 920 PCS。

成功发展贸易有限公司

SUCCESS DEVELOPMENT TRADING LTD.

39/FL，FLATF，TIANHE PLAZA SHANGHAI, CHINA

COMMERCIAL INVOICE

TEL：0086-21-65658933

FAX：0086-21-65658932

INV. NO：CG2003118

DATE：FEB. 19，2009

S/C NO：2008KG02350

L/C NO：667-01-3042855

TO：JYSK AB

　　FOERETA 6 S-23237 ARLOEV SWEDEN

FROM：SHANGHAI PORT, CHINA　　TO：GOTHENBURG　BY：SEA

MARKS&.NOS.	DESCRIPTION OF GOODS	QUANTITY	UNIT PRICE	AMOUNT
			CIF	GOTHENBURG
	LEATHER GLOVE		USD 1. 25/PC	USD 10 500. 00
JYSK	ART 3900300	8 400 PCS	USD 1. 02/PC	USD 15 830. 40
GOTHENBURG	ART 3901400	15 520 PCS		
VOS. 1-1196	TOTAL	23 920 PCS		USD 26 330. 40

TOTAL AMOUNT：U. S. DOLLARS TWENTY SIX THOUSAND THREE HUNDRED AND THIRTY AND CENTS FOURTY ONLY.

SUCCESSDEVELOPMENTTRADING LTD.

（二）根据信用证以及相关资料缮制以下单据

INVOICE

NO. 07INC9988　　　　　　　　　　　MAY5, 2007

TO: DIRAMODE

3 RUE DU DUREMONT

BP 21, 59531 NEUVILLE EN FERRAIN FRANCE　**SHIPPED S. S.**　FUXING V. 196

　　　　　　　　　　　　　　　　　　SHIPMENT DATE　MAY 20, 2007

　　　　　　　　　　　　　　　　　　DESTINATION DUNKIRK FRANCE

Marks & Nos.	Description of Goods	Amount
DIRAMODE	500 CARTONS (10 000 PCS)OF	CIF DUNKIRK
DUNKIRK	LADIES DRESS　　USD 8. 00/PC	USD 80 000. 00
C/NO. 1~500	LESS 3% CIMMISION	USD　2 400. 00
		======================
		TOTAL　　USD 77 600. 00

SAY TOTAL U. S. DOLLARS SEVENTY-SEVEN THOUSAND SIX HUNDRED
ONLY.

PACKED IN CARTONS OF 20PCS EACH, 500CARTONS TOTAL.

G. W.: 21 KGS/CARTON TOTAL GROSS WEIGHT: 10 500 KGS

N. W.: 20 KGS/CARTON TOTAL NET WEIGHT: 10 000 KGS

MEST: 0. 1 M³/CARTON TOTAL MEASUREMENT: 50 M³

L/C NO.: 00001LCC0603814

CONTRACT NO.: SCGD2007001

　　　　　　　　　GUANGDONG FENG QING TRADING CO.

PACKING LIST

Commodity　LADIES DRESS　　　Destination　　DUNKIRK FRANCE

Contract No.　SCGD2007001　　　Consignee DIRAMODE

　　　　　　　　　　　　　　　　3 RUE DU DUREMONT

　　　　　BP 21,59531 NEUVILLE EN FERRAIN FRANCE

Means of Transportation FROM GUANGZHOU TO DUNKIRK FRANCE BY SEA

Marks &. Nos.	Description of goods	Quantity	Package	Gross Weight	Net Weight	Measurement
DIRAMODE	LADIES DRESS	10 000 PCS	500 CARTONS	10 500 KGS	10 000KGS	50 M³
DUNKIRK						
C/NO. 1~500						
		========================				
TOTAL		10 000 PCS	500 CARTONS	10 500 KGS	10 000 KGS	50 M³

SAY TOTAL FIVE HUNDRED CARTONS ONLY.

PACKED IN CARTONS OF 20 PCS EACH，500CARTONS TOTAL.

G. W.：21 KGS/CARTON TOTAL GROSS WEIGHT：10 500 KGS

N. W.：20 KGS/CARTON TOTAL NET WEIGHT：10 000 KGS

MEST：0. 1 M³/CARTON TOTAL MEASUREMENT：50 M³

L/C NO.：00001LCC0603814

CONTRACT NO.：SCGD2007001

GUANGDONG FENG QING TRADING CO.

GUANGDONG FENG QING TRADING CO.

NO. 31 ZHONG SHAN ROAD GUANGZHOU. CHINA

FAX：+88-20-8331 5567

INVOICE NO.

DATE：MAY 20，2007

TO MESSRS：DIRAMODE

3 RUE DU DUREMONT

BP 21，59531 NEUVILLE EN FERRAIN FRANCE

SHIPPING ADVICE

(1) NAME OF COMMODITY：LADIES DRESS

(2) QUANTITY：10 000 PCS

(3) INVOICE VALUE：USD 77 600. 00

(4) NAME OF STEAMER：FUXING V. 196

(5) DATE OF SHIPMENT：MAY 20，2007

(6) CREDIT NO.：00001LCC0603814

(7) S/C NO.：SCGD2007001

(8) PORT OF LOADING：GUANGZHOU

(9) PORT OF DISCHARGE：DUNKIRK FRANCE

(10) SHIPPING MARK：DIRAMODE

DUNKIRK

C/NO. 1~500

（三）根据资料缮制发票

Issuer ZHEJIANG CLOTHING IMP. AND EXP. CO., LTD. 902 WULIN ROAD, HANGZHOU,CHINA	商 业 发 票 **COMMERCIAL INVOICE**		
To ORCHID TRADING LTD. UNIT 513, CHINACHEM BLDG., 78 MODY ROAD, TST, KOWLOON,HONG KONG	No. 04DL0F015		Date APR. 22, 2008
Transport details FROM SHANGHAI CHINA TO ROTTERDAM BY SEA	S/C No. B04ED121		L/C No. 540370
	Terms of payment BY L/C		
Marks and numbers	Number and kind of packages Description of goods	Quantity	Unit price	Amount
ORCHID B04ED121 ROTTERDAM C/NO. 1-224	LADIES WEARS STYLE NO. 1484521 112 CARTONS OF ROUNDNECK STYLE NO. 1484521 112 CARTONS OF JACKET	1 568 PCS 1 568 PCS	CIF ROTTERDAM USD 5.40/PC USD 6.20/PC	USD 8 467.20 USD 9 721.60
	TOTAL 313 6PCS			USD 18 188.80

SAY TOTAL U.S. DOLLARS EIGHTEEN THOUSAND ONE HUNDRED AND EIGHTY-EIGHT POINT EIGHTY ONLY.

L/C NO.: 540370

STYLE NO.1484020 ROUNDNECK 1 568 PCS

STYLE NO.1484521 JACKET　1 568 PCS

ZHEJIANG CLOTHING IMP. AND EXP. CO., LTD.

（四）根据信用证缮制下列单据

ISSUER HEBEI MACHINERY IMP. AND EXP. CORP (GROUP) 720 DONGFENG ROAD, SHIJIAZHUANG, CHINA		COMMERCIAL INVOICE			
TO LUCKY VICTORY INTERNATIONAL STUTTGART STIR. 5, D-84618, SCHORNDORF, GERMANY		NO. INOV 080220		DATE FEB. 20, 2008	
TRANSPORT DETAILS FROM TIANJIN CHINA TO HAMBURG GERMANY		S/C NO. 08HM256		L/C NO. 08-4-1520	
		TERMS OF PAYMENT BY L/C AT 30 DAYS SIGHT			
Marks & Numbers	Description of goods	Quantity	Unit Price		Amount
LUCKY VICTORY S/C NO. 08HM256 HAMBURG GERMANY	STAINLESS STEEL SPADE HEAD ART. NO. S569 ART. NO. F671 **TOTAL**	4 800 PCS 3 200 PCS 8 000 PCS	CIF USD 5. 60/PC USD 9. 60/PC		HAMBURG USD 26 880. 00 USD 30 720. 00 USD 57 600. 00

SAY TOTAL: U. S. DOLLARS FIFTY-SEVEN THOUSAND SIX HUNDRED ONLY.

L/C NO.: 08-4-1520

HEBEI MACHINERY IMP. AND EXP. CORP (GROUP)

ISSUER HEBEI MACHINERY IMP. AND EXP. CORP (GROUP) 720 DONGFENG ROAD, SHIJIAZHUANG，CHINA		PACKING LIST		
TO LUCKY VICTORY INTERNATIONAL STUTTGART STIR. 5， D-84618，SCHORNDORF, GERMANY		INVOICE NO. INOV 080220		DATE FEB. 20，2008
Marks&Numbers	Number and kind of package Description of goods	N. W.	G. W.	MEASUREMENT
LUCKY VICTORY S/C NO. 08HM256 　HAMBURG 　GERMANY	 STAINLESS STEEL SPADE HEAD 　　ART. NO. S569 　　ART. NO. F671 100 PCS/CTN 80 CTNS	6 000 KGS	6 300 KGS	18 CBM
	TOTAL 6 000 KGS		6 300 KGS	18 CBM
	HEBEI MACHINERY IMP. AND EXP. CORP (GROUP)			

(五) 阅读信用证及相关资料并制作单据

1. 下面是一张已经填好的装箱单，请根据上面的 L/C 和补充资料将错误修改在空白处。

PACKING LIST

S/C NO.: P. O. 2007-018　　　　　　　　SHIPPING MARK：
INVOICE NO.: CFF-016　　　　　　　　　　　　N/M
L/C NO.: 078230CDI1117LC

C/NOS.	NOS&KIND OF PKGS	QTY(BAGS)	G. W. (KGS)	N. W. (KGS)	MEAS. (M³)
TROPIC ISLE CANED MANDARIN ORIANGES LS—WHOLE SEGMENTS 950 CTNS					
		5 760	17 138	16 188	183. 65
TOTAL		5 760	17 138	16 188	183. 65

TOTAL AMOUNT：SAY US DOLLARS TEN THOUSAND EIGHT HUNDRED AND THIRTY ONLY.

　　　　　　　　　　　　　　HUNAN CEREALS, OILS &FOODSTUFFS
　　　　　　　　　　　　　　IMPORT & EXPORT CORPORATION

装箱单缮制错误的地方有：

(1) 装箱单中 SHIPPING MARK 标为 N/M，应该为 W. F. L.
　　　　　　　　　　　　　　　　VANCOUVER
　　　　　　　　　　　　　　　　C/NO.：1-950

(2) 信用证中要求"除了发票和汇票，所有的单据中都不能显示信用证号码"，但是在装箱单中标注了信用证的号码。

(3) 货物的体积应该是 18. 365 M³，不是 183. 65 M³。

(4) 货物的数量应该是 5 700 BAGS，不是 5 760 BAGS。

(5) 在 NOS&KIND OF PKGS 一项中应写为 950 CTNS OF TROPIC ISLE CANNED MANDARIN ORIANGES LS-WHOLE SEGMENTS。

(6) 在体积和数量的总计（即 TOTAL 部分）中应写为 18. 365 和 5 700。

(7) 装箱单中不应该写总金额的大写，应该是外包装总数量的大写，即：TO-TAL SAY NINE HUNDRED AND FIFTY CARTONS ONLY.

2. 填制下列单据：

COMMERCIAL INVOICE

TO：WENSCO FOODS LTD.，　　　　　　　　　INVOICE NO.：CFF-016

　　RUA DE GREENLAND STREET，68-A　　　　DATE：FEB. 1，2007

　　1260-297 WELL D. COQUITLAM，B. C.　　　　S/C NO.：P. O. 2007-018

　　CANADA　　　　　　　　　　　　　　　L/C NO.：078230CDI1117LC

FROM：HUANGPU　　　　　　　TO：VANCOUVER B. C.

MARKS&NOS.	DESCRIPTIONS OF GOODS	QUANTITY (CTNS)	UNIT PRICE (USD/CTN)	AMOUNT
W. F. L. VANCOUVER C/NO.：1~950	950 CTNS OF TROPIC ISLE CANNED MANDARIN ORIANGES LS-WHOLE SEGMENTS WE HEREBY CERTIFY THAT THE GOODS ARE OF CHINESE ORIGIN. P/I NO. CF07018 PACKING：IN PLASTIC BAGS OF 2. 84 KGS EACH THEN SIX BAGS IN A CARTON	950 CTNS (5 700 BAGS)	CIF USD 11. 40/CTN	VANCOUVER B. C. USD 10 830. 00
TOTAL AMOUNT：	SAY U. S. DOLLARS TEN THOUSAND EIGHT HUNDRED AND THIRTY ON-LY.			

TOTAL NUMBER OF PACKAGE：SAY NINE HUNDRED AND FIFTY CARTONS ONLY.

　　　　　　　　　　　　　　　　　　HUNAN CEREALS，OILS &FOODSTUFFS

　　　　　　　　　　　　　　　　　　IMPORT & EXPORT CORPORATION

(六) 根据信用证缮制发票和装箱单

SHANGHAI FOREIGN TRADE CORP.
SHANGHAI, CHINA
COMMERCIAL INVOICE

To: MOUN CO., LTD
   NO. 443, 249 ROAD
   BANGKOK
THAILAND
From:

Invoice No.: INV 001020
Invoice Date: DEC. 5, 2000
S/C No.: SC001020
S/C Date: OCT. 20, 2000

To:

SHANGHAI, CHINA   BANGKOK, THAILAND

Letter of Credit No.: BKKB1103043   BANGKOK BANK PUBLIC

Issued By: COMPANY LIMITED
                 BANCKOK

Marks and Numbers	Number and kind of package Description of goods	Quantity	Unit Price	Amount
MOUN SC001020 BANGKOK NO. 1-40	CFR BANGKOK			
	40 DRUM OF . ISONIAZID BP98	2 000 KGS	USD 9.00 PER KG	USD 18 000.00
	PACKED IN 50 KGS/DRUM TOTAL 40 DRUMS			FOB=USD 16 500 FREIGHT= USD 1 500.00

TOTAL: 2 000 KGS   USD 18 000.00

SAY TOTAL: U.S. DOLLARS EIGHTEEN THOUSAND ONLY.
L/C NUMBER: BKKB1103043

SHANGHAI FOREIGN TRADE CORP.

SHANGHAI FOREIGN TRADE CORP.

SHANGHAI, CHINA

PACKING LIST

To：MOUN CO.，LTD

　　NO. 443,249ROAD BANGKOKTHAILAND

Invoice No.：INV 01020

Invoice Date：DEC. 5，2000

S/C No.：SC001020

S/C Date：OCT. 20，2000

From：SHANGHAI, CHINA

To：BANGKOK，THAILAND

Letter of Credit No.：BKKB1103043　　　　Date of Shipment：DEC. 20，2000

Marks and Numbers	Number and kind of package Description of goods	Quantity	Package	G. W.	N. W.	Meas.
MOUN SC001020 BANGKOK NO. 1-40	40 DRUM OF . ISONIAZID BP98 PACKED IN 50 KGS/DRUM TOTAL 40 DRUMS	2 000 KGS	40 DRUMS	2 300 KGS	2 000 KGS	
	TOTAL：	2 000 KGS	40 DRUMS	2 300 KGS	2 000 KGS	

SAY TOTAL：FORTY DRUMS ONLY

SHANGHAI FOREIGN TRADE CORP.

（七）依据销售合同和信用证以及有关资料缮制商业发票、装箱单

ABC 纺织品进出口有限公司
ABC TEXTILES IMP. & EXP. CORPORATION
127ZHONGSHAN RD. E. 1 SHANGHAI P. R. OF CHINA

商 业 发 票
COMMERCIAL INVOICE

Messers:TOMSCN TEXTJLES INC.

 3384 VINCENT ST

 DOWNSVIEW. ONTARIO

 M3J. 2J4 CANADA

INVOICE NO: D2C4193

INVOICE DATE: APR. 4，2008

L/C NO.: T-017641

L/C DATE: MAR. 25，2008

S/C NO.: 23CA1006

Exporter: ABC TEXILES IMPORT AND EXPORT CORPORATION

 127 ZHONGSHAN RD. E. 1

 SHANGHAI P. R. OF CHINA

Transport details:	Terms of payment:
FROM SHANGHAI TO TORONTO	BY L/C 30 DAYS AFTER SIGHT

MARKS AND NUMBERS	DESCRIPTION OF GOODS	QUANTITY	UNIT PRICE	AMOUNT
TOMSON	ART. NO. 77111		CIF	TORONTO
23CA1006	TRUERAN DYED JEAN			
TORONTO	POLYESTES 65%, COTTON 35%			
NO. 1-60	20×20，94×60，112/114cm,			
	40M AND UP ALLOWING 15% 27. 432 M			
	AND UP IN IRREGULAR CUTS			
COL.		M.	USD/M	USD
RED		4 000	1. 56	6 240. 00
SILVER		3 000	1. 32	3 960. 00
FIESTA		4 000	1. 56	6 240. 00
DKNAVY		3 000	1. 62	4 860. 00
WINE		2 200	1. 62	3 564. 00
ELEPHANT		3 000	1. 44	4 320. 00
BLACK		4 800	1. 62	7 776. 00
TOTAL:		24 000		36 960. 00

TOTAL AMOUNT IN WORDS:SAY U. S. DOLLARS THIRTY-SIX THOUSAND NINE HUNDRED AND SIXTY ONLY.

TOTAL GROSS WEIGHT: SAY SEVENTY-FIVE HUNDRED KGS ONLY

TOTAL NUMBER OF PACKAGE: SAY SIXTY CARTONS ONLY

ABC TEXILES IMPORT AND EXPORT CORPORATION

ABC 纺织品进出口有限公司

ABC TEXTILES IMP. & EXP. CORPORATION

127ZHONGSHAN RD. E. 1 SHANGHAI P. R. OF CHINA

装　箱　单

PACKING LIST

Exporter：ABC TEXILES IMPORT AND EXPORT
CORPORATION
127 ZHONGSHAN RD. E. 1
SHANGHAI P. R. OF CHINA

DATE：APR. 4，2008
INVOICE NO. :D2C4193
S/C NO. :23CA1006

BUYER：TOMSCN TEXTJLES INC.
3384 VINCENT ST
DOWNSVIEW. ONTARIO
M3J. 2J4 CANADA

TRANSPORT DETAILS：FROM SHANGHAI CHINA TO TORONTO CANADA

C/NOS.	NOS& KINDS OF PACKS	ITEM	QTY.	G. W.	N. W.	MEAS.
	ART. NO. 77111 TRUERAN DYED JEAN POLYESTES 65%，COTTON 35% 20×20，94×60，112/114cm， 40M AND UP ALLOWING 15% 27. 432 M AND UP IN IRREGULAR CUTS					
1—10	10 CTNS	RED	4 000 M	1 250 KGS	1 170 KGS	0. 410 M³
11—17	7 CTNS	SILVER	2 800 M	875 KGS	819 KGS	0. 287 M³
18—27	10CTNS	FIESTA	4 000 M	1 250 KGS	1 170 KGS	0. 410 M³
28—34	7CTNS	DK. NAVY	2 800 M	875 KGS	819 KGS	0. 287 M³
35—39	5CTNS	WINE	2 000 M	625 KGS	585 KGS	0. 205 M³
40—46	7CTNS	ELEPHANT	2 800 M	875 KGS	819 KGS	0. 287 M³
47—58	12CTNS	BLACK	4 800 M	1 500 KGS	1 404 KGS	0. 491 M³
59	1CTNS	SILVER 200 M DK. NAVY 200 M		125 KGS	117 GKS	0. 041 M³
60	1CTNS	WINE 200 M ELEPHANT 200 M		125 KGS	117 KGS	0. 041 M³
TOTAL :60CTNS			24 000 M	7 500 KGS	7 020 KGS	2. 459 M³

TOTAL NUMBER OF PACKAGE：SAY SIXTY CARTONS ONLY

TOTAL QUANTITY：SAY TWENTY-FOUR THOUSAND METERS ONLY

TOTAL GROSS WEIGHT：SAY SEVENTY-FIVE HUNDRED KGS ONLY

TOTAL NET WEIGHT：SAY SEVEN THOUSAND AND TWENTY KGS ONLY

TOTAL MEASUREMENR：SAY TWO POINT FOUR HUNDRED AND FIFTY-NINE M³ ONLY

ABC TEXILES IMPORT AND EXPORT CORPORATION

(STAMP)

（八）根据信用证、合同和补充资料的内容缮制商业发票

商业发票：

SHANGHAI IMPORT & EXPORT TRADE CORPORATION.
1321 ZHONGSHAN ROAD SHANGHAI, CHINA
COMMERCIAL INVOICE

TEL：021-65788877

FAX：021-65788876

INV NO：_XH056671

DATE：FEB. 01, 2005

S/C NO.：HX050264

TO：TKAMLA CORPORATION

  6-7KAWARA MACH

  OSAKA, JAPAN

FROM SHANGHAI,CHINA   TO OSAKA, JAPAN

DRAWN UNDER FUJI BANK LTD   L/C NO. 33416852

MARKS & NO	DESCRIPTION OF GOODS	QUANTITY	U/PRICE	AMOUNT
T. C	250 CTNS OF		CIF OSAKA	
OSAKA	COTTON SHIRT			
C/NO. 1~250	ART NO. H666	500 PCS	USD 5. 50	USD 2 750. 00
	ART NO. HX88	500 PCS	USD 4. 50	USD 2 250. 00
	ART NO. HE21	500 PCS	USD 4. 80	USD 2 400. 00
	ART NO. HA56	500 PCS	USD 5. 20	USD 2 600. 00
	ART NO. HH46	500 PCS	USD 5. 00	USD 2 500. 00
	TOTAL	2500 PCS		USD 12 500. 00

TOTAL AMOUNT：SAY U. S. DOLLARS TWELVE THOUSAND FIVE
          HUNDRED ONLY.

PACKED IN CARTONS OF 10 PCS, TOTAL 250 CARTONS.

PACKED IN TWO 20'CONTAINER(NO. TEXU2263999；TEXU2264000)

G. W.：20. 5 KGS/CTN TOTAL G. W.：5 125 KGS

N. W.：20 KGS/CTN TOTAL N. W.：5 000 KGS

MESUREMENT：0. 456 M³ TOTAL MEAS：114 M³

          SHANGHAI IMPORT & EXPORT TRADE CORPORATION

          李明

（九）根据信用证以及相关资料缮制发票和装箱单

COMMERCIAL INVOICE		
1) SEELER CHINA SHAANXI TEXTILE IMPORT N EXPORT CORPORATION. NO.A-113 BEIKOU JIANGUO ROAD, XIAN, CHINA.	**3) INVOICE NO.** SHAANXITEX08/03/A	**4) INVOICE DATE** APRIL 15, 2008
	5) L/C NO. 01080099-C	**6) DATE** MARCH 03, 2008
	7) ISSUED BY THE CITY BANK LIMITED BANGABANDHU AVENUE BRANCH, DHAKA, BANGLADESH.	
2) BUYER F.K.TRADING 26, AHSANULLAH ROAD, NAWAB BARI, HAKA-1100, BANGLADESH.	**8) CONTRACT NO.** 08STRY040	**9) DATE** FEBURARY 25, 2008
	10) FROM XIANGGANG CHINA	**11) TO** CHITTAGONG BANGLADESH
	12) SHIPPED BY JINXING V.788	**13) PRICE TERM** CFR CHITTAGONG

14) MARKS	15) DESCRIPTION OF GOODS	16) QTY.	17) UNIT PRICE	18) AMOUNT
F.K. CHITTAGONG NOS.1-600	600 CTNS OF TEXTILE INDUSTRIES "TAYEN PAGDOA" BRAND POLYESTER 65, VISOSE 35 ART NO. TR40S/1	60 000 LBS	USD 0.68/LB	CFR CHITTAGONG USD 40 800
H.S. CODE : 5509. 11	TOTAL:	60 000 LBS		USD 40 800

PACKING/ IN CARTONS 100LBS PER CARTON
TOTAL 600 CARTONS

TOTAL AMOUNT IN WORDS:
SAY U. S. DOLLARS FORTY THOUSAND EIGHT HUNDRED ONLY
TOTAL GROSS WEIGHT:
SAY TWENTY-NINE THOUSAND SEVEN HUNDRED KGS ONLY
TOTAL NUMBER OF PACKAGE:
SAY SIX HUNDRED CARTONS ONLY

19) ISSUED BY
　　CHINA SHAANXI TEXTILE IMPORT N EXPORT CORPORATION.

20) SIGNATURE

PACKING LIST

1) SEELER	3) INVOICE NO.	4) INVOICE DATE
CHINA SHAANXI TEXTILE IMPORT N EXPORT CORPORATION. NO.A-113 BEIKOU JIANGUO ROAD, XIAN, CHINA.	SHAANXITEX08/03/A	APRIL 15, 2008

	5) FROM	6) TO
	XIANGGANG CHINA	CHITTAGONG BANGLADESH

7) TOTAL PACKAGES (IN WORDS)
SAY SIX HUNDRED CARTONS ONLY

2) BUYER	8) MARKS & NOS.
F.K.TRADING 26, AHSANULLAH ROAD, NAWAB BARI, HAKA-1100, BANGLADESH.	F.K. CHITTAGONG NOS.1-600

9) C/NOS. 10) NOS. & KINDS OF PKGS. 11) ITEM 12) QTY. 13) G.W. 14)N.W.
15) MEAS(M³)

1-600   600 CTNS OF TEXTILE INDUSTRIES 60 000 LBS 29 700 KGS 27 240 KGS 109.98 M^3

     "TAYEN PAGDOA" BRAND

     POLYESTER 65, VISOSE 35

     ART NO. TR40S/1

            TOTAL:60 000 LBS 29 700 KGS 27 240 KGS 109.98M^3

PACKING/ IN CARTONS 100LBS PER CARTON

TOTAL GROSS WEIGHT:
SAY TWENTY-NINE THOUSAND SEVEN HUNDRED KGS ONLY

TOTAL NET WEIGHT:
SAY TWENTY-SEVEN THUSAND TWO HUNDRED AND FORTY KGS ONLY

TOTAL NUMBER OF PACKAGE:
SAY SIX HUNDRED CARTONS ONLY

16) ISSUED BY
    CHINA SHAANXI TEXTILE IMPORT N EXPORT CORPORATION.
17) SIGNATURE

（十）根据下列所提供资料和信用证有关信息缮制单据

发票

KUNSHAN HUACHENG WEAVING AND DYEING CO.,LTD
HUANGLONG RD., LIUJIA ZHEN, SUZHOU,JIANGSU, CHINA
COMMERCIAL INVOICE

TO:	YOU DA TRADE CO.,LTD., 101 QUEENS ROAD CENTRAL, HONGKONG TEL：852-28566666		INVOICE NO.:	INV080210
			INVOICE DATE:	FEB. 10, 2008
			S/C NO.:	99WS061
			S/C DATE:	DEC. 10, 2007
FROM:	SHANGHAI CHINA	TO:	HONGKONG	
LETTER OF CREDIT NO.:	HK1112234	ISSUED BY:	BANK OF CHINA HONGKONG BRANCH	

MARKS AND NUMBERS	DESCRIPTION OF GOODS	QUANTITY	UNIT PRICE	AMOUNT
YOU DA HONGKONG R/NO.：1-3298	3298 ROLLS OF 100 PCT NYLON FABRICS	100 000 YARDS	CIF USD 0. 3368/YD	HONGKONG USD 33 680. 00
	L/C NO.：HK1112234 CONTRACT NO. 99WS061			
TOTAL:		100 000 YARDS		USD 33 680. 00

SAY TOTAL U. S. DOLLARS THIRTY-THREE THOUSAND SIX HUNDRED AND EIGHTY ON-LY.

KUNSHAN HUACHENG WEAVING AND DYEING CO.,LTD

装箱单

KUNSHAN HUACHENG WEAVING AND DYEING CO.,LTD
HUANGLONG RD., LIUJIA ZHEN, SUZHOU,JIANGSU, CHINA

PACKING LIST

TO:	YOU DA TRADE CO.,LTD., 101 QUEENS ROAD CENTRAL,HONGKONG TEL：852-28566666		INVOICE NO.：	INV080210
			INVOICE DATE：	FEB. 10，2008
			S/C NO.：	99WS061
			S/C DATE：	DEC. 10，2007
FROM：	SHANGHAI CHINA	**TO：**	HONGKONG	
LETTER OF CREDIT NO.：	HK1112234	**ISSUED BY：**	BANK OF CHINA HONGKONG BRANCH	

MARKS AND NUMBERS	DESCRIPTION OF GOODS	QUANTITY	PACKAGE	G. W.	N. W.	MEAS.
YOU DA HONGKONG R/NO.：1-3298	3298 ROLLS OF 100PCT NYLON FABRICS	100 000 YARDS	3 298 ROLLS	14 077 KGS	12 584 KGS	35 CBM
	L/C NO.：HK1112234 CONTRACT NO. 99WS061					
TOTAL		100 000 YARDS	3 298 ROLLS	14 077 KGS	12 584 KGS	35 CBM

SAY TOTAL THREE THOUSAND TWO HUNDRED AND NINETY-EIGHT ROLLS ONLY

KUNSHAN HUACHENG WEAVING AND DYEING CO.,LTD

受益人证明

KUNSHAN HUACHENG WEAVING AND DYEING CO.,LTD
HUANGLONG RD., LIUJIA ZHEN, SUZHOU,JIANGSU, CHINA

BENIFICIARY'S LETTER

MESSERS:YOU DA TRADE CO.,LTD.,

101 QUEENS ROAD CENTRAL,HONGKONG

TEL:852-28566666

DEAR SIRS:

RE:CONTRACT NO.:99WS061

L/C NO.:HK1112234

WE HEREBY INFORM YOU THAT THE GOODS UNDER THE ABOVE MENTIONED CREDIT HAVE BEEN SHIPPED. THE DETAILS OF THE SHIPMENT ARE AS FOLLOWS:

COMMODITY:100 PCT NYLON FABRICS

QUANTITY:100 000 YARDS

TOTAL AMOUNT:USD 33 680.00

OCEAN VESSEL:DANUBHUM/S009

PORT OF LOADING:SHANGHAI

PORT OF DESTINATION:HONGKONG

DATE OF SHIPMENT:APR.1, 2008

KUNSHAN HUACHENG WEAVING AND DYEING CO.,LTD

（十一）根据信用证审核相关单据,找出不符点

发票中的错误：

1. 运输方式中删掉贸易术语

2. 单价中的术语应该是 CIF 不是 CFR

3. 发票中缺少订单号

4. 发票中缺少总计

装箱单中的错误：

1. 发票号填写错误

2. 缺少订单号

3. 缺少商品的数量

（十二）根据信用证的内容和相关资料制作信用证指定的议付发票和装箱单

Issuer： DESUN TRADING CO.,LTD 224 JINLIN ROAD，NANJING，CHINA	商业发票 **COMMERCIAL INVOICE**	
To： WAV GENEAL TRADING CO.，OSAKA，JAPAN	No： SH25586	Date： APR. 20TH，2008
Transport details： FROM NANJING TO OSAKA BY SEA	S/C No： SHL553	L/C No： JST-AB12
	Terms of payment： L/C AT SIGHT	

Marks and numbers	Description of goods	Quantity	Unit price	Amount
ITOCHU OSAKA NO. 1-200	LADIES GARMENTS PACKING：10 PCS/CTN STYLE NO. ROCOCO STYLE NO. ROMAN- TICO	1 000 PCS 1 000 PCS	CIF OSAKA USD 5. 50 USD 4. 80	USD 5 500. 00 USD 4 800. 00

TOTAL：2 000 PCS USD 10 300. 00

DESUN TRADING CO.,LTD
LI MING

ISSUER	装箱单				
DESUN TRADING CO., LTD 224 JINLIN ROAD, NANJING, CHINA	**PACKING LIST**				
TO WAV GENEAL TRADING CO., OSAKA, JAPAN					
	INVOICE NO. SH25586		DATE APR. 20TH, 2008		
Marks and Numbers	Number and kind of package Description of goods	Quantity	Package	G. W.	N. W.	Meas.
ITOCHU OSAKA NO. 1-200	LADIES GARMENTS PACKING; 10 PCS/CTN STYLE NO. ROCOCO STYLE NO. ROMANTICO	2 000 PCS	200 CARTONS	3 080 KGS	2 600 KGS	24 CBM
TOTAL:	2 000 PCA	200 CARTONS	3 080 KGS	2 600 KGS	24 CBM

DESUN TRADING CO., LTD
LI MING

（十三）根据托收指示书和合同缮制发票、装箱单、装船通知和受益人证明

Issuer： HUBEI TWIN HORSE TRADE CO.,LTD 1ST XUDONG ROAD,WUCHANG,430077,WU- HAN,CHINA	商业发票 **COMMERCIAL INVOICE**	
To： HANWA CO. LTD. KYOTO,JAPAN.	No： HW003	Date： MAY. 15TH,2006
Transport details：	S/C No： HW003	
	Terms of payment： D/P AT SIGHT	

Marks and numbers	Description of goods	Quantity	Unit price	Amount
N/M	FASTENERS 2000 M. JIS FASTENERS BLACK TREATED IN WOODEN CASE OF 25 KG EACH. /GROSS WT 26 KG.	100 M/T	CIF YOKOHAMA USD 6 000. 00	USD 600 000. 00
	TOTAL：100 M/T			USD 600 000. 00

HUBEI TWIN HORSE TRADE CO.,LTD

LI MING

ISSUER HUBEI TWIN HORSE TRADE CO.,LTD 1ST XUDONG ROAD,WUCHANG,430077,WUHAN,CHINA	装箱单 PACKING LIST				
TO HANWA CO. LTD. KYOTO, JAPAN.					
	INVOICE NO. HW003		**DATE** MAY. 15TH,2006		
Marks and Numbers	**Number and kind of package Description of goods**	**Quantity**	**Package**	**G. W.**	**N. W.**	**Meas.**
N/M	FASTENERS 2000 M. JIS FASTENERS BLACK TREATED IN WOODEN CASE OF 25 KG EACH. / GROSS WT 26 KG. 4000WODEN CASES	100 M/T	4 000WODEN CASES	104 000 KGS	100 000 KGS	156 CBM
TOTAL:		100 M/T	4 000 WODEN CASES	104 000 KGS	100 000 KGS	156 CBM

HUBEI TWIN HORSE TRADE CO.,LTD
LI MING

受益人证明

HUBEI TWIN HORSE TRADE CO.,LTD

1ST XUDONG ROAD,WUCHANG,430077,WUHAN,CHINA

CERTIFICATE

NO. HW003

MAY. 20TH, 2006

TO WHOM IT MAY CONCERN:

RE: S/C NO. HW003

WE CERTIFY THAT ONE SET OF NON-NEGOTIABLE SHIPPING DOCU. HAS BEEN SENT DIRECTLY TO HANWA CO. LTD 24 HOURS AFTER THE SHIPMENT IS EFFECTED.

HUBEI TWIN HORSE TRADE CO.,LTD

HUBEI TWIN HORSE TRADE CO.,LTD

1ST XUDONG ROAD,WUCHANG,430077,WUHAN,CHINA

SHIPPING ADVICE

INVOICE NO. HW003

DATE:MAY. 15TH,2006

TO: HANWA CO. LTD. KYOTO, JAPAN.

RE: S/C NO. HW003

DEAR SIRS:

We'd like to advise you that the following mentioned goods has been shipped out,full details are shown as follows:

1. Commodity: FASTENERS JIS FASTENERS BLACK TREATED

2. Quantity:100 M/T

3. Gross weight:104 000 kgs

4. Net weight:100 000 kgs

5. Port of loading: shanghai

6. Port of destination:YOKOHAMA

7. Vessel NO.:BUTTERFLY V. 089

8. B/L NO. KGES5825691

9. Date of shipment:May. 20TH,2006

10. Total value: USD 600 000. 00

11. Estimated time of arrival: May. 25TH,2006

12. Shipping mark:N/M

We hope you are satisfied with the quality of our goods and look forward to receiving your repeat order soon.

Sincerely yours,

HUBEI TWIN HORSE TRADE CO.,LTD

（十四）根据信用证及相关资料缮制发票和装箱单

发票

COMMERCIAL INVOICE

TO:	LAIKI PERAGORA ORPHANIDES LTD. 020 STRATIGOU TIMAGIA AVE.,6046, LARNAKA,CYPRUS		INVOICE NO.:	:04SHGD3029
			INVOICE DATE:	20080209
			S/C NO.:	NO. E03FD121
			S/C DATE:	
FROM:	SHANGHAI GARDEN PRODUCTS IMP. AND EXP. CO., LTD. 27 ZHONGSHAN DONGYI ROAD, SHANGHAI, CHINA	TO:	FROM SHANHAI TO LIMASSOL PORT	
LETTER OF CREDIT NO.:	186/04/10014	ISSUED BY:	CYPRUS POPULAR BANK LTD, LARNAKA	

MARKS AND NUMBERS	DESCRIPTION OF GOODS	QUANTITY	UNIT PRICE	AMOUNT
L. P. O. L. DC NO. 186/04/10014 MADE IN CHINA	WOODEN FLOWER STANDS AND WOODEN FLOWER POTS	350PCS 600PCS	CFR LIMASSOL USD 8. 90/PC USD 5. 00/PC	USD 3 115 USD 3 000
	WE HEREBY CERTIFY THAT THE ABOVE GOODS ARE OF CHINESE ORIGIN			
TOTAL:				USD 6 115

SAY US DOLLAR SIX THOUSAND ONE HUNDRED AND FIFTEEN ONLY

装箱单

PACKING LIST

TO:	LAIKI PERAGORA ORPHANIDES LTD. 020 STRATIGOU TIMAGIA AVE., 6046, LARNAKA, CYPRUS	INVOICE NO.:	04SHGD3029
		INVOICE DATE:	20080209
		S/C NO.:	E03FD121
		S/C DATE:	

FROM:	T SHANGHAI GARDEN PRODUCTS IMP. AND EXP. CO., LTD. 27 ZHONGSHAN DONGYI ROAD, SHANGHAI, CHINA	TO:	FROM SHANHAI TO LIMASSOL PORT
LETTER OF CREDIT NO.:	186/04/10014	ISSUED BY:	CYPRUS POPULAR BANK LTD, LARNAKA

MARKS AND NUMBERS	DESCRIPTION OF GOODS	QUANITY	PACKAGE	G. W.	N. W.	MEAS.
L. P. O. L. DC NO. 186/04/10014 MADE IN CHINA	WOODEN FLOWER STANDS AND WOODEN FLOWER POTS WE HEREBY CERTIFY THAT THE ABOVE GOODS ARE OF CHINESE ORIGIN + EACH PACKING UNIT BEARS AN INDELIBLE MARK INDICATING THE GOODS ARE OF CHINESE ORIGIN	350 PCS 600 PCS	175 CARTONS NO. 1-175 CARTONS, 2 PCS TO A CARTON 150 CARTONS NO. 176-325 CARTONS 4 PCS TO A CARTON	1 925 KGS 2 250 KGS	1 575 KGS 1 950 KGS	12. 1968 CBM 11. 907 CBM
TOTAL			325 CARTONS	4 175 KGS	3 525 KGS	24. 1038 CBM

SAY THREE HUNDRED AND TWENTY FIVE CARTONS ONLY

(十五) 按照下列信用证回答问题并制作发票

回答下列问题(根据信用证)：

1. 信用证的有效期20090115，装运期20081231，交单期20090115。

2. 如装运日为12月20日，则最迟的交单日是20090110。

3. 该封信用证是什么类型的信用证：是不可撤销的、可转让的、指定议付行的跟单信用证。

4. 该封信用证项下外贸交易的成交条件是：CFR DAMMAN PORT。

5. 该封信用证所需提单的抬头人是TO ORDER。

6. 信用证的开证费由开证申请人支付，议付费由受益人支付，通知费由受益人支付。

7. 开证行在审单时如发现单单不符，有三个不符点，则开证行将收取不符点费用USD 162.00。

8. 本信用证有一处不合理的需要修改的地方，请找出并修改：DATE AND PLACE OF EXPIRY 31D：20090115 IN OUR COUNTER 应改为 IN BENEFICIARY'S COUNTRY。

9. 请分析该信用证是否存在风险？

   是存在风险的。

   原因何在？如何处理？

   信用证要求将一套正本提单直接寄给申请人，将会货款两失. 应改为将一套副本提单直接寄给申请人。

COMMERCIAL INVOICE

SELLER INHAI IMP. & EXP. GROUP CORP.		
	INVOICE NO. JH57868	**INVOICE DATE**
	L/C NO. LCF776FV333324	**DATE** 081119
NO. 233, TAIPING ROAD, QINGDAO, CHINA		

BUYER HOPE TRADING EST		
	CONTRACT NO. 564676	**DATE** NOV.10, 2008
	FROM ANY CHINESE PORT	**TO** **DAMMAN**
P.O. BOX 0000 DAMMAN 31491,SAUDI ARABIA	**SHIPPED BY** VESSEL,PRETTY V.11	**PRICE TERM** CFR DAMMAN PORT

MARKS DES. OF GOODS	QTY.	UNIT PRICE	AMOUNT

HOPE
 564676
 	
      FROZEN CHICKEN
      BREAST MEAT, A GRAD
 DAMMA
 N
 	
 CTN.1-20
 00
	24 MTS	USD 1 945.57 /MT CFR
		 DAMMAN
			USD 46 693.68

SAY US DOLLAR FORTY SIX THOU SAND SIX HUNDRED AND NINTY THREE
AND SIXTY EIGHT CENT S ONLY

ISSUED BY JINHAI IMP. & EXP. GROUP CORP.

SIGNATURE

（十六）按以下材料缮制商业发票

COMMERCIAL INVOICE

TO:	SAKA INTERNATIONAL FOOD CO. 26 TORIMI-CHO NISHI-PU, NAGOYA 546, JAPAN		INVOICE NO.:	
			INVOICE DATE:	2007 年 6 月 19 日
			S/C NO.:	NP94051
			S/C DATE:	
FROM:	NINGBO NATIVE PRODUCTS CO. NO. 115 DONGFENG ROAD, NING- BO, CHINA	TO:	FROM NINGBO CHINA TO NAGOYA, JAPAN	
LETTER OF CREDIT NO.:	L/C NO.: 9426	ISSUED BY:	TOKYO BANK LTD., TOKYO	

MARKS AND NUMBERS	DESCRIPTION OF GOODS	QUANTITY	UNIT PRICE	AMOUNT
NO MARKS	FRESH BAMBOO SHOOTS	20M/T	CIF NAGOYA USD 1 080. 00 PER M/T	USD 21 600. 00
	FRESH ASPARAGUS WE HEREBY CERIFY THAT THE ABOVE GOODS ARE OF CHINESE ORIGIN THIS INVOICE IS ISSUED BY NINGBO NATIVE PROD- UCTS CO.	30M/T	USD 1 600. 00 PER M/T	USD 48 000. 00
TOTAL:		50 M/T		USD 69 600. 00

SAY US DOLLAR SIXTY NINE THOUSAND AND SIX HUNDRED ONLY

（十七）按以下材料缮制装箱单

PACKING LIST

TO:	HONGKONG ABC COMPANY NO. 18 BUILDING BROADSTONE STREET, HONGKONG, CHINA		INVOICE NO.:	SY22
			INVOICE DATE:	APR. 15, 2008
			S/C NO.:	SYA2000663
			S/C DATE:	
FROM:	NINGBO SHANYA IMP&. EXP CO. NO. 12 ZHISHAN ROAD, NINGBO	TO:		HONGKONG
LETTER OF CREDIT NO.:	CMD 20808	ISSUED BY:		THE HONGKONG AND SHANGHAI BANKING CORPORATION, HONGKONG

MARKS AND NUMBERS	DESCRIPTION OF GOODS	QUANTITY	PACKAGE	G. W.	N. W.	MEAS.
A B C SYA2000663 HONGKONG CTN/NO. 1-500	FROZEN SOYABEANS	10 M/T	500 SEAWO RTHY CARTONS	10 500 KGS 21 KGS PER CTN	10 000 KGS 20 KGS PER CTN	18 CBM
	THIS PACKING LIST IS ISSUED BY NINGBO SHANYA IMP&. EXP CO.					
TOTAL		10 M/T	500 CARTONS	10 500 KGS	10 000 KGS	18 CBM

SAY FIVE HUNDRED CARTONS ONLY.

（十八）单选题

1	2	3	4	5	6	7	8
A	B	D	D	B	A	C	A
9	10	11	12	13	14	15	16
C	D	B	C	C	B	C	B
17	18	19	20	21	22	23	24
D	C	C	C	C	B	D	C
25	26	27	28	29	30	31	32
C	C	A	B	A	B	B	B
33	34	35	36	37	38	39	40
C	C	D	C				

（十九）多选题

1	2	3	4	5	6	7	8
ABD	AB	ABC	ABCD	ACD	BCDE	ABCD	BCE
9	10	11	12	13	14	15	16
BCD	ABC	ABD	ABEG	AD			

（二十）判断题

1	2	3	4	5	6	7	8
F	F	T	F	F	T	F	T
9	10	11	12	13	14	15	16
T	F	F	T	T	F	F	F
17	18	19	20	21	22	23	24
F	T	F	F	F	F	T	

二、官方单据的制作与审核

(一) 保险单制作

中保财产保险有限公司

发票号码

INVOICE NO.CG2003118

海洋货物运输保险单 NO.2003SH25066

MARINE CARGO TRANSPORTATION INSURANCE POLICY

被保险人：INSURED (已知条件) SUCCESS DEVELOPMENT TRADING LTD

待签发本保险单

保险货物项目	包装、单位 数量	保险金额
LEATHER GLOVE	20 PAIRS TO A CARTON	USD 28 963.44
ART 3900300	8400PAIRS/420 CARTONS	
ART 3901400	15520PAIRS/776 CARTONS	

承保险别 货物标记

INSURANCE : BE EFFECTED BY THE SELLERS FOR 110% INVOICE VALUE,COVERING

F.P.A RISKS AS PER PICC CLAUS

JYSK

GOTHENBURG

VOS.1-1196

总保险金额：

TOTAL AMOUNT INSURED:US DOLLAR TWENTY EIGHT THOUSAND NINE HUNDRED SIXTY THREE AND FORTY FOUR CENTS ONLY

保费： AS ARRANGED 运输工具： MOON V.252 开航日期： AS PER B/L

起运港：CHINESE PORTS TO GOTHENBURG, SWEDEN

中保财产保险有限公司

赔款偿付地点： CLAIMS PAYABLE IF ANY IN SWEDEN.

日期：FEB.26 2009 AT GOTHENBURG, SWEDEN

地址：

（二）根据信用证以及相关资料缮制结汇单据

1. Consignor GUANGDONG FENG QING TRADING CO. NO. 31 ZHONG SHAN ROAD GUANGZHOU. CHINA	中远集装箱运输有限公司 **Cosco container lines** **Port-to-Port or combined transport** **BILL OF LADING**
2. Consignee TO ORDER OF SHIPPER	No. SIO5789666
3. Notify party EXPEDITORS INTERNA- TIONAL-BAT L-ROUTE DES FAMARDS-59818 LESQUIN FRANCE	

4. Combined transport	5. Combined transport
6. Ocean vessel voy. no. FUXING V. 196	7. Port of loading　S/C NO. SCGD2007001 GUANGZHOU L/C NO. 00001LCC0603814
8. Port of discharge 　DUNKIRK FRANCE	9. Combined Transport

Marks & nos. Container/seal no. DIRAMODE DUNKIRK C/NO. 1~500	No. of Container or package 500CARTONS	Description of Goods LADIES, DRESS 21 KGS/CARTON 10 000 PCS	Gross 21 KGS/CARTON TOTAL: 10 500 KGS	Means. M³ 50 CBM

10. Total Number of Container and/or Package(in words) five hundred cartons only.

11. freight & charges	Revenue tons	Rate	Per	Prepaid	Collect
FREIGHT PREPAID **ORIGINAL B/L THREE**			Place and date of issue MAY 20，2007 GUANGZHOU		

Signed for or on behalf of the Carrier Cosco container lines

Original

1. Exporter 2. GUANGDONG FENG QING TRADING CO. 3. NO. 31 ZHONG SHAN ROAD, GUANZHOU, CHINA	Certificate No. **CERTIFICATE OF ORIGIN** **OF** **THE PEOPLE'S REPUBLIC OF CHINA**
4. Consignee DIRAMODE 3 RUE DU DUREMONT BP 21, 59531 NEUVILLE EN FERRAIN FRANCE	**ISSUED DATE: MAY 17, 2007**
5. Means of transport and route **OCEAN VESSEL FUXING V. 196**	6. For certifying authority use only
7. Country/region of destination 8. DUNKIRK, FRANCE	

9. Marks and numbers DIRAMODE DUNKIRK C/NO. 1~500	10. Number and kind of packages; description of goods LADIES DRESS, 10 000 PCS. 21 KGS/CARTON 20 PCS PER CARTON S/C NO. SCGD2007001 L/C NO. 00001LCC0603814	11. H. S. Code 6401. 0058	12. Quantity **10000 PCS** **500 CTNS**	13. Number and date of invoices **NO. O71NC9988** **MAY 5, 2007**

14. Declaration by the exporter
    The undersigned hereby declares that the above details and statements are correct, that all the goods were produced in China and that they comply with the Rules of the People's Republic of China
 	
GUANGDONG FENG QING
TRADING CO.
NO. 31 ZHONG SHAN ROAD,
GUANZHOU, CHINA
MAY 17, 2007, GUANZHOU
	15. Certification
	    It is hereby certified that the declaration by the export is Correct.

Place and date, signature and stamp of authorized signatory	Place and date, signature of authorized signatory

中保财产保险有限公司
The people's insurance (Property) Company of China, Ltd
No.of Original, one
保险单号次
Policy No

发票号码
Invoice No. 07INC9988

海 洋 货 物 运 输 保 险 单
MARINE CARGO TRANSPORTATION INSURANCE POLICY

被保险人 GUANGDONG FENG QING TRADING CO.

Insured:

中保财产保险有限公司(以下简称本公司)根据被保险人的要求,及其所缴付约定的保险费,按照本保险单承保险别和背面所载条款与下列条款承保下述货物运输保险,特签发本保险单

This POLICY OF Insurance witnesses that The People's Insurance (Property) Company of China, Ltd. (hereinafter called "The Company"), at the request of the Insured and in consideration of the agreed premium paid by the Insured, undertakes to insure the under-mentioned goods in transportation subject to the conditions of this Policy as per the Clauses printed overleaf and other special clauses attached hereon.

保险货物项目 Descriptions of Goods	包装 单位 数量 Packing Unit Quantity	保险金额 Amount Insured
LADIES DRESS, 10 000 PCS. 21KGS/CARTON	PACKED IN CARTONS OF 20 PCS EACH, 500 CARTONS TOTAL	USD 88 000.00

承保险别:
Conditions
ALL RISKS AND WAR RISK AS PER CIC

货物标记
Marks of Goods
DIRAMODE
DUNKIRK
C/NO. 1~500

总保险金额 SAY US DOLLAR EIGHTY EIGHT THOUSAND ONLY.
Total Amount Insured:

保 费   运输工具 FUXING V. 196   开航日期
Premium: as arranged   Per conveyance S. S.   Slg. On or abt. AS B/L

起运港 GUANGZOU, PORT   目的港
From   To   DUNKIRK PORT

所保货物,如发生本保险单项下可能引起索赔的灭失或损坏,应立即通知本公司下属代理人查勘。如有索赔,应向本公司提交保险单正本(本保险单共有 份正本)及有关文件。如一份正本已用于索赔,其余正本则自动失效。

In the event of loss or damage which may result in a claim under this Policy, immediate notice must be given to the Company's Agent as mentioned hereunder. Claims, if any, one of the Original Policy which has been issued in Original(s) together with the relevant documents shall be surrendered to the Company, If one of the Original Policy has been accomplished, the others to be void.

中保财产保险有限公司
THE PEOPLE'S INSURANCE (PROPERTY) COMPANY OF CHINA LTD.

赔付地点
Claim payable at   DUNKIRK, FRANCE

日期   在
Date   MAY 18, 2007   at   GUANGZHOU
地址

（三）根据资料缮制提单

Shipper ZHEJIANG DONGFANG FOOD CO.,LTD NO. 124 QINGCHUN ROAD HANGZHOU, CHINA	B/L NO 中国远洋运输(集团)总公司 **CHINA OCEAN SHIPPING (GROUP)CO.**
Consignee TO ORDER OF NATIONAL BANK, NAGO-YA NO. 145 FIRST ROAD NAGOYA, JA-PAN	Combined Transport BILL OF LADING
Notify Party NATIONAL BANK, NAGOYA NO. 145 FIRST ROAD NAGOYA, JAPAN	
Pre-carriage by Place of receipt	
Ocean Vessel Voy No. Port of Loading **NINGBO** YURONG VOY. NO. E244	

Port of Discharge NAGOYA	Place of Delivery NAGOYA			Final Destination	
Marks &. nos container Seal no. N/M	No. of Containers or P'kgs 210 CASES	Kind of Packages; Description of Goods 3 000 CANS CANNED MEAT	Gross Weight 3 300 KGS	Measurement 76. 43 M³	

TOTAL NUMBER OF CONTAINERS OR PACKAGES(IN WORDS)
SAY TWO HUNDRED AND TEN CASES ONLY.

FREIGHT &. CHARGES	Revenue Tons	Rate	Per	Prepaid	Collect
Ex Rate	Prepaid at NINGBO	Payable at		Place and date of Issue NINGBO 2008-01-22	
	Total Prepaid YES	No. Of Original B(S)/L THREE		Signed for the Carrier **CHINA OCEAN SHIPPING (GROUP)CO.**	

（四）根据信用证缮制保险单

中国人民保险公司河南省分公司
The People's Company of China Henan Branch
总公司设于北京 一九四九年创立
Head Office Beijing Established in 1949
货物运输保险单 ORINGINAL
CARGO TRANSPORTATION INSURANCE POLICY

INVOICE NO. 08HM248

POLICY NO.

L/C NO. 08-4-1520

INSURED: HEBEI MACHINERY IMP. AND EXP. CORP (GROUP)

中国人民保险公司（以下简称本公司）根据被保险人的要求，由被保险人向本公司缴付约定的保险费，按照本保险单承保险别和背面所载条款与下列特别条款承保下述货物运输保险，特立本保险单。

THIS POLICY OF INSURANCE WITNESSES THAT THE PIOPLE'S INSURANCE COMPANY OF CHINA(HEREINAFTER CALLED "THE COMPANY")AT THE REQUEST OF THE INSURED AND IN CONSIDERATION OF THE AGREED PREMIUM PAID TO THE COMPANY BY THE IN-SURED, UNDERTAKES TO INSURE THE UNDERMENTIONED GOODS INTRANSPORTATION SUBJECT TO THE CONDITONS OF THIS POLICY AS PER THE CLAUSES PRINTED OVERLEAF AND OTHER SPECIAL CLAUSES ATTACHED HEREON.

标记 MARKS & NOS	包装及数量 QUANTITY	保险货物项目 DESCRIPTION OF GOODS	保险金额 AMOUNT INSURED
LUCKY 08HM256 HAMBURG NO. 1-UP	S569/480 CTN F671/160 CTN TOTAL 640CTN	STAINLESS STEEL SPADE HEAD, ART. NO. S569, 4 800 PCS, ART. NO. F671, 3 200 PCS	USD 63 360. 00

总保险金额　　　SAY US DOLLAR SIXTY THREE THOUSAND THREE HUNDRED AND SIXTY ONLY
TOTAL AMOUNT INSURED
保费：　　　　　费率：　　　　装载运输工具：HUAFENG V.
PREMIUM：AS ARRANGED RATE：AS ARRANGED PER CONVEYANCE S. S. 872W
开航日期　2008年03月20日　自　TIANJIN　至　HAMBURG
SLG. ON OR ABT. MAR. 20, 2008 FROM TIANJIN TO HAMBURG
承保险别：　INSTITUTE CARGO CLAUSE (A)　L/C NO. 08-4-1520
CONDITONS
　　所保货物，如发生本保险单项下可能引起赔偿的损失或损坏，应立即通知本公司下属代理人查勘。如有索赔，应向本公司提交保险单正本（本保险单共有正本　份）及有关文件。如一份正本已用于索赔，其余正本自动失效。
　　IN THE EVENT OF LOSS OR DAMAGE WHICH MAY RESULT IN A CLAIM UNDER THIS POLICY, IMMEDIATE NOTICE MUST BE GIVEN TO THE COMPANY'S AGENT AS MEN-TIONED HEREUNDER. IN THE EVENT OF CLAIMS, IF ANY, ONE OF THE ORIGINAL POLICY WHICH HAS BEEN ISSUED IN ORIGINAL(S) WITH THE RELEVANT DOCUMENTS SHALL BE SURRENDERED TO THE COMPANY. IF ONE OF THE ORIGINAL POLICY HAS BEEN ACCOL-PLISHED, THE OTHERS SHALL BE VOID.
赔款偿付地　　　HAMBURG
CLAIM PAYABLE AT：　　　　　　　　　　中国人民保险公司河南省分公司
出单日期　　　　MARCH 20, 2008
ISSUING DATE：　　　　　　　　　　THE PIEPLE'S INSURANCE COMPANY OF
　　　　　　　　　　　　　　　　　CHINA, HENAN BRANCH

（五）根据信用证制作下列单据

Shipper HUNAN CEREALS, OILS & FOODSTUFFS MPORT & EXPORT CORPORATION			B/L No. B/L NO. 6180		
Consignee or order TO ORDER OF SHIPPER			中国对外贸易运输总公司 CHINA NATIONAL FOREIGN TRADE TRANSPORTATION CORP. 直运或转船提单 BILL OF LADING DIRECT OR WITH TRANSHIPMENT		
Notify address WENSCO FOODS LTD., RUA DE GREENLAND STREET, 68-A 1260-297 WELL D. COQUITLAM, B. C. CANADA			SHIPPED on board in apparent good order and condition（unless otherwise indicated）the goods or packages specified herein and to be discharged at the mentioned port of discharge or as near thereto as the vessel may safely get and be always afloat.		
Pre-carriage by	Port of loading HUANGPU				
Vessel S. S "DEWEI V. 213"	Port of transshipment		In WITNESS whereof the number of original Bills of Lading stated below has been signed one of them being accomplished, the other(s) to be void.		
Port of discharge VANCOUVER B. C	Final destination				
Container, seal No. or Marks and Nos. W. F. L. VANCOUVER C/NO. 1-950	Number and kinds of packages 950 CARTONS	Description of goods "TROPIC ISLE CANNED MANDARIS ORIANGES LS-WHOLE SEGMENTS" AS PER P/I NO. CF07018	Gross weight(kgs.) 17 138 KGS		Measurement (m) 18 365 CBM
Freight and charges FREIGHT PREPAID			REGARDING TRANSHIPMENT INFORMATION PLEASE CONTACT		
Ex. rate	Prepaid at HUANGPU	Freight payable at	Place and date of issue 070220 HUANGPU		
	Total Prepaid YES	Number of original Bs/L THREE	Signed for or on behalf of the Master ABC CO., LTD, FOR THE AGENT, COSCO AS THE CARRIER as Agent		

SUBJECT TO THE TERMS AND CONDITIONS ON
BACK 93A NO. 0241877
ORIGINAL

1. Goods consigned from (Exporter's business name, address, country) HUNAN CEREALS, OILS & FOODSTUFFS IMPORT & EXPORT CORPORATION	Reference No. 1283890096 **GENERALIZED SYSTEM OF PREFERENCES** Issued in .... **P. R. CHINA**(country)
2. Goods consigned to (Consignee's name, address, country) WENSCO FOODS LTD., RUA DE GREENLAND STREET, 68A, 1260-297 WELLD COQUITLAM, B. C.	**See Notes overleaf**
3 Means of transport and route (as far as known) S. S "DEWEI V. 213" FROM HUANGPU PORT TO VANCOUVER B. C	4. For official use

5. Item number	6. Marks and numbers of package	7. Number and kind of packages; description of goods	8. origin criterion	9. G. W.	10. INVOICES
					DATE: 070201

PACKING: IN PLASTIC BAGS OF 2. 84 KGS EACH THEN SIX BAGS IN A CARTON.

950 CARTONS   "W"   INV. NO.: CFF-016
"TROPIC ISLE CANNED
W. F. L.   MANDARIS ORIANGES   GROSS WEIGHT: 17 138 KGS
VANCOUVER   LS-WHOLES
C/NO. 1-950   EGMENTS" AS PER
           P/I NO. CF07018

11. Certification	12. Declaration by the exporter
It is hereby certified, on the basis of control carried out, that the declaration by the exporter is correct. 张三 FEB. 15, 2007 Place and date, signature and stamp of certifying authority	The undersigned hereby declares that the above details and statements are correct, that all the goods produced in .... **P. R. CHINA**(country) and that they comply with the origin requirements specified for those goods in the Generalized System of Preferences for goods exported to **CANADA** .... FEB. 18, 2007 Place and date, signature and stamp of authorized signatory

（六）根据信用证改正下列单据中你认为填错的日期或出单人

经修改有如下错误：

单据名称	出单日期	出单机构
出口许可证	5 月 12 日	商务部驻各地特派员办事处
形式发票	4 月 08 日	出口方
商业发票	5 月 10 日	出口方
装箱单	5 月 10 日	出口方
G. S. P FORM A	5 月 17 日	出入境检验检疫局
熏蒸证书	5 月 17 日	出入境检验检疫局
报关单	5 月 26 日	中国海关
保险单	5 月 24 日	保险公司
受益人证明	6 月 02 日	出口方
汇票	6 月 10 日	出口方
备运提单	5 月 26 日	船公司

（七）根据信用证缮制提单

SHANGHAI FOREIGN TRADE CORP. SHANGHAI, CHINA 62, JIANGXI RD, SHANGHAI CHINA	B/L No.

2. Consignee Insert Name, Address and Phone
TO ORDER OF BANGKOK BANK PUBLIC COMPANY LIMITED, BANGKOK

3. Notify Party Insert Name, Address and Phone
(It is agreed that no responsibility shall attach to the Carrier or his agents for failure to notify)
MOUN CO., LTD
NO. 443, 249 ROAD
BANGKOK THAILAND

中远集装箱运输有限公司
COSCO CONTAINER LINES

TLX: 33057 COSCO CN
FAX: +86(021) 6545 8984

ORIGINAL

Port-to-Port or Combined Transport

BILL OF LADING

RECEIVED in external apparent good order and condition except as other-

4. Combined Transport * Pre-carriage by	5. Combined Transport * Place of Receipt
6. Ocean Vessel Voy. No. CHANGAN V. 018	7. Port of Loading SHANGHAI
8. Port of Discharge BANGKOK	9. Combined Transport * Place of Delivery

Marks & Nos. Container/Seal No.	No. of Containers or Packages	Description of Goods (If Dangerous Goods, See Clause 20)	Gross Weight Kgs	Measurement
M. C. L. BANGKOK NO. 1-40DRUMS CONTAINER NO. TTBU7038062 SEAL NO. B0090958 2×20'CY/CY	40 DRUMS	ISONIAZID BP98 FREIGHT PREPAID SHIPPED ON BOARD DATE: DEC. 20, 2000	2 200 KGS	20M³
		Description of Contents for Shipper's Use Only (Not part of This B/L Contract)		

10. Total Number of containers and/or packages (in words) SAY FORTY DRUMS ONLY
Subject to Clause 7
Limitation

11. Freight & Charges Declared Value Charge	Revenue Tons	Rate	Per	Prepaid	Collect
Ex. Rate:	Prepaid at	Payable at		Place and date of issue SHANGHAI DEC. 20, 2000	
	Total Prepaid	No. of Original B(s)/L THREE		Signed for the Carrier, COSCO CONTAINER LINES JOHN DOE	

LADEN ON BOARD THE VESSEL

DATE　　　　BY

（八）依据销售合同和信用证以及相关资料缮制提单、产地证、保险单

BILL OF LADING

Shipper ABC TEXILES IMPORT AND EXPORT CORPORATION 127 ZHONGSHAN RD. E. 1 SHANGHAI P. R. OF CHINA	**COSCO** B/L NO. 0811676 CHINA OCEANS SHIPPIGN COMPANY 总公司 HEAD OFFICE. 北京 BELJNG
CONSIGNEE TO SHIPPER'S ORDER	CABLE： TALEX： **ORIGINAL**
Notify TOMSCN TEXTJLES INC. 3384 VINCENT ST, DOWNSVIEW. ONTARIO M3J. 2J4 CANADA	
Vessel Voy. POSSESSION V16	

Port of Loading SHANGHAI	Port of Discharge TORONTO	TRANSPORT THROUGH OR VIA：

Nationality THE PEOPLE'S REPUBLIC OF CHINA	Freight Payable at

Particular furnished by the Shipper

Marks and Number	No. Of Packages	Description of Goods	Gross Weight	Measurement
T. T. I. TORONTO CTN NO. 1-1 200 CONTAINER NO. APLU2911562 SEAL NO. 30224 1×40′FCL/FCL	1 200 CARTONS	TRUERAN DYED JEAN FREIGHT PREPAID TO TORONTO SHIPPED ON BOARD DATE APR. 20TH, 2008 FREIGHT CHARGES： USD 2 341. 00	18 000 KGS	36 M³

Total Packages (in words) SAY ONE THOUSAND TWO HUNDRED CARTONS ONLY

Freight and Changes	NO OF ORIGINAL B/LTHREE	PLACE AND DATE OF ISSUE Dated … APR. 20TH, 2008 … at … SHANGHAI … CHINA OCEANS SHIPPIGN COMPANY HEAD OFFICE. BELJNG
LOADING ON BOARD THE VESSEL DATE BY		_____ SIGNED For the CARRIER

中保财产保险有限公司
The people insurance (Property) Company of China，LTD.
PICC PROPERTY

发票号码
Invoice No. C0015

保险单号次
Policy No. 053125

海洋货物运输保险单
MARINE CARGO TRANSPORTATION INSURANCE POLICY

被保险人：
Insured： ABC TEXILES IMPORT AND EXPORT CORPORATION 127
ZHONGSHAN RD. E. 1 SHANGHAI P. R. OF CHINA 。

中保财产保险有限公司(以下简称本公司)根据被保险人的要求，及其所缴付约定的保险费，按照本保险单承担险别和背面所载条款与下列特别条款承保下列货物运输保险，特签发本保险单。
This policy of Insurance witnesses that The People Insurance (Property) Company of China, Ltd. (hereinafter called the Company), at the request of the Insured and in consideration of the agreed premium paid by the Insured, undertakes to insure the under mentioned goods in transportation subject to the conditions of this Policy as per the Clauses printed overleaf and other special clauses attached hereon.

保险货物项目 Descriptions of Goods	包装 单位 数量 Packing Unit Quantity	保险金额 Amount Insured
TRUERAN DYED JEAN	1 200 CARTONS	USD 40 656. 00

承 保 险 别
Conditions

货物标记
Marks of Goods AS PER INVOICE NO. C0015

COVERING ALL RISKS AND WAR RISKS AS PER OCEAN
MARINE CARGO CLAUSES (WAREHOUSE TO WAREHOUSE CLAUSE
IS INCLUDED) AND OCEAN MARINE CARGO WAR RISK
CLAUSES OF THE PEOPLES INSURANCE COMPANY OF CHINA (1/1/1981)

总保险金额：
Total Amount Insured： SAY US DOLLARS FORTY THOUSAND. SIX HUNDRED AND FIFTY SIX ONLY.

保险   载运输工具   开航日期
Premium AS ARRANGED Per. conveyance S. S POSSESSION V16 Sig. on or abt. AS PER B/L

起运港   目的港
From SHANGHAI   To   TORONTO

所保货物，如发生本保险单项下可能引起索赔的损失或损坏，应立即通知本公司下属代理人查勘。如有索赔，应向本公司提交保险单正本(本保险单共有 2 份正本)及有关文件。如一份正本已用于索赔，其余正本则自动失效。
In the event of damage which may result in a claim under this Policy, immediate notice be given to the Company Agent as mentioned hereunder? Claims, if any, one of the Original Policy which has been issued in (15) 2 Original(s) together with the relevant documents shall be surrendered to be Company, if one of the Original Policy has been accomplished, the others to be IN void.

ABC COMPANY IN CANADA

中保财产保险有限公司
THE PEOPLE INSURANCE (PROPERTY) COMPANY OF CHINA, LTD.

赔款偿付地点
Claim payable at TORONTO IN USD

日期   (17)   在
Date… APR. 17TH, 2008   at   SHANGHAI

Address：地址：

1. Goods consigned from (Exporter's business name, address, country) ABC TEXILES IMPORT AND EXPORT COR-PORATION 127 ZHONGSHAN RD. E. 1 SHANGHAI P. R. OF CHINA…	Reference No.　062-0003 GENERALIZED SYSTEM OF PREFERENCES
2. Goods consigned to (Consignee's name, address, country) TOMSCN TEXTJLES INC. 3384 VINCENT ST, DOWNSVIEW. ONTARIO M3J. 2J4 CANADA	Issued in ‑‑‑‑‑‑‑‑‑‑‑‑‑‑‑‑‑‑‑‑‑‑‑‑‑‑‑‑‑‑‑‑ 　　　　　　(country) 　　　　See Notes overleaf
3. Means of transport and route (as far as known) FROM SHANGHAI TO TORONTO CANADA BY SEA	4. For official use

5. Item number 6. Marks and numbers of packages 7. Number and kind of packages; description of goods 8. Origin criterion(see Notes overleaf) 9. Gross weight or other quantity 10. Number and date of invoices 　T. T. I. TORONTO CTN NO. 1-1200　　TRUERAN DYED	P　18 000 KGS NO. C0015 APR. 10，2000

11. Certification It is hereby certified, on the basis of control carried out, that the declaration by the exporter is correct.	12. Declaration by the exporter The undersigned hereby declares that the above details and statements are correct, that all the goods were produced in ‑‑‑‑‑‑‑‑‑‑‑‑‑‑‑‑‑‑‑‑‑‑‑‑‑‑‑‑‑‑‑‑‑‑ 　　　　　CHINA(country) and that they comply with the origin requirements specified for those goods in the Generalized System of Preferences for goods exported to 　　　　CANADA ‑‑ 　　　　(country)
SHANGHAI APR. 10，2000 Place and date, signature and stamp of certifying authority	SHANGHAI　APR. 10，2000 Place and date, signature and stamp of authorized signatory

（九）根据信用证、合同和补充资料的内容缮制提单和产地证

提单

Shipper SHANGHAI IMPORT & EXPORT TRADE CORPORATION 1 321 ZHONGSHAN ROAD SHANGHAI, CHINA		B/L No.COCSO 511861
.Consignee TO ORDER		中远集装箱运输 有限公司 COSCO CONTAINER LINES
Notify Party TKAMLA CORPORATION 6-7, KAWARA MACH OSAKA, JAPAN		Port-to-Port or Combined Transport

Pre-carriage by	Place of Receipt SHI JIA ZHUANG	
Ocean Vessel Voy. No. NANGXING V.068	.Port of Loading SHANGHAI	**BILL OF LADING**
.Port of Discharge OSAKA,	Place of Delivery	

	Marks & Nos. Container / Seal No.	No. of Containers or Packages	Description of Goods (If Dangerous Goods, See Clause 20)	Gross Weight Kgs	Measurement
Particulars Furnished by	T. C. OSAKA C/NO.1-250	250 CARTONS	COTTON SHIRT FREIGHT PREPAID SHIPPED ON BORAD DATE:FEB.26, 2005,	5 125 KGS	114 CBM
			Description of Contents for Shipper's Use Only (Not Part of This B/L Contract)		

.**Total Number Of Containers and/or Packages (In Words)**
SAY TWO HUNDRED AND FIFTY CARTONS ONLY.

Freight & Charge	Revenue Tons	Rate	Per	Prepaid	Collect

Ex.Rate:	Prepaid at	Payable at	Place and date of Issue
	Total Prepaid	No. of Original B(s)/L	Signed for the Carrier: COSCO CONTAINER LINES WAN HAI SHIPPING CO.
			LI MING AS AGENT FOR THE CARRIER: COSCO CONTAINER LINES

产地证

ORIGINAL

1. Exporter SHANGHAI IMPORT & EXPORT TRADE CORPORATION 1321 ZHONGSHAN ROAD SHANGHAI, CHINA	Certificate No. QDCD118
2. Consignee TKAMLA CORPORATION 6-7, KAWARA MACH OSAKA, JAPAN	**CERTIFICATE OF ORIGIN** **OF** **THE PEOPLE'S REPUBLIC OF CHINA**

3. Means of transport and route FROM SHANGHAI TO OSAKA BY SEA	5. For certifying authority use only
4. Country/region of destination OSAKA, JAPAN	

6. Marks and numbers T. C. OSAKA C/NO. 1-250	7. Number and kind of packages; description of goods 250CTNS	8. H. S. Code 551.000	9. Quantity 2 500 PCS	10. Number and date of Invoices INVOICE

SAY TWO HUNDRED AND FIFTY CTNS ONLY   NO. XH056671

FEB. 01, 2005

****

11. Declaration by the exporter The undersigned hereby declares that the above details and statements are correct, that all the goods were produced in China and that they comply with the Rules of Origin of the People's Republic of China. SHANGHAI FEB. 20, 2005 Place and date, signature and stamp of authorized signatory	12. Certification It is hereby certified that the declaration by the exporter is correct. SHANGHAI FEB. 20, 2005 Place and date, signature and stamp of certifying authority

（十）根据信用证以及相关资料缮制提单

BILL OF LADING	
1) SHIPPER CHINA SHAANXI TEXTILE IMPORT N EXPORT CORPORATION. NO. A-113 BEIKOU JIANGUO ROAD, XIAN, CHINA.	10) B/L NO. COS0816787 CARRIER： **C O S C O** 中国远洋运输(集团)总公司 **CHINA OCEAN SHIPPING (GROUP) CO.** **ORIGINAL** Combined Transport BILL OF LADING
2) CONSIGNEE TO THE ORDER OF CITY BANK LIMITED	
3) NOTIFY PARTY F. K. TRADING, 26, AHSANULLAH ROAD, NAWAB BARI, DHAKA-1100, BANGLADESH THE CITY BANK LIMITED, BANGABANDHU AVENUE BRANCH, DHAKA, BANGLADESH.	

4) PLACE OF RECEIPT	5) OCEAN VESSEL JINXING	
6) VOYAGE NO. V. 788	7)PORT OF LOADING XIANGANG CHINA	
8) PORT OF DISCHARGE CHITTAGONG	9) PLACE OF DELIVERY	

11) MARKS 12) NOS. & KINDS OF PKGS. 13) DESCRIPTION OF GOODS 14) G. W. (kg)
15) MEAS(m³)

F. K.
CHITTAGONG
NO. S1-600

   600CARTONS RAW MATERIALS FOR TEXTILE INDUSTRIES 29 700 KGS 109. 98 m³
        "TAYEN PAGDOA" BRAND 60 000 LBS
        GREY TR40S/1YARN ON COVES
        POLYESTER 65 VISOSE 35.

COSU7854436/1234567

            FREIGHE PREPAID
            SHIPPED ON BOARD
           DATE：APRIL 25, 2008

16)

17) TOTAL NUMBER OF CONTAINERS OR PACKAGES (IN WORDS)
    SAY SIX HUNDRED CARTONS ONLY.

FREIGHT & CHARGES	REVENUE TONS	RATE	PER	PREPAID	COLLECT
PREPAID AT	PAYABLE AT	21) PLACE AND DATE OFISSUE TIANJIN APRIL 25 2008			
TOTAL PREPAID	18) NUMBER OF ORIGINAL B(S)L THREE				

LOADING OF BOARD THE VESSEL		22) C O S C O
		  CHINA OCEAN SHIPPING
		    (GROUP) CO			

19) DATE, APRIL 25, 2008	20) BY				

（十一）根据所提供资料和信用证有关信息缮制单据产地证

1. Exporter KUNSHAN HUACHENG WEAVING AND DYEING CO., LTD HUANGLONG RD., LIUJIA ZHEN, SUZHOU, JIANGSU, CHINA TEL：86-520-7671386	Certificate No. 040377950 **CERTIFICATE OF ORIGIN** **OF** **THE PEOPLE'S REPUBLIC OF CHINA**			
2. Consignee YOU DA TRADE CO., LTD., 101 QUEENS ROAD CENTRAL, HONGKONG TEL：852－28566666				
3. Means of transport and route FROM SHANGHAI TO HONGKONG BY SEA	5. For certifying authority use only			
4. Country/region of destination HONGGANG				
6. Marks and numbers YOU DA HONGKONG R/NO.：1-3298	7. Number and kind of packages；description of goods 100PCT NYLON FABRICS —3298—ROLLS SAY THREE THOUSAND TWO HUNDRED NINTY EIGHT ROLLS ONLY. *********************	8. H. S. code 5407. 1010	9. Quantity —100 000— YARDS	10. Number and date of invoices INV. 0804123 APR. 10, 2008
11. Declaration by the exporter 　The undersigned hereby declares that the above details and statements are correct；that all the goods were produced in china and that they comply with the rules of origin of the people's republic of china. 　　SHANGHAI APR. 10, 2008	12. Certification 　It is hereby certified that the declaration by the exporter is correct. 　　SHANGHAI APR. 10, 2008			
Place and date, signature and stamp of certifying authority	Place and date, signature and stamp of certifying authority			

（十二）根据信用证审核相关单据，找出不符点

提单不符点	应修改为
1. 提单收货人栏错误 Consignee：CHO HUNG BANK 2. 没有填写船名 3. 交货地点填写错误 Port of delivery：PUSAN，KOREA 4. 集装箱号码填制位置错误 5. 运费条款错误 FREIGHT TO COLLECT 6. 大写件数不应填在件数一栏中 7. 毛重 5 000 KGS 错误 8. 提单签发日期 21 JUN，2006 错误	1. Consignee： TO THE ORDER OF CHO HUNG BANK 2. 船名应为 TIAN SHUN V. 329N 3. 交货地点不应填写，没有就应空着 4. 集装箱号码应填制在唛头一栏中 5. 运费条款应为 FREIGHT PREPAID 6. 大写件数应填在"SHIPPER'S LOAD COURT & SEAL"此栏中 7. 毛重应为 7 654 KGS 8. 应为 20 JUN，2006
保险单不符点	应修改为
1. 赔款偿付地点没有填赔款币值 Claim Payable at　　　PUSAN 2. 保险金额大小写错误 USD 35 500（SAY US DOLLARS THIRTY FIVE THOUSAND FIVE HUNDRED ONLY） 3. 承保条件错 COVERING MARINE ALL RISKS AS PER INSTITUTE CARGO CLAUSES（A）DATED1/1/1982	1. 赔款偿付地点后面应注明赔款的币值为信用证上的币值即：美元 Claim Payable at PUSAN IN USD 2. 保险金额 USD 39 050（SAY US DOLLARS THIRTY NINE THOUSAND AND FIFTY ONLY） 3. 承保条件中的"一切险"是中国人民保险公司的保险险别，而不是伦敦协会保险条款 INSURANCE：COVERING ALL RISKS AND WAR RISKS AS PER OCEANMARINE CARGO CLAUSES（WAREHOUSE TO WAREHOUSE CLAUSE IS INCLUDED）AND OCEAN MARINE CARGOCLAUSES OF THE PEOPLES INSURANCE COMPANY OF CHINA（1/1/1981）

（十三）根据提供的信用证的内容和相关资料制作信用证指定的议付提单和产地证

DESUN TRADING CO,LTD 224 JINLIN ROAD,NANJING,CHINA				B/L No.		
2. Consignee Insert Name，Address and Phone TO ORDER OF SHIPPER				中远集装箱运输有限公司 COSCO CONTAINER LINES TLX：33057 COSCO CN FAX：＋86(021) 6545 8984 ORIGINAL		
3. Notify Party Insert Name，Address and Phone (It is agreed that no responsibility shall attach to the Carrier or his agents for failure to notify) WAV GENEAL TRADING CO.， RUA DE，98-OSAKA, JAPAN				Port-to-Port or Combined Transport **BILL OF LADING**		
4. Combined Transport ＊ Pre - carriage by	5. Combined Transport ＊ Place of Receipt			RECEIVED in external apparent good order and condition except as other-Wise noted. The total number of packages or unites stuffed in the container, the description of the goods and the weights shown in this Bill of Lading are furnished by the Merchants, and which the carrier has no reasonable means of checking and is not a part of this Bill of Lading contract. The carrier has Issued the number of Bills of Lading stated below, all of this tenor and date. One of the original Bills of Lading must be surrendered or endorsed or signed against the delivery of the shipment and whereupon any other original Bills of Lading shall be void. The Merchants agree to be bound by the terms and conditions of this Bill of Lading as if each had personally signed this Bill of Lading. SEE clause 4 on the back of this Bill of Lading (Terms continued on the back hereof, please read carefully). ＊ Applicable Only When Document Used as a Combined Transport Bill of Lading.		
6. Ocean Vessel Voy. No. DAFENG V3336	7. Port of Loading NANJING PORT					
8. Port of Discharge OSAKA，JAPAN	9. Combined Transport ＊ Place of Delivery					
Marks &. Nos. Container/Seal No. ITOCHU OSAKA NO. 1-200	No. of Containers or Packages 200CARTONS	Description of Goods（If Dangerous Goods, See Clause 20） LADIES GARMENTS FREIGHT PREPAID SHIPPED ON BOARD DATE MAY 15，2008		Gross Weight Kgs 3 080 KGS		Measurement 24 CBM
		Description of Contents for Shipper's Use Only（Not part of This B/L Contract)				
10. Total Number of containers and/or packages（in words)SAY TWO HUNDRED CARTONS ONLY. Subject to Clause 7 Limitation						
11. Freight &. Charges Declared Value Charge	Revenue Tons	Rate	Per	Prepaid		Collect
Ex. Rate：	Prepaid at		Payable at	Place and date of issue NANJING MAY 15，2008		
	Total Prepaid		No. of Original B(s)/L THREE	Signed for the Carrier, COSCO CONTAINER LINES		

ORIGINAL

1. Goods consigned from (Exporter's business name, address, country) DESUN TRADING CO.,LTD 224 JINLIN ROAD,NANJING,CHINA	Reference No. 062-0003 GENERALIZED SYSTEM OF PREFERENCES
2. Goods consigned to (Consignee's name, address, country) WAV GENEAL TRADING CO., RUA DE,98-OSAKA, JAPAN BY SEA	Issued in .... (country) See Notes overleaf
3. Means of transport and route (as far as known) FROM NANJING PORT, CHINA TO OSAKA,JAPAN	4. For official use

5. Item number	6. Marks and numbers of packages	7. Number and kind of packages; description of goods	8. Origin criterion (see Notes overleaf)	9. Gross weight or other Quantity	10. Number and date of invoices
1	ITOCHU OSAKA NO. 1-200	LADIES GARMENTS ------- 200CTNS ------- SAY TWO HUNDRED CARTONS ONLY * * * * * * * * * *	P	3 080 KGS	SH25586 APR. 20，2008

11. Certification It is hereby certified, on the basis of control carried out, that the declaration by the exporter is correct. C. I. Q NANJING APR. 20, 2008	12. Declaration by the exporter The undersigned hereby declares that the above details and statements are correct, that all the goods were CHINA produced in ----------------------------------- (CPOUNTRY) and that they comply with the origin requirements specified for those goods in the Generalized System of Preferences for goods exported to JZPAN (IMPORTING COUNTRY) NANJING APR. 20, 2008
PLACE AND DATE SIGNATURE AND STAMP OF AUTHORIZED	PLACE AND DATE SIGNATURE AND STAMP OF AUTHORIZED

（十四）根据托收指示书和合同制作全套清关单证和全套结算单证

SHIPPING NOTE

经营单位 （托运人）	HUBEI TWIN HORSE TRADE CO.,LTD. 1ST XUDONG ROAD, WUCHANG, 430077, WUHAN,CHINA		公司 编号	3100056412	
提/运单项目	发货人（SHIPPER）HUBEI TWIN HORSE TRADE CO.,LTD. 　　　　1ST XUDONG ROAD, WUCHANG,430077,WUHAN,CHINA				
	收货人（CONSIGNEE）TO ORDER				
	通知人（NOTIFY ）HANWA CO.,LTD H. K. 　　　　TEL/FAX：008522678556				

运费（√） FREIGHT	预付（√）或到付（　　） PREPAID/COLLECT		提单 份数	3/3	寄送 地址	
起运港 SHANGHAI	目的港	YOKOHAMA	可否转船	YES	可否分批	YES

标记 唛码	包装 件数	中英文货名 DESCRIPTION	毛重 KGS	尺码 CBM	成交条件（总价）
H. C. L. YOKOHAMA NO. 1-4000	4 000 WOODEN CASES	FASTENERS 2000M JIS FASTENERS BLACK TREATED	KGS 104 000 KGS	156 CBM	CIF YOKOHAMA USD 600 000. 00

声明事项		结算方式	D/P AT SIGHT
		代办项目	
		预配运输 工具名称	BUTTERFLY V. 089
		提/运单号	KGES5825691
		签名：	

中华人民共和国出口货物报关单

预录入编号　　　　　　　　　　海关编号

出口口岸 SHANGHAI	备案号	出口日期 MAY. 20，2006	申报日期 MAY. 19，2006
经营单位 湖北双马贸易公司	运输方式 江海运输/2	运输工具 BUTTERFLY V. 089	提运单号 KGES5825691
发货单位 湖北双马贸易公司	贸易方式 一般贸易 0110	征免性质 一般征税	结汇方式 承兑交单/5
许可证号	抵运国（地区） 日本/116	指运港 YOKOHAMA	境内货源地 武汉市洪山区
批准文号	成交方式 CIF/1	运费	保费	杂费
合同协议号 HW003	件数 4 000	包装种类 木箱	毛重 104 000 KGS	净重 100 000 KGS

集装箱号 SOCU6689721/CUS600341 5×20′	随附单据 B	生产厂家 武汉汽车标准件有限公司

标记唛码及备注
H. C. L.　　　　　SOCU6689722/CUS600342
YOKOHAMA　　　SOCU6689723/CUS600343
NO. 1-4000　　　SOCU6689724/CUS600344
　　　　　　　　SOCU6689725/CUSO600345

项号	商品 编号	商品名称	规格 型号	数量 及单位	最终目的国 （地区）	单价	总价	币制	征免
01		FASTENERS JIS FASTENERS BLACK TREATED	2000 M	100 MT	日本	USD 6 000.00 PER MT	600 000.00	USD	全免

税费征收情况

录入员　录入单位	兹申明以上申报无讹并承担法律责任	海关审单批注及放行日期（签章）	
		审单	审价
报关员　　申报单位（签章） 单位地址		征税	统计
查验　　放行　　MAY. 19，2006			

出口收汇核销单
存根
(鄂)编号:315808954

出口单位:	
单位代码:	
出口币种汇总	
收回方式	
预计收款日期	出口单位盖章
报关日期	
备注	
此单报关有效期截止到	

出口收汇核销单
(鄂)编号:315808954

出口单位:			
单位代码:			
类别	币种金额	日期	盖章
海关签注栏			
外汇局签注栏			

(出口单位盖章)

出口收汇核销单
(鄂)编号:315808954

出口单位:		
单位代码:		
货物名称	数量	币种总价
报关单编号:		
外汇局签注栏:		

年　月　日(盖章)

(出口单位盖章)

出口收汇核销单
(存根)
编号:315808954

出口单位:湖北双马贸易公司
单位代码:
出口币种总价:USD 600 000
收方式:D/P AT SIGHT
预计收款日期:20060519
报关日期:20060519
备注:
此单报关有效期截止到:

年　　月　　日

出口收汇核销单
(正联)
编号:315808954

银行签审	类别	币种金额	日期	盖章
		USD 60 000		

出口单位:湖北双马贸易公司

单位代码:

海关签注栏:

外汇局签注栏:

年　　月　　日(盖章)

出口收汇核销单
(出口退税专用联)
编号:315808954

出口单位:湖北双马贸易公司		
单位代码:		
货物名称	数量	币种总价
	100公吨	USD 600 000

报关单编号:

外汇局签注栏:

年　　月　　日(盖章)

中华人民共和国出入境检验检疫
出境货物通关单

编号：3100034568729

1. 发货人 湖北双马贸易公司			5. 标记及号码 H. C. L. YOKOHAMA NO. 1-4000	
2. 收货人 HANWA CO., LTD. KYOTO, JAPAN.				
3. 合同/信用证号 HW003		4. 输往国家或地区 日本		
6. 运输工具名称及号码 BUTTERFLY V. 089		7. 发货日期 MAY. 20，2006	8. 集装箱规格及数量 SOCU6689721/CUS600341 5×20'	
9. 货物名称及规格 FASTENERS 2000M JIS FASTENERS BLACK TREAT- ED	10. H. S. 编码 6201.0922	11. 申报总值 USD 600 000	12. 数、重量、包装数量及种类 100 公吨　　4 000 木箱	
13. 证明 　　上述货物业经检验检疫，请海关予以放行 　　　　　　　　　　本通关单有效期至　　　2006 年 6 月 19 日 　　　　　　　　　　签字				
14. 备注				

中华人民共和国出入境检验检疫
ENTRY-EXIT INSPECTION AND QUARNTINE
OF THE PEOPLE'S REPUBLIC OF CHINA

熏蒸/消毒证明书   编号 NO. 005988

FUMIGATION/DISINFECTION CERTIFICATE

发货人名称及地址

Name and address of consignor WUHAN TWIN HORSE TRADING CO.,
LTD, 1ST XUDONG ROAD, WUCHANG, 430077. WUHAN, CHINA.

收货人名称及地址

Name and address of consignee HANWA CO. LTD. KYOTO, JAPAN

品名   产地

Description of goods FASTENERS 2000M Place of origin 武汉市洪山区

报验数量

  Quantity declared   100 MT

启运地

Place of dispatch   SHANGHAI

到达口岸

Port of destination   YOKOHAMA

运输工具

Name of conveyance BUTTERFLY V. 089

标记及号码

Mark & no.   H. C. L.
      YOKOHAMA
      No. 1-4000

ORIGINAL

1. Goods consigned from (Exporter's business name, address, country) WUHAN TWIN HORSE TRADING CO., LTD, 1ST XUDONG ROAD, WUCHANG, 430077. WUHAN, CHINA.	Reference No.　　HU-3748 **GENERALIZED SYSTEM OF PREFERENCES**
2. Goods consigned to (Consignee's name, address, country) HANWA CO. LTD. KYOTO, JAPAN	Issued in .... (country) See Notes overleaf
3. Means of transport and route (as far as known) FROM SHANGHAI TO YOKOHAMA JAPAN BY SEA	4. For official use

5. Item number	6. Marks and numbers of packages	7. Number and kind of packages; description of goods	8. Origin criterion (see Notes overleaf)	9. Gross weight or other quantity	10. Number and date of invoices
1	H. C. L YOKOHAMA NO. 1-4 000	FASTENERS 2000M JIS FASTENERS BLACK TREATED	P	G. W. 104 000 KGS	INV. HW003
		——4000——WOOODEN CASES			MAY 15, 2006
		SAY FOUR THOUSAND WOODEN CASES ONLY			

＊＊＊＊＊＊＊＊＊＊＊＊＊＊＊＊

11. Certification It is hereby certified, on the basis of control carried out, that the declaration by the exporter is correct. SUANGHAI　MAY 15, 2006 .... Place and date, signature and stamp of certifying authority	12. Declaration by the exporter The undersigned hereby declares that the above details and statements are correct, that all the goods were CHINA produced in -------------------------------------- (country) and that they comply with the origin requirements specified for those goods in the Generalized System of Preferences for goods exported to JAPAN -- (country) SHANGHAI　MAY 15, 2006 .... Place and date, signature and stamp of certifying authority

INSURANCE POLICY

PICC 中国人民保险公司湖北分公司
The People's Insurance Company of China, Shanghai Branch
货物运输保险单
CARGO TRANSPORTATION INSURANCE POLICY

发票号: (INVOICE NO.)INV. HW003   保单号次:
合同号: (CONTRACT NO.)HW003   POLICY NO. 04-2988956
信用证号: (L/C NO.)
被保险人:
Insured: WUHAN TWIN HORSE TRADING CO., LTD,
      1ST XUDONG ROAD, WUCHANG, 430077. WUHAN, CHINA.
中国人民保险公司(以下简称本公司)根据被保险人的要求,由被保险人向本公司缴付约定的保险费,按照本保险单承保险别和背面所列条款与下列特别条款承保下述货物运输保险,特立本保险单。
THIS POLICY OF INSURANCE WITNESSES THAT THE PEOPLE'S INSURANCE COMPANY OF CHINA(HEREINAFTER CALLED THE COM-
PANY) AT THE RQUEST OF THE INSURED AND IN CONSIDERATION OF THE AGREED PRE-MIUM PAID TO THE COMPANY BY THE INSURED.
UNDERTAKES TO INSURE THE UNDERMENTIONED GOODS IN TRAN-SPORTATION SUB-JECT TO THE CONDITIONS OF THIS POLICY AS PER THE CLAUSES PRINTED OVERLEAF AND OTHER SPECIAL CLAUSES ATTACHED HEREIN.

标记 MARKS & NOS.	包装、数量及保险货物项目 PACKING, QUANTITY, DESCRIPTION OF GOODS	保险金额 AMOUNT INSURED
AS PER INVOICE NO. INV. HW003	FASTENERS 2000M JIS FASTENERS BLACK TREATED	USD 66 000. 00

总保险金额
TOTAL AMOUNT INSURED: SAY US DOLLARS SIXTY SIX THOUSAND ONLY
保费   启运日期
PREMIUM   AS ARRANGED   DATE OF COMMENCEMENT   AS PER B/L
装载运输工具
PERCONVEYANCE: BUTTERFLY V. 089
自   经   至
FROM   SHANGHAI   VIA _____ TO   YOKOHAMA
承保险别:
CONDITIONS:
    COVERING ALL RISKS AND WAR RISK AS PER THE OCEAN MARINE CARGO CLAUSES OF THE PEOPLE'S INSURANCE COMPANY OF CHINA, DATED JAN. 1ST,1981.
所保货物,如发生保险单项下可能引起索赔的损失或损坏,应立即通知本公司下属代理人查勘。如有索赔应向本公司提交保险单正本(共   份正本)及有关文件。如一份正本已用于索赔,其余正本自动失效。
IN THE EVENT OF LOSS OR DAMAGE WHICH MAY RESULT IN A CLAIM UNDER THIS POLICY. IMMEDIATE NOTICE MUST BE GIVEN TO THE COMPANY'S A-GENT AS MENTIONED HEREUNDER. IN THE EVENT OF CALIMS IF ANY, ONE OF THE ORIGINAL POLICY WHICH HAS BEEN ISSUED IN   ORIGINALS TO-GETHER WITH THE RELEVANT DOCUMENTS SHAL BE SURRENDERED TO THE COMNPANY. IF ONE OF THE ORIGINAL POLICY HAS BEEN ACCOMPLISHED, THE OTHERS SHALL BE VOID.

中国人民保险公司湖北分公司
The People's Insurance Company of China
Shanghai Branch

赔款偿付地点
CLAIM PAYABLE AT   YOKOHAMA. IN USD
出单日期
ISSUING DATE   MAY 18, 2006
Authorised Signature
地址: 中国湖北武汉   电话: 027 77889900
ADDRESS: WUHAN, HUBEI, CHINA.   TEL: 027 77889900

（十五）按照下列信用证制作海运提单、原产地证书

ORIGINAL

1. EXPORTER JINHAI IMP. & EXP. GROUP CORP. NO. 233，TAIPING ROAD，QINGDAO，CHINA	CERTIFICATE NO. 8767544，
2. CONSIGNEE HOPE TRADING EST.， P. O. BOX 0000 DAMMAN 31491， SAUDI ARABIA	**CERTIFICATE OF ORIGIN** **OF** **THE PEOPLE'S REPUBLIC OF CHINA**
3. MEANS OF TRANSPORT AND ROUTE FROM QINGDAO TO DAMMAN PORT， SAUDI ARABIA BY SEA	5. FOR CERTIFYING AUTHORITY USE ONLY
4. COUNTRY/REGION OF DESCRIPTION SAUDI ARABIA	

6. MARKS AND NUMBERS	7. NUMBER AND KIND OF PACKAGES；DESCRIP- TION OF GOODS	8. H. S. CODE	9. Quantity or weight	10. NUMBER AND DATE OF INVOICES
H. T. E. DAMMAN PORT NO. 1-2000	FROZEN CHICKEN BREAST MEAT, A GRADE ——2000——CARTONS SAY TWO THOUSAND CARTONS ONLY *************	5674. 8374	24 000 KGS	JH57868 DEC. 10，2008

11. DECLARATION BY THE EXPORTER THE UNDERSIGNED HEREBY DECLARES THAT THE ABOVE DETAILS AND STATEMENTS ARE CORRECT THAT ALL THE GOODS WERE PRODUCED IN CHINA AND THAT THEY COMPLY WITH THE RULES OF ORIGIN OF THE PEOPLES REPUBLIC OF CHINA. QINGDAO DEC. 10，2008	12. CERTIFICATION IT IS HEREBY CERTIFIED THAT THE DECLARATION BY THE EXPORTER IS CORRECT. QINGDAO DEC. 10，2008
PLACE AND DATE SIGNATURE AND STAMP OF AUTHORIZED SIGNATORY	PLACE AND DATE SIGNATURE AND STAMP OF AUTHORIZED SIGNATORY

BILL OF LADING

1) SHIPPER JINHAI IMP. & EXP. GROUP CORP. NO. 233，TAIPING ROAD，QINGDAO，CHINA	7) B/L NO.　BL3888 **CARRIER** 　**C O S C O**
2) CONSIGNEE TO ORDER	
3) NOTIFY PARTY HOPE TRADING EST., P. O. BOX 0000 DAMMAN 31491，SAUDI ARABI- A	中国远洋运输(集团)总公司 CHINA OCEAN SHIPPING (GROUP) CO.

PRE-CARRIAGE	PLACE OF RECEIPT	Combined Transport BILL OF LADING
4) VESSEL　VOY NO. PRETTY V. 116	5) PORT OF LOADING QINGDAO	
6)PORT OF DISCHARGE DAMMAN PORT， SAUDI ARABIA	PLACE OF DELIVERY	

8) MARKS　9) NO. OF PACKAGE　10) DESCRIPTION OF GOODS　11) G. W.（kg）　12) MEAS(m³)

8) MARKS	9) NO. OF PACKAGE	10) DESCRIPTION OF GOODS	11) G. W. (kg)	12) MEAS(m³)
H. T. E. DAMMAN PORT NO. 1-2000 FBZU876551 FBZU876552 FBZU876553 FBZU876554 FBZU876555 FBZU876556 FBZU876557 FBZU876558	2000 CARTONS	FROZEN　CHICKEN　BREAST MEAT，A GRADE	28 000 KGS	118. 08 CBM

PREPAID AT	FREIGHT PREPAID
14) PAYABLE AT	SHIPPED ON BOARD
15) PLACE AND DATE OF ISSUE	DATE：DEC. 20，2008

TOTAL PREPAID	16) NUMBER OF ORIGINAL B(S)L THREE	17) SIGNATURE CHINA OCEAN SHIPPING (GROUP) CO. 王彬 AS AGENT FOR THE CARRIER： CHINA OCEAN SHIPPING (GROUP) CO.

（十六）单选题

1	2	3	4	5	6	7	8
C	B	A	C	C	D	D	A
9	10	11	12	13	14	15	16
D	A	D	B	B	A	C	D
17	18	19	20	21	22	23	24
	D	C	A	B	B		

（十七）多选题

1	2	3	4	5	6
BC	AC	BCD	AB	AB	

（十八）判断题

1	2	3	4	5	6
T	F	F	F	F	F
7	8	9	10	11	12
F	T	F	T	F	

三、金融单据的制作与审核

（一）根据信用证以及相关资料缮制汇票

1. **No.** 07INC9988

Exchange for　USD 80 000.00　　GUANGDONG　，MAY 25，2007

　　　　　　At _____×××_____ sight of this **Second** of Exchange

（**First** of the same tenor and date unpaid），pay to the Order of

BANK OF CHANA，GUANGDONG BRANCH_____the sum of

SAY U. S. DOLLARS EITHTY THOUSAND ONLY

Drawn under　BNP PARIBAS ZI DE LA PILATERIE

　　　　　　59442 WASQUEHAL FRANCE

　　　　　　L/C NO. 00001LCC0603814，DATED 12-APR-2007

To   BNP PARIBAS

    ZI DE LA PILATERIE   GUANGDONG FENG QING TRADING CO

   59442 WASQUEHAL FRANCE

2.

BILL OF EXCHANGE

凭 Drawn Under	BANGKOK BANK PUBLIC COMPANY LIMITED	不可撤销信用证 Irrevocable L/C No.	BKKB1103043

日期 Date   3ʳᵈ, NOV, 2000   支取 Payable With interest   @   %   按   息   付款

号码 No.   ×××××   汇票金额 Exchange for   USD 18000.00   南京 Nanjing

见票 at   ××××××××   日后(本汇票之副本未付)付交 sight of this FIRST of Exchange (Second of Exchange

Being unpaid) Pay to the order of   BANK OF CHINA

金额 the sum of   SAY U.S. DOLLARS EIGHTEEN THOUSAND ONLY

此致 To   BANGKOK BANK PUBLIC COMPANY LIMITED   SHANGHAI FOREIGN TRADE CORP.

     BANCKOK

（二）根据资料缮制汇票

No. BP0600636

Exchange for USD 21 600.00   NOV. 25，2006   ,   NINGBO，CHINA

    At   ×××   sight of this **Second** of Exchange

(**First** of the same tenor and date unpaid)，pay to the Order of

BANK OF CHINA   the sum of

SAY U. S. DOLLARS TWENTY-ONE THOUSAND SIX HUNDRED ONLY

Drawn under AUSTRALIA AND NEW ZEALAND BANKING GROUP

       LIMITED NORTH SHORE AREA 8 RAILWAY ST

       CHATSWO OD NSW2067 L/C NO. AND DATE：LC06067

       NOV. 5，2006

    To AUSTRALIA AND NEW ZEALAND BANKING GROUP LIMITED

NORTH SHORE AREA 8 RAILWAY ST CHATSWO OD NSW2067

           NINGBO YITONG LEATHER CO., LTD.

（三）根据信用证缮制汇票

BILL OF EXCHAGE

No. 08HM248

Exchange for USD 57 600. 00

AT ___30 DAYS AFTER___ sight of this **FIRST** of Exchange(Second of Exchange being unpaid)

Pay to the order of BANK OF CHINA, TIANJIN BRANCH_____ the sum of

SAY U. S. DOLLARS FIFTY-SENEN THOUSAND SIX HUNDRED ONLY

Drawn under VOLKSBANK SCHORNDORF

HAMBURG, GERMANY

L/C NO.: 08-4-1520, DATE: 1ST, FEB, 2008

To VOLKSBANK SCHORNDORF

HAMBURG, GERMANY

HEBEI MACHINERY IMP. AND EXP. CORP (GROUP)

（四）根据销售合同和信用证以及相关资料缮制汇票

BILL OF EXCHANGE

DRAWN UNDER BANK OF NOVA SCOTIA, TORONTO, CANADA　　1

L/C NO.: ___078230CDI1117LC___

DATED ___18 JAN, 2007___

NO CFF-016 EXCHANGE FOR U. S. D 10 830. 00 CHANGSHA. CHINA 25TH, FEB, 2007

AT 45 DAYS AFTER B/L DATE: 20TH, FEB, 2007 OF THIS FIRST OF EXCHANGE (SECOND OF EXCHANGE BEING UNPAID). PAY TO THE ORDER OF BANK OF CHINA

THE SUM OF SAY U. S. DOLLARS TEN THOUSAND EIGHT HUNDRED AND THIRTY ONLY

TO: BANK OF NOVA SCOTIA, TORONTO, CANADA

550 WEST GEORGIA ST ., PO BOX 172 TORONTO, CANADA

FOR: HUNAN CEREALS, OILS & FOODSTUFFS IMPORT & EXPORT CORPORATION

(五) 根据信用证和有关信息资料缮制汇票

凭   <u>CANADIAN INPERIAL BANK</u> OF COMMERCE
Drawn under

信用证   第   号
L/C   No. T-017641

日期   <u>2008</u> 年 <u>3</u> 月 <u>25</u> 日
Dated   25TH , MAR, 2008

按   息   付款
Payable with interest @   ‰ per annum

号码   汇票金额   中国 年 月 日
No.   D2C4193   Exchange for   USD 36 960. 00 China

见票   日后(本汇票之副本未付)付
At <u>30DAYS AFTE</u> sight of this **FIRST** of Exchange (Second of exchange being unpaid)
Pay to the order of   <u>BANK OF CHINA</u>   或其指定人

金额
The sum of
SAY U. S. DOLLARS THIRTY-SIX THOUSAND NINEHUNDRED AND SIXTY ONLY

此致
To
CANADIAN INPERIAL BANK OF COMMERCE
TORONTO   ABC TEXILES IMPORT AND EXPORT CORPORATION

(六) 根据信用证和相关资料制作议付汇票

Inv. No.   SHAANXITEX08/03/A

Exchange for   USD 40 800

At   ×××   sight of this First of Exchange
(Second of the same tenor and date unpaid), pay to the Order of
THE BANK OF CHINA, SHAANXI BRANCH the sum of
SAY U. S. DOLLARS FORTY THOUSAND EIGHT HUNDRED ONLY

Drawn under THE CITY BANK LIMITED, BANGABANDHU AVENUE BRANCH,
        CREDIT NO. 01080099-C DATED 2008, MARCH, 03
To   THE CITY BANK LIMITED,
      BANGABANDHU AVENUE BRANCH,
      DHAKA, BANGLADESH.

              CHINA SHAANXI TEXTILE IMPORT N EXPORT CORPORATION

（七）按照信用证制作汇票

BILL OF EXCHANGE

DRAWN UNDER BANK OF CHINA，HONGKONG BRANCH

L/C NO HK1112234　DATED 1ST ，JAN，2008

PAYABLE WITH INSTERST @ .... ‰ PER ANMUM

NO： ×××　EXCHANGE FOR　USD33,680.00

AT　×××　SIGHT OF HIS FIRST OF EXCHANGE（SECOND OF EXCHANGE BEING UNPAID）PAY TO THE ORDER OF　　BANK OF CHINA，SUZHOU BRANCH

THE SUM OF SAY U. S. DOLLARS THIRTY-THREE THOUSAND SIX HUNDRED AND EIGHTY ONLY

TO　BANK OF CHINA，HONGKONG BRANCH

KUNSHAN HUACHENG WEAVING AND DYEING CO.,LTD

（八）根据信用证要求制作全套结汇单证

BILL OF EXCHANGE

凭 Drawn Under	THE ROYAL BANK,TOKYO		不可撤销信用证 Irrevocable　L/C No.		JST-AB12

日期　　　　5TH,APR, 2008
Date

支取　Payable With interest　　@　　%　　按　　息　　付款

号码　×××　汇票金额　　　　　　　　　南京
No.　　　　Exchange for　　USD 10300.00　Nanjing

见票　　　　×××　　　　　　日后(本汇票之副本未付)付交
at　　　　　　　　　　　　　sight of this FIRST of Exchange（Second of Exchange

Being unpaid) Pay to the order of　BANK OF CHINA

金额　　SAY U.S. DOLLARS
the sum of　TEN THOUSAND THREE HUNDRED ONLY

此致　　　　　　　　　　　　　　　　　DESUN TRADING CO,LTD
To　THE ROYAL BANK.

TOKYO

（九）根据信用证和其他资料制作全套结汇单据

凭　　　　　　　　　　　　　　　　　信用证

Drawn under <u>CYPRUS POPULAR BANK LTD, LARNAKA</u>　L/C NO. <u>186/04/10014.</u>

日期　　　　　　支取　　　　　　　　　　　　按......息......付款

Dated <u>5TH JAN,2008V</u> Payable with interest　　@............ %.....................

号码　　汇票金额　　　　　　　　　　　　　上海

NO <u>04SHGD3029</u>　Exchange for USD 6115.00 Shanghai　_____

见票　　　日后（本汇票之正本未付）付交　　　　　　　　金额

At　<u>XXX</u>　　　　　　　　　　sight of this **SECOND** of Exchange (First of Exchange

being unpaid)　　　　　　　　Pay to the order of BANK OF CHINA, SHANGHAI BRANCH

the sum of　**SAY U.S.DOLLARS SIX THOUSAND ONE HUNDRED AND**

FIFTEEN ONLY.

款已付讫

Value received...

....

此致：

To: <u>CYPRUS POPULAR BANK LTD ,</u>

　　<u>LARNAKA</u>　_____

　　　　　　　　　　SHANGHAI GARDEN PRODUCTS IMP. AND EXP. CO., LTD.

（十）根据信用证及有关业务资料缮制全部结汇单据

Issuer： QINGDAO BRIGHT CO. LTD. 66，SHANDONG ROAD, QINGDAO, CHINA	商业发票 COMMERCIAL INVOICE		
To： W/W TEXTILES P. O. BOX9CEMEERYROAD LONDON U. K.	No： QB12	Date： NOV. 10TH,2007	
Transport details： FROM QINGDAO TO LONDON BY SEA	S/C No： 27SGB062018	L/C No： CR2594/183865	
	Terms of payment： L/C AT SIGHT		

Marks and numbers	Description of goods	Quantity	Unit price	Amount
W/W LONDON NO. 1-96	837 MEN'S RAIN JACKET 840 LADIES' RAIN JACKET ONE PC IN A PLASTIC BAG, ONE HUNDRED BAGS TO A CARTON GR. WT：2 400 KGS NET WT：2 208 KGS MEASUREMENT：96. 000 M³ 96CARTONS	5 200 PCS 4 400 PCS	FOBQINGDAO @USD 28. 60 @USD 26. 55	USD 148 720. 00 USD 116 820. 00
	TOTAL	9 600 PCS		USD 265 540. 00

QINGDAO BRIGHT CO. LTD.

LI MING

ISSUER QINGDAO BRIGHT CO. LTD. 66，SHANDONG ROAD, QINGDAO, CHINA			装箱单 PACKING LIST			
TO W/W TEXTILES P. O. BOX9CEMEERYROAD LONDON U. K.			**INVOICE NO.** QB12		**DATE** NOV. 10TH，2007	

Marks and Numbers	Number and kind of package Description of goods	Quantity	Package	G. W.	N. W.	Meas.
W/W LONDON NO. 1-96	837 MEN'S RAIN JACKET 840 LADIES' RAIN JACK- ET ONE PC IN A PLASTIC BAG, ONE HUNDRED BAGS TO A CARTON GR. WT：2 400 KGS NET WT：2 208 KGS MEASUREMENT：96 000 M³ 96CARTONS	9 600 PCS	96 CARTONS	2 400 KGS	2 208 KGS	96 000M³
TOTAL：		9 600 PCS	96 CARTONS	2 400 KGS	2 208 KGS	96 000 M³

QINGDAO BRIGHT CO. LTD.

LI MING

ORIGINAL

1. Exporter	Certificate No.
QINGDAO BRIGHT CO. LTD. 66, SHANDONG ROAD, QINGDAO, CHINA	
2. Consignee	**CERTIFICATE OF ORIGIN** **OF** **THE PEOPLE'S REPUBLIC OF CHINA**
W/W TEXTILES P.O.BOX9CEMEERYROAD LONDON U.K	
3. Means of transport and route	**5. For certifying authority use only**
FROM QINGDAO TO LONDON BY SEA	
4. Country/region of destination	
U.K.	

6. Mrks and numbers	7. Number and kind of packages; description of goods	8. H.S.Code	9. Quantity	10. Number and date of invoices
W/W LONDON NO.1-96	837 MEN'S RAIN JACKET 840 LADIES' RAIN JACKET 96CARTONS (NINTY SIX CARTONS) ****************	87596215	9 600 PCS	QB12 NOV.10TH,2007

11. Declaration by the exporter	12. Certification
The undersigned hereby declares that the above details and statements are correct，that all the goods were produced in china and that they comply With the rules of Origin of the People's Republic of china.	Lt is hereby certified that the declaration by the exporter is correct
NOV.10TH,2007　QIGNDAO-------LIMING----------- Place and date，signature and stamp of authorized signatory	Place and date，signature and stamp of certifying authority

1. Consignor QINGDAO BRIGHT CO. LTD. 66, SHANDONG ROAD, QINGDAO CHINA		B/L NO.GB211		
2. Consignee TO ORDER		中远集装箱运输有限公司 **Cosco container lines** **Port-to-Port or combined transport**		
3. Notify party W/W TEXTILES P.O.BOX9CEMEERYROAD LONDON U.K		**BILL OF LADING**		
4. Combined transport		5. Combined transport		
6. Ocean vessel voy.no. "MAYOR" V.26		7. Port of lading QINGDAO		
8. Port of discharge LONDON		9. Combined Transport		
Marks&nos. **Container /seal no.** W/W LONDON NO.1-96	**No.of** **Container or package** 96CARTONS	**Description of Goods** MEN'S RAIN JACKET LADIES' RAIN JACKET FREIGHT COLLECT	**Gross WEIGHT** 2 400 KGS	**Means.M^3** 96 000 M^3

10. Total Number of Container and/or Package(in words) NINTY SIX CARTONS

11. freight&charges	Revenue tons	Rate	Per	Prepaid	Collect
		Place and date of issue QINGDAO JAN.10TH,2008			
		Signed for or on behalf of the Carrier LI MING			

汇票

NO. _____QB12_____QINGDAO_____

EXCHANGE FOR　　　USD 265 540. 00_____

AT _____*******_____ **SIGHT OF THIS FIRST OF EXCHANGE**

（SECOND OF THIS SAME TENOR AND DATE UNPAID）,

THE SUM OF US DOLLORS TWO HUNDRED AND SIXTY FIVE THOU-SAND FIVE HUNDRD AND FORTY

PAY TO THE ORDER OF _____BANK OF CHINA QINGDAO BRANCH_____

DRAWN UNDER __MIDLAND BANK PLC, LONDON__

　　L/C NO. CR2594/183865 **DATED** NOV. 7TH, 2007

TO __MIDLAND BANK PLC, LONDON__

QINGDAO BRIGHT CO. LTD.

LI MING

（十一）根据资料信息制单

Issuer： HEBEI ×××× TRADING CO.,LTD. BLDG. NO. ×××× STREET SHIJIAZHUANG， HEBEI,CHINA		商业发票 COMMERCIAL INVOICE	
To： ×××× CO SRL VIA VENTIQUATTRO ×××××,35 20099 ×××××××××-ITALY		No： 09HD1042	Date： MAR. 15TH,2009
Transport details： FROM XINGANG TO LA SPEZIA PORT,ITALY BY SEA		S/C No： 09HM1042	L/C No： 32390CI006500700
		Terms of payment： L/C AT SIGHT	

Marks and numbers	Description of goods	Quantity	Unit price	Amount
×××× IMPORT ESTO DAN GIO-VANNI CS MEDIA GROUPORSA	MICROFIBER TRAVEL BAG-SIZE 50 × 70 × 20CM BLACK AND WHITE EACH FOLDED IN SIN-GLE POLIBAG ONE PC IN A POLY-BAG,30 PCS IN A CTN 　TOTAL：2833CTNS ONE PC IN A POLY-BAG,10 PCS IN A CTN 　TOTAL：1CTN G.W.： 42 500.50 KGS N.W.： 39 666.50 KGS MEA.：191 907 M³	85 000 PCS	FOBXINGANG @USD 1.99	USD 169 150.00
TOTAL：85 000 PCS　　　　　　　　　　USD 169 150.00 　　　　　HEBEI ×××× TRADING CO.,LTD. 　　　　　　　　LI MING				

ISSUER						
HEBEI ×××× × TRADING CO.,LTD. BLDG. NO. ×××× × STREET SHIJIAZHUANG, HEBEI,CHINA	装箱单 PACKING LIST					
TO ×××× CO SRL VIA VENTIQUATTRO ×××× ×,35 20099 ××××××××××-ITALY	**INVOICE NO.** 09HD1042		**DATE** MAR. 15TH,2009			

Marks and Numbers	Number and kind of package Description of goods	Quantity	Package	G. W.	N. W.	Meas.
×××× IMPORT ESTO DAN GIO-VANNI CS MEDIA GROUPORSA	MICROFIBER TRAVEL BAG-SIZE 50×70×20CM BLACK AND WHITE EACH FOLDED IN SIN-GLE POLIBAG ONE PC IN A POLYBAG, 30 PCS IN A CTN TOTAL:2 833 CTNS ONE PC IN A POLYBAG, 10 PCS IN A CTN TOTAL:1 CTN G.W.: 42 500. 50 KGS N.W.: 39 666. 50 KGS MEA.:191 907 M³	85 000 PCS	2834 CTNS	42 500. 50 KGS	39 666. 50 KGS	191 907 M³
TOTAL:		85 000 PCS	2 834 CTNS	42 500.50 KGS	39 666.50 KGS	191 907 M³

HEBEI ×××× × TRADING CO.,LTD.

LI MING

ORIGINAL

1. Exporter	Certificate No.154879658
HEBEI ×××× TRADING CO., LTD. BLDG. NO.×××× STREET SHIJIAZHUANG, HEBEI , CHINA	**CERTIFICATE OF ORIGIN** **OF** **THE PEOPLE'S REPUBLIC OF CHINA**

2. Consignee	
×××× CO SRL VIA VENTIQUATTRO ××××, 35 20099 ××××××××× –ITALY	

3. Means of transport and route	5. For certifying authority use only
FROM XINGANG TO LA SPEZIA PORT, ITALY BY SEA	

4. Country/region of destination	
ITALY	

6. Marks and numbers	7. Number and kind of packages；description of goods	8. H.S. Code	9. Quantity	10. Number and date of invoices
×××× IMPORT ESTO DAN GIOVANNI CS MEDIA GROUPOR SA	MICROFIBER TRAVEL BAG-SIZE 50×70×20CM BLACK AND WHITE 2834CARTONS (TWO THOUSAND EIGHT HUNDRED AND THIRTY FOUR CARTONS) **********************************	98547584	85 000 PCS	09HD1042 MAR.15TH,2009

11. Declaration by the exporter	12. Certification
The undersigned hereby declares that the above details and statements are correct，that all the goods were produced in china and that they comply With the rules of Origin of the People's Republic of china. MAR.15TH,2009 SHIJIAZHUANG LI MING --- Place and date，signature and stamp of authorized signatory	Lt is hereby certified that the declaration by the exporter is correct --- Place and date，signature and stamp of certifying authority

1. Consignor HEBEI ×××× TRADING CO.,LTD. BLDG. NO. ×××× STREET SHIJIAZHUANG, HEBEI , CHINA		中远集装箱运输有限公司 **Cosco container lines** **Port-to-Port or combined transport**
2. Consignee TO ORDER		
3. Notify party ×××× CO SRL VIA VENTIQUATTRO ×××××, 35 20099 ×××××××××× –ITALY		**BILL OF LADING**

4. Combined transport	5. Combined transport
6. Ocean vessel voy.no. 　HANJIN AMSTERDAM　　0056W	7. Port of lading 　XINGANG
8. Port of discharge 　LA SPEZIA PORT, ITALY	9. Combined Transport

Marks&nos. Container /seal no. BMOU4106754/40'HQ CS5031766 HJCU7896930/40'HQ CS5031777 SENU4246407/40'GP CS5031778 ×××× IMPORT ESTO DAN GIOVANNI CS MEDIA GROUPORSA	No.of Container or package 2834CARTONS	Description of Goods MICROFIBER TRAVEL BAG FREIGHT COLLECT	Gross Weight 42 500.50 KGS	Means.M³ 191.907 M³

10. Total Number of Container and/or Package(in words) TWO THOUSAND EIGHT HUNDRED THIRTY FOUR CARTONS					
11. freight&charges	**Revenue tons**	**Rate**	**Per**	**Prepaid**	**Collect**

Place and date of issue **TIANJIN** MAR.20TH,2009
Signed for or on behailf of the Carrier 　**LI MING**

汇票

NO. _____TIANJIN_____

EXCHANGE FOR _____

AT _____ SIGHT OF THIS FIRST OF EXCHANGE

（SECOND OF THIS SAME TENOR AND DATE UNPAID），

PAY TO THE ORDER OF _____BANK OF CHINA JIANGSU_____

DRAWN UNDER _____STANDARD CHARTERED BANK，LONDON_____

L/C NO. 327984XY 070623DATED 23，JUNE，2007

TO _____STANDARD CHARTERED BANK，LONDON_____

HEBEI ×××× × TRADING CO.，LTD.

Issuer: JIANGXI INTERN ATIONAL IMP. & EXP. CORP. 8TH FLOOR FOREIGN TRADE BUILDING 200 ZHANQIAN ROAD, NANCHANG, CHINA	商业发票 **COMMERCIAL INVOICE**	
To: NICHIMEN CORPORATION 2-2 NAKANOSHIMA 3-CHOME, KITA-KU, NAGOYA, 632-8620,JAPAN	**No:** 05AO-P001	**Date:** MAR.10, 2005
Transport details: FROM SHANGHAI TO NAGOYA BY SEA	**S/C No:** J515	**L/C No:** DCMTN55123
	Terms of payment: L/C AT SIGHT	

Marks and numbers	Description of goods	Quantity	Unit price	Amount
J-515 NAGOYA PKG.NO.1-166	100 PCT COTTON GREIGE PRINT CLOTH L/C NO. DCMTN55123 ART.NO.3042 　　　FIRST QUALITYSIZE：30×30 68×68 50″ EXPORT PACKING IN SEAWORTHY BALES 　1 200 YDS/BALE166BALES	199 200 YDS	CIF NAGOYA USD 0.32	USD 63 744.00
TOTAL		199200YDS		USD 63 744.00

JIANGXI INTERNATIONAL IMP. & EXP. CORP.

LI MING

ISSUER JIANGXI INTERNATIONAL IMP. & EXP. CORP. 8TH FLOOR FOREIGN TRADE BUILDING 200 ZHANQIAN ROAD, NANCHANG, CHINA			装箱单 **PACKING LIST**			
TO NICHIMEN CORPORATION 2-2 NAKANOSHIMA 3-CHOME, KITA-KU, NAGOYA, 632-8620,JAPAN			**INVOICE NO.** 05AO-P001		**DATE** MAR.10, 2005	

Marks and Numbers	Number and kind of package Description of goods	Quantity	Package	G.W.	N.W.	Meas.
J-515 NAGOYA PKG.NO.1-166	100 PCT COTTON GREIGE PRINT CLOTH ART.NO.3042 FIRST QUALITY SIZE: 30×30 68×68 50″ EXPORT PACKING IN SEAWORTHY BALES 1 200 YDS/BALE 166BALES GW141 KGS/BALE NW139 KGS/BALE MEAM:95×68×50CM/BALE L/C NO. DCMTN55123	199 200 YDS	166 BALES	23 406 KGS	23 074 KGS	53 618 CBM
TOTAL:		199 200 YDS	166 BALES	23 406 KGS	23 074 KGS	53 618 CBM

JIANGXI INTERNATIONAL IMP. & EXP. CORP.

LI MING

ORIGINAL

1. Exporter JIANGXI INTERNATIONAL IMP. &. EXP. CORP. 8TH FLOOR FOREIGN TRADE BUILDING 200 ZHANQIAN ROAD, NANCHANG, CHINA	Certificate No. 12587965258 **CERTIFICATE OF ORIGIN** **OF** **THE PEOPLE'S REPUBLIC OF CHINA**
2. Consignee NICHIMEN CORPORATION 2-2 NAKANOSHIMA 3-CHOME, KITA-KU, NAGOYA, 632-8620, JAPAN	
3. Means of transport and route FROM SHANGHAI TO NAGOYA BY SEA	5. For certifying authority use only
4. Country/region of destination JAPAN	

6. Marks and numbers	7. Number and kind of packages; description of goods	8. H. S. Code	9. Quantity	10. Number and date of invoices
J-515 NAGOYA PKG. NO. 1-166	100 PCT COTTON GREIGE PRINT CLOTH ART. NO. 3042 166BALES (ONE HUNDRED SIXTY SIX BALES) L/C NO. DCMTN55123 ***********	96528745	199 200 YDS	05AO-P001 MAR. 10, 2005

| 11. Declaration by the exporter

   The undersigned hereby declares that the above details and statements
are correct, that all the goods were produced in china and that they comply
With the rules of Origin of the People's Republic of china.

  MAR. 10, 2005 NANCHANG LI MING
Place and date, signature and stamp of authorized signatory | 12. Certification

Lt is hereby certified that the declaration by the exporter is correct

----
Place and date, signature and stamp of certifying authority |

PICC 中国人民保险公司天津分公司

货物运输保险单

CARGO TRANSPORTATION INSURANCE POLICY

发票号：Invoice NO. 05AO-P001

合同号：S/CNo.：J515

信用证号：L/C NO. DCMTN55123

保险单次号：POLICY NO. SH058812

被保险人：Insured __ JIANGXI INTERNATIONAL IMP. & EXP. CORP.

中国人民保险公司(以下简称本公司)根据被保险人的要求，由被保险人向本公司交付约定的保险费，按照本保险单承保险别和背面所列条款与下列条款承保下述货物运输保险，特立本保险单。

标记 MARKS & NOS.	包装及数量 QUANTITY	保险货物项目 DESCRIPTION OF GOODS	保险金额 AMOUNT INSURED
J-515 NAGOYA PKG. NO. 1-166	199 200 YDS	100 PCT COTTON GREIGE PRINT CLOTH L/C NO. DCMTN55123	USD 70 119

保费 　　　　　　　　　　启运日期

PREMIUM AS ARRENGED DATE OF COMMENCEMENT AS PER B/L

装载运输工具

PER CONVEYANCE MSC SARAH V. 6A

自　　　　　经　　　　　至

PROM　SHANGHAI　TO　NAGOYA

承保险别

CONDITIONS：OCEAN MARINE CARGO CLAUSEA（ALL RISKS），OCEAN MARIEN CRIGO WAR RISK CLAUSES OF THE P. I. C. C.（SUBJECT TO C. I. C.）

所保货物，如果发生保险单项下可能引起索赔或损坏，应立即通知本公司下属代理人查勘，如有赔偿，应向本公司提交保单正本（保险单共有 2 份正本）及有关文件，如一份正本已用于索赔，其余正本自动失效。

赔款偿付地点 　　　　　　　THE PEOPLE'S INSURANCE OSAKA BRANCH

Claim Payable at NAGOYA IN USD　　98 LSKL MACH NAGOYA JAPAN

　　　　　　　　　　　　　TEL：028-543657

出单日期：　　　　　中国人民保险公司天津分公司

Issuing at 　　MAR. 10TH, 2005　　The people's Insurance Company of China

1. Consignor JIANGXI INTERNATIONAL IMP. & EXP. CORP. 8TH FLOOR FOREIGN TRADE BUILDING 200 ZHANQIAN ROAD, NANCHANG, CHINA	B/L NO. DMDF2390
2. Consignee 　TO ORDER	中远集装箱运输有限公司 Cosco container lines Port-to-Port or combined transport
3. Notify party NICHIMEN CORPORATION 2-2 NAKANOSHIMA 3-CHOME, KITA-KU, NAGOYA, 632-8620,JAPAN	BILL OF LADING
4. Combined transport	5. Combined transport
6. Ocean vessel voy.no. 　MSC SARAH V.6A	7. Port of lading 　SHANGHAI
8. Port of discharge 　NAGOYA	9. Combined Transport

Marks&nos. Container /seal no.	No.of Container or package	Description of Goods	Gross WEIGHT	Means.M³
J-515 NAGOYA PKG.NO.1-166 CONTAINER NO. MSCU4201437	166BALES	100　PCT　COTTON GREIGE PRINT CLOTH FREIGHT PREPAID L/C NO. DCMTN55123	23 406 KGS	53 618 CBM

10. Total Number of Container and/or Package(in words) ONE HUNDRED SIXTY SIX BALES

11. freight&charges	Revenue tons	Rate	Per	Prepaid	Collect
		Place and date of issue 　MAR,20ᵀᴴ,2005　TIANJIN			
		Signed for or on behalf of the Carrier CHINA NATIONAL FOREIGN TRADE TRANSPORT CORPORATION COSCO CONTAINER LINES			

汇票

NO. 05AO-P001 **NANCHANG**

EXCHANGE FOR USD63 744. 00
AT *********** **SIGHT OF THIS FIRST OF EXCHANGE**

(SECOND OF THIS SAME TENOR AND DATE UNPAID)

THE SUM OF US DOLLORS SIXTY THREE THOUSAND SEVEN HUNDRED FORTY FOUR

PAY TO THE ORDER OF BANK OF CHINA, NAN CHANG BRANCH

DRAWN UNDER THE NORINCHUK BANK TOKYO

L/C NO. DCMTN55123 **DATED** FEB. 12TH , 2005
TO THE NORINCHUK BANK TOKYO

JIANGXI INTERNATIONAL IMP. & EXP. CORP.
LI MING

Issuer:	商业发票
CHINA NATIONAL METALS AND MINERALS EXP AND IMP CORP., JIANGSU201 ZHUJIANG ROAD, NAN JING, JIANGSU,CHINA	COMMERCIAL INVOICE

To:	No:	Date:
ALEXANDER FRASERE AND SON LTD FRAKLAND MOORE HOUSE, 185/187 HIGH ROAD, BERN. SWITZER LAND	TSW15	25, JUNE, 2007

Transport details:	S/C No:	L/C No:
FROM SHANG HAI TO HAMBURG TRANSIT TO BERN, SWITZER LAND	SPGS45	327984XY 07062

Terms of payment:
L/C AT SIGHT

Marks and numbers	Description of goods	Quantity	Unit price	Amount
N/M	ORDER NO. PTC5 POLISHED MARBLE TILES, 30.5×30.5× 1CM.(PLUS OR MINUS0.3 MM) ARTNO.176: 312.56 SQM ARTNO..178: 312.56 SQM TOTAL: 625.12 SQM AS PER S/C SPGS45		CIF BERN	
	ARTNO.176: 312.56 SQM	312.56 SQM	USD 18.00	USD 5626.08
	ARTNO..178: 312.56 SQM	312.56 SQM	USD 18.00	USD 5626.08
TOTAL:		625.12 SQM		USD 11 252.16

CHINA NATIONAL METALS AND MINERALS EXP AND IMP CORP., JIANGSU

LI MNIG

ISSUER CHINA NATIONAL METALS AND MINERALS EXP AND IMP CORP., JIANGSU 201 ZHUJIANG ROAD, NAN JING, JIANGSU, CHINA				装箱单 **PACKING LIST**		
TO ALEXANDER FRASERE AND SON LTD FRAKLAND MOORE HOUSE, 185/187 HIGH ROAD, BERN. SWITZER LAND						
				INVOICE NO. TSW15	DATE 25, JUNE, 2007	

Marks and Numbers	Number and kind of package Description of goods	Quantity	Package	G.W.	N.W.	Meas.
N/M	ORDER NO. PTC5 POLISHED MARBLE TILES, 30.5×30.5× 1CM.(PLUS OR MINUSO.3 MM) ARTNO.176: 312.56 SQM ARTNO..178: 312.56 SQM TOTAL: 625.12 SQM AS PER S/C SPGS45	312.56 SQM 312.56 SQM	12 CRATES 12 CRATES	8.800 KG 8.800 KG	8.480 KG 8.480 KG	3.6 CBM 3.6 CBM
TOTAL:		625.12 SQM	24 CRATES·	17.6 KGS	16.96 KGS	7.2 CBM

CHINA NATIONAL METALS AND MINERALS EXP AND IMP CORP., JIANGSU
LI MNIG

ORIGINAL

1. Exporter CHINA NATIONAL METALS AND MINERALS EXP AND IMP CORP., JIANGSU 201 ZHUJIANG ROAD, NAN JING, JIANGSU, CHINA	Certificate No.CQS5147 **CERTIFICATE OF ORIGIN** **OF** **THE PEOPLE'S REPUBLIC OF CHINA**			
2. Consignee ALEXANDER FRASERE AND SON LTD FRAKLAND MOORE HOUSE, 185/187 HIGH ROAD, BERN. SWITZER LAND				
3. Means of transport and route FROM SHANG HAI TO HAMBURG TRANSIT TO BERN, SWITZER LAND	5. For certifying authority use only			
4. Country/region of destination 　SWITZER LAND				

6. Marks and numbers	7. Number and kind of packages；description of goods	8. H.S. Code	9. Quantity	10. Number and date of invoice
N/M	POLISHED MARBLE TILES 24CRATES(TWENTY FOUR CRATES)	95021245	625.12 SQM	TSW15 25, JUNE, 2007

11. Declaration by the exporter 　The undersigned hereby declares that the above details and statements are correct，that all the goods were produced in china and that they comply With the rules of Origin of the People's Republic of china. NANJING　25 JUNE, 2007---------LI MING------------- Place and date，signature and stamp of authorized signatory	12. Certification 　Lt is hereby certified that the declaration by the exporter is correct --- Place and date，signature and stamp of certifying authority

PICC 中国人民保险公司天津分公司

货物运输保险单
CARGO TRANSPORTATION INSURANCE POLICY
发票号：Invoice NO. TSW15
合同号：S/CNo.：SPGS45
信用证号：L/C NO. 327984XY 070623
保险单次号：POLICY NO. 1528794625879
被保险人：InsuredCHINA NATIONAL METALS AND MINERALS EXP AND IMP CORP., JIANGSU
中国人民保险公司（以下简称本公司）根据被保险人的要求，由被保险人向本公司交付约定的保险费，按照本保险单承保险别和背面所列条款与下列条款承保下述货物运输保险，特立本保险单。

标记 MARKS&NOS.	包装及数量 QUANTITY	保险货物项目 DESCRIPTION OF GOODS	保险金额 AMOUNT INSURED
N/M	625. 12 SQM	POLISHED MARBLE TILES	USD 12 378

保费   启运日期
PREMIUM AS ARRANGED DATE OF COMMENCEMENT AS PER B/L
装载运输工具
PER XNGBAO V. 0716
自   经   至
PROM   SHANG HAI VIA   HAMBURG **TO**   BERN
承保险别
CONDITIONS：COVERING ALL RISKS AND WAR RISKS
所保货物，如果发生保险单项下可能引起索赔或损坏，应立即通知本公司下属代理人查勘，如有赔偿，应向本公司提交保单正本（保险单共有 2 份正本）及有关文件，如一份正本已用于索赔，其余正本自动失效。
赔款偿付地点
Claim Payable at BERN IN USD
出单日期   中国人民保险公司天津分公司
Issuing at   AUG. 10，2007   **The people's Insurance Company of China**

1. Consignor CHINA NATIONAL METALS AND MINERALS EXP AND IMP CORP., JIANGSU 201 ZHUJIANG ROAD, NAN JING, JIANGSU, CHINA	B/L NO.OUS45879521635 中远集装箱运输有限公司 **Cosco container lines** **Port-to-Port or combined transport**
2. Consignee TO ORDER	
3. Notify party PETRICO INTERNATIONAL TRADING CORP., 1110 SHEPPARD AVENUE EAST SUITE 406 BERN, SWITZERLAND..	**BILL OF LADING**

4. Combined transport	5. Combined transport HAMBURG
6. Ocean vessel voy.no. XNGBAO V.0716	7. Port of lading SHANG HAI
8. Port of discharge BERN, SWITZER LAND	9. Combined Transport

Marks&nos. Container /seal no. N/M	No.of Container or package 24CRATES	Description of Goods POLISHED MARBLE TILES	Gross WEIGHT 17.6 KGS	Means.M³ 7.2 CBM

10. Total Number of Container and/or Package(in words) TWENTY-FOUR CRATES

11. freight&charges	Revenue tons	Rate	Per	Prepaid	Collect
		Place and date of issue SHANGHAIAUG.17, 2007			
		Signed for or on behalf of the Carrier LI MING			

汇票

NO. ___TSW15___ **NANJING**

EXCHANGE FOR ___USD11252.16___

AT ___＊＊＊＊＊___ **SIGHT OF THIS FIRST OF EXCHANGE**

(SECOND OF THIS SAME TENOR AND DATE UNPAID),

THE SUM OF US DOLLORS ELEVEN THOUSAND TWO HUNDRED AND FORTY-TWO POINT ONE SIX ONLY

PAY TO THE ORDER OF ___BANK OF CHINA JIANGSU BR.___

DRAWN UNDER ___STANDARD CHARTERED BANK，LONDON___

L/C NO. 327984XY 070623 **DATED** 23，JUNE，2007

TO ___STANDARD CHARTERED BANK，LONDON___

CHINA NATIONAL METALS AND MINERALS EXP AND
IMP CORP.，JIANGSU
LI MING

（十二）单选题

1	2	3	4	5	6
A	B	A	C	B	A
7	8	9	10	11	12
B	A	A	A	B	D
13	14	15	16	17	18
C	B				

（十三）多选题

1	2	3	4	5	6
ABCD	ABD	BCDE	ABCDE	ABD	ADE
7	8	9	10	11	12
ACD	ABC	ABCDE	BCD		

（十四）判断题

1	2	3	4	5	6
T	F	F	F	T	T
7	8	9	10	11	12
F	F	T	T	F	F

（十五）问答题

7月1日付款。6月1日见票，承兑后即取得单据。

综 合 篇

综合练习一

（一）根据合同审核信用证，并填写审单记录

信用证审核结果

信用证号	101465
合 同 号	20406
审证结果	1. 信用证中规定汇票的付款期限为"见票后30天"，与合同中规定不符，应改为"见票即付"。
	2. 信用证要求提供保险单，与贸易术语CFR含义不一致，应删除保险单条款。
	3. 信用证要求提供买方出具的质量检验证书，属于软条款，应删除。
	4. 信用证中对货物的描述与合同不符，应将"JA-103"改为"JA-13"。
	5. 信用证中引用的合同号为"95406"，应改为"101465"。
	6. 信用证中规定的装运期与合同不符，应改为"DURING OCT. /NOV. 2009"，装运港应改为天津。
	7. 信用证规定不允许转船，应改为允许。

（二）根据交易信息及信用证制作结汇单据及托收项下的汇票

COMMERCIAL INVOICE

1) SELLER TIANJIN IMPORT AND EXPORT CORPORA-TION NO. 29 JIEFANG ROAD TIANJIN CHINA	3) INVOICE NO 41120	4) INVOICE DATE NOV. 22TH, 2009
	5) DO NO. C-788520	6) DATE JAN 12TH, 2009
	7) ISSUED BY JPMORCAN CHASE BANK, NY	
2) BUYER COMETALS 222 BRIDGE PLAZA SOUTH FORTLEE. NJ 07024	8) CONTRACT NO. JZIE041101	9) DATE NOV 1ST, 2008
	10) FROM TIANJIN, CHINA	11) TO BALTIMOREMD
	12) SHIPPED BY VESSEL	13) PRICE TERM CIF BALTIMORE

14) MARKS	15) DESCRIPTION OF GOODS	16) QTY	17) UNIT PRICE	18) AMOUNT
CHROMIUM METAL PC-14228 COMETALS MADE IN CHINA	CHROMIUM METAL	200 METRIC TONS	CIF BALTIMORE USD 35 550. 00	USD 7 110 000. 00 TOTAL: USD 7 110 000. 00

TOTAL AMOUNT: US. DOLLARS SEVEN THOUSAND ONE HUNDRED AND TEN THOUSAND O

GOODS ARE PACKED IN STEEL DRUMS OF 250 KGS NET KACH ON
FUMIGATED WOODEN PALLETS, IN SEAWORTHY OCEAN CONTAINERS
CREDIT NUMBER: C-788520
WE CERTIFY THAT THE CONTENTS OF THIS INVOICE IS TRUE ANDCORRECT

19) ISSUED BY
　　TIANJIN IMPORT AND EXPORT CORPORATION
20) SIGNATURE

PACKING LIST

1) SELLER TIANJIN IMPORT AND EXPORT CORPORATION NO. 29 JIEFANG ROAD TIANJIN CHINA	3) INVOICE NO. 41120	4) INVOICE DATE NOV 22TH, 2009
	5) FROM TIANJIN, CHINA	6) TO BALTIMORE MD
	7) TOTAL PACKAGES(IN WORDS) EIGHTY EIGHT STEEL DRUMS ONLY	
2) BUYER COMETALS 22 BRIDGE PLAZA SOUTH FORT LEE NJ07024	8) MARKS &. NOS. CHROMIUM METAL PC-14228 COMETALS MADE IN CHINA	

9) C/NOS.	10) NOS. &. KINDS OF PKGS.	11) ITEM	12) QTY. (pcs.)	13)G. W. (kg)	14) N. W. (kg)	15) MEAS(m³)
			DRUMS	M/T	M/T	CBM
1-800	800STEEL DRUMS CHROMIUM METAL		800			0. 0375
		TOTAL:	800	42. 4	40. 00	30. 000

SAY TOTAL: EIGHT HUNDRED STEEL DRUMS ONLY

20′ CBHU0611758/25783 CY/CY
20′ CBHU2765381/25784 CY/CY

CREDIT NUMBER C-788520
WE HEREBY CERTIFY THAT EACH EXPORT PACKAGE CARRIES A "MADE IN CHINA" LABEL
GOODS ARE SUPPLIED IN STEEL DRUMS OF 250 KGS NET EACH ON FUMIGATED
WOODEN PALLETS, IN SEAWORTHY OCEAN CONTAINERS

16) ISSUED BY
TIANJIN IMPORT AND EXPORT CORPORATION

17) SIGNATURE

中国人民保险公司
THE PEOPLE'S INSURANCE COMPANY OF CHINA
总公司设于北京　　一九四九年创立
Head office BEIJING　　　Established in 1949

保险单　　　　　　　　　　保险单号次 PICC000369
INSURANCE POLICY　　　　POLICY NO. ××××××

中国人民保险公司（以下简称本公司）
THIS POLICY OF INSUPANCE WITNESSES THAT THE PEOPLES INSURANCE COMPANY OF CHINA（HEREINAFTER CALLED THE COMPANY）

根据
AT THE REQUEST OF　TIANJIN IMPORT AND EXPORT CORPORATION

（以下简称被保险人）的要求，由被保险人向本公司缴付约定的保险，按照本保险单承保险别和背面所载条款下列特别条款承保下述货物运输保险，特签本保险单
（HEREINAPTER CALLED "THE INSURED"）AND IN CONSIDERATION OF THE AGREED PREMIUM PAID TO THE COMPANY BY THE INSURED UNDERTAKES TO INSORE THE UNDERMENTIONED GOODS IN TRANSPORTATION SUBJECT TO THE CONDITIONS OF THIS POLICY AS PER THE CLAUSES PAINTED OVERLEAF AND OTHER SPECIAL CLAUSES ATTACHED HEREON

标记 MARKS & NOS	包装及数量 QUANTITY	保险货物项目 DESCRIPTION OF GOODS	保险金额 AMOUNT INSURED
ASPER INVOICE NO. 41120	200 METRIO TONS	CHROMIUM METAL	USD7 821 000. 00

总保险金额：
TOTAL AMOUNT INSURED：SAY TOTAL US. DOLLARS SEVEN HUNDRED AND ELEVEN THOUSAND ONLY

保费　　　　　　　费率　　　　　装载运输工具
PREMIUMAS ARRAGED　RATE AS ARRAGED　PER CONVEYANCE SS　BULE SKY V. 312E

开航日期　　　　　　　　自　　　　　　　　　　至
SLG. ON OR ABT AS PER B/L　　　FROM TIANJIN, CHINA　　　　　　TO BALTIMORE MD

承保险别：
CONDITIONS
COVERING ALL RISKS, WAR RISKS AND S. R. C. C.

CREDIT NUMBER：C-788520

所保货物，如遇出险，本公司凭本保险单及其他有关证件给付赔款。所保货物，如发生本保险单项下负责赔偿的损失或事故，应立即通知本公司下属代理人查勘。
CLAIMS. IF ANY, PAYABLE ON SURRENDER OF THIS POLICY TOGETHER WITH OTHER RELEVANY DOCUMENTS IN THE EVENT OF ACCIDENT WHEREBY LOSS OR DAMAGE MAY RESULT IN A CLAIM UNDER THIS POLICY IMMEDIATE NOTICE APPLYING FOR SURVEY MUST BE GIVEN TO THE COMPANYS AGENT AS MENTIONED HEREUNDER.

CLAIMS SETTING AGENT
ABCD THE UNITED STATES

赔款偿付地点　　　　　　　　　　　　中国人民保险公司天津分公司
CLAIM PAYABLE AT/IN　AT DE STINATION　THE PEOPLE'S INSURANCE CO. OF CHINA
PORT, BALTIMOREM IN USD　　　　　　　SHANGHAI BRANCH
DATE　TIANJIN, CHINA

地址：中国天津中山东一路 23 号　TEL：3234305 3217466-44 Telex：33128 PICCS CN
Address：23 Zhongshan Dong Yi Lu Shanghai China，Cable：42001，Shanghai

　　　　　　　　　　　　　　　　××××
　　　　　　　　　　　　　　　General Manager

BILL OF LADING

1) SHIPPER TIANJIN IMPORT AND EXPORT CORPORATION NO. 29 JIEFANG ROAD TIANJIN CHINA	10) B/L NO. BS04112823
	CARRIER
2) CONSIGNEE TO ORDER OF SHIPPER	**COSCO** 中国远洋运输(集团)总公司 **CHINA OCEAN SHIPPING (GROUP) CO.**
3) NOTIFY PARTY JOHN S. CONNOR, INC.	

4) PLACE OF RECEIPT	5) OCEAN VESSEL BLUE SKY	
6) VOYAGE NO. V. 312E	7) PORT OF LOADING TIANJIN, CHINA	*ORIGINAL*
8) PORT OF DISCHARGE BALTIMORE MD	9) PLACE OF DELIVERY	**Combined Transport BILL OF LADING**

11)MARKS 12) NOS. & KINDS OF PKGS. 13) DESCRIPTION OF GOODS 14) G. W. (kg) 15) MEAS(m³)

CHROMIUM METAL
PC-14228   800STEEL DRUMS   CHROMIUM METAL   42 400. 00 KGS 30 000 CBM
COMETALS
MADE IN CHINA

CBHU2765381/25784   FREIGHT PREPAID
CBHU0611758/25783   **CREDIT NUMBER: C-788520**
CY/CY
2×20′

16) TOTAL NUMBER OF CONTAINERS	
OR PACKAGES(IN WORDS)	**SAY EIGH HUNDRED STEELDRUMS ONLY**

FREIGHT & CHARGES	REVENUE TONS	RATE	PER	PREPAID	COLLECT

PREPAID AT	PAYABLE AT	17) PLACE AND DATE OF ISSUE
TOTAL PREPAID	18) NUMBER OF ORIGINAL B/L	TIANJIN. CHINA NOV. 28TH, 2009
LOADING ON BOARD THE VESSEL		21)
19) DATE NOV. 28TH, 2009	20) BY	×××××××AS AGENT FOR CARRIER

地址：天津市中山东一路 13 号
Address：13 Zhongshan Road
（E. 1.）Tianjin

检验证书
INSPECTION CERTIFICATE

日期 Date：
NOV. 21TH，2009

电报：天津 2914
Cable：2914. TIANJIN

电话 Tel：63211285

QUALITY

发货人：
Consignor TIANJIN IMPORT AND EXPORT CORPORATION

受货人：
Consignee *** *** ***

品　名：
Commodity CHROMIUM METAL

标记及号码：
Marks & No： CHROMIUM METAL
PC-14228
COMETALS
MADE IN CHINA

报验数量/重量：
Quantity/Weight
Declare 40M/T　　　　0

检验结果：
RESULTS OF INSPEOTION： OK

We hereby certify that the goods are of the above-mentioned quantity and of sound quality.

CREDIT NUMBER：C-788520

主任检验员
Chief Inspector：

CERTIFICATE OF ORIGIN

1. Exporter TIANJIN IMPORT AND EXPORT CORPORATION NO. 29，JIEFANG ROAD TIANJIN CHINA	Certificate No. ××××××
2. Consignee COMETALS 222 BRIDGE PLAZA SOUTH FORT LEE. NJ 07024	CERTIFICATE OF ORIGIN OF THE PEOPLE'S REPUBLIC OF CHINA
3. Means of transport and route FROM TIANJIN. CITO BALTIMORE MD BY SEA	5. For certifying authority use only
4. Country/region of destination BALTTMORE,MD	

6. Marks and numbers	7. Number and kind of packages; description of goods	8. H. S. Code	9. Quantity	10. Number and date of invoices
CHROMIUM METAL PC-14228 COMETALS MADE IN CHINA CBHU2765381/25784 CBHU0611758/25783 CY/CY 2×20′	800（EIGHTY HUNDRED）STEEL DRUMS CHROMIUM METAL ＊＊＊　＊＊＊　＊＊＊ CREDIT NUMBER C-788520	81122100	200 M/T	INVOICE NO. 411 INVOICE DATE： NOV. 22

11. Declaration by the exporter The numbersigned hereby declares that the above details and statements are correct，that all the goods were produced in China and that they comply with the rules of Origin of the People's Republic of China. TIANJIN，CHINA NOV. 23TH，2009 Place and date，signature and stamp of authorized signatory	12. Certification. Lt is hereby certified that the daclaration by the exporter is correct TIANJIN，CHINA NOV. 23TH，2009 Place and date，signature and stamp of certifying authority

TIANJIN IMPORT AND EXPORT CORPORATION，

BENIFICIARY'S CERTIFICATION

DATE：

NOV. 30TH，2009

TO：COMETALS

RE： INVOICE. NO. 41120　　　L/C NUMBER. C-788520

WE HERE CERTLFY THATONE SET OF NON-MEGOTLABLE BL TOGETHER WITH INVOICE AND PACKING LIST HAS BEEN SENT TO APPLICANT BY DHL BY BENEFICIANY WIIHIN

24 HOURS AFIER SHIFMENT.

CREDIT NUMBER：C-788520

TIANJIN IMPORT AND EXPOET CORPORATION.

BILL OF EXCHANGE

No. 41120

For USD 6 399 000. 00　　　　　　　TIANJIN. CHINA NOV. 30TH 2009

At　＊＊＊　＊＊＊　＊＊＊　　　 sight of this FIRST Bill of exchange（SECOND being unpaid）

pay to　CHINA CONSTRUCTION BANK. TIANJIN BRANCH　　or order the sum of

SAY US DOLLARS SIX THOUSAND THREE HUNDRED AND NINTY NINE THOU-SAND ONLY

Value received for　　　　　　of

　　　　　　（quantity）　　　（name of commodity）

Drawn under JPMORCAN CHASE BANK. NY

L/C No.　C-788520　　　　　　dated　JAN. 12TH，2009

To：JPMORCAN CHASE BANK，NY　　　　　For and on behalf of

CREDIT NUMBER：C-788520

TIANJIN IMPORT AND EXPORT CORPORATIO

（Signature）

综合练习二

(一) 根据成交资料审核信用证,列明不符点,并说明应如何修改

1. ISSUING BANK 通常在出口地议付行。

2. USD17 250.00 未注明 5% 增减。

3. SAY US DOLLARS SEVENTEEN THOUSAND 大写有误。

4. DATED 3 OCT 2009 开证日错。

5. 10 OCT 2009 签约日有误。

6. TYDAC036 合约号与下面不符。

7. 5INSURANCE POLICY COVERING ICC(A) CLAUSE IN 2 COPIES CFR 价格条款不应含有保险单据。

8. TYPAC036 合约号与上述不符。

9. 数量漏写溢短装。

10. WITHIN 2 DAYS 提交单据的时间通常为 15~21 天。

11. FOR ACCOUNT OF BENEFICIARY. 建议修改为由开证人支付。

(二) 单据制作

第一题:

1. 出口商名称错;2. 开证日期有误;3. 装运港和卸货港与信用证不符;4. 价格术语与信用证不符;5. 开立信用证年份有误。

第二题:

1. 托运人 shipper 名称有误;2. 收货人栏应为:to order of shipper;3. 装运港和卸货港名称有误;4. 唛头(运输标志)与信用证不符;5. 开证年份有误;6. 没有注明目的港船方代理的名称和电话;7. 签发提单的地点和年份有误。

ISSUER					
Tianjin Bluebird Import & Export Corporation	装箱单				
No.249, Sanguan Road, Tianjin China	PACKING LIST				
TO Lieane Trading Corp. Unit87, Fareast Building, Los Angeles, U.S.A.					
	INVOICE NO. LK-LTIV7923		**DATE** 22-DEC-2009		
Marks and Numbers	Number and kind of package Description of goods	Quantity	Package	G.W.	N.W.	Meas.
LIEANE LK-LTSC0738 LOS ANGELES NO.1-600	600CARTONS N&A LAMPS ART NO. JIE-452 HEQ-349 VPU-875 PNC-684	500SETS 200SETS 200SETS 300SETS	250CTNS 100CTNS 100CTNS 150CTNS	2500KGS 1000KGS 1200KGS 1800KGS	2000KGS 800KGS 1000KGS 1500KGS	18.000M³ 7.200M³ 7.200M³ 14.850M³
TOTAL:		1200SETS	600CTNS	6500KGS	5300KGS	47.250M³

Tianjin Bluebird Import & Export Corporation
LI MING

汇票

NO. LK-LTIV7923 **TIANJIN**

DATE: 22-DEC-2009

EXCHANGE FOR USD80,500.00
SAY US DOLLARS EIGHTY THOUSAND FIVE HUNDRED ONLY
AT ***** **SIGHT OF THIS FIRST OF EXCHANGE**

(SECOND OF THIS SAME TENOR AND DATE UNPAID),

PAY TO THE ORDER OF BANK OF CHINA TIANJIN

DRAWN UNDER AMERICAN BANK, LOS ANGELES BRANCH

L/C NO. LT-LKLC9375 **DATED 15-NOV-2009**

TO AMERICAN BANK, LOS ANGELES BRANCH

Tianjin Bluebird Import & Export Corporation
LI MING